the

GOURMET GARAGE®

cookbook

**200 Everyday Recipes Using Fresh and Exotic
Ingredients from Around the World**

Sheryl and Mel London

Illustrations by Kathleen Skelly-Kurka

Henry Holt and Company   New York

Henry Holt and Company, LLC
Publishers since 1866
115 West 18th Street
New York, New York 10011

Henry Holt® is a registered
trademark of Henry Holt and Company, LLC.

Published in Canada by Fitzhenry & Whiteside Ltd.,
195 Allstate Parkway, Markham, Ontario L3R 4T8.

Library of Congress Cataloging-in-Publication Data
London, Sheryl.
The Gourmet Garage cookbook: 200 everyday recipes using fresh and
exotic ingredients from around
the world / Sheryl and Mel London.—1st ed.
p.   cm.
Includes index.
ISBN 0-8050-5411-1
1. Cookery.   2. Gourmet Garage (Store)   I. London, Mel.
TX714.L812   2000   99-15022
641.5—dc21   CIP

Henry Holt books are available for special
promotions and premiums. For details contact:
Director, Special Markets.

First Edition 2000

Designed by Paula Russell Szafranski
Illustrations by Kathleen Skelly-Kurka

Printed in the United States of America

1   3   5   7   9   10   8   6   4   2

For
Susan Solomita and N. D. Wruble
Friends by chance . . . family by choice

Contents

Acknowledgments

We are grateful . . .

to our original editor, Beth Crossman, a conscientious, straightforward lady, for her support, praise, and encouragement, and to David Sobel, who volunteered to support this project when Beth left;

to Madeleine Morel, our delightful agent and dear friend, who returns our telephone calls immediately and who always has an encouraging word to carry us through the dark, lonely days of developing a manuscript;

to the helpful, pleasant, and always available people in the many departments of Gourmet Garage;

to our dear friends, who graciously sampled, commented on, rejected, or accepted our frequent invitations to last-minute taste tests;

to the strengths of our long marriage, which has allowed two symbiotic personalities to coauthor this book—one a morning person and one a night owl.

Introduction

IT IS 3 A.M. IN NEW YORK . . .

In the SoHo district of lower Manhattan, the cobblestone streets are empty except for the occasional late-night taxi echoing between the darkened cast-iron buildings, its tires making a soft rumble on the uneven road.

On one corner, at Broome and Mercer streets, a slow hum of activity soon becomes a roaring terminal of trucks, each one's produce unloaded, only to be replaced by another truck, another delivery of boxes, crates, bulging burlap bags:

- Five hundred kilos of French and Spanish and Italian cheeses now stand on Broome Street, delivered from the import broker at Newark Airport.
- A second truck, still partially loaded, leaves for Greenwich Village.
- One hundred and fifty cases of organic California mesclun, 450 pounds, a single day's supply, just arrived from Kennedy Airport, now sit on the curb at Broadway and Ninety-sixth Street.
- And a trailer filled with vine-ripened Florida tomatoes squeezes down the narrow block of East Sixty-fourth Street and rumbles to a halt in front of what was once a parking garage, to be transformed in just a few hours into a bustling, thriving market.

The activities at the four locales go on for hours, with arrivals from airports, from farmers directly, and from cargo points across the country. There is oven-fresh bread from local bakers, still warm. There is the ordinary: skeins of garlic, chiles, onions, a vast diversity of oils and vinegars, fruits and nuts. And the extraordinary: wild mushrooms—hedgehog, shiitake, oyster, cremini, Portobello, pompom, morel—Charantais melons,

Beluga caviar, game pâtés, coriander and cornichons, imported mustards, and a range of fragrant herbs, tied together as though they were bouquets of elegant flowers. Smoked fish. Fresh fish. Salsas. Spices. White truffles. Pastas. Grains. The energy reaches a peak and then melts away at the thin light of daybreak.

By 8 A.M. it is all over, and twenty-four empty heavy-duty trucks leave, to be back the next day. The traffic in the city changes to what is considered normal by New York standards. The streets are now lit by sunlight. The curtain rises on a bright, warm, sunny day. It is "showtime" at the four most exciting stores in all of New York City.

What is now a booming enterprise with four hundred employees was originally hatched from a very simple idea. For, as alien as it seems today, fine produce and the specialty items that are so common now, had never been brought into the United States until about 1981. On a trip to France in that year, partner and cofounder Andy Arons became intoxicated with items rarely seen in the United States. He came up with what he thought might be a practical idea: Why not fly these foods fresh to the United States and make them available to the chefs of New York, one of the most innovative cities in the culinary world? And so, in 1981, in a chilly warehouse in an isolated industrial section of Long Island City, a company called Flying Foods was born.

Their first customer was Andre Soltner of Lutèce. He ordered a case of Dover sole and some *haricots verts*. Flying Foods flew them over on ice and immediately hit a roadblock. In order to get credit from the shipping company, they had to show some financial backing. So they started a bank account with $5!

Soltner told his fellow chefs, and they told their professional friends. From a handful of knowledgeable clients the company began to grow and flourish. Flying Foods was the first bulk importer of European produce that we now take for granted: radicchio lettuce, peppers from Holland, fresh wild mushrooms, and Dover sole. By 1987 the company was grossing almost $10 million. Andy was then only twenty-eight. Eventually, Flying Foods was sold to Kraft Foods, but the idea remained very much alive, and in 1992, Andy Arons, John Gottfried, and Ned Visser formed one of the most perfect partnerships we've ever seen in order to conceive and create the reality that is now Gourmet Garage.

Their backgrounds could not have been more diverse. Andy Arons, who had been accepted at law school but turned it down, was the dynamo who scoured the globe for Flying Foods, his success fueled by a charismatic personality and an enthusiasm that is unmatched by most entrepreneurs. John Gottfried was a founder of the parent company, Metropolitan Agribusiness, back in 1978. It supplied fresh specialty foods to restaurants and was one of the first large-scale distributors of fresh mushrooms in the United States. But he too came to his calling through a winding road after degrees in finance from Wharton and Columbia, followed by a background in banking, real estate, restaurant reviewing, and food writing. Ned Visser, with a background in architecture that would later aid him in building new Gourmet Garage stores, had also developed products for supermarkets and had been an exporter of unusual foods as diverse as sea urchins and monkfish roe. He had gotten his experience in dealing with the public by managing such upscale restaurants as Maxwell's Plum in New York. The common demoninator that brought them together is their love of good food and quality.

The first location (their original warehouse) was an ex-garage in a neglected neighborhood on the edge of Manhattan's fashionable SoHo district. Almost immediately Gourmet Garage became a boon to chefs from 180 major hotels and restaurants that make up New York City's top dining places: Daniel, Le Cirque, Le Bernardin, and the Four Seasons, to name a few. Gourmet Garage was a boon to them because very few chefs have the time to go to New York's wholesale market at Hunt's Point. It is a murderous enough profession without having to get up at three o'clock in the morning in order to find top-quality ingredients.

With the exception of Flying Foods, no one had ever sold food in the way that Gourmet Garage was conceived—discounting high-quality fresh produce in down-to-earth warehouse style, a no-frills environment in which the products were displayed in ordinary cut cardboard boxes rather than being treated as high-priced jewels. And, above all, the unusual and the very best quality that the seasons had to offer were always reflected. The chefs and caterers loved it!

But the general public—the authors included—pressed their noses to the battered double doors of the garage and wondered why *they* couldn't buy tomatoes that tasted like tomatoes, culinary herbs that had been delivered by air that very morning, greens that beckoned with fresh, unwilted crispness. Why only chefs?

In what we home cooks believe was a decision worthy of Solomon, the three partners decided to open the place to the general public after 1 P.M. when the chefs had departed for their kitchens. No one, certainly not the three founders, ever expected to see the avalanche of customers that followed.

New York was being battered by one of the stormiest, rainiest, windiest days of the year. Subways were flooded, tunnels closed, and it was a good day to stay home with the newspapers and a hot cup of coffee. In spite of that, when the doors were finally opened to the public, twelve hundred eager shoppers showed up. Within less than an hour the supposedly adequate supply of 70 shopping bags had run out, and the owners had to borrow more from the neighborhood pet store. Since then, Gourmet Garage has never stopped growing. And though Day One had caught them all by surprise, by Day Two they were adapting well.

A vast range of new products and departments were added, new vendors appeared, and a weekly ritual of tastings by the partners (to which the authors were occasionally invited) increased the offerings that would be displayed for the general public. The wholesale and retail operations outgrew the space immediately, and finally wholesale moved to a giant warehouse building on Greenwich Street in Manhattan's Tribeca section. The four currently operating retail stores are now busy seven days a week, and in the very near future—probably close to the publication of this cookbook—there are plans for three more locations in New York plus mail order availability for customers across the country. Amazingly, only two years after their founding, they won the "Entrepreneur of the Year" Award from their industry peers.

But, despite the astounding growth, the philosophy of Gourmet Garage has not changed: It is a retail store that is close to the source, one step away from the farmer, with no compromise on quality and with value at fair prices in a no-frills environment. Essentially its credo—"What the chefs can buy, the public can too"—is to make readily available to the general public the quality and variety of food that first-class chefs demand for their own customers.

We, of course, have been there since the beginning, and probably this book was bound to happen. It started as we shopped and then stopped to speak to the partners. We gathered around the cheese counter and spoke of our mutual love for food, of the excitement that was now our favorite food store, of our philosophy of cooking, and, particularly, of our shopping for that evening's menu. We had completed ten cookbooks up to that time, and we don't know who said it first, but somehow the question was asked: Why don't you guys write the *Gourmet Garage Cookbook* for us? The answer is in the next few hundred pages!

Along the way we have realized over and over again that the philosophy behind Gourmet Garage concerning food and quality is also ours. We are, first of all, totally sympathetic to the pressures of today's busy lifestyle. We read with amusement some time ago an article about shoppers trying to save time and effort by ordering through a shopping service on the Internet—ordering $130 worth of groceries in only fifteen minutes and doing it anytime of the day or night. The title told the story: "Stop Squeezing the Cyber Melons!" We believe the first step toward good cooking is finding the perfect raw materials. We love the feeling of actually seeing, questioning, touching, and selecting as we wander the aisles of our markets, be they the major supermarket chains, the specialty shops, or the outdoor stalls of the local farmer's markets that have sprouted in the urban parks and plazas across the country. Many of us have had the experience of visiting the local markets of the world—the Boqueria of Barcelona or Cordoba's Sánchez Peña, now housed in an old city jail, and Pike's Market in our own Seattle. Having worked in over sixty countries filming our documentaries and writing food articles and cookbooks, we still carry with us the images of those bustling markets alive with the color, aroma, and bounty of their wares. Indeed, many of our recipes reflect those trips.

There was a time not too long ago when shoppers were confined to vegetables and fruits that had been brought to outward (if not inward) perfection by the use of gas and then wrapped in touch-proof plastic containers so that the probing finger was unable to tell what really lay beneath. But we have seen the world of food change dramatically. Many of us now travel more and are able to sample the joys of other cultures, and we have therefore become more demanding shoppers at home. In response, with amazing rapidity, specialty shops such as Gourmet Garage, patisseries, charcuteries, epicurean cheese shops, and farmer's markets have sprouted—like mung beans, as one writer described it.

Much of what we once saw in only a few cities has become commonplace throughout the United States and Canada—in Harry's in Atlanta, Wild Oats in Chicago, Whole Foods in Texas, Bread & Circus in Boston, and Giraldi's in Pennsylvania. We have seen change in the typical chain supermarkets from Grand Rapids, Michigan, and Gillette, Wyoming, to Hendersonville, North Carolina. They now offer produce that is organically grown as well as a staggering array of cheeses, oils, tropical fruits, seafood, grains, and beans.

And the current culinary chronicle goes on. Today's cooks are also demanding the end of tortured food. They long for simple fare, clean and uncomplicated dishes that allow honest, fresh ingredients to speak for themselves and recipes that respect the full flavor of the ingredients. There is also a growing concern for health and nutrition.

We wanted to give guidance on how to choose wisely when you visit your local market, and throughout the book you will find a whole range of tips under the heading:

SHOP SMART

Since so many formerly rare ingredients from Asia, Europe, and Latin America are now available in the marketplace, we wanted to echo these ethnic influences. Some are new and strange to us, and since we have heard so many times in the market, "Gee, they're lovely. I wish I knew what to do with them," we hope to answer some of the questions about them.

We want to stress our own nutritional philosophy based on healthful eating without sacrificing taste or presentation. We have cut back or eliminated large amounts of butter, eggs, and cream in most our recipes while retaining their full flavors by using culinary herbs and spices.

Our recipes offer suggestions for attractive presentations with simple, detailed instructions for any home cook to achieve success. Each one has been created and tested by us in our own kitchens on equipment that is probably very close to what is in your home.

So take a voyage with us to the everyday marketplace and roam the aisles with us. What we finally decide to cook should come as a natural outgrowth of how we shop— traveling from department to department, checking our lists, changing and planning the menus as we go. Thus, in the structure of this book, we have avoided moving through the usual categories of appetizers through soups, entrees, salads, and desserts; instead, we have tried to organize our recipes to reflect the actual departments of a specialty shop or supermarket.

Like us, the three partners of Gourmet Garage believe that good cooking is an act of love, a sensual experience, and a source of true happiness. They asked that this book reflect their philosophy, which was communicated to us at our first meeting at the Gourmet Garage cheese counter:

> We want to take the best things we know about food and share them with our friends. . . . We'd like the book to be as accessible as our stores.

The market basket is empty. The rest is up to you.

the
gourmet garage
cookbook

The Old Basics:
Herbs and Spices, Flavor Boosters

Sometimes when we cook, the simple, old basic pointers can make a difference in the end result. How much salt, and when do we put it into the recipe if the instructions read, "Salt to taste"? When do you add spices or fresh herbs for best results? Since peppercorns come in all colors and intensities, which do we use for what? Here is a brief synopsis of some of the rules and techniques we have used in testing the recipes in this book.

THE RECIPE INSTRUCTIONS

We have tried to be very exact and specific about our instructions in all the recipes, and we hope they are not daunting. For example, how big is a "large" onion or a "medium" one? Each recipe gives a suggested weight. How do you get all the grit out of mushrooms? Check the cleaning details we've given for each variety. Throughout the book we have also given exact pot and pan sizes for each recipe.

And should you come across an instruction that tells you to use a blender rather than a food processor (or vice versa), don't panic if your kitchen boasts just one of those wonderful machines. We prefer to use a blender for a really smooth puree for soups and for fine bread crumbs. A food processor can be substituted, but the texture will be somewhat coarser.

SALT

Our recipes call for "salt to taste." Professional cooks usually add tiny amounts of salt during each step in a recipe. For example, a bit of salt is added when sautéeing onions or other vegetables, then another after the next ingredient is added, and still another after the next few.

If in doubt about the amounts, use less salt and then add more later if you feel it is needed. We use coarse (or kosher) salt because we find it less salty per teaspoon than table salt. If you're using table salt, use only half the amount. However, we do use the finer-grain salt in baking.

PEPPER

It was an amazing revelation to us that black peppercorns come from berries that are green and then dried in the sun, while white peppercorns come from berries that have ripened to red, and the skin and fleshy part are then removed. And both are from the same plant.

White peppercorns give milder flavor and are generally used for light-colored dishes. Green peppercorns come in various forms—dried so that they can be ground just like black pepper, or water-packed so that they can be easily mashed.

We have used several different kinds of pepper in this book, all of them freshly ground with a mill that can be adjusted from very fine to very coarse. If you don't already have one, we recommend buying a really good pepper mill.

OLIVE OIL AND BUTTER

When butter is called for, we always use sweet butter, not salted. And the olive oil we use for both salads and cooking is extra-virgin (see page 181).

STOCK

Some cooks who are purists prefer to make their own stock, but when a recipe calls for vegetable, chicken, or beef stock, we think that canned or frozen is a great time saver and quite acceptable. Commercial fish stock is only available frozen in specialty shops.

THE FLAVOR BOOSTERS: HERBS AND SPICES

We believe culinary herbs and spices can not only redefine food flavors but can provide startling and unusual accents to almost any recipe. A simple change in seasoning can create an entirely new and unusual dish.

The ancient Romans were familiar with the range of spices. In fact, the Roman chef Apicius, who was cooking and writing at the dawn of the Christian era, was using cloves, pepper, nutmeg, lovage, aniseed, and coriander in his recipes. The barbarian Goths used spices (probably dried berries) in their religious rites, and the Egyptians were quite familiar with herbal treatments in medicine as well as using spices for both food preparation and embalming.

The earliest use of culinary herbs and spices was mostly directed toward disguising the flavor of decaying foods. Then, after the discovery of air drying and salting to preserve foods, as well as the leap forward of refrigeration, chefs began to move away from camouflage and began to discover that herbs and spices could alter, improve, and expand the taste of many of their dishes.

Herbs are the leafy parts of bushes or plants, all grown in the temperate zones of the world, whereas spices are the dried parts of tropical plants and trees—roots, berries, bark—all grown in the Far East, with the exception of allspice, a product of the New World.

Until about fifty or sixty years ago, almost every home kitchen boasted a mortar and pestle with which to grind whole spices. In some places such as India we still find them today, but not in the United States and Canada where by and large they have disappeared. Fresh herbs and spices began to be used again in the late forties, after World War II, and within the last fifteen or twenty years just about everyone seems to be using the fresh culinary herbs that are available almost everywhere.

The spice shelf, too, has been undergoing a minor revolution, with the tastes of the home chef becoming more and more sophisticated. People are traveling more extensively and discovering new taste sensations. The interest in fresh foods, nutrition, and organic farming has grown steadily as well, and possibly the most exciting development has been the growth of Chinese, Thai, Greek, French, Vietnamese, Japanese, and Ethiopian restaurants from coast to coast, introducing us to new flavors.

Throughout this book we have used fresh herbs and spices as flavor enhancers.

How to Use Fresh Herbs

For the truest and best flavors we much prefer to use fresh herbs where possible. We are convinced that some herbs are decidedly better only when used fresh rather than dried—basil, parsley, chives, chervil, borage, and cilantro, for example. On the other hand, if some fresh herbs are not available in the marketplace at a given time, then dried herbs and spices may be used.

- ◆ When choosing fresh herbs, it is best to select just one for the dominant flavor, adding other milder herbs in smaller amounts.

- Dried herbs have a more intense flavor than fresh, so the rule is to use one tablespoon of fresh to one teaspoon of dried.
- Taste as you go. Use your seasoning sparingly at first. You can always add more later on.
- For hot foods, sprinkle the fresh herbs on at the last minute since the heat of the food helps release their flavor. Also, the vivid green colors of the herbs will be maintained.
- For cold dishes, add the fresh herbs a few hours before serving or even the night before if possible so that their flavors permeate the dish completely.
- Set some of the fresh herbs aside to sprinkle over the top of the completed dish. You'll be pleasantly surprised at how a few pinches of chopped parsley can add sparkle to a bubbling brown stew or how a few sprigs of fresh rosemary can add a decorative touch.
- Mince the larger herbs very finely to release their fullest flavor. Even as you mince, you'll begin to discover the aroma.
- For the smaller herbs such as thyme and French tarragon, strip the tiny leaves from the tough stems.
- For delicate, wispy herbs such as chives, dill, chervil, and fennel leaves, use a pair of scissors to snip them into the recipe ingredients or salad.
- If you have room in your refrigerator, a good way to keep culinary herbs fresh is to place the stems in a glass of water, cover loosely with a plastic bag, and place the glass on the top shelf. Or store the herbs in a tightly closed, flat plastic container on the bottom shelf; each herb should be wrapped separately in a plastic bag so that the flavors are not exchanged.

Dried Herbs and Savory Spices: How to Buy Them and How to Use Them

- Replace ground herbs and spices once a year or at least every two years. If you're in doubt, smell them. If the scent is just a memory or they smell and look like tea, they've lost their vitality and it's time to replace them.
- Keep dried herbs and spices in a cool, dry, dark place, tightly sealed. When you need a particular herb or spice, open the jar, take what you need, and reseal the jar at once. They will keep well in a freezer, but if they're hidden away, you'll probably forget to use them.

- Some dried herbs can be bought with their whole leaves more or less intact, such as Greek oregano and mint. They last longer this way, and when you want to use them, you can easily crush them between your fingers to release the flavor before adding them to the dish.
- The flavor of whole dried spices (cloves, nutmeg, peppercorns, and coriander) is more pronounced, and they keep longer than the ground or powdered form.
- If you're using whole spices, grind them just before using them. The finer the grind, the richer the flavor.
- When using whole spices, place them in a little cheesecloth sack before dropping them into the pot. That way they are easily retrieved when the dish is done, and your teeth are safe from a wayward peppercorn.

A Word About Commercial Blends

Aside from the vast array of pure dried herbs and spices now on the shelves of supermarkets and specialty stores, there are a great many commercial blends available. Many of these have become basic standbys: poultry seasoning, herbs de Provence, pumpkin pie spice, five-spice powder, curry powders, and crab boil, to name just a few. The best advice we can give you is that when you decide to use one of these products, read the label carefully.

Some commercially prepared herb and spice salts may contain MSG, monosodium glutamate, which is to be avoided by people who are highly allergic to it. Other blends vary depending upon the manufacturer, and we have found some with the same generic name varying considerably. For example, serious Indian cooks resent the designation of "curry powder" since their spice blends of curry are as personal as fingerprints. Every Indian cook's treasured family recipe can combine as many as twenty different spices, usually including turmeric, ginger, fenugreek seed, cumin, mustard seed, red and black peppers, and, occasionally, cinnamon and cloves. The spices are usually lightly toasted first to bring out their flavors, and then they are freshly ground.

GINGER ROOT

Although ginger is not an herb or spice, we use it frequently in our recipes as an important flavor booster. Technically, fresh ginger is a rhizome and has its own roots, very much like a tuberous begonia. It has an intense, tongue-tingling quality that adds zip to many foods and beverages. It is available in many forms, each one with different properties.

MATURE GINGER: The skin (usually peeled before using in a recipe) is creamy tan in color, with a slight sheen, and is firm and smooth in texture. Grating mature ginger results in a fibrous mass. Therefore, chop it finely with a knife or in a small food processor after peeling. To keep it fresh, wrap it in a paper towel or aluminum foil and keep in the crisper drawer of your refrigerator.

YOUNG GINGER: Paler, cream colored, and with a lavender blush, the sheer skin does not need peeling. It is much milder in flavor and more delicate in texture than the mature ginger. It can be used in greater quantities because of its delicacy, can be grated or finely chopped, and can be kept fresh in the same way as the mature ginger (above). It can generally be found in Asian markets.

POWDERED GINGER: Ginger root is usually dried in the sun before being ground into a powder. It is used primarily in baked goods and desserts.

PICKLED GINGER: Used in Japanese cuisine and known as "gari," it is prepared from freshly peeled ginger and cut into thin shavings or sometimes thin julienne. Pickled ginger is steeped in a bath made from rice vinegar, sugar, salt, and sometimes coloring agents. Most commonly it is served with sushi and sashimi.

STEM GINGER IN SUGAR SYRUP: Sometimes called preserved ginger, young ginger is cut into various shapes and sizes, cooked, and then marinated in sugar syrup.

CRYSTALLIZED GINGER: Prepared as ginger in syrup and then drained and coated with granulated sugar, crystallized ginger is eaten out of hand as candy. We find it addictive. Cut into tiny pieces, it is added to cakes, tarts, and other sweets, creating new realms of tingling bursts of flavor.

LEMONGRASS

It resembles clipped beach grass with a fat bulb at one end or a 24-inch atrophied scallion and is a common ingredient in the cuisines of Southeast Asia. The flavor of lemongrass is similar to that of lemon or lemon verbena, yet it has its very own unique and haunting piquancy.

The technique for using lemongrass as well as the end results are very different from lemon juice. Lemon juice can curdle a cream sauce and after long cooking the lemon taste becomes invisible, so we usually add it toward the end in most recipes. Lemongrass, on the other hand, results in a noticeable but more subtle infusion when it is cooked, so we add it at the start. It will not curdle cream sauces.

SHOP SMART

Buy lemongrass that is heavy and green, with a fat bulb and not dried out. Wrap it in plastic and refrigerate. It will keep for about two weeks. Allow one or two fat stalks per dish.

Notes for the Cook

ON LEMONGRASS . . .

◆ If the lemongrass is to be removed from the dish after it infuses its flavor, as in some soups, sauces, rice, pasta, or vegetables, do the following: Remove the tough outer layers until the pale core is revealed. Cut these outer leaves into long pieces and bruise them to release some of their flavor. Then add them to the dish. Remove and discard the leaves after cooking, just as you would a bay leaf.

◆ If the lemongrass is to be eaten as part of the dish, use the pale, more tender inner core and bulb with their slightly fibrous texture. They do not soften after cooking, so cut them into two- or three-inch pieces and crush them with a mallet or the side of a heavy knife in order to release their volatile oils. Then finely mince them by using a mini-chop or spice grinder.

Garlic and Its Sisters: Onions, Leeks, Shallots, Scallions, and Ramps

Provençal Garlic Soup with Sage, Thyme, and Cloves

Cipolline Agridulce with Raisins and Pine Nuts

Spanish Leek Gratin with Cabrales Cheese and Olives

Caramelized Red Onions with Red Wine, Honey, and Thyme

Roasted Vidalia Onions with Goat Cheese

Ramp and Potato Soup with Saffron, Chives, and Tomatoes

The words of one anonymous nineteenth-century epicure still ring true for us today. He stated, "Banish the onion and garlic from the kitchen and all pleasure of eating flies with it. Their presence lends color and enchantment to the most modest dish; its absence reduces the rarest dainty to hopeless insipidity and the diner to despair."

GARLIC

It is actually of the *Allium* genus and a member of the lily family, as are leeks, onions, chives, shallots, and scallions. All are indispensable to the cook. Garlic is said to have fed the slaves that built the great pyramid at Giza in 2900 B.C., made fierce fighters of the Roman legions, was supposed to be able to kill vampires, and was capable of curing everything from the common cold to cardiovascular disease.

Today it is still a love-it-or-leave-it vegetable. Those who hate it mention its ferocious odor and taste; those who cannot live without it think its perfume rivals Chanel No. 5. There is no dish (except dessert) that does not benefit from some member of the *Allium* genus either in a supporting role or as a featured player.

In the last few years, many types of garlic have appeared in our markets, just a few of the three hundred known varieties. A head of garlic will vary from season to season and from variety to variety, but it is exactly these varietal differences that cause us to select different wines, cheeses, apples, or, for that matter, our mates.

Most garlic is either hardneck or softneck. Hardnecks send up a central woody stalk that would flower if left to grow but is removed as soon as it appears. A single circle of garlic cloves, between six and eleven bulbs, forms around this stalk while still underground. The cloves are loose-skinned and easy to peel. These small cloves are reputed to have a more intense "half-wild" flavor and will not keep as long as softneck garlic.

Some Hardneck Types

ROCAMBOLE: With blotchy, purplish, plump, moist cloves, this young, thin-skinned summer garlic has a strong outstanding flavor and no trace of bitterness.

RED REZAN: A glazed, purple blush with a tinge of gold distinguishes this garlic that originated near the town of Rezan in the Republic of Russia. The bulb has fewer and shorter individual cloves and slightly more zip than the similar Rocambole.

PURPLE ITALIAN AND PURPLE TIP: The bulbs have reddish purple streaks with easy-to-peel large cloves. They have a vigorous flavor, yet they leave a sweet aftertaste.

Some Softneck Types

Sometimes referred to as "braiding garlic," the softneck types are descendants of the hardneck variety that have lost their ability to flower. Their bulbs are large and have tightly overlapping layers all the way to the center. Their skins prevent rapid dehydration, so they store longer—for up to a year under proper conditions. They are frequently sold with their dried tops braided attractively, to be used as gifts or for ornamental display. Their flavor is a bit spicier, and they are adaptable to a wider range of climatic conditions.

In the United States, the softneck types grow in the Deep South, on the Gulf of Mexico, and in southern California. They are the most commonly grown garlic in the world. Here are some popular varieties:

SILVERSKIN: This is the American supermarket favorite and the favorite with the braiders. The bulbs are slightly elliptical and have smooth, tight, papery wrappers and a very mild flavor.

ELEPHANT GARLIC: With a much, much larger garlic head, many weighing over a pound, most of these are grown in California and the State of Washington. It is a good garlic for tempting a confirmed garlic hater because its flavor is very mild, and slow roasting makes it even milder.

Notes for the Cook

ON GARLIC . . .

- ◆ To peel a clove, hit the flat side of the clove with a meat pounder or the side of a heavy-duty chef's knife. This will slightly smash the clove, and the peel should easily slip away.
- ◆ For just a hint of garlic, do not peel before adding to a recipe.

- For a mild flavor, peel the garlic clove, slit it lengthwise, and cut out and discard the innermost green heart.
- Slow simmering of peeled garlic tames the intensity.
- For a stronger garlic flavor, peel and mince the cloves.
- For the most intense flavor, peel and crush or mash the garlic. This releases the oil-containing compounds that oxidize on contact with the air and give it a more "violent" flavor. It will be two to three times stronger than minced garlic.

GARLIC'S SISTERS

Rare is a dish in any universal cuisine that does not owe a debt of flavor to an onion. The onion's sweetly pungent personality and its astonishing versatility make it the ally of every cook. Many onion varieties are available today, so knowing their characteristic pungency and sweetness can help you choose the one best suited for your use.

SWEET ONIONS

The sweet onion season begins early in the year when the Oso onions arrive from Chile. Their season ends when the other varieties begin to appear in late March: Maui onions from Hawaii, Walla Wallas from Washington State, Vidalias from Georgia, and several other sweet varieties from Texas. They are incredibly sweet—sweet enough, in fact, to eat out of hand if you are a raw onion lover. Their high water content is responsible for their sweetness, but unlike other onions, they are more perishable. They now account for 15 to 20 percent of all onions sold in the United States. They are often milder and larger than other varieties, and have a high sugar content and less sulfur.

Spanish Onions

Tagged as a globe-shaped gentle giant, these sensationally sized onions weigh between eight ounces and one pound each. They are much like the Bermuda onion, another large, mild white onion that is flatter in shape. Both are great for eating raw or baking, or for making fried onion rings.

Red Onions

Sometimes called "purple onions," these are available in a variety of sizes, shapes, and flavors, as well as names. They are very mild and can be eaten raw in salads or sandwiches and are delicious and attractive when grilled or made into a caramelized conserve with red wine.

YELLOW ONIONS

These humble, earthy, firm-fleshed, and highly flavored onions are multipurpose. Their tan paper skins can cover a globe shape or a flat-topped *(granex)* onion. The small, appealing granex-shaped yellow and white onions from Italy are marketed as Cipolline onions and are good roasted.

WHITE ONIONS

These come in a variety of shapes, sizes, and tastes. They include the small ones labeled "boiling onions" and the even smaller white ones called "pearl onions." Pearl onions are less than one inch in diameter and have papery white (and sometimes papery red) skin, much like garlic. They have a strong flavor, but they become mellow when sautéed, boiled, pickled, or used in hearty sauces.

Why Cry Over Onions?

Peeling onions under running water is said to dilute the chemical compounds found in onions—the stuff that makes you cry. Since the root end releases more of those juices, we always cut and peel an onion from the stem end first.

Chopping onions and garlic is an odiferous business, and the "fragrance" may well linger on your fingers. We suggest the method of rubbing your hands with toothpaste and cold water, then soaping to get rid of the scent. Or wash your hands with salt and lemon juice. Rubbing with used coffee grounds may also do the trick.

These remedies were offered to us by others. They may not do the trick, so keep a box of tissues handy when peeling onions!

SHOP SMART

For all globe onions:

- Buy firm, heavy, unblemished onions with dry, papery skins.
- Avoid damp, bruised, sprouting soft onions or those with black mold.
- Onions should keep well for two months (depending on their condition when purchased) if stored in a well-ventilated place out of the light.
- Humidity in the kitchen and in a refrigerator will encourage decay.

Notes for the Cook

ON ONIONS . . .

- In a pinch, if you're down to your last few onions and they have sprouted, the sprouts can be used like scallions.
- Burned onions are acrid onions. Keep adjusting the heat and stirring them while cooking so they don't burn.

SHALLOTS

Bulblets with a French cachet. Once these robust, full-bodied alliums were hard to come by, and because of their scarcity, they earned a reputation for elegance. They range in size from ½ to 2 inches and have dry, papery, reddish brown to gray skin with a slight surface sheen. They cook down and thicken sauces such as the classic French *beurre blanc*. They are a tradition with steamed mussels, poached seafood, and poultry, and raw shallots flavor vinaigrettes in a delightful manner.

SCALLIONS

This name is given to the young, immature plant of any variety of onion. It is known for its interchangeable terms: green onion, spring onion, or bunch onion. Production is not limited to spring, however, for they are plentiful year-round. Their leaves should be fresh, crisp, and blue-green, with their stem ends either straight or bulbous and tipped with a hairy root. They are often eaten raw, and their taste ranges from mild to strong as their size increases. They are used in salads and for crudités, and are indispensable raw. They are also cooked until wilted in Chinese and Japanese cuisines. More perishable than dry onions, they should be wrapped in paper towels, placed in a plastic bag, and kept in the refrigerator for only a few days. Before using, cut off and discard the wilted green parts.

LEEKS

The leek has been claimed as an emblem of national pride to the Welsh, who wore them in their caps to easily distinguish friend from foe in battle. The Welsh still wear a leek on March 1, Saint David's Day, and soldiers in the Welsh regiments are required to eat raw leek on that day.

With a lustier taste than the scallion, which they vaguely resemble, leeks are heavier, coarser, larger, thicker, and more cylindrical in shape. White for two to three inches above the root end, they have broad, flat, dark green leaves. Leeks have always grown profusely in temperate climates and are plentiful in the fall through the spring.

They are indispensable for stocks and are excellent braised, served as an hors d'oeuvre, or cut into julienne to garnish fish. Leeks contain a gelatin-like substance that holds and binds cream and eggs beautifully, so they are good in custardy quiches. Also, individual leaves can be blanched and used to wrap other foods.

Notes for the Cook

ON LEEKS . . .

Leeks are not difficult to clean, but you need to do a thorough job or you'll be crunching on sand:

- ◆ Trim off the shaggy root end only, leaving the white part intact.
- ◆ Cut off the topmost greener, tougher leaves, leaving 5 to 8 inches of mostly white vegetable with some paler green leaves.
- ◆ Split the top lengthwise to within an inch of the root base. Fan out the leaves and run your fingers gently over them under cold running water to get rid of any hidden dirt.
- ◆ Dry them thoroughly.

RAMPS

These native wild leeks grow throughout the Appalachian Mountains, and ramp festivals are held in their honor in West Virginia. With their purple-streaked stalks and leaves that look like lily-of-the-valley, they resemble a dainty spring bouquet. They don't smell exactly like violets, however, but have a notorious lingering odor. They are slimmer and shorter than scallions and have a slightly bitter edge and a taste that is a cross between a leek and garlic. Cook them as you would leeks for a new taste sensation. Newly marketed nationally, their season is short—from March to early May.

CHIVES

The most tender and delicate member of the onion clan has a soft springtime flavor. Cut chives are sold in bunches and in little pots of growing chives. Rarely cooked (except in omelets), they are usually snipped with a scissors and sprinkled on a finished dish just before serving to preserve their mildness. Their delicacy sets off creamy white cheeses, egg dishes, potatoes, soups, salads, fish, poultry, and cream soups. The lavender blossoms are a stronger, very attractive version of the chive flavor and look stunning in a dark green fresh spinach salad. They're a bit more flavorful than sweet red onions. Chinese chives, a flat-leaf, more assertive variety, are used in a similar manner.

PROVENÇAL GARLIC SOUP WITH SAGE, THYME, AND CLOVES

A liberal amount of garlic is used in this soup, but it is not at all assertive since the garlic loses its strong flavor when gently simmered.

SERVES 4

8 cups chicken broth
24 medium cloves garlic, peeled and
    coarsely chopped
1 bay leaf
4 whole cloves
6 sprigs fresh thyme
10 large fresh sage leaves
Pinch of saffron
2 egg yolks
4 tablespoons olive oil

8 slices French or sourdough baguette
2 tablespoons butter, melted
2 to 3 tablespoons grated Gruyère
    cheese
3 to 4 drops Tabasco
1 tablespoon lemon juice (about
    ½ large lemon)
Salt to taste
⅓ cup finely minced fresh parsley

In a 4- to 6-quart pot over medium heat, bring the broth to a boil, then lower the heat. Add the garlic and simmer, uncovered, for 5 minutes. Put the bay leaf, cloves, thyme, and sage into a small piece of cheesecloth and tie with string. Add it to the soup along with the saffron. Simmer the soup, uncovered, for 30 minutes.

Meanwhile, whisk the egg yolks in a small bowl. Add the olive oil, a little at a time, and whisk constantly until the mixture is thick. Set aside.

While the soup is simmering, preheat the oven to 325 degrees. Spread the slices of bread in 1 layer on a jelly roll pan. Trickle the bread with the melted butter and bake for 10 minutes, or until crisp and dry. Sprinkle with the cheese and slip under the broiler for 1 minute or so, until the cheese melts.

When the soup is cooked, remove the cheesecloth bag and discard it. Puree the soup in a blender or food processor in batches, then add 1 cup of hot soup slowly to the egg and oil emulsion, whisking constantly until combined. Return this mixture to the pot and heat over low heat, stirring occasionally. Do not allow it to boil, or it will curdle.

Just before serving, add the Tabasco and lemon juice, and taste for salt. Ladle the soup into bowls, sprinkle liberally with parsley, and float 2 slices of the cheese toasts on top of each serving.

CIPOLLINE AGRIDULCE WITH RAISINS AND PINE NUTS

These tiny, flat Italian onions have a Sicilian accent when pan-roasted until golden in a reduced balsamic and white wine glaze with a shower of raisins and nuts. Try them with a steak or pork or as part of an antipasto.

SERVES 4

1 pound Cipolline onions with skins
3 tablespoons black raisins
Warm water
2 tablespoons olive oil
3 tablespoons sugar

Salt to taste
¼ cup dry white wine
¼ cup balsamic vinegar
2 tablespoons cold water
1 tablespoon toasted pine nuts

In a 1½-quart saucepan, add the onions to boiling salted water and cook, covered, over medium heat for 3 minutes. Drain and cool. When cool enough to handle, cut off the small tail at the top of the onions and peel the skin back to the root. Closely trim the root ends, leaving enough root to hold the onions together. Dry them on paper towels.

In a small cup, add the raisins to warm water to plump them up. In a 12-inch non-reactive (stainless steel or nonstick) skillet, heat the oil over medium heat for 1 minute. Add the onions and cook, sliding the skillet frequently so they brown without burning. Cook for 5 to 8 minutes, turning them over with wooden tongs. (Metal tongs don't grab slippery onion surfaces well.) When the onions are brown, sprinkle them with sugar and salt, and continue to cook, sliding the pan until the sugar melts and the onions are coated. Add the wine and cook for 1 minute. Add the vinegar and cold water, and cook over low heat until the liquid is reduced to a glaze, about 5 or 6 minutes. Baste once with the glaze and transfer the onions to a serving dish. Scatter the drained raisins and pine nuts over the onions and serve at room temperature.

SPANISH LEEK GRATIN WITH CABRALES CHEESE AND OLIVES

The strongly flavored, blue-veined Spanish cabrales cheese beautifully sauces young leeks poached in chicken broth and polka-dotted with black and green olives.

SERVES 4

1 ½ pounds thin leeks, including 2 inches of green tops (about 8 leeks)

2 cups chicken broth

6 ounces cabrales cheese, cut up

½ cup heavy cream

2 teaspoons cornstarch

16 assorted black and green olives such as Kalamata and Manzanilla, pitted

Freshly ground black pepper to taste

Trim the beards from the leeks and split them halfway down from the green end. Separate the leaves as you rinse them under cold water. Dry on paper towels and tie with string into 2 bundles.

In a 10-inch skillet, bring the chicken broth to a boil over medium heat. Add the leek bundles, cover the skillet, and poach for 5 minutes. Turn the bundles over and cook 5 minutes more, or until the leeks are tender when pierced with the point of a knife.

While the leeks are poaching, place the cheese and cream in a 2-quart saucepan and whisk over low heat until the cheese melts. When the leeks are cooked, remove the bundles, place on paper towels to drain, and then transfer them to a heat-proof gratin dish. Cut off and discard the string and pour off ¼ cup of the poaching broth into a small cup. Dissolve the cornstarch in this broth, then add it to the cheese mixture and whisk over very low heat until thickened.

Preheat the broiler. Spoon the sauce over the leeks, scatter the olives over the sauce, and grind some fresh pepper over all. Slip the gratin dish under the broiler and broil for about 3 minutes, or until the gratin is dappled with brown flecks. Serve hot.

CARAMELIZED RED ONIONS WITH RED WINE, HONEY, AND THYME

We always try to keep these onions on hand for multiple uses: to add to broccoli raab, to sauce a pasta, and to top a pissaladière (see page 450). We used them with grilled meats, in an omelet, or just as a spread on a crostini for a quick hors d'oeuvre.

MAKES ABOUT 2½ CUPS

2 tablespoons olive oil

2 tablespoons butter

3 tablespoons mild light honey

2½ pounds red onions (about 6 or 7), peeled and sliced into ½-inch slices (about 8 cups)

3 sprigs thyme

1 small bay leaf

¼ teaspoon ground allspice

Salt and pepper to taste

2 cups dry red wine

⅓ cup red wine vinegar or sherry vinegar

Heat the oil and butter in a 12-inch skillet over medium heat. Stir in the honey and cook for 1 to 2 minutes, until it starts to brown slightly. Stir in the onions and sauté, stirring occasionally, until wilted and transparent, about 5 minutes. Add the thyme, bay leaf, allspice, salt, and pepper. Add the wine and vinegar, cover the skillet, lower the heat to a slow simmer, and cook for 1 to 1½ hours, until whatever liquid remains is syrupy.

Stir occasionally during cooking and if the mixture seems to require liquid, add a bit of water and continue cooking. Remove and discard the thyme sprigs and bay leaf. The onions will keep, covered, in the refrigerator for up to 10 days. Use at room temperature.

ROASTED VIDALIA ONIONS WITH GOAT CHEESE

Slow-roasting releases more of the natural sugars of these already sweet onions, which are so mild and succulent even when raw that they can supposedly be chomped on like an apple. It also makes an unusual first course or side dish.

SERVES 4

4 medium Vidalia or other sweet
    onions such as Maui, Oso, or Walla
    Walla, unpeeled
2 tablespoons olive oil

1 cup chicken broth
4 ounces fresh goat cheese such as
    Montrachet
Cayenne pepper to taste

Preheat the oven to 300 degrees. Dip the onions in the olive oil and rub the oil evenly over the skins. Place them in a shallow baking dish 1 inch apart. Pour the chicken broth over them and roast, uncovered, for 1 to 1½ hours, or until the broth is absorbed.

Spread the onion layers open a bit like the petals of a flower and add 1 ounce of cheese to the top of each onion. Sprinkle with some cayenne and return to the oven with the heat off until the cheese melts and is slightly warm.

RAMP AND POTATO SOUP WITH SAFFRON, CHIVES, AND TOMATOES

A lovely, creamy soup made golden with saffron and redolent with ramps. Delicate chives and tiny bits of tomato float on the surface, creating a medley of colors and flavors. You can substitute leeks if ramps are not available.

SERVES 6

½ teaspoon saffron threads

2 tablespoons boiling water

2 tablespoons butter

8 ounces washed ramps, root end trimmed and thinly sliced (about 4 cups)

1 pound russet potatoes (about 2 potatoes), peeled and diced (about 2½ cups)

5 cups chicken broth

2 cups milk

Salt and pepper to taste

⅛ teaspoon Tabasco

¼ cup finely snipped chives

12 cherry tomatoes, cut into quarters

Combine the saffron and boiling water in a small cup and steep for 10 minutes. In a 5-quart Dutch oven, melt the butter over medium heat. Add the ramps and sauté for 5 minutes, stirring until wilted. Add the potatoes and cook, stirring, for 1 to 2 minutes. Add the chicken broth, saffron, and saffron water, and bring to a boil. Turn the heat to low, cover the pot, and simmer for 30 minutes.

Puree in a blender, a few batches at a time, and return to the same Dutch oven. Stir in the milk and simmer over low heat until hot, about 10 to 15 minutes. Season with salt, pepper, and Tabasco. Ladle into bowls and sprinkle each serving with some chives and tomatoes. Serve hot.

Artichokes, Asparagus, and Avocados

*Braised Baby Artichokes with New Potatoes, Carrots, and
Pearl Onions (Greek Style)*

Roasted Asparagus Wrapped in Prosciutto with Asiago Cheese

*Avocado, Fennel, and Anchovy Salad with a
Tomato and Olive Vinaigrette*

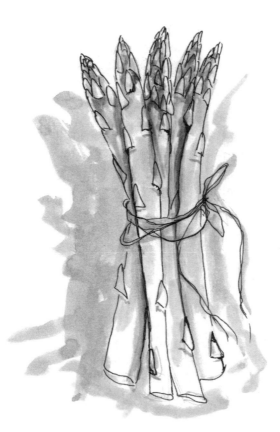

THE ARTFUL ARTICHOKE

Since 1922, Castroville, California, about one hundred miles south of San Francisco, has been the undisputed green globe artichoke center of the United States, duly celebrated with a September festival that always includes a lovely local radiant young woman who is carried on a float as Artichoke Queen. The 1949 queen was an unknown starlet named Marilyn Monroe. At that time the artichoke was considered a daunting, hostile, perplexing vegetable. Its globe shape and smooth, tight, scale-like leaves tipped with small thorns resembled a weapon more than an edible plant. And so the young Monroe was immediately dispatched around the country on a publicity tour designed to counteract the public image.

The United States grows about 12,000 acres of globe artichokes annually, but this is "small potatoes" compared to Italy's 150,000 acres, Spain's 60,000 acres, and France's 30,000 acres—not to mention Greece and Algeria. Artichokes have been enjoyed in Europe and North Africa for centuries. There are about fifty different varieties that range in a spectrum of colors, from the blanched white to the small purple of France and Italy.

Botanically defined as a prickly thistle, this perennial plant can grow up to six feet in diameter and three to four feet tall. What we eat are the flower buds, the base of the firm green leaves. The fuzzy, fibrous parts, called the choke, are the petals of the flowers, which must be scraped away before eating the heart. The choke is surrounded by a sharp purple-tipped cone of leaves that must also be discarded.

Artichokes come in various sizes depending on which part of the stem they grew on; the largest are from the top of the plant.

SHOP SMART

Artichokes reach their seasonal peak from March to May, with a secondary crop around October and November. Along with the size, the shapes also change slightly with the seasons:

In spring, a slightly rounded shape with tightly folded leaves.

In summer, more cone-shaped with pointier leaves that splay out slightly.

In the fall and winter, either conical or round, and sometimes kissed by frost, leaving a brown-streaked scarring.

No matter what the size or the seasonal shape, all artichokes should be freshly green, compact, and heavy for their size. If the leaves look dried out or yellowed or have any brown mottled spots (not frost kissed), avoid them. And when you get your prize home, keep them unwashed in a plastic bag in the refrigerator for only three or four days.

Medium artichokes weigh about 8 ounces.

Baby artichokes weigh anywhere from 2 to 4 ounces.

One medium or large or four to five babies = 1 serving.

Artichokes are also available marinated, canned, and frozen. Time savers, yes, but the fresh ones will always taste the best.

Notes for the Cook

ON ARTICHOKES . . .

- Fill a glass, ceramic, or stainless-steel bowl with water. Squeeze the juice of a medium lemon into the water and add the lemon shells to the bowl. This will help prevent discoloration of the artichokes.
- Before cooking artichokes, you must remove the inedible to get to the edible parts.

FOR WHOLE ARTICHOKES:

- Cut off ½ inch from the base of the stem.
- Remove the small leaves from the base of the globe.
- Lay the artichoke on its side and slice off 1 inch from the top.
- Use scissors to trim off the thorny tips of the remaining leaves.
- Drop the artichoke into the bowl of acidulated water until ready to cook.

TO COOK WHOLE ARTICHOKES:

◆ Cooking artichokes in chicken broth and lemon juice adds extra flavor, but salted cold water with lemon juice is fine.

◆ Place the artichokes tightly in the pot, cover with liquid, and bring to a boil. Lower the heat to medium and boil gently, uncovered, for 20 to 45 minutes, depending on size. Test for doneness by piercing the bottom with the tip of a knife, and then see if you can pull off a leaf with ease.

◆ When the artichokes are cooked, remove with tongs and turn them upside down to drain on paper towels.

◆ Serve whole with dishes of salted lemon juice or garlic butter for dipping.

◆ Serve warm or cold with a vinaigrette sauce.

◆ To stuff, spread the leaves open and scoop out the choke and cone, leaving a cavity for stuffing. Bake as directed. A bit of stuffing can also be forced between each leaf.

◆ Hearts and babies, as well as bottoms, cook in about 15 minutes. Infants, once trimmed of outer leaves (or the purple imports from Italy), can be sliced paper thin, dressed with oil and lemon juice, and eaten raw.

FOR ARTICHOKE HEARTS:

The heart is the tender part under the covering cone of leaves, with the chokes removed.

◆ After cooking, to get to the heart, remove the outer leaves until a central core of pale yellowish leaves is reached. Slice the artichoke in half vertically and trim the thorny tips.

◆ Scoop out the fuzzy center at the base of the artichoke bottom, using a spoon or a melon ball scoop.

◆ If the hearts are large, cut them into quarters.

FOR ARTICHOKE BOTTOMS:

The bottom is the cup or disc-shaped base, with all the center leaves and the choke cut out. Cut off the cone with a sharp knife, then cut out the fuzzy center choke and scrape the surface.

FOR ARTICHOKE BABIES (2 TO 3 INCHES) OR INFANTS (1 INCH OR THE SIZE OF A WALNUT):

- Trim the stem end and the tough outer leaves.
- Cut off the tips.
- When small enough (1 to 2 inches), the whole artichoke can be eaten since the fuzzy chokes have not yet developed.
- Cook whole, halved, or quartered.
- About 8 to 10 babies = 1 pound.

Notes for the Artichoke Eater

Whole artichokes are possibly the world's best finger food. Pull off a cooked leaf and dip the broad base, the fleshy end, into a sauce. Draw the leaf through your front teeth, scraping off the small, edible part, then discard the leaf. Continue until you get to the purple-tipped cone. Pull or cut it out and scrape off the fuzzy choke with a spoon or knife. What remains is the heart and the meatiest part, the bottom. Cut it up, dip it in the sauce, and enjoy!

Some Artichoke Don'ts

To prevent discoloration: Don't use a carbon-steel knife to cut artichokes. Use only stainless steel.

Don't use cast-iron or aluminum pots to cook artichokes; use only enamel, stainless-steel, or nonstick pots.

Don't wrap artichokes in aluminum foil after cooking. Only use plastic wrap.

ASPARAGUS = SPRINGTIME!

For those of us who cook by nature's calendar, the inspiring, graceful green shoots of asparagus emerging from the awakened thawing earth signify that winter is finally over, that springtime is definitely here. Although asparagus is usually available in the marketplace all year round, the peak season is brief: from mid-February to June.

There are basically three varieties of asparagus:

1. *Green* is available in three sizes that range from pencil thin to standard to the very fat spears as the season progresses.
2. *White* touched with a hint of purple is milder in flavor and has a

slightly bitter edge. It is more popular in Europe but is now appearing more frequently in specialty markets in the United States.

3. *Red/Purple* is a new variety now found occasionally in the markets. It is very sweet, and the stalks cook up green.

SHOP SMART

- ◆ When shopping for the best asparagus, check the stem ends first to make sure they are not dried out. They should look freshly cut. Select firm, tightly closed spears with vivid green color and slightly purple tips.
- ◆ If the spear tips are open or spongy, the asparagus will be bitter.
- ◆ Try to choose them all in the same thickness for even cooking.
- ◆ Store them at home by cutting ⅛ inch from the base and placing them upright in a wide-mouthed jar with 1 inch of water. Cover the tops loosely with a plastic bag and refrigerate. Or wrap the stem ends only in a damp paper towel before bagging. Cook the asparagus within three or four days for best flavor.
- ◆ Allow about 8 ounces per person, untrimmed. There are about fifteen to twenty thick asparagus spears to the pound and about thirty pencil-thin spears to the pound.

Notes for the Cook

ON ASPARAGUS . . .

- ◆ To prepare, rinse the asparagus under cold water and gently bend the stalks. They will break naturally at the point where the stem gets tough. Or cut about 1½ inches off the bottoms for a neater look. The trimmings can be used in a vegetable stock or an asparagus soup.
- ◆ Peeling the stems just under the tips, as some restaurants do, is a matter of preference or is necessary if the skin is fibrous. We usually like our asparagus in thin to medium spears, cooked tender/crisp and bright green by steaming them over boiling water in a wide skillet with a rack or boiling them in salted water.
- ◆ Slim spears take about two to three minutes; medium spears about five to seven minutes; fat spears eight to ten minutes for steaming. Boiling takes one to two minutes less time.
- ◆ Fat spears invite roasting to make them nutty sweet. Medium-size asparagus rolled in butter or olive oil and some salt and layered on a baking pan will usually

be tender in ten to twelve minutes in a 425 degree oven. Keep testing by inserting the point of a knife into the thickest end until they are the texture you prefer. Remove them with tongs to paper towels to drain for a moment.

◆ Asparagus can be dressed simply in a vinaigrette or added to risottos, pastas, and frittatas.

THE ALLURE OF THE AVOCADO

This New World subtropical tree fruit, which we look upon as a vegetable, has been growing in the Americas for about seven thousand years. And long before the arrival of the conquistadors, the Aztecs were eating this protein-rich, buttery-textured fruit, which they called *ahuacatl.* Loosely translated it means "the fruit of the testicle tree" because of the shape of the fruit and its typically double-clustered pendulant growth pattern. Of course, it was then reputed to have aphrodisiac qualities.

Of the 300 million pounds of avocados harvested annually, 80 percent are shipped by California growers; most of the remainder come from Florida, and there are some Mexican and Guatemalan hybrids.

The variety needed depends upon its use:

HASS: This is the most popular California variety, originally a Guatemalan and Mexican hybrid. Small and with rough, pebbly, thick skin and a dark greenish black color, it gets blacker as it ripens. The fruit is creamy rich, high in oil (but not the high-cholesterol kind), and full flavored. It is best used for purees. Added to rice and crab, wrapped in seaweed, and served in sushi bars, it is called "California Roll." Cut in half and filled with any variety of seafood, vegetables, or poultry, it can be served as a salad. The flesh crushes easily, so the Hass avocado is more difficult to dice or slice neatly. Its peak season is from May to November.

FUERTE: Also from the same growing regions but more elongated and pear-shaped, this variety has a slightly smoother, dark green skin than Hass and a creamy texture. The varieties called Bacon and Zutano have smooth, bright green skins that remain green as they ripen. These avocados are available from November through May.

FLORIDA AVOCADOS: Larger in size, these are sometimes called "alligator pears." They are bright green and have a smooth skin and a milder flavor than the others. The flesh is also firmer, so it takes to dicing and slicing without falling apart.

SHOP SMART

The avocado tree acts as a "holding pattern," and the fruit matures but does not ripen fully until picked. Once picked, early-season avocados take longer to ripen than the later-season ones.

How will you know if an avocado is ripe? Press gently. If the avocado yields easily and doesn't leave finger marks, it's ripe. A rock-hard avocado is one that has been picked too soon; and many times it will rot before ripening.

Buy avocados a few days before you plan to use them. Select unbruised fruit that yields to gentle pressure without being mushy. Keep them at room temperature for two to three days.

Two small or one large avocado = about 1 pound.
When mashed it makes about 1 cup.

Notes for the Cook

ON AVOCADOS . . .

- To ripen an avocado at home if it does not yield to the touch, wrap it in newspapers or a brown paper bag for one to two days.
- Once peeled, cut, and stored, the flesh of the avocado darkens rapidly. It is not attractive, but the darkness doesn't affect the taste. To combat darkening, brush the cut surface with citrus.
- Keep the pit intact for leftovers and cover the unused part with plastic wrap, pressing it directly on all surfaces to omit any contact with the air.
- Avocados are best eaten raw. When they're cooked for any length of time, their flavor is diminished and they frequently take on a bitter, unpleasant edge.

BRAISED BABY ARTICHOKES WITH NEW POTATOES, CARROTS, AND PEARL ONIONS (GREEK STYLE)

This is a classic Greek vegetable dish starring the artichoke: It is bathed in a lemon sauce thickened with egg yolk and then flavored with either fresh fennel or dill fronds.

SERVES 6

8 to 10 baby artichokes (2 to
    3 inches)
3 tablespoons olive oil
½ cup thinly sliced scallions (about
    2 medium)
12 tiny white pearl onions, blanched
    for 2 minutes and peeled
¼ cup dry white wine
3 tablespoons lemon juice
2 tablespoons butter

3 tablespoons flour
3 cups hot chicken broth
8 small whole red potatoes
    (8 ounces), scrubbed
8 ounces baby carrots, scrubbed and
    left whole
1 egg yolk
Salt and pepper to taste
3 tablespoons coarsely snipped fennel
    fronds or dill

Prepare the artichoke hearts (see page 28). Heat the oil in a heavy 6-quart Dutch oven over medium-high heat. Add the scallions and pearl onions, and stir and cook for 2 minutes. Add the wine and 2 tablespoons of the lemon juice. Cook and stir until most of the liquid evaporates. Add the butter, and when it melts, sift the flour over it. Lower the heat and cook, stirring constantly, for 2 minutes. Add the hot broth gradually, stirring until smooth. Add the artichoke hearts and potatoes. Simmer, uncovered, for 20 minutes, then add the carrots and simmer 10 minutes more.

When the vegetables are tender, transfer them with a slotted spoon to a large serving dish and keep warm. Beat the egg yolk with a whisk in a small bowl and slowly add a ladleful of the sauce to the egg, whisking constantly. Return it to the sauce and simmer over very low heat, stirring constantly, for 2 minutes, until slightly thickened. Add the remaining tablespoon of lemon juice, season with salt and pepper, and stir in the fennel or dill. Spoon the sauce over all the vegetables and serve hot or at room temperature.

ROASTED ASPARAGUS WRAPPED IN PROSCIUTTO WITH ASIAGO CHEESE

Fat, green spears of asparagus enrobed in paper-thin slices of prosciutto are roasted in the oven and then sprinkled with a lovely melting cheese before they are slipped under the broiler for a few minutes. A wonderful first course.

SERVES 4

3 tablespoons butter

1 pound fat asparagus (about 12), bottoms trimmed

4 ounces paper-thin slices prosciutto (12 slices)

salt and pepper to taste

¼ cup grated asiago (*pressato;* see page 43) or Parmigiano-Reggiano cheese (about 2 ounces)

1 small wedge lemon

Preheat the oven to 425 degrees. Put the butter in a heavy oven-to-table casserole large enough to accommodate the asparagus in 1 layer. Place in the oven for a few minutes until the butter melts. Remove from the oven and set aside.

Wrap a slice of prosciutto in a spiral fashion around each spear of asparagus and roll it in the melted butter. Repeat with all the asparagus and place in 1 layer in the pan. Season lightly with salt and grind some fresh pepper over all. Cover the dish with aluminum foil and roast for 12 to 15 minutes, or until the asparagus are tender-crisp. (Test with the point of a knife.)

Remove the foil and sprinkle with the cheese. Tilt the pan and baste with some of the butter. Raise the heat to broil and slip the dish under the broiler for 1 to 2 minutes, or until the cheese has melted and is slightly dappled with brown. Squeeze lemon juice over all and serve.

◆ Prosciutto ◆

Prosciutto is the hind quarter of ham that has been seasoned, cured, and then air dried. The best is Prosciutto di Parma from Italy. Its melting texture and just the right salt/sweet balance is ethereal when very thinly sliced and paired with vegetables, fruits, and cheese. When prosciutto is cooked by itself, it takes on a leathery, tough texture, so stir it into pasta sauces, soups, and stews at the end of the cooking time.

AVOCADO, FENNEL, AND ANCHOVY SALAD WITH A TOMATO OLIVE VINAIGRETTE

A first-course salad with crisp, licoricy fennel and soft, buttery avocado that offers a textural contrast with the briny anchovies and olives and just a touch of tomato in a sparkling vinaigrette.

SERVES 4

2 small bulbs fennel (about 1 pound)
1 teaspoon finely minced garlic
   (1 clove)
6 tablespoons red wine vinegar
1 teaspoon crushed dried oregano,
   preferably Greek
Salt and pepper to taste
6 tablespoons olive oil
¾ cup ¼-inch diced plum tomatoes
   (about ½ pound)

12 pitted Kalamata olives, cut into
   quarters
12 flat anchovy fillets, rinsed, dried, and
   cut in half crosswise
1 large ripe Florida avocado or 2 ripe
   Hass avocados
Fennel fronds for garnish

Trim the base of the fennel bulbs, pulling off any large, tough outer leaves. Cut the bulbs lengthwise into twelve ¼-inch slices. Place 3 slices on each of 4 plates.

In a small bowl, combine the garlic, vinegar, oregano, salt, and pepper. Slowly whisk in the oil and then whisk rapidly to combine. Stir in the tomatoes and olives, then set aside.

Arrange 2 pieces of anchovy in a V shape on each slice of fennel. Peel, pit, and slice the avocados lengthwise and arrange them on the plates between the fennel slices. Whisk the sauce again and spoon it over the avocado and fennel slices. Scatter the fennel fronds over all.

Leafy Greens: Just for the Health of It

Shredded Kale with Pickle Relish and Kielbasa

Crustless Mixed Greens Tart with Jalapeño Pepper Cheese

Portuguese Caldo Verde with Collard Greens and Linguiça Sausage

Red Swiss Chard Bundles with Lemon, Olive Oil, and Scallions

Greens have always had a nutrient-dense profile. In the age of innocence many years ago when cholesterol was not even a word in our vocabularies, no less a dirty word, it was mostly American southerners who ate their greens without complaint, usually with lengthy cooking and copious amounts of fatty pork. Greens are now trendy in both the North and the South. However, we now cook them with just a touch of oil or butter for flavor, maintaining their nutrients, clean taste, and bright color.

And there are now all sorts of wonderful greens available, many of them with lots of character and unusual, assertive flavors: hot peppery mustard, milder turnip greens, earthy collard greens, kale with just a hint of its cabbage relative, salty Swiss chard, bitter dandelion greens, chicory and escarole, tart lemony sorrel, red-veined sweet-top beet leaves, and, of course, spinach.

We can also find a slew of wild and semi-wild greens such as lamb's-quarters, nettles, purslane, miner's lettuce. Some of these are easily subdued and do well with other bold, assertive, flavored greens. Many greens are interchangeable as well, so if one is not available, a decent substitute can easily be found.

TENDER AND DELICATE LEAFY GREENS

SPINACH: This misunderstood vegetable has finally overcome its bad press and is now appreciated for its versatility. It accepts other flavors gracefully and is compatible as a bed for eggs, fish, and poultry. It can also be partnered with a variety of herbs, spices, cheeses, mushrooms, nuts, and raisins. Two varieties are easily available: Crinkly-leaf Savoy spinach, which has a hardy texture and earthy flavor and is used for cooking or salads with heavy dressings, and the smooth, tender, flat-leaf spinach of spring with its delicate, mildly herbaceous flavor that is delicious in light salads.

CHINESE SPINACH: Really a leaf amaranth, it is mild, slightly sweet, and tinged with red. It is now becoming more available.

BEET GREENS: Fresh leafy green tops of beet roots can replace spinach in some recipes, although their red stems bleed like beets. They are known for their tender texture and mild flavor.

Two pounds of beet roots yields about 12 ounces of trimmed leaves.

SWISS CHARD: Two varieties can be found in the marketplace: chard with white veins and stems and large oval green leaves, and the red-stemmed variety. Chard is related to the beet but has a mild, saltier edge. Both stems and leaves are eaten, with the stems usually removed and cooked separately and a bit longer than the leaves. Whole large leaves can be blanched and used to wrap grains, meat, fish, poultry, and a variety of vegetables, much like cabbage leaves. They are interchangeable with beet greens and spinach in most recipes.

TOUGHER, MORE ASSERTIVE GREENS

MUSTARD GREENS: The two most available varieties of this hot and peppery green are the yellowish greens with feathered edges and those that are reddish purple. When cooking mustard greens, trim and discard the fibrous stems and cook them long enough to tenderize them and to mellow their pungency. Braising or boiling are the preferred cooking methods. Tender young leaves, sparingly used raw in salads, add a perky dimension. You can use broccoli raab as a substitute for mustard greens.

TURNIP GREENS: These are usually the tops of the turnip roots and have oval green leaves and cream-colored veins. They have a distinct, peppery edge when cooked but are not quite as assertive as mustard greens. Trim and discard the fibrous stems before cooking slowly and longer, much like mustard greens. Turnip greens are excellent as an accompaniment for strong-tasting fish such as tuna and mackerel as well as with pork and duck. Broccoli raab is also a good substitute here.

COLLARD GREENS: Fleshy and with a dusty green color, these leathery, roundish leaves have tough stems. They are similar to kale in flavor but have a more muted quality.

This southern U.S. staple can be cooked in the same manner as turnip and mustard greens—braised in liquid. They are excellent in soups.

One pound of trimmed and shredded leaves in ½-inch strips = 8 cups.

KALE: This attractive, substantial, hearty, crinkly, ruffled dark blue or green leaf with tough stems and ribs does not reduce in volume as much as spinach does during cooking. It requires more water and a lengthier cooking time.

RED RUSSIAN KALE: This is smaller and frilly, and has lavender-veined leaves. It is milder and more tender than regular kale, and cooks to tenderness in a shorter time.

> For 1 pound of trimmed kale, allow 1 cup of water and at least twenty
> minutes of cooking time, depending on the age and toughness of the
> leaves. The yield is about 2 cups when cooked.

DANDELION GREENS: This strong, bitter spring green should be eaten very young when the leaves are less bitter. They can be used with bold flavors such as hot chiles, garlic, and oil. The slim, spiky, tooth-edged greens are cultivated; they are not the ubiquitous weeds with yellow flowers that grow where they're not wanted. Dandelion greens are best braised or used raw in salads.

SORREL: Also known as sour grass, this spring green makes its debut along with early peas and asparagus. It has an intriguing lemony taste that is a very pleasant addition to purees, classic French sauces, and French and Russian soups. Select young, unwilted leaves, fold each leaf in half, and cut out and discard the center stem and vein, which can become stringy when cooked. Sorrel turns olive green after cooking.

> One pound of trimmed leaves will reduce to about ⅔ cup of puree
> when cooked with just a bit of water or quickly stirred in some
> butter to wilt.

 ## SHOP SMART

The growing season is long for most greens, and therefore they are fairly inexpensive as well as being distinctive, so you can get a lot of bang for your buck. All greens hate hot weather, when they get bitter and go to seed. They are really cool-season vegetables and are best in early spring when they are most tender and flavorful, as well as in the cooler months of autumn and early winter.

- It is best to buy spinach tied in bundles or loose leaves rather than the prepackaged variety, which tends to be tired.
- Buy vibrantly colored leaves; avoid limp, yellowed ones or any with a slimy sign of decay.
- Although greens are best when used quickly, they can be stored, unwashed and wrapped in paper towels, in a plastic bag for three days.

- Remember, except for kale, the volume of greens reduces considerably after cooking, so make sure you buy enough.

Three pounds of spinach after trimming (about 1½ pounds) yields
about 2 cups cooked.

Notes for the Cook

ON LEAFY GREENS . . .

- Silver and aluminum create an unpleasant metallic reaction with spinach. Use stainless-steel knives and pots or nonstick pots.
- Trim away tough stems or root clusters and discard them. Usually, stems less than an eighth of an inch thick can be kept and cooked just a bit longer.
- Most greens grow in sandy soil, so they must be cleaned carefully and properly.
- Submerge greens in cold water in either a sink or a large bowl. Swish them around in the water so that any particles of grit fall to the bottom. Lift out the leaves, discard the water and grit, and repeat the process several times until no more dirt is left on the bottom.
- As a rule, tender greens such as spinach, beet greens, and Swiss chard can be sautéed with only the water clinging to them. However, blanching in a large amount of boiling salted water or steaming sets the flavor and intensifies the color. Tougher greens require longer cooking time to become tender, but avoid overcooking or the texture can turn mushy and the flavor muddy.
- Most greens profit from a touch of something acidic, such as citrus or a few drops of vinegar, added just before serving. And they stand up well to hot peppers, ginger, and salty things such as anchovies, olives, and soy sauce.
- Very young greens, delicate or assertive, and a step up from a seedling, can be eaten raw. In fact, many of these young greens are included in mesclun salad mixes.

Kale

SHREDDED KALE WITH PICKLE RELISH AND KIELBASA

We all hail kale! Kale is one of those mega-nutrient-rich vegetables that has been sorely overlooked in favor of its more popular vegetable cousins. Its hearty flavor takes well to any kind of pork. It is really quite wonderful with just a touch of acidity.

SERVES 4

1 pound curly kale or Red
   Russian kale
Salt and pepper to taste
4 ounces kielbasa sausage, cut into
   ½-inch pieces

1 tablespoon olive oil
3 tablespoons chopped India pickle
   relish (from a jar)

Trim and discard the stems and ribs of the kale. Wash the leaves and cut them finely into a chiffonade. Place them in a steamer basket over boiling water, sprinkle with salt and pepper, cover tightly, and steam for 20 to 25 minutes. (See Note.)

Meanwhile, sauté the kielbasa in a 10-inch nonstick pan over medium-low heat, just until it begins to brown. When the kale is cooked, put it into a serving dish. Add the olive oil and combine. Add the relish and combine again. Stir in the kielbasa and serve.

Note: If Russian kale is used, steam for 10 to 15 minutes.

CRUSTLESS MIXED GREENS TART WITH JALAPEÑO PEPPER CHEESE

Similar to the Italian vegetable pie called Torta di Verdura, this is a sort of crustless quiche with a Mexican accent. The eggs and cheese mellow the greens and give them a peppery bite. It's a lovely lunch or dinner party first course.

SERVES 4 TO 6

2 tablespoons olive oil

1¾ cups thinly sliced leeks (2 thin leeks), white parts plus 1 inch green part

1 tablespoon finely minced garlic (2 medium cloves)

3 tablespoons coarsely chopped parsley

1 pound mixed assertive-flavored greens, any combination: mustard, turnips, Russian kale, and/or collard greens, trimmed of coarse stems and roughly chopped

1 pound milder greens: Swiss chard, beet greens, or spinach, trimmed and roughly chopped.

3 eggs

Salt and pepper to taste

½ cup sour cream

½ teaspoon ground cumin

⅔ cup coarse, dry bread crumbs

½ cup (2 ounces) shredded Jalapeño Pepper Jack cheese

Heat the oil in a 12-inch skillet over medium heat. Add the leeks and garlic, and sauté, stirring frequently, until wilted, about 4 to 5 minutes. Stir in the parsley and set aside.

In a 7½-quart pot, bring salted water to a boil. Add the assertive-flavored greens and cook for 5 minutes. Add the milder greens to the pot and cook 5 more minutes. Drain them well in a colander, pressing the greens against the side with a wooden spoon to drain as much liquid as possible. There should be about 2 cups. Add the greens to a bowl along with the leek mixture.

Preheat the oven to 350 degrees. Place the eggs, salt, pepper, and sour cream in a food processor and combine. Stir in the cumin. Add the mixture to the greens. Butter a 10-inch quiche or tart pan without a removable bottom and sprinkle with bread crumbs. Spoon the greens mixture into the pan and scatter shredded cheese on the surface. Bake for 15 minutes, then lower the heat to 325 degrees and continue to bake until the cheese is melted and the torte is firm, about 15 minutes more.

PORTUGUESE CALDO VERDE WITH COLLARD GREENS AND LINGUIÇA SAUSAGE

Simple and hearty, this is practically the national soup of Portugal. The variety of green, which grows in every Portuguese garden, is called tron-chuda, *or Portuguese cabbage. It looks and tastes most like collards. As with most hearty soups and stews, the flavors intensify with time, so prepare this soup one or two days before serving.*

SERVES 4

8 ounces garlic sausage such as linguiça or kielbasa (precooked)

2 tablespoons olive oil

¾ cup coarsely chopped sweet Spanish onion

1 teaspoon finely minced garlic (1 clove)

2 medium white or red boiling potatoes (about 12 ounces to 1 pound), peeled, cut into chunks, and placed in cold water

4 cups chicken broth

6 cups trimmed and coarsely shredded leaves of collard greens, Portuguese cabbage, or kale, stems removed

14-ounce can cannellini beans, drained and rinsed

Salt and pepper to taste

Lemon wedges

Pierce the sausage, cover with water in a small saucepan, and bring to a boil. Turn the heat to low and simmer for 5 minutes to remove the excess fat. Drain and discard the water. Slice the sausage into ¾-inch pieces and set aside.

In a 6-quart Dutch oven, heat the oil over medium heat. Add the onion and garlic, and sauté, stirring, for 2 or 3 minutes. Drain the potatoes and add them to the pot. Stir and cook for 1 or 2 minutes. Add the broth and bring to a boil. Lower the heat and simmer for 15 to 20 minutes.

Using a potato masher, crush the potatoes lightly in the pot. Add the shredded greens and simmer 15 minutes more. Stir in the beans, salt, pepper, and reserved sausage, and simmer 5 to 10 minutes more, until hot. Serve hot and with a wedge of lemon, to be squeezed into the soup at the table. If made in advance, just reheat and serve.

RED SWISS CHARD BUNDLES WITH LEMON, OLIVE OIL, AND SCALLIONS

Red Swiss chard, shaped into bright green and red-veined balls (bietola) *were sold in the market place in Florence. After sampling them in Italy, we tried to duplicate them at home—and everyone seemed to love them.*

SERVES 4

1 pound red Swiss chard with large leaves (or white-stemmed can be substituted)

½ cup finely sliced scallions, green part only (about 2 to 3 thin scallions)

½ cup shredded Provolone cheese (about 1 ounce)

salt and pepper to taste

2 tablespoons lemon juice (half a medium lemon)

4 tablespoons olive oil

1 tablespoon long shreds lemon zest made with a zester tool

Wash and drain the chard. Remove any discolored stem tips. Cut off the stems, reserving the leaves, and chop them finely. There should be about 1 cup. Any remaining stems can be saved for another use.

In a 5-quart Dutch oven, bring ¾ pot of salted water to a boil over high heat. Place the chopped stems in a steamer basket and submerge in the boiling water. Cook until tender, about 4 to 5 minutes. Then lift out the basket, drain the stems, and add them to a bowl along with the scallions and cheese. Keep the water boiling.

Then, take 12 to 14 of the best whole leaves and gently push them down into the same boiling water. Blanch them until limp, about 1 minute. Carefully lift out the leaves with tongs and spread them out gently on paper towels to dry and cool.

Add about 1 tablespoon of the stem mixture to each leaf. Then wrap the leaf around the filling to enclose it, starting from the stem end, and form it into a ball. Place them, seam side down, in a serving dish with a rim to contain the sauce.

In a small bowl, whisk the lemon juice, salt, pepper, and oil together, and spoon the mixture over all. Scatter the lemon zest shreds over the chard balls and serve at room temperature. Don't let them stand too long in their sauce before serving or the bright green color will turn dull.

The Extended Cabbage Family

Italian Braised Savoy Cabbage with Wine and Pancetta

*Bavarian Sweet-and-Sour Red Cabbage with
Apples, Cloves, and Allspice*

Roasted Brussels Sprouts with Shallots and Pine Nuts

Macco: Broccoli Raab and Dried Fava Bean Puree

*Cauliflower and Broccoli with Chèvre Sauce and
Anchovy Bread Crumbs*

Originating from a hardy wild plant that was grown more than twenty-five hundred years ago, there are now over sixty closely related members of the cabbage family on every continent. It has a place in every cuisine of the world, but this vast extended family can be confusing to the consumer.

There are two main groups of cabbage: Asian or Eastern vegetables and the Western ones, and these two can be further divided into three general categories:

1. Those with heads, such as cabbages, Brussels sprouts, broccoli, and cauliflower
2. Edible roots such as turnips, kohlrabi, and rutabagas
3. Leafy greens such as kale, mustard greens, and collard greens

This chapter deals only with the first category. For edible roots see page 61, and for leafy greens see page 38.

CABBAGE

Head cabbage has suffered an image problem for years. This is the result of overcooking, a process that unfortunately releases hydrogen sulfide, which is the culprit that causes malodorous smells. (And mushy textures as well!) However, with more information on how to prepare them, all the vegetables in this extended cabbage family have now been elevated by medical researchers into a health cure akin to a miracle drug.

Cabbage is best in cooler weather when the chill enhances their sweeter flavor by turning the plant's starch into sugar.

GREEN CABBAGE: Also known as Dutch White, this round, firm cabbage with tight leaves is solid and heavy for its size. Choose those that have loose dark green outer leaves attached. Make sure there are no brown spots or cracked leaves. Many markets trim them as they wilt, leaving only the pale inner head exposed. Usable but not as tasty.

RED CABBAGE: Actually purple-rose colored, it has a more peppery flavor than the green variety and is used in salads and braised. The same criteria should be followed when selecting and storing as for green cabbage.

SAVOY CABBAGE: This is more tender, mellow, and mild than green head cabbage. The crenelated leaves are softer in texture and have delicate veins showing. It's a very popular variety in Italy and France. More attractive and delicate, it can be used interchangeably with regular cabbage in a pinch. Savoy cabbage is fragile, so keep it wrapped and refrigerated for only three or four days.

CHINESE CABBAGE: Also known as napa cabbage and michihli cabbage, these are actually two different varieties of head cabbage:

1. Napa is stubby, short, and pale, and its darker, frilly tipped leaves fan away slightly from the top of its squat head.
2. Michihli, also called celery cabbage, has a taste reminiscent of cabbage tinged with a bit of celery. Its loose, thinner, elongated leaves are a bit greener in color than napa cabbage, and they curve slightly inward toward the top.

Both kinds are shredded and eaten raw or lightly braised or quickly stir-fried. Allow 1¼ pounds shredded for four people.

SHOP SMART

- ◆ Green cabbage goes a long way. A 2-pound head, cored and shredded, equals 10 to 12 cups. One-half of a medium 1-pound head, shredded, equals about 4 cups.
- ◆ Refrigerate it in a loose plastic bag for one to two weeks, but for best flavor when eaten raw, use it within a few days.

Napa Cabbage

Notes for the Cook

ON CABBAGE . . .

There are as many ways to prepare cabbage as there are cooks who use it.

- ◆ Besides cole slaw, sauerkraut, and corned beef accompaniment, there is cabbage stuffed with meat or grains, braised with pasta, combined with beets for borscht, and many newer lightly cooked uses, such as wraps for chicken and fish.
- ◆ For simply steaming wedges, allow about 12 minutes and test the tenderness so that the cabbage doesn't overcook.
- ◆ The center core is usually fibrous and tough, so it's best to remove it. If whole leaves are needed for blanching individually or stuffing, just cut out the conical-shaped core in its entirety with a sharp knife. Once the core is removed, the leaves can be removed separately.
- ◆ Another method for blanching whole cabbage leaves is to stick a long-handled fork or corkscrew into the bottom core of the cabbage. It acts as a handle as you lower the whole head into boiling water for a few minutes at a time to soften the outer leaves. Then gently pull off the blanched leaves with tongs and repeat the process for the number of leaves needed for the recipe.
- ◆ If you plan to shred or chop cabbage, cut the head in half and then cut out the triangular core.
- ◆ Cutting by hand with a large, sharp knife rather than in a food processor results in better texture for both raw and cooked cabbage dishes.

BRUSSELS SPROUTS: Also known as rosenkohl (or rose cabbage in German or *petit choux* in French), these little blue-green cabbage buds have growth habits that are totally different from their bigger brothers and sisters. They grow on a fat stalk in spiraling rows.

SHOP SMART

Brussels sprouts are basically a cold weather crop—October through March—though there is year-round availability. Their sprightly robust flavor is best when used very fresh. Sometimes they're sold complete with the little buds nesting on an entire stalk, but for some unknown marketing reason, they are usually packaged in little 10-ounce cartons. The smaller (1- to 1½-inch) sprouts are usually the sweetest, but however you buy them, try to get them sized about the same for even cooking.

Allow about 1 pound for 4 people.

Avoid yellowing, insect-damaged, or loose heads. Keep them refrigerated for no more than two days before using.

Notes for the Cook

ON BRUSSELS SPROUTS . . .

◆ Thinly trim the base of the sprouts. Some cooks make a small X in the base to promote even cooking.

◆ For best color, taste, and texture (depending on size) steam about 7 minutes for the smallest sprouts. Add 1 minute more for medium size and 2 minutes for extra-large ones.

◆ Brussels sprouts take well to nuts of all kinds as well as butter and cream sauces. And they're a wonderful accompaniment for game, poultry, and pork.

BROCCOLI: One of the cabbage incarnations, broccoli has thick stalks topped by tight masses of dark blue-green flower buds; it is harvested before the buds open. A bunch of broccoli resembles a miniature forest of trees, and, indeed, *brocco* means "branch" in Italian.

SHOP SMART

Broccoli is available year-round, though it is not as good in the heat of the summer.

◆ Buy fresh, tight, dark green heads that are not blooming and with no wilt or yellowing.
◆ Avoid woody or hollow stalks.
◆ Keep in a plastic bag in the refrigerator for two or three days.

One and a half pounds or 1 large head is more than enough to feed 4 people.

Some Other Family Members

Alas, broccoli is no longer just plain old broccoli. There is purple broccoli, a soft-textured, dusky red-purple variety that turns brownish green when cooked. And there are varieties that some geneticists say are masquerading as broccoli but are really cauli-flowers, such as broccoflower and broccoli Romanesco, which comes in various shades of chartreuse. To our taste, these varieties are not noticeably special, nor are they widely available. There is one exception: a new seed hybrid variety called asparation, which is also known as broccolini. A young delicate broccoli, it has long thin stems (about 6 inches long) and small, loosely flowering heads. It's a cross between Chinese broccoli (*gai lan*; see below) and broccoli, and it's available year-round. It's delicate, milder, and slightly more peppery than broccoli.

There are also some young upstarts, such as broccoli sprouts, that are merely three days old. They have a combined slight sweetness of alfalfa sprouts and the slightly spicy bitterness of radish sprouts. One ounce of these sprouts is claimed by researchers to protect you by stimulating your own fighting mechanisms against cancer. That one ounce also has the equivalent nutritional value of two pounds of plain old broccoli, which may even make them acceptable to broccoli hater and former president George Bush.

And now, of course, there is the popular broccoli raab, also known as *cime di rabe*, which has been embraced by specialty stores and supermarkets everywhere. Its name in Italian means "top" or "flower shoots" of the turnip. It is unique and pungent, and has a slightly bittersweet flavor. It has firm stalks 12 to 18 inches long and dark green leaves topped with small green florets that show a few fresh yellow flowers. It also resembles its Chinese cousin, Chinese broccoli, but they are both quite different in taste and recipe treatment.

CHINESE BROCCOLI: Also called *gai lan*, it is identified by its creamy white flowering buds, leathery leaves, and smooth, round stems that resemble slim broccoli. This ancient Chinese cultivar is best when bright, fresh, and young, and it can be eaten raw.

Notes for the Cook

ON BROCCOLI . . .

- Trim the bottom 2 inches from the stalks. Peeling the stalks is optional. Cut off the florets and separate them into small pieces.
- Blanching or steaming maintains the vegetable's vivid color if it is not overcooked.
- For steaming florets to tender/crisp, allow 3 minutes. Steam the sliced, diced, or julienned stems 1 minute before adding the florets.
- We like the stems raw and thinly sliced—like an amoeba-shaped flower—for crudités.
- Acid marinades turn broccoli yellowish, so when vinegar or lemon is to be used, add just before serving.

ON BROCCOLI RAAB . . .

◆ Trim the stem ends of the broccoli raab if very tough, then cut the tops into bite-size pieces. Allow 2 pounds for four people.

◆ Braise and cook slowly with a bit of broth or water, covered, for twenty-five to thirty minutes after first quickly sautéeing with oil, garlic, and a few hot pepper flakes.

◆ Broccoli raab is wonderful when combined with pasta.

◆ It is never eaten raw.

ON CHINESE BROCCOLI . . .

◆ Trim the stem ends and separate the tops. Cut them into bite-size pieces.

◆ Its juicy crunch can be maintained by quickly stir-frying.

◆ When eaten raw in salads, blanch it quickly and then refresh the whole stalks before cutting them as required for the recipe.

CAULIFLOWER: Also known as flowering cabbage or queen of cabbages or *chou-fleur*. After being introduced by Louis XI, *chou-fleur* became the darling of the chefs, and the cheese-sauced cauliflower is still identified with the name of his mistress, Madame du Barry. Recently, chefs have resurrected and rethought the cauliflower in new dishes, and it is fast becoming a highbrow version of its lowly relative, the cabbage. In the south of Italy, a common purple variety is grown that turns green after cooking.

Each plant grows only a single head, and to maintain and protect its white center (the curd) from the sun, the outer leaves need to be individually tied up to enclose the curd. However, one cauliflower goes a long way.

SHOP SMART

Buy fresh, firm heads with no bruised or brown spots on the curd and with no wilted leaves.

They are available year-round. One medium head weighs about 2 pounds after trimming, and it will keep for two weeks, untrimmed, in a plastic bag in the refrigerator.

Notes for the Cook

ON CAULIFLOWER . . .

◆ Trim the stem ends of the leaves by cutting the head stem side up. Cut out the cone-shaped core to keep the head intact. Or, alternately, slice the stem part near the base of the head and break the curds into florets.

◆ When sliced horizontally into paper-thin slices, the curds look like fine lace and are lovely in a salad, blanched and eaten raw.

◆ Some cooks believe that lemon juice added to the cooking water helps keep the curds white.

◆ We prefer steaming florets and sliced stems for six to eight minutes until just crisp/tender.

◆ Cauliflower can be used for cream soups (Crème du Barry), fritters, Dutch pickles, and Indian curries.

ITALIAN BRAISED SAVOY CABBAGE WITH WINE AND PANCETTA

Delicately mellow Savoy cabbage, scented with just a hint of garlic and rosemary, is slowly wine-braised in this vegetable dish from Apulia. It is simplicity exemplified.

SERVES 4

I tablespoon olive oil

I medium clove garlic, peeled and crushed

I sprig rosemary

2 ounces pancetta, or slab bacon diced (see box)

⅔ cup finely chopped onion (1 medium)

I pound Savoy cabbage, quartered, cored, and thinly sliced (about 6 cups)

Salt and pepper to taste

½ cup dry white wine

I tablespoon finely minced parsley

In a 10-inch skillet over medium heat, heat the olive oil and add the garlic and rosemary. Stir and cook until the oil is fragrant and the garlic is golden. Remove both with a slotted spoon and discard. Add the pancetta to the skillet. Stir and sauté for about 2 minutes, then add the onion and sauté 2 minutes more. Stir in the cabbage, season with salt and pepper, and cook, stirring, until the cabbage begins to wilt. Add the wine, cover the skillet, and lower the heat. Braise for 10 minutes, stirring once. If there is not enough liquid, add 1 to 2 tablespoons of water and continue to cook until the cabbage is tender but not too soft. Transfer to a serving dish and stir in the parsley.

◆ Pancetta ◆

The Italian version of bacon, made from the pork belly, is curled and wrapped into a cylinder. Like prosciutto, it is salt-cured and peppered before being made into its final shape, whereas American bacon is smoked and only partially cured.

Pancetta tastes best cooked first since it is a fattier cut of meat. Cut it into fine dice (to prevent it from unrolling while cooking) to add to vegetable dishes, sauces, stews, and soups. It gives an extra flavor dimension that is totally different from American bacon.

BAVARIAN SWEET-AND-SOUR RED CABBAGE WITH APPLES, CLOVES, AND ALLSPICE

This red cabbage dish always tastes better when cooked the day before. Serve it with goose or duck or sauerbraten, as the Bavarians do. For hearty winter eating it is perfect—and even better when it's snowing outside!

SERVES 4 TO 6

1½ pounds red cabbage

3 tablespoons butter or goose fat

3 tablespoons light brown sugar

⅔ cup coarsely chopped onion (1 medium)

½ teaspoon black pepper

Salt to taste

¼ cup water, or more as needed

2 tablespoons red wine vinegar

2 large tart green apples such as Granny Smith, peeled, cored, and thickly sliced (about 3 cups)

⅛ teaspoon ground cloves

½ teaspoon ground allspice

1 tablespoon lemon juice (optional)

Cut the cabbage lengthwise into quarters. Cut out and discard the core and trim any tough outer center rib parts. Shred the cabbage thinly with a sharp knife. (A food processor can be used, but the texture is better when cut by hand.) There should be about 6 cups.

Melt the butter over low heat in a 5-quart nonreactive Dutch oven with a tight-fitting lid. Add the sugar to the butter and cook, stirring, until the sugar dissolves. Add the onion, pepper, and salt, and cook, stirring constantly, for about 2 minutes.

Stir in the cabbage, water, and vinegar, and combine well. Cover the pot and simmer for 10 minutes. Stir in the apple slices, cloves, and allspice, and continue to simmer for 30 minutes, or until the apples have dissolved into the cabbage.

Check after 30 minutes and add more water while the cabbage is cooking if it seems dry. Cook 10 minutes more. Taste and add the lemon juice or more brown sugar to adjust the sweet-sour balance to your own taste. Add more salt and pepper if needed.

ROASTED BRUSSELS SPROUTS WITH SHALLOTS AND PINE NUTS

Tiny, tightly furled Brussels sprouts no bigger than the tip of a man's thumb have the best flavor. Roasting them in high heat brings out their sweetness.

SERVES 4

¼ cup finely diced pancetta
　(2 ounces) (see page 55)
¼ cup finely minced shallots (2 to
　3 large)
4 cups very small Brussels sprouts
　(about 1 pound)

Salt and pepper to taste
⅛ teaspoon freshly ground nutmeg
1 tablespoon butter
2 tablespoons pine nuts
2 teaspoons sherry vinegar

Preheat the oven to 400 degrees. Add the pancetta to a 9 x 12-inch oven-to-table baking dish and heat for about 5 minutes, until the pancetta starts to melt. Add the shallots and sprouts, and stir to combine. Roast about 10 minutes, stirring occasionally, until tender/crisp when tested with the point of a knife. (Larger sprouts will take a bit longer to roast.) Season with salt, pepper, and nutmeg.

While the sprouts are roasting, melt the butter in a small skillet and add the pine nuts. Sauté over medium heat, stirring, for 1 to 2 minutes, or until the nuts are golden. Sprinkle them over the roasted sprouts. Add the vinegar and toss. Serve hot.

MACCO: BROCCOLI RAAB AND DRIED FAVA BEAN PUREE

Macco is a classic southern Italian staple in the Apulia region. Calabrians add pasta to their version, sparking a controversy as to which is the best. We find both divine—and, besides, Garibaldi had enough trouble uniting Italy once before!

SERVES 4 TO 6

8 ounces dried, peeled, split fava beans, soaked overnight

1 cup coarsely chopped onion (about 1 medium onion)

½ cup coarsely chopped celery (about 1 large rib)

Water

Salt and freshly ground black pepper to taste

3 tablespoons olive oil

1 tablespoon coarsely chopped garlic (2 medium cloves)

1½ pounds broccoli raab, trimmed of coarse stems and cut into 2-inch pieces (about 10 cups)

⅛ teaspoon hot pepper flakes

2 tablespoons toasted pine nuts (optional)

4 lemon wedges

Drain the soaked beans and add to a 3-quart saucepan with the onion, celery, and enough water to cover by about 1 inch. Bring to a boil over medium heat, then lower the heat and simmer for about 40 minutes, or until the beans are very soft. Add salt and pepper during the last 10 minutes of cooking. Add more water if needed.

While the beans are cooking, heat 1 tablespoon of the olive oil in a 12-inch skillet over medium-high heat. Add the garlic and stir for 30 seconds. Add the broccoli raab and stir constantly until wilted. Season with salt and hot pepper flakes. Add ⅓ cup of water, cover the pan, and cook for 4 or 5 minutes, until tender.

When the beans are soft, drain them well and transfer to a food processor. Add salt, pepper, and the remaining 2 tablespoons of olive oil. Puree and transfer to a serving platter. Spoon the greens over and scatter the surface with pine nuts if you wish. Serve with lemon wedges to be squeezed over at the table.

CAULIFLOWER AND BROCCOLI WITH CHÈVRE SAUCE AND ANCHOVY BREAD CRUMBS

A wreath of green broccoli florets rings a white cauliflower center livened with a goat cheese béchamel and a scattering of crisp garlic and anchovy–scented bread crumbs.

SERVES 4 TO 6

8 ounces cauliflower florets, trimmed
1 pound broccoli florets, trimmed
Salt to taste
2 tablespoons butter
1 tablespoon finely minced scallion, green part only (1 thin scallion)
2 tablespoons flour
1½ cups milk
4 ounces goat cheese such as Montrachet, crumbled

½ teaspoon black pepper
⅛ teaspoon cayenne pepper
1 teaspoon olive oil
½ teaspoon finely minced garlic (1 small clove)
1 flat anchovy, coarsely chopped
¼ cup coarse dry bread crumbs

In a 5-quart pot with a steamer insert, steam the cauliflower about 6 or 7 minutes, until crisp/tender. Transfer to a buttered 2½-quart oven-to-table baking dish, piling it up in the center. Add the broccoli to the steamer basket and steam for 6 to 8 minutes, until crisp/tender. Remove with tongs and surround the cauliflower. Season with salt and set the dish aside.

Prepare the sauce: Melt the butter in a 2-quart nonstick saucepan over low heat. Add the scallion and stir for 30 seconds. Sift the flour, a little at a time, into the scallion mixture, stirring constantly to prevent lumps. Cook, stirring, for 1 minute. While stirring, slowly add the milk. Simmer over low heat for 5 minutes, stirring occasionally, until the mixture is slightly thickened. Add the goat cheese, black pepper, cayenne, and salt. Raise the heat to medium and stir vigorously to melt the cheese and thicken the sauce, about 5 minutes, until bubbles form.

Spoon most of the sauce over the cauliflower and trickle some over the broccoli. In a small skillet, heat the olive oil over medium-low heat. Stir in the garlic and anchovy, and sauté, stirring, for 1 minute. Remove from the heat and stir in the bread crumbs. Sprinkle over the cheese sauce.

This dish can be made ahead up to this point. When ready to serve, put it in a preheated 400-degree oven and heat for 5 to 8 minutes.

Broccoli & Cauliflower with Chèvre Sauce and Anchovy Bread Crumbs

Discovering Your Humble Roots

Kohlrabi with Pancetta, Carrot, and Onion

Baby Beets Filled with Sorrel

Spiced Carrot, Orange, and Ginger Soup with Yogurt

Braised Fennel with Sausage and Parmesan Cheese

Moroccan Radish and Orange Salad with Mint

Rutabaga and Apple Bisque with Thyme

Roasted Turnips on Turnip Greens with Orange and Crispy Ginger

Maple-Glazed Parsnip Pennies with Sweet Marsala

Céleri Rave Rémoulade

KOHLRABI

If, after that last wonderful trip to Paris, you returned raving about that popular French vegetable *chou-rave*, you had eaten kohlrabi. Cultivated since the fifteenth century in Europe, it came to our shores along with the Chinese and the early German settlers.

Kohlrabi possesses uniquely unconventional growing habits. As it matures, the stem swells into a clean, round shape that sits above the earth; this is the part that we eat. From this round shape a thin taproot or "true root" grows downward into the earth. This is the part that is discarded. The top part sends up thin stems that grow randomly from the round vegetable and are topped with edible green leaves; the stems are discarded.

In addition to pale green, kohlrabi now appears in a rose-purple hue. Both are available from June to November.

SHOP SMART

Large kohlrabi can be fibrous, so choose the smallest sizes (about 2 inches in diameter) before the skin gets thickened. They will keep in a plastic bag in the refrigerator for about one week.

Notes for the Cook

ON KOHLRABI . . .

♦ Peel them before cooking. If overcooked, they become mushy. A bite test should reveal a certain bit of crunch. Check after cooking 12 to 15 minutes.

♦ Small ones can be very thinly sliced and eaten raw in salads. Soak them in iced water for additional crispness.

♦ An unusual addition to soups and stews or pureed, kohlrabi is interchangeable with turnips in many recipes.

♦ The leaves can be steamed or sautéed, much like beet or turnip greens.

BEETS

The sweet, earthy flavor and hardy texture of the "beetroot" (as they are known in the British Isles) make this a beloved vegetable throughout the world.

Beets are also available in a golden orange hue as well as the more familiar red. They're ultra sweet and don't leach their color, as do their red brothers and sisters. Another choice is the mild *chioggia* (also known as candy cane) beet, which is cherry red on the outside and has concentric red-and-white circles within.

SHOP SMART

Most beets appear from fall through spring. If possible, buy firm, smooth-skinned beets with their fresh greens still attached and get two vegetables for the price of one.

♦ A 2-inch size is a good one to select for best flavor and texture, and choosing all the same size helps them to cook evenly.

♦ Leave 1 to 2 inches of the stems attached to the beet tops and keep the taproot intact. Store them in the refrigerator in a plastic bag with holes punched in it to keep them dry. The beets will keep for about two weeks, while the green tops will keep in a plastic bag for two to three days.

About ten 2-inch beets = 1 pound (4 servings).

Notes for the Cook

ON BEETS . . .

- ◆ If the skins break, the beets will bleed, so wash them well but don't scrub.
- ◆ It is best to keep the skins on when cooking in order to get the best flavor.
- ◆ The size of the beets will determine the cooking time, which can be anywhere from ten to forty minutes. When they're tender, plunge them into cold water for a few seconds, then trim the tops and bottoms. The skins should slip off while still warm.
- ◆ You can steam or boil beets, but roasting them in their skins with a bit of oil and salt brings out their natural sugars. One to 1½ hours in a 400-degree oven with 1 inch of water and the pan covered with foil should do the trick. Remove the foil for the last twenty minutes.
- ◆ The greens, if young, can be eaten raw in salads or blanched for two to three minutes in boiling water and drained. Or they can be sautéed with oil, shallots, and lemon or orange juice.
- ◆ Red beet stains are tenacious, so when peeling or slicing, *don't* use a wooden cutting board. Try a china plate. Rubber gloves will keep your manicure intact.

CARROTS

Very versatile and very much the rival of beets and parsnips for sweetness, carrots add color and sparkle to everything: soups, stews, salads, pickles, cakes, breads, and puddings. Although carrots are grown wherever soil and climate are best, we are most partial to the organically grown carrots for best flavor and sweetness.

SHOP SMART

- ◆ Select long, slender, young golden orange carrots—firm and smooth, not lumpy or withered. Preferably they should still have their green tops to assure freshness.
- ◆ Older, fatter carrots hold up well in stews and need to be peeled before cooking, but young ones need only to be scrubbed.
- ◆ The 1-inch peeled and packaged baby carrots, because of their lack of maturity, seem to lack a good carrot flavor, though they certainly are a convenience.

◆ Store carrots in the refrigerator in a plastic bag. They will keep for about two weeks.

One pound of carrots should serve four.

FENNEL BULBS

An exceptional multi-use vegetable, fennel is reminiscent of a bunch of celery in appearance, but one that has gone astray and has developed a big, fist-sized bulbous bottom. From this pearly white–ribbed squat bulb grow narrow stalks topped with feathery frondlike tips, resembling dill but tasting like licorice when it is snipped and added to salads or used as a garnish.

All parts are used in this refreshing vegetable, and many methods of cooking are applicable. Fennel can be breaded, fried, sautéed, roasted, braised, or eaten raw in salads. Since it lends itself to such a multitude of dishes, the method of cooking greatly influences its flavor and, of course, its texture.

The slivered bulbs, eaten raw in salads, are clean, sweet, crisp, and fresh, and have a subtle aniselike flavor. Slowly braised with other ingredients, fennel acquires a flavor complexity that is fabulous. The stalks can be used to flavor vegetable stocks and as an aromatic "rack" when roasting poultry or fish. Fish and fennel seem to have such an affinity for each other that every Mediterranean country puts them together.

 SHOP SMART

◆ Choose large, firm bulbs with no brown spots and make certain that the feathery leaves and stalks are not limp. This will guarantee more flavor since all parts of the fennel bulb can be used.
◆ Sometimes the bulbs are flattened and elongated. This means the fennel is younger and thus more tender and delicate—a personal choice.
◆ Wrap the bulbs in a plastic bag and place in the crisper. They'll keep for a few days.

Notes for the Cook

ON TRIMMING AND SLICING FENNEL . . .

◆ Cut the stalks and fronds close to the bulb. Trim a very thin slice from the base of the bulb and remove any tough or discolored outer fibrous leaves.

- When the fennel is to be used for eating raw or sautéeing or braising, slice the bulb in half and remove the pyramid-shaped core.
- If slicing wedges, don't remove the core. It keeps the individual layers together.
- If you are making fan-shaped slices, keep the core intact when you slice the fennel bulb vertically. That way, the slices will hold together and not break apart.

RADISHES

Their names are descriptive and euphonious: cherry belle, white icicle, French breakfast. They are marble-sized and all white, cherry red, long red with white tips, or the white Japanese daikon "killer radishes" that can weigh up to 2 pounds apiece and are usually eaten raw in minute slivers or grated. Then there is the round black radish that we associate with Germany and the Slavic countries, where it is grated or thinly sliced to accompany sandwiches and sausages, or is piled on dark pumpernickel bread with goose fat and coarse salt. The flavors vary, too, from crisply mild to aggressive with a peppery hot tingle. And older radishes are hotter still. Four hundred million pounds of radishes are consumed annually.

SHOP SMART

- Radishes are available year-round, with the best coming to the marketplace in early spring. We like those that are organically grown.
- Select smooth, firm skins with bright, fresh green tops. Store them in plastic bags in the refrigerator and wash and trim them before using.

RUTABAGAS AND TURNIPS

Rutabagas

Also known as yellow turnips or Swedes, rutabagas are a natural cross between turnips and wild cabbage. They're about the size of a grapefruit but with a fatter neck than a turnip. Grown for fall harvest—October through April—their skins are creamy tan to lavender, and their flesh is firm and yellow.

SHOP SMART

- Medium-size rutabagas are best. The large ones can be woody and fibrous.
- They occasionally appear in the marketplace coated with wax to hold in the moisture.
- Store them unwrapped in a cool, dry place. They will keep for a month.

Turnips

This vegetable is best when no bigger than a golf ball. The skin is either all white (a Japanese variety) or white blushed with rose-purple at the neck. The flesh is crisp and sweet, and it can be eaten raw, thinly sliced, grated, or julienned.

SHOP SMART

- Try to choose smooth, firm roots that are not rubbery and preferably have fresh green leaves attached.
- Turnip greens are not only edible but downright delicious and have a slight mustardy bite.
- The cool months in spring and fall produce the crispest, sweetest, and most tender roots.
- The Japanese white turnips, the size of a walnut, appear in the spring; these are our favorites.
- Store turnips in plastic bags in the refrigerator for no more than one week.

Notes for the Cook

ON RUTABAGAS AND TURNIPS . . .

- Rutabagas love apples, and they make wonderful soups and purees when paired (see page 75).
- Turnips are able to cut fatty meats such as duck and short ribs. The Scots pair mashed turnips (which they call "bashed neeps") with haggis, their rich national dish.

PARSNIPS

Parsnips are the most unassuming of the root vegetables and have a subtle, earthy sweetness—one that is again being rediscovered by some of the best chefs in the country. Although they resemble faded beige carrots, their flavor is much deeper, and their uses are curtailed only by a lack of imagination.

SHOP SMART

Parsnips are available year-round, but in fall and through spring they are at their flavorful best. Since the first frost improves flavor, farmers leave their crops in the ground, where the cold weather turns the carbohydrates in the root to sugar.

- ◆ Select long, straight, smooth, and preferably small roots that are not limp or wilted.
- ◆ If only larger parsnips are available in the marketplace, after peeling and trimming them, quarter them and cut out the dark, woody center core.

Notes for the Cook

ON PARSNIPS . . .

- ◆ Don't overcook them. A limp parsnip, like a limp carrot, is not appealing.
- ◆ Steaming rather than boiling locks in parsnips' taste. Add a few herbs and shreds of orange peel when they are being steamed.
- ◆ As an alternative to potatoes, they make unusual French fries.
- ◆ Grated raw, young parsnips make a different salad when tossed with bitter greens such as arugula, frisée, or mizuna.
- ◆ Parsnips add a lovely note to soups and stews or roasted alongside a chicken.

CELERIAC

Known as knob or root celery, and ranging in size from an orange to a grapefruit, this large, tan, misshapen gnarled root with its crunchy white flesh and intense celery flavor is more popular throughout Europe than here. It is roasted and mashed with potatoes, added to soups and stews, and cut into fine julienne and eaten raw in a mustard dressing. Céleri Rave Rémoulade is a true classic French bistro first course.

SHOP SMART

Celeriac is a fall and winter specialty but is sometimes available year-round. Buy firm, not spongy roots and store them in the refrigerator in a plastic bag for up to one week.

Notes for the Cook

ON CELERIAC . . .

◆ Use stainless-steel knives when peeling away the thick skin and do not use aluminum pots. Celeriac discolors once it is cut, so it should be dropped into acidulated water to prevent darkening.

◆ Keep the crunch when cooking unless you intend to puree the root.

Celeriac

KOHLRABI WITH PANCETTA, CARROT, AND ONION

Kohlrabi is a winter root vegetable and a very much underutilized delicacy in the United States. Its taste combines both the sweetness of turnips and a hint of cabbage.

SERVES 4 TO 6

2 pounds kohlrabi (as small as possible), with leaves

2 ounces pancetta or slab bacon, cut into ¼-inch dice

⅔ cup finely chopped onion (1 small onion)

⅓ cup coarsely shredded carrot (1 thin carrot)

Salt and pepper to taste

Trim both ends of the kohlrabi. Peel the roots with a vegetable peeler and cut them vertically into half-moon slices ¼ inch thick. Trim and shred the leaves ¼ inch wide as well. Add both roots and leaves to a 3-quart saucepan and cover with salted water. Bring to a boil over medium-high heat, then cover. Lower the heat to medium and cook for about 15 minutes, or until tender.

While the kohlrabi is cooking, fry the pancetta in an 8-inch skillet over medium heat until crisp. Transfer the pancetta pieces to a paper towel using a slotted spoon, and reserve. Add the onion and carrot to the same skillet and sauté over medium heat for 5 minutes, stirring frequently.

When the kohlrabi is tender, drain and return to the same saucepan. Stir and combine the onion mixture with the kohlrabi and cook over low heat 2 minutes more. Season with salt and pepper, transfer to a serving dish, and scatter the reserved pancetta bits over all.

BABY BEETS FILLED WITH SORREL

It couldn't be simpler—or better. In the early spring when the first tiny beets appear alongside the tongue-shaped leaves of fresh lemony sorrel, this is a healthful and unusual one-bite morsel for a cocktail party or side dish.

SERVES 4

12 ounces very small beets (about 16), about 1½ inches in diameter, washed well

1 tablespoon butter

⅓ pound fresh sorrel, center stems removed and cut into very fine julienne (see Note)

Salt and pepper to taste

Steam the beets for about 20 minutes, or until tender. Place them on paper towels to drain and cool. Peel them and then, using a small melon scoop, cut out a scoop from each beet to make a cavity for the sorrel. Cut a tiny slice off the bottom of each beet to keep it upright and steady. Place them on a serving plate.

Melt the butter in an 8-inch nonstick skillet. Add the sorrel and stir until wilted. Season with salt and pepper. Fill the beets with ¼ teaspoon each of the sorrel. Serve at room temperature.

Note: If sorrel is not available, substitute trimmed leaf spinach and 1 teaspoon of lemon juice.

Baby Beets filled with Sorrel

SPICED CARROT, ORANGE, AND GINGER SOUP WITH YOGURT

This delightful soup has sparkling color and flavor, the natural goodness and sweetness of organic carrots, and the snap of two kinds of ginger: ginger root and slivers of pickled Japanese ginger.

SERVES 6

2 tablespoons butter

1 teaspoon minced garlic
   (1 large clove)

1½ tablespoons peeled and grated
   ginger root

1 cup coarsely chopped onion
   (1 medium onion)

4 cups thoroughly scrubbed, thickly
   sliced carrots (1¼ pounds; about
   7 large carrots, preferably organic)

¼ teaspoon ground cardamom

¼ teaspoon ground coriander

4 cups chicken broth, homemade or
   canned

2 tablespoons finely grated
   orange zest

1½ cups milk

½ cup heavy cream

Salt and pepper to taste

Pinch of sugar

Plain yogurt, slivers of Japanese pickled
   ginger, drained, and a few leaves of
   cilantro for garnish

In a 5-quart Dutch oven, melt the butter over medium heat. Add the garlic and ginger, and sauté, stirring, for 1 minute. Add the onion and sauté, stirring 2 to 3 minutes more. Add the carrots, cardamom, and coriander, and sauté 2 minutes more. Add the broth and orange zest. Bring to a boil, lower the heat, and simmer for 25 to 30 minutes, or until the carrots are very tender.

Strain over a bowl and reserve the broth, pouring it back into the pot.

Puree the vegetables in a food processor, adding a ladle of broth to moisten them. Return the pureed vegetables to the pot. Stir in the milk and cream, and add salt, pepper, and sugar. Heat over medium-low heat. Do not allow it to boil.

Serve with a dollop of yogurt and sprinkle a few shreds of the pickled ginger over the yogurt. Add a cilantro leaf if you wish.

BRAISED FENNEL WITH SAUSAGE AND PARMESAN CHEESE

Fennel bulbs are widely used in Italian cooking. Here they are intensified with an additional touch of fennel seed–flavored sausage and Parmesan cheese.

SERVES 6

2 pounds fennel bulbs (6 small or
  3 medium bulbs)
1¼ cups chicken broth, homemade or
  canned
2 fennel pork sausages or other pork
  sausages (about 8 ounces)

Salt and freshly ground pepper
  to taste
2 tablespoons butter, cut into small
  pieces
4 tablespoons grated Parmesan cheese
4 tablespoons finely minced parsley

Cut a thin slice from the bottom of each fennel bulb, then cut the bulb into quarters and put them in a shallow 10 x 22-inch flame-proof baking dish. Pour the chicken broth over the fennel and bring to a boil over high heat. Lower the heat to medium, cover the dish with aluminum foil, and simmer for 10 minutes.

When the fennel is cooking, remove the sausage casings and crumble the sausage into a small nonstick skillet. Sauté over low heat for 5 to 6 minutes, stirring occasionally, until the sausage is no longer pink in color. Drain the sausage on paper towels. Remove the aluminum foil from the fennel dish and scatter the sausage over the fennel. Season with salt and pepper. Dot with the butter and sprinkle with the cheese. (This can all be prepared ahead up to this point.)

When ready to finish cooking, preheat the oven to 400 degrees and bake, uncovered, for 15 to 20 minutes. Test with the point of a knife. When tender, raise the oven temperature and slip the dish under the broiler for 2 minutes, or until it is dappled brown.

Remove from the oven, tilt the pan, and spoon any remaining sauce over the fennel. Sprinkle with parsley and serve hot.

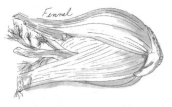

MOROCCAN RADISH AND ORANGE SALAD WITH MINT

Moroccans are ingenious users of mint. Here is a cool summer salad straight from the kitchens of Rabat.

SERVES 4

2 large navel oranges
¼ cup lemon juice (about
    I large lemon)
2 teaspoons light honey
2 bunches radishes (12 ounces to
    I pound)

¼ teaspoon salt or to taste
12 soft lettuce leaves (such as Bibb or
    Boston)
I tablespoon finely minced fresh mint

Peel the oranges, removing the bitter white pith. Cut out the orange segments from between the membranes and then cut each segment into 2 or 3 small pieces. Place in a medium-size bowl and set aside.

In a small cup, mix the lemon juice and honey together and set aside. Coarsely shred the radishes in a food processor using the shredder blade. Combine the radishes and salt with the oranges and the honey-lemon dressing.

Line 4 plates with lettuce leaves and mound the orange-radish mixture over the leaves. Distribute the mint evenly over each portion and serve at once.

Note: If the salad is allowed to stand, liquid will accumulate at the bottom of the plate and the crispness of the radishes will be lost, so prepare just before serving.

RUTABAGA AND APPLE BISQUE WITH THYME

This is a favorite: a full-flavored winter soup with rutabaga, sweet apples, and a touch of tart lemon and yogurt to round out the flavors.

SERVES 6

2 pounds rutabaga (also known as
    yellow turnip), peeled and cut into
    1-inch cubes (about 5 cups)
5 sprigs fresh thyme, reserving
    2 sprigs for garnish
2 tablespoons butter
1 pound eating apples (such as
    Braeburn, Fuji, or Yellow Delicious),
    peeled and sliced (about 3 cups)

1 medium lemon wedge
2 tablespoons dark brown sugar
1/8 teaspoon freshly grated nutmeg
5 cups chicken broth
Salt and pepper to taste
1 cup plain yogurt

In a 5-quart Dutch oven, cover the rutabaga with salted water and 3 sprigs of the thyme. Bring to a boil over medium heat, then turn the heat to medium-low, cover, and cook for 25 to 30 minutes, or until tender.

While the rutabaga is cooking, use a 2-quart nonstick saucepan to melt the butter over medium heat. Add the apples and squeeze the lemon juice over the apples. Add the sugar and nutmeg, and cook, stirring frequently, for about 10 minutes, or until the apples are tender. When the rutabaga is tender, drain and place in a bowl along with the apples and chicken broth. Remove and discard the thyme sprigs. Puree the mixture in a blender, a few batches at a time, and return each batch to the pot. Bring to a simmer, covered, over medium heat. Stir in the yogurt, lower the heat, and simmer until hot. Taste to correct the seasoning and serve hot with the thyme leaves sprinkled on top.

ROASTED TURNIPS ON TURNIP GREENS WITH ORANGE AND CRISPY GINGER

Tiny globes of sweet pearl white turnips nest on a bed of their own spicy greens, showered with crisply fried shreds of ginger and tempered with refreshing oranges.

SERVES 4

2 tablespoons olive oil
1½ pounds small white Japanese or
    other small white turnips with
    green tops
1 large red onion, sliced ¼ inch thick
Salt and pepper to taste
1 large navel orange

Corn oil for frying
2-inch piece of ginger root, peeled and
    cut into very fine julienne (about
    ⅓ cup)
1 teaspoon thyme honey
1 teaspoon balsamic vinegar

Preheat the oven to 425 degrees. Place the olive oil in a bowl. Scrub but do not peel the turnips. Trim the tails and slice the turnips ¼ inch thick. Add them to the bowl. Wash and trim the green tops and steam in a basket over boiling water for 5 minutes.

Add the onion to the turnips and toss to cover with the oil. Add salt and pepper, and transfer to a jelly roll pan. Roast the onion and turnips for about 15 minutes, turning once until they begin to color.

Peel the orange, remove the bitter white pith, and cut into 4 thick slices. When ready to serve, arrange the greens on one side of each of 4 plates. Spoon some of the turnip-onion mixture on the other side and tuck in one slice of orange.

In a small skillet, heat ½ cup of corn oil until hot but not smoking. Add the ginger and fry for 30 seconds, until golden. Remove with a slotted spoon and sprinkle some on each serving. Trickle the honey on each orange slice and trickle the vinegar over the greens. Season with additional salt and pepper if you wish.

MAPLE-GLAZED PARSNIP PENNIES WITH SWEET MARSALA

If you have always underestimated the humble parsnip, try this easy recipe and change your mind. Just a touch of sharp mustard cuts the sweetness of the glaze in an unexpected way.

SERVES 4

1¼ pounds young parsnips
2 tablespoons butter
¼ cup water
Salt and pepper to taste
⅓ cup maple syrup

1 teaspoon extra-strong Dijon mustard
2 tablespoons sweet Marsala wine
¼ cup broken toasted walnuts
1 tablespoon finely minced parsley

Trim and scrub the parsnips with a stiff brush. (No need to peel since the skin is very thin.) Slice the parsnips ¼ inch thick on the diagonal. You should have about 4 cups.

In a 10-inch nonstick skillet over medium heat, melt the butter, add the parsnips, and toss to coat. Add the water, salt, and pepper, cover the skillet, and turn the heat to medium-low. Cook for 10 to 12 minutes, or until tender, stirring occasionally.

Combine the maple syrup, mustard, and Marsala, and add the mixture to the skillet. Cook, uncovered, over medium-high heat for 2 to 3 minutes, or until the parsnips are glazed. Stir frequently to coat. Stir in the walnuts and transfer to a serving dish. Sprinkle with parsley and serve.

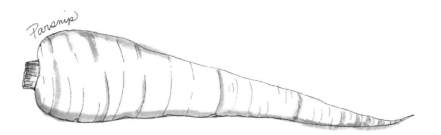
Parsnip

CÉLERI RAVE RÉMOULADE

We always order this favorite as a salad or first course when it appears on a bistro menu. The secret to its sharply appealing mustardy tang is advance preparation, so it's great for a dinner party or buffet. Adding shredded apple and endive plus a few shrimp can make this a main course salad.

SERVES 6 TO 8

SALAD:

1 pound celery root

2 cups water

½ cup white wine vinegar

1 tablespoon tarragon vinegar

2 tablespoons olive oil

Salt and pepper to taste

¼ teaspoon powdered mustard such as Colman's English

RÉMOULADE SAUCE:

1 cup mayonnaise

1 tablespoon extra-strong Dijon mustard

¼ teaspoon powdered mustard

1 tablespoon nonpareil capers, rinsed and dried

1 teaspoon finely snipped chives

¼ teaspoon crushed dried tarragon

1 tablespoon finely minced parsley or watercress leaves

Salt and pepper to taste

To make the salad: Peel and cut the celery root into ⅛-inch fine julienne, either by hand, in a food processor fitted with a julienne blade, or with a mandoline. Combine the water and white wine vinegar in a 3-quart saucepan, and as the celery root is cut, drop it into the pot to prevent discoloration. Bring to a boil over medium-high heat and cook for 30 seconds. Drain and put in a medium-size bowl.

In a cup, whisk together the tarragon vinegar, oil, salt, pepper, and mustard. Pour this mixture over the warm celery root and stir to combine. Cover with plastic wrap and refrigerate for several hours or overnight.

To make the sauce: Combine all the sauce ingredients, cover with plastic wrap, and refrigerate.

Combine the celery root with the remoulade sauce, cover, and chill once again for 2 hours to let the flavors blend before serving.

When ready to serve, Céleri Rave Rémoulade looks perfect on a base of frilled red lettuce leaves with a sprinkle of paprika and a pinch of minced parsley for color if you wish.

Demystifying the Unfamiliar Vegetables

Jicama Salad with Blood Oranges and Mizuna

White Salsify with Chicken, Roasted Red Peppers, and Peas

Scorzonera (Black Salsify) all'Italiana with Prosciutto, Capers, and Parmesan Curls

Roasted Sunchokes and Garlic with Oregano, Bay Leaf, and Cloves

Cardoon and Cherry Tomatoes in a Honey-Lemon Vinaigrette

Corn Spoon Bread with Okra and Tomato

Beef with Burdock and Shiitake Mushrooms, Japanese Style

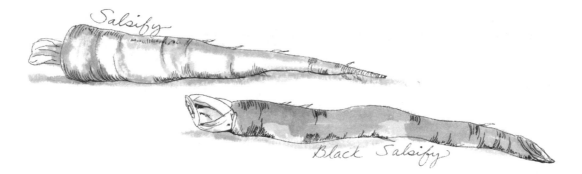

Salsify

Black Salsify

At various times of the year they appear in the markets, nestled among the familiar potatoes, spinach, or broccoli. Their names and even their shapes are daunting. We study them, pondering what on earth we can do with them: sunchokes, jicama, cardoons, salsify, scorzanera, burdock, and even (for northerners) okra. And so we pick them up, feel their texture, comment on their unusual shapes, smell them, give them a final squeeze, and then put them back in the bin, moving on to the potatoes, spinach, and broccoli.

Sometimes a little daring may be required to nudge a jaded palate out of the familiar and into the realm of the unfamiliar. Remember, it has been said that it took a brave man to eat the first oyster!

◆ Some Tips ◆

Certain vegetables—sunchokes, cardoons, salsify, burdock, artichokes, and celeriac—will darken rapidly when peeled or cut and exposed to the air. As you peel or cut them, add them to acidulated water to prevent this from occurring.

Don't use an aluminum or cast-iron pot when cooking them. The chemical reaction between the metal and the vegetables will cause them to turn black.

JICAMA

It is pronounced *hic-ah-ma*, and it's a tuber that hails from Mexico and Central and South America. It tastes like a cross between a crisp Chinese water chestnut and a faintly sweet Bosc pear. In Mexico it is sometimes sold as "street food" with just a few drops of lime juice, a few sprinkles of salt, and a fiery chile powder.

SHOP SMART

A satisfyingly delicate, crunchy, pristine white flesh is hidden beneath a sort of dusty brownish skin. It is slightly flat in shape, and the sizes vary from ounces to pounds. It is available year-round. Choose the small or medium ones with the thinnest skins. A thick skin means that the jicama is old, and the very large ones may be slightly woody. It will keep in the refrigerator for five to seven days. If you cut off a portion, rub the cut side with lemon and cover the jicama tightly with plastic wrap. Once peeled, store it in iced water or water with lime or lemon juice added.

Twelve ounces will make 4 to 6 servings.

Notes for the Cook

ON JICAMA . . .

◆ It is one of those wonderful vegetables that is best when eaten raw. Just peel and cut it into very thin slices or julienne. It becomes a crunchy rival for tortilla chips (with many fewer calories). It is wonderful with guacamole or spicy salsas, and it absorbs marinades beautifully.

◆ You can also mince it or shred it and add it to fruit and vegetable salads. Cut into sticks, it makes a great crudité for use with dips and an unusual, tasty, and texturally interesting garnish for soups and stews.

SALSIFY: WHITE AND BLACK

Although highly prized on the Continent, white salsify, also called oyster plant, is relatively little known in the United States and Canada. The roots look like long, thin, hairy parsnips, and they can grow up to 10 inches long. When their creamy pale skin is peeled, a white sweet-tasting flesh is revealed. The black salsify (*Scorzonera*) is covered with rough brownish black skin, and it is interchangeable with the white.

SHOP SMART

These natives of central and southern Europe are available from October through April. Buy firm, crisp roots. If they are limp, they are too old.

One and a half pounds = four servings.

Notes for the Cook

ON SALSIFY . . .

◆ After peeling with a vegetable peeler, drop the salsify into acidulated water to prevent discoloration.

◆ Boil with some lemon juice in the water for 10 to 12 minutes, depending on the size they've been cut.

◆ Their mild, sweet flavor is best brought out in lightly seasoned dishes with creamy sauces or in an early spring salad with new potatoes and baby artichokes in a vinaigrette sauce.

SUNCHOKES

The sunchoke, also known as the Jerusalem artichoke, is not related to the globe artichoke, which is a thistle, nor does it have any vegetable relatives in Israel's city of Jerusalem. In fact, the sunchoke is as American as a Yankee Doodle dandy. The settlers found them growing in the fields that had been cultivated by the Native Americans in the Cape Cod area as early as the 1600s.

Although they resemble a coarser, more bulbous-looking fresh ginger root, they have the nutty sweet taste and the crisp texture of the Chinese water chestnut mellowed by an artichoke.

SHOP SMART

The sunchoke is an autumn and winter vegetable and is best from October to March, though they can usually be found year-round. Just like Brussels sprouts, parsnips, and collard greens, they need a touch of frost while still in the earth for the carbohydrates to break down into sugars, giving them their characteristic sweet, nutty flavor.

◆ Buy firm sunchokes, free of soft spots.

◆ Store them in plastic bags in the refrigerator. Room-temperature storage makes them limp because they quickly lose moisture.

One pound serves four to five people.

Notes for the Cook

ON SUNCHOKES . . .

- ◆ To prepare, scrub them with a stiff brush. If they are to be roasted, the skins can be left on to add additional flavor.
- ◆ If you puree them by putting them through a food mill, the skins will be left behind.
- ◆ Lightly steamed, sunchokes make an unusual addition to salads, slaws, and pickles.

CARDOONS

In Italian it's *cardone*, a favorite in Italy since the Roman Empire. In French it's *cardon*, a staple in Provence where it is traditionally eaten on Christmas Eve. In North America many of us turn up our noses at anything with such a bitter edge. But if you're game and curious to try what looks like an obscenely overgrown, weathered bunch of celery with wide, deeply ribbed strings and silvery stalks, your daring will be well rewarded.

The cardoon is part of the thistle family and a relative of the artichoke. But instead of the globe or flower part of the plant, the celery look-alike stalks are eaten.

SHOP SMART

- ◆ Cardoons are in season from winter to early spring, and when you buy them, look for the ones that are the palest silvery green. It means that they were hilled up (covered from the light) for a few weeks.
- ◆ Don't purchase limp cardoons. They should be rigid. Wrap the base in damp paper towels and slip them into a plastic bag when you get home.
- ◆ After a week you will have to trim off any bruised, brownish parts before you use them.

Allow 2 pounds untrimmed or 1½ pounds trimmed for four servings.

Notes for the Cook

ON CARDOONS . . .

◆ Like the artichoke, the cardoon does require trimming. Cut off any leaves, trim the base end, and remove and discard the tougher outside stalks.

◆ Using a vegetable peeler, pare off the prickly strings, much like stringing celery. Slice the hearts crosswise into the size you need for your recipe. (In Italy they are sliced very thin, dipped in coarse salt and olive oil, and eaten raw.)

◆ Drop the pieces into acidulated water (1 teaspoon of either lemon juice or vinegar) to prevent discoloring.

◆ When cooking, lemon juice, or vinegar and salt is added to the water. They are boiled for anywhere from 20 to 40 minutes, depending on the size of the pieces, or until tender.

OKRA

To any southerner, okra is most familiar. This hot-climate vegetable is a staple in the Deep South where it was first introduced by African slaves, who called it "gumbo." In Louisiana it was rapidly embraced as a part of Cajun and Creole cooking, and it is found on every menu in that state.

But okra is also much beloved and ubiquitous in the cuisines of India, the Middle East, Turkey, and Greece, where it is dried and reconstituted before use, very much like mushrooms. But northern Europeans as well as many northern and midwestern Americans are unfamiliar with okra or have been turned off by the texture. When okra is cut, it exudes a slippery fluid quite similar to nopales (cactus paddles). We hasten to add, however, that it can be easily rinsed off.

 SHOP SMART

◆ The best okra, the smallest pods, are found from mid to late summer, and earlier in the hot southern climates. The larger 3- to 4-inch pods are generally around most of the year.

◆ They're green-ridged, have a tiny cap on top, and taper to a point. Buy the smallest, unblemished, under-2-inch pods that you can find. The large ones tend to be fibrous.

◆ Store them in a plastic bag for no more than three days since they start to brown at the edges after that.

One pound = four servings.

Notes for the Cook

ON OKRA . . .

◆ Wash and trim a tiny slice from the stem ends just before cooking. Very little, if any, gummy substance will be released.

◆ Blanch tiny pods quickly and toss them in salads. Okra pickles are another specialty in Texas and Tennessee, and they're wonderful when combined with tomatoes, garlic, and rosemary. In many Middle Eastern stews, okra is combined with meat, made into an omelet, or roasted for 10 minutes in a 500-degree oven and tossed in olive oil and oregano.

◆ The pods tend to discolor if cooked in an iron or copper pot. Even though they're edible, they're just not bright green and gorgeous.

BURDOCK ROOT

With origins in southern Russia, this long, slender root with a length that sometimes reaches 36 inches has a mild, neutral flavor and a crunchy texture. It has been a part of ancient diets for as far back as the tenth century. In China it is believed to have medicinal properties that help the immune system and increase energy for those who are recuperating from an illness.

In Japan burdock root is called *gobo*, and it appears in many Japanese dishes—slivers for crunch in sushi rolls and for textural contrast in soft noodle dishes. It is also pickled and served as an accompaniment for many dishes.

You'll find that its neutral taste acts as a carrier for other flavors that will be absorbed during cooking or marinating.

SHOP SMART

- ◆ Select the slimmest pale or tan burdock you can find that has no soft spots.
- ◆ Only buy burdock that is no more than 1 inch in diameter since the center part of thick burdock can be woody in texture.

Notes for the Cook

ON BURDOCK . . .

To prepare:

- ◆ Scrub the burdock with a stiff brush and trim away the ends and any hair-like roots.
- ◆ Drop the burdock in vinegared water and cook it in the same water to prevent discoloration.
- ◆ Parboil before sautéeing and slice paper thin or julienne either before or after par-boiling. A pleasant, desirable crunch remains after cooking.

JICAMA SALAD WITH BLOOD ORANGES AND MIZUNA

Refreshing raspberry-colored citrus and sweet, crisp, white jicama contrast with the pungent bite of young mustard greens in a salad with no oil. A cholesterol watcher's delight.

SERVES 4

3 medium oranges, preferably blood oranges
1 lime
8 ounces mizuna or young mustard greens

8 ounces jicama, peeled and cut into ¼-inch julienne (about 4 cups)
¼ teaspoon coarse salt
⅛ teaspoon cayenne pepper
1 tablespoon cilantro leaves

With a zester tool, zest 1 orange and the lime and set aside. Squeeze the juice of 1 orange (about 4 tablespoons) and place in a small bowl. Peel the remaining oranges, remove the bitter white pith, and slice thinly crosswise. Squeeze the juice from the lime (about 2 tablespoons) and add it to the orange juice.

Line 4 salad plates with the greens. Arrange the orange slices in a circle toward the outer rim of the plates and mound the julienned jicama in the center. Spoon the orange-lime juice over the jicama and sprinkle with the salt and cayenne. Scatter cilantro leaves and shredded zest over all.

WHITE SALSIFY WITH CHICKEN, ROASTED RED PEPPERS, AND PEAS

Remember a dish from the '50s called Chicken à la King? Well, this recipe is that family favorite updated and gone sophisticated with the addition of wonderful white salsify cooked in chicken broth.

SERVES 4

2 teaspoons lemon juice

8 ounces white salsify, thin roots peeled

4 cups chicken broth

½ cup tiny frozen peas

7-ounce jar roasted red peppers, drained and cut in ¼-inch pieces (about ½ cup)

12 ounces to 1 pound chicken breasts, skinned and boned

3 tablespoons butter

3 tablespoons flour

2 tablespoons dry sherry

⅛ teaspoon freshly ground nutmeg

Salt and pepper to taste

3¼ cups cooked white jasmine rice

2 tablespoons finely minced chives

Add 1 teaspoon of lemon juice to a bowl of water. Cut the salsify diagonally into 1-inch pieces and add the pieces to the bowl. Set aside. In a 3-quart nonstick saucepan, bring the broth and the remaining teaspoon of lemon juice to a boil over medium-high heat. Drain, add the salsify to the saucepan, and cook, uncovered, for 12 minutes. Add the peas and continue to cook 2 to 3 minutes more. Remove the salsify and peas from the broth with a slotted spoon and place in a large bowl. Add the red peppers and set aside.

Return the broth in the pot to a boil. Add the chicken breasts and poach over medium heat for about 8 minutes, or until the breasts are just cooked through. Do not overcook. Transfer the chicken breasts to a work surface, let cool slightly, and cut into bite-size pieces. Add them to the bowl with the salsify mixture.

Strain the broth, reserving 2 cups. Wipe out the saucepan, then add the butter and melt over medium heat. When the butter has melted, sift in the flour, stirring constantly. Slowly add the reserved broth, stirring constantly to keep the mixture smooth. Turn the heat to medium-low and simmer the sauce for 5 to 8 minutes, stirring frequently, until the mixture is slightly thickened. Add the sherry, nutmeg, and salt to taste and season liberally with pepper. Add the contents of the bowl and continue to simmer until heated through. Ladle over a bed of white rice and scatter the chives over the surface.

SCORZONERA (BLACK SALSIFY) ALL'ITALIANA WITH PROSCIUTTO, CAPERS, AND PARMESAN CURLS

When we first tried this unusual vegetable in Italy, we said, "Where has this been all our lives?" Now it has become a seasonal treat in our local marketplace, and we eagerly look forward to it in the cold-weather months.

SERVES 4

1 pound scorzonera (black salsify) (about 5 roots, 1 inch in diameter and 12 inches long)	4 tablespoons coarse fresh bread crumbs
2 cups cold water	2 tablespoons olive oil
2 tablespoons lemon juice	1 ounce prosciutto di Parma, cut in small dice
1 teaspoon salt	1 teaspoon rinsed nonpareil capers
2 tablespoons butter	1 tablespoon finely minced parsley
1 tablespoon thinly sliced garlic (about 1 large clove)	Parmesan cheese in 1 piece
	Freshly ground black pepper

Peel the roots with a vegetable peeler, working quickly so that the salsify doesn't discolor. Rinse in cold water, cut into 1-inch pieces, and drop into cold water mixed with

1 tablespoon lemon juice. Transfer the salsify, water, and lemon juice to a non-reactive (not aluminum or cast iron) 2-quart saucepan. Add the salt and bring to a boil. Lower the heat to medium and cook, covered, for 8 minutes, or until the salsify is crisp/tender.

While the vegetable cooks, melt 2 tablespoons of butter in a small skillet. Add the garlic and sauté over medium heat for 1 to 2 minutes, stirring. Stir in the bread crumbs and continue to stir for 30 seconds. Turn off the heat and set the skillet aside.

When the vegetable is cooked, drain and add the remaining tablespoon of lemon juice and the olive oil. Stir to combine and transfer to a serving dish. Scatter the prosciutto and the reserved garlic crumbs over the surface and sprinkle with parsley. Cut cheese curls with a paring or cheese knife over the surface. Add a few grinds of pepper and serve hot.

ROASTED SUNCHOKES AND GARLIC WITH OREGANO, BAY LEAF, AND CLOVES

If you have never eaten sunchokes, they certainly merit a try. Roasting them with garlic, herbs, and spices gives fine flavor to this mellow, nutty-tasting vegetable. Whole garlic cloves, roasted with the sunchokes, can be spread on crisp sourdough toasts and served alongside.

SERVES 4

2 tablespoons olive oil
1 whole garlic head, cloves separated
   and peeled
½ lemon
4 cups cold water
1 pound sunchokes (Jerusalem
   artichokes)
1½ teaspoons dried Greek oregano
Salt and black pepper to taste

1 dried bay leaf
2 whole cloves
2 tablespoons butter, cut into small
   pieces
1 to 2 tablespoons lemon juice
¼ cup minced parsley
Several slices toasted
   sourdough bread

Preheat the oven to 375 degrees. Place the olive oil and peeled garlic in a small bowl. In another bowl, squeeze the lemon into the water. Peel the sunchokes and drop them into the acidulated water to prevent discoloration. If some tubers are larger than others, cut them so that they are all approximately the same size. Drain the water and blot the sunchokes with paper towels. Add them to the garlic and oil along with the oregano, salt, and pepper.

Transfer to a medium-size baking dish in a single layer. Stir in the bay leaf and cloves, and dot with the butter. Roast for 40 minutes, stirring once or twice, or until the sunchokes are tender when pierced with the point of a knife. Remove and discard the bay leaf and cloves. Sprinkle with lemon juice and parsley. Accompany with sourdough toasts at the table, spreading the toasts with the roasted garlic cloves.

CARDOON WITH CHERRY TOMATOES IN A HONEY-LEMON VINAIGRETTE

Each country that has made the "cardoon connection" has its own particular subtlety. The French boil and then bake them in a béchamel sauce laced with Gruyère cheese. The Italians either fry them or boil them and serve them with the warm Piedmontese dipping sauce called bagna cauda. *The Spaniards include diced Serrano ham and almonds in their béchamel. Here we've used cardoon in a simple salad with a marinade made with honey to counteract any bitter edge.*

SERVES 4 TO 6

CARDOON:

2 quarts water

1 bay leaf

5 whole peppercorns

4 sprigs parsley

2 sprigs thyme

1 large onion, peeled and cut in half

3 whole cloves garlic, peeled

1 teaspoon white vinegar

1 teaspoon sugar

1 teaspoon salt

2 pounds cardoon, trimmed, strings removed, and cut into bite-size pieces (see page 86 for basic preparation)

6 cherry tomatoes

HONEY-LEMON VINAIGRETTE:

½ cup olive oil

½ cup lemon juice (about 2 medium lemons)

1 teaspoon finely minced lemon zest

2 teaspoons light mild honey (such as thyme honey)

⅛ teaspoon cayenne pepper

¾ teaspoon salt

2 tablespoons coarsely chopped fresh mint

Fresh black pepper to taste

Place the water in a 5-quart Dutch oven. For easy removal, gather the bay leaf, peppercorns, parsley, thyme, onion, and garlic into a cheesecloth bag and tie it. Place in the pot and add the vinegar, sugar, salt, and drained cardoon. Bring to a boil over medium heat, then turn the heat to medium-low and simmer for about 30 minutes, or until the cardoons are tender. While cooking, prepare the vinaigrette.

To make the vinaigrette: Whisk all the ingredients together and set aside.

When the cardoons are tender, drain well and add to a serving bowl along with the cherry tomatoes. Pour the vinaigrette over all while warm. Stir to combine and let marinate at room temperature for at least 2 hours or overnight. Stir every so often while marinating. Taste and add more honey to counteract any slight bitterness if you wish.

Cardoon

CORN SPOON BREAD WITH OKRA AND TOMATO

This is a West Indian version of a traditional southern colonial bread. It is not quite a bread because it is much lighter, and it is not quite a soufflé because it is denser in texture. But one thing it is: a hearty pudding-like dish that would make any vegetarian happy. And it is also a terrific side dish with grilled chicken.

SERVES 4 TO 6

3 scallions, finely sliced (about ¾ cup)

1 cup corn kernels, cut from 2 ears of corn

1 large plum tomato, diced (½ cup)

6 ounces okra, stem tips cut off and discarded, then sliced ½ inch thick (about 1 cup)

1½ cups low-fat milk

1 teaspoon sugar

1 teaspoon salt or to taste

1 cup stone-ground yellow cornmeal

3 tablespoons soft butter

1 cup buttermilk

3 eggs, separated

½ teaspoon baking soda

¼ teaspoon cayenne pepper

2 teaspoons baking powder

1 tablespoon finely minced fresh sage

¼ teaspoon black pepper

Preheat the oven to 375 degrees. Butter a 2-quart baking dish. In a large bowl, combine the scallions, corn, tomato, and okra, and set aside. In a 3-quart nonstick saucepan over medium heat, bring the milk, sugar, and salt to the boiling point. Slowly add the cornmeal and stir constantly with a wooden spoon until the mixture is smooth and thick and leaves the sides of the pan. Transfer the mixture to the bowl of a food processor, add the butter, and process for a few strokes until the butter is incorporated. Add the buttermilk, and then the egg yolks, and process.

In a small cup, whisk together the baking soda, cayenne, and baking powder. Add it to the food processor and combine. Add the sage and pepper, and combine. Scrape the mixture into the bowl with the reserved vegetables and set aside.

In another deep bowl, beat the egg whites with a hand beater until stiff. Fold ⅓ of the beaten egg whites into the cornmeal mixture, then fold in the remaining beaten egg whites. Scrape the mixture into the prepared dish and bake until the top is golden and puffy, about 35 to 40 minutes. Serve warm.

BEEF WITH BURDOCK AND SHIITAKE MUSHROOMS, JAPANESE STYLE

Our local Japanese restaurant worked out this recipe with us on a snowy winter night just before closing time. It was a remarkable experience to watch these knife-skilled wizards at work, deftly slivering the burdock in two seconds flat! Serve this with a sticky short-grain rice to make it fully authentic.

SERVES 4

8 ounces burdock (about
   30 inches long)

4 cups water

1 tablespoon rice wine vinegar

3 tablespoons mirin (sweet rice wine)

3 tablespoons light soy sauce

2 tablespoons sake

1 tablespoon sugar

¼ teaspoon Japanese red chile pepper
   mix (see Note)

8 ounces boneless sirloin; freeze slightly
   before slicing into paper-thin slices

2 tablespoons corn oil

3 ounces shiitake mushrooms, wiped
   clean and stems removed and
   discarded

2 tablespoons diagonally sliced scallion,
   green part only (about
   1 scallion)

Scrub the burdock with a stiff brush and cut it into 2-inch chunks. Place in a 2-quart saucepan with the water and vinegar. Let stand for 15 minutes, then bring to a boil over medium heat and cook for 20 to 25 minutes, until tender. It will maintain a slight crunchiness. Drain and cut the burdock into julienne.

In a medium-size bowl, combine the mirin, soy sauce, sake, sugar, and red pepper mix. Add the julienned burdock and marinate for 2 hours. After the first hour, remove ¼ cup of the marinade, transfer it to a small bowl, and add the sliced beef. Continue to marinate both for the allotted time.

When ready to cook, drain the beef and burdock, reserving the marinade. In a large nonstick skillet, heat the oil until it is very hot. Add the beef and mushrooms, and stir-fry for 30 seconds. Transfer the beef and mushrooms to a bowl using a slotted spoon. Quickly add the burdock and marinade to the skillet and bring to a boil. Stir constantly until the sauce is reduced a bit, about 1 to 2 minutes. Return the meat and mushrooms, and stir-fry 1 minute more.

Transfer to a serving dish and scatter the scallion slices over the surface. Serve with sticky short-grain rice.

Note: Japanese red chile pepper mix, *Schichimi Togarashi,* is a combination of powdered chile, Japanese black pepper (*sancho*), black and yellow sesame seeds, roasted hemp and poppy seed, orange peel, and seaweed.

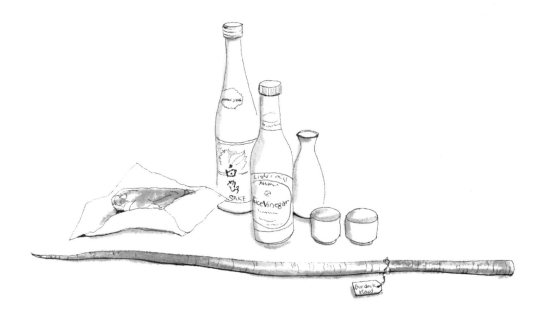

Mushroom Mania

Cremini Mushroom Caps Stuffed with Scallops, Chives, and Rosemary

Wild Mushroom Pie with an Herb and Cheese Crust

Ramekins Forestière with Ham and Parmesan Cheese

Farro with Wild Mushrooms and Butter-Toasted Almonds

Linguini with Roquefort, Basil, and White Truffle Oil

Chicken Breasts with Morels, Asparagus, Peas, and Marjoram

Enoki Mushroom Salad with Radicchio, Watercress, and Sesame Seeds

There is truly something magical about the cultivation of mushrooms—the wonder of how they suddenly spring up in the dark, snowy and tightly capped. And there is also the magic of what seems to take place in our kitchens when we use them. Of course, in this day and age of nutrition awareness, we know they contain a minimal 14 to 18 calories per cup, are cholesterol and fat free, and are available all year round, a boon to vegetarians who laud their meatlike texture and flavor.

The word "mushroom" comes from the French word *moisseron*—the moss in which they are grown. It is also the name of a tiny French wild mushroom. Mushrooms were first cultivated in Japan over two thousand years ago. At the beginning of the eighteenth century they were grown in limestone quarries outside of Paris.

We find them irresistible, as do most home cooks; They have soft, fleshy textures; an endless variation of myriad, attractive shapes; fragrant woodsy aromas; and an infinite choice of individual flavors.

There has been an explosion in mushroom sales that has had a side effect: total confusion. Some merchants actually invent names for lesser-known varieties. Some mushrooms are called by different names in other countries and even in other parts of our own. With more than ten thousand species (by the reckoning of some mycologists), each with its own distinct characteristics, no wonder it is difficult to be "mushroom specific" at times. But take heart. All the varieties of mushrooms are still mushrooms, and freely substituting one for another because of availability or season will still work out well.

POPULAR WILD AND CULTIVATED MUSHROOMS AT A GLANCE

This chart includes information on only the most popular mushrooms, those easily available in supermarkets and specialty outlets around the country. Note also that some wild mushrooms are also being cultivated.

CODE:

W= Wild **C**= Cultivated **S**= Spring **F**= Fall **Y**= Year-round or Sporadic

VARIETY	DESCRIPTION	USE
BLACK TRUMPET **W F S** *AKA* HORNS OF PLENTY, BLACK CHANTERELLE, TRUMPET OF DEATH	Marketed as "Horns of Plenty" since Trumpet of Death (because of its looks, not its effects) is understandably a turnoff. Hollow, black, limp, and lightweight, with cap and stem merged like a musical horn instrument. Lively, somewhat deep fruity flavor.	The color is lovely in risottos and white creamy sauces.
CAULIFLOWER **W F**	Can grow very large, up to several pounds. Convoluted shape like a piece of gathered fabric, making it difficult to clean. Firm, rubbery texture, slight licorice flavor, and very fragrant.	Folds up well but needs long cooking time in soups and stews. Good textural contrast for fish, and when it's grilled, it gets crunchy and crisp.

VARIETY	DESCRIPTION	USE
CHANTERELLE **W F S** *AKA* GIROLLE, EGG MUSHROOM	Golden apricot color; trumpet- or lily-shaped. Chewy, somewhat leathery texture. Buttery, delicate flavor	Prepare simply so flavor is not masked. Sauté for deeper flavor and use in omelets and with poultry, seafood, or creamy pasta sauces. They pick up other flavors, so go easy on garlic. Use citrus or fresh herbs to enhance its delicate flavor.
CREMINI **C Y** *AKA* ROMAN, PRATAIOLI, BABY BELLA, GOLDEN ITALIAN	Cocoa-colored variant of the familiar white button mushroom but with more intense flavor and firmer texture. Same umbrella shape as the white button. The cap should extend to the gills so that the gills are concealed.	Excellent all-purpose mushroom for soups; sautéed for pastas and stews; added to risotto or other grain dishes along with wild mushrooms.
ENOKI **W AND C Y** *AKA* ENOKITAKE, "SNOW PUFF," SNOW PEAK	Bright yellow when found in the wild. When cultivated, white clusters with very thin long stems and tiny caps that resemble carpenter's nails. Moist and slightly acidic bland flavor. Cultivated enoki are sold in vacuum-packed plastic and clear plastic boxes.	Only cultivated white eroki can be eaten raw in salads. They can be seasoned with lemon and dill, and wrapped in buttered foil and baked. Very decorative in clear or cream soups and when used as garnishes.
HEDGEHOG **W S** *AKA* SWEET TOOTH, PIED-DE-MOUTON	Harbinger of spring. Fragile, salmon-colored, and a bristly look-alike for golden chanterelles in both color and flavor. Underside of cap looks like layers of crooked teeth that need orthodontic work. Deep, woodsy flavor.	Does well in stews, soups, and sauces for veal, chicken, or seafood. Can be cooked and substituted for golden chanterelles.

HEN-OF-THE-WOODS **W** *AKA* Maitake (no relation to Chicken-of-the-Woods)	Grayish tan color layered with frilly edges. Pleasant aroma, mild flavor, fragile flesh. Edible stems have more firmness.	Cook in sauces for pasta with sausage, chicken, or veal. Toss with wild wilted braising greens or as part of a wild mushroom ragout.
MOREL **W S Y** *AKA* Sponge mushroom	Hollow, honey-combed dunce caps. Two varieties: dark brown with heftier flavor, and pale golden with more delicate, meatier texture. Dried morels: smoked lightly over wood, have deeper flavor and smoky taste.	Can be cut in half lengthwise or horizontally into rings. Whole caps can be batter-fried or stuffed. Best appreciated in creamy sauces with poultry, veal, fish, or pasta, where texture picks up and holds sauces.
OYSTER **W** and **C F Y** *AKA* Tree Oyster, Shemeji, Pleurotte, Abalone	Pale, ivory to soft gray, and joined in clusters. They resemble Ping-Pong paddles and range in size from tiny to the size of a quarter. Soft, fragile, with the silky feel of a chamois cloth. Has a mild, rather bland taste.	Best cooked quickly over high heat. After cooking, texture is somewhat like al dente pasta. Sauté or fry in batter. Use the "paddles" as garnish for soups or use as stuffing with seafood.
PORCINI **W F Y** *AKA* Cèpes, Boletes	The Italian favorite. Large, umbrella-shaped. Cap is tan to darker brown. Thick stems. Fleshy, firm, plump texture and full flavored. When sliced and dried, resemble cedar bark mulching chips with intense winy flavor and bosky aroma.	Cutting off the gills from the underside of the caps before cooking gives them a more delicate flavor and doesn't darken the dish. Can braise, sauté, or grill, brushed with olive oil or enhanced with truffle oil.

VARIETY	DESCRIPTION	USE
PORTOBELLO **C Y** *AKA* "KING OF THE GRILL"	An overgrown cremini and an extremely popular, meaty giant. Caps are usually 4 to 6 inches, but some are the size of dinner plates. Brown, slightly flattened umbrella shape with dense, heavy flesh and a sometimes fibrous, thick stem and dark brown gills on the underside of the cap.	Stems can be removed and finely chopped for duxelles or flavoring sauces. Caps are best grilled, baked, stuffed or sliced, and sautéed. Some chefs cut away the gills from under the caps before cooking to prevent plates and cooking utensils from being discolored.
SHIITAKE **W** AND **C F Y** *AKA* BLACK FOREST, GOLDEN OAK. (IN JAPANESE *SHIA* MEANS OAK AND *TAKE* MEANS MUSHROOM.)	Surface skin is pale tawny to dark brown with dome-shaped umbrella cap that curls under at the edges. Interior is cream colored. Firm, supple texture and slightly earthy mild flavor. Dried Chinese Black Forest shiitakes have a cracked tortoise shell pattern on the caps and are deeper in flavor than the fresh.	Can be used for flavoring soups and sauces. A versatile mushroom amenable to most dishes—in soups, with vegetables, poultry, fish, or Oriental dishes—or stuffed and baked. Note: Soak dried Shiitakes for one hour to reconstitute them before using in stir fries or any Oriental dish.
WHITE **C Y** *AKA* DOMESTIC, CULTIVATED, BUTTON, CHAMPIGNON DE PARIS	White, umbrella-shaped, with the same characteristics as the cremini but with less flavor.	Used as an all-purpose mushroom for mild, blander dishes. Large caps can be stuffed and baked. Available from 1-inch to 2½-inch cap sizes.

FRESH MUSHROOMS

SHOP SMART

- Wild and cultivated mushrooms come in different sizes and weights, so buy accordingly for your recipe needs. A rough guide: Allow 4 ounces per person before cleaning.
- Mushrooms contain 85 percent water, so expect shrinkage and plan your purchase to allow for it. For example:

One pound of trimmed, cleaned, thickly sliced
raw wild mushrooms = about 6 cups.
After sautéeing, equals 2 cups.

- Buy tight, firm mushrooms with solid color and no mottling, insect holes, or slimy surfaces.
- Freshness counts! Purchase your mushrooms no more than one or two days before using them since they are highly perishable. They wither and shrivel with age.

Notes for the Cook

ON CLEANING FRESH MUSHROOMS . . .

- Fresh mushrooms, both wild and cultivated, span a wide spectrum of textures and shapes, and cleaning them can take different paths. Some are very fragile—the black trumpets, for example. The golden chanterelles and hedgehogs harbor clingy dirt on their undersides, while morels have little nooks and crannies that require meticulous cleaning.
- Many articles suggest using soft brushes and no water. However, from our own experience, the best advice we can give is that brushes are the quickest way to destroy fresh mushrooms. We agree with Jack Czarnecki, the well-respected mushroom hunter and mycologist, that dirt can be washed away by rinsing mushrooms briefly under warm tap water. Some mushrooms with underside gills should be carefully examined and quickly rinsed. The caps should then be wiped with damp paper towels. Here are some specifics:

BLACK TRUMPET: Rinse under warm running water a few at a time and blot dry on paper towels. Trim the coarse ends and pull apart to examine for foreign matter. Place on clean paper towels and blot dry.

CAULIFLOWER: Rinse in warm water to remove dirt from crevices. Trim end, pull it apart, and examine again for any dirt.

CREMINI: Trim stem ends and wipe clean with damp paper towels.

GOLDEN CHANTERELLES: Rinse in warm water. Use your fingers to gently dislodge clinging dirt, especially on the undersides. Blot dry with paper towels, trim the tough part of the caps, and wipe with damp paper towels.

HEDGEHOG: Trim tough ends, examine the underside for foreign matter, and wipe with damp paper towels.

MORELS: Trim stem ends. Soak in hot water for five minutes to dislodge hidden insects or dirt and swish them around. Drain in a colander. Scrape away any dirt while rinsing under lukewarm tap water. Blot dry on paper towels.

OYSTER: Trim and discard tough stem ends. Pull apart, examine for foreign matter, and wipe clean with damp paper towels. Place on dry paper towels.

PORTOBELLO: Cut off stems and wipe caps carefully with damp paper towels.

SHIITAKE: Cut off tough stems, leaving cap, and wipe with damp paper towels.

WHITE CULTIVATED: Trim stem ends and wipe clean with damp paper towels.

DON'T THROW THOSE STEMS AWAY . . .

Use them in sauces for steak, veal, or poultry by making a wild mushroom essence with 4 cups of stem trimmings, cleaned, and 2 cups of water.

Put the mushroom stems and the water into a 2-quart saucepan and bring to a boil over high heat. Skim off the surface foam and discard it. Cover the pot, lower the heat, and simmer for 30 minutes. Strain into a cup or small bowl by pressing the solids against a paper coffee filter–lined strainer. Discard the solids.

Makes about ¾ cup.

DRIED MUSHROOMS

They are a pantry staple always at your beck and call. The best thing about them is that when mushrooms are dried, the flavor characteristics are actually intensified rather than diminished.

SHOP SMART

Choose mushrooms in see-through bags or containers. There should be no broken pieces and no dirty residue. Much like grains, dried mushrooms can harbor insects, so it is best to store them in the freezer where they'll keep for years and can be used without defrosting.

Notes for the Cook

ON DRIED MUSHROOMS . . .

- Rinse the dried mushrooms to rid them of any grit or sand.
- Put them in a bowl with warm water to cover or use warm chicken stock with or without a bit of Madeira or sherry. It takes between 30 and 40 minutes for soaked, dried mushrooms to be pliable. Hot water speeds up the timing but will dilute the flavor intensity. If the mushrooms absorb all the liquid before becoming soft, merely add some additional warm liquid.
- After soaking, remove the mushrooms with a slotted spoon without disturbing any residue that has settled on the bottom of the bowl. Gently squeeze any excess liquid from the mushrooms into the bowl. If there are hard or woody stems (as with shiitakes), they should be removed and discarded.
- Line a strainer with a dampened paper coffee filter and pour the liquid through to remove the sediment. The liquid will be filled with flavor, so don't discard it.
- Add mushrooms to your recipe at the beginning of your cooking to allow their highly concentrated flavor to permeate.
- Unlike their fresh counterparts, dried mushrooms are not used on their own as a vegetable but rather as an accent or seasoning (like an herb or spice). They can enhance a dish with remarkable complexity and nuance, be it poultry, meat, or grain dishes.

THE FOUR NEVERS OF WILD MUSHROOMS

Never store wild mushrooms in plastic bags. To prevent rot, refrigerate them in paper bags or in one layer on a plate, loosely covered with damp paper towels.

Never wash mushrooms before storing them. Wash and clean them right before using.

Never eat mushrooms raw except for the white cultivated buttons and enoki mushrooms. Experts advise that the others are not hygienically acceptable when eaten raw.

Mushrooms contain compounds that are not lethal but can cause stomach distress, rumblings, and indigestion. After cooking, these compounds break down. An additional culinary benefit to cooking is that it brings out their full flavor.

Never forage for mushrooms in the wild. It can be a life-threatening activity unless you are accompanied by a mycologist "with the credentials equivalent of a brain surgeon," according to Gourmet Garage's in-house mushroom maven John Gottfried, a member of the American Mycological Society. You may suffer the risk of food poisoning or even death. It is prudent to have complete faith in the integrity of your supplier.

CREMINI MUSHROOM CAPS STUFFED WITH SCALLOPS, CHIVES, AND ROSEMARY

Mushrooms, deemed "food for the gods" by the ancient Greeks, have never lost their appeal over the centuries. Mycologists reckon that there are over ten thousand species. When you, too, succumb to "the call of the wild," try this hearty earth mother, the firm and coffee-colored cremini mushroom that has a creamy scallop tucked into its cuplike cap.

SERVES 4

8 large cremini mushrooms
1 tablespoon balsamic vinegar
1 medium clove garlic, peeled and crushed
1 teaspoon fresh rosemary leaves
2 tablespoons olive oil
2 tablespoons butter
3 tablespoons fresh bread crumbs

A few grindings of black pepper
Salt to taste
1 teaspoon lemon juice
2 drops white Worcestershire sauce
4 sea scallops or 4 ounces bay scallops
1½ teaspoons minced fresh chives
1 teaspoon finely minced fresh parsley

Remove the mushroom stems and save for another use. Clean the caps with damp paper towels and place them, hollow side up, in a tempered glass pie plate. Combine the vinegar, garlic, rosemary, and olive oil, and spoon the mixture over the mushrooms. Most of the marinade should be absorbed.

In a small skillet, melt the butter and add the bread crumbs, pepper, and salt. Add the lemon juice and Worcestershire sauce. Stir and cook over medium heat for 1 minute, then set aside.

Cut each sea scallop in half horizontally. Place 1 piece in each mushroom cap. If using small bay scallops, put 3 or 4 in each mushroom cap. Spoon a bit of the bread crumb mixture over each one. When ready to serve, preheat the broiler and broil the mushrooms for 5 to 7 minutes, until the bread crumbs are golden brown. Remove from the broiler and sprinkle with the chives and parsley. Serve hot.

WILD MUSHROOM PIE WITH AN HERB AND CHEESE CRUST

Exquisitely rich, tender, fragrant mushrooms sit happily beneath an herbal crisp crust in a sublime contrast of textures and flavors. With a salad, this pie could make four people ecstatic when you serve it for lunch or a light supper.

SERVES 4

CRUST:
½ cup fresh coarse sourdough bread crumbs
2 tablespoons freshly grated Parmesan cheese
3 tablespoons freshly grated Gruyère cheese
2 tablespoons finely minced parsley
1 tablespoon finely minced basil
1 teaspoon fresh thyme leaves

MUSHROOM FILLING:
8 ounces cremini mushroom caps (after trimming stems and cleaning)
8 ounces assorted wild mushrooms (after trimming and cleaning; use any combination of 3 or 4 with contrasting flavors and textures, such as shiitake, black trumpet, oyster, golden chanterelle, hedgehog)
2 tablespoons butter
¼ cup finely minced shallots (about 2 ounces)
1 teaspoon minced garlic (1 medium clove)
3 tablespoons dry Madeira
2 tablespoons dry sherry
1 cup heavy cream
1 tablespoon finely minced parsley
Salt and pepper to taste
⅛ teaspoon Tabasco

To make the crust: In a small bowl, combine all the ingredients, then set aside.

To make the filling: Slice the mushrooms thickly. In a 12-inch nonstick skillet, melt the butter over medium heat. Add the shallots and garlic, and sauté for 2 minutes, stirring until wilted. Add the mushrooms, raise the heat to high, and cook, stirring frequently, until the mushrooms release and then absorb most of their liquid, about 6 to 8 minutes. Scrape into a bowl and set aside.

Return the skillet to medium heat, add the Madeira, sherry, and cream, and cook for about 5 minutes, until reduced to half a cup. Return the mushrooms to the skillet and turn off the heat. Mix in the parsley, salt, pepper, and Tabasco. Spoon the mixture into a 9-inch pie pan, preferably tempered glass or ceramic. Sprinkle the crust mixture over the surface.

Preheat the broiler and slip the pie pan under the source of heat for about 2 minutes, until the crust mixture is nicely browned. Watch carefully so it doesn't burn. Serve hot.

RAMEKINS FORESTIÈRE WITH HAM AND PARMESAN CHEESE

Your food processor does most of the work for this delicate, elegant little side dish or first course. Or served with a mesclun salad, it is lunch.

MAKES FOUR 6-OUNCE SERVINGS

3 tablespoons butter

2 medium shallots (about 2 ounces)

1 large garlic clove

8 ounces cremini mushrooms, trimmed and cleaned

4 ounces mixed wild mushrooms such as black trumpet or chanterelles, trimmed and cleaned

½ teaspoon grated lemon zest

1 teaspoon fresh thyme leaves

3 or 4 large basil leaves

8 to 10 sprigs parsley leaves

2 ounces cooked ham, coarsely cut

⅓ cup Parmesan cheese

Salt and black pepper to taste (see Note)

3 eggs

1 cup milk

Preheat the oven to 325 degrees and boil a kettle of water. In a 12-inch nonstick skillet, melt the butter over medium heat. Put the shallots and garlic in the bowl of a food processor and process until fine. Add to the butter in the skillet and sauté, stirring, for 2 minutes. Remove the pan from the heat and set aside.

Place the mushrooms in the food processor and process until finely chopped. Add to the skillet, return it to medium heat, and cook for 10 minutes, stirring occasionally. Remove the pan from the heat and add the lemon zest.

Place the thyme, basil, and parsley in the food processor and process until fine. Add to the mushroom mixture.

Place the ham in the food processor and process until fine (there should be about ½ cup). Stir into the mushroom mixture along with the cheese and black pepper. Let cool slightly.

Put the eggs and milk in the food processor and process. Add to the cooled mushroom mixture and combine with a few strokes.

Coat four 6-ounce ramekins with olive oil spray and set them into a 9 x 12 x 2½-inch roasting pan. Ladle the mixture into the ramekins and pour boiling water into the pan, halfway up the sides of the ramekins. Bake in the preheated oven for 45 minutes, until set.

Remove the ramekins from the water with tongs. Cool for about 5 minutes. Run the tip of a small knife around the edges of the ramekins to loosen the custards. Unmold them on the center of a serving plate or serve right in the baking cups.

Note: In the ingredients, both ham and cheese contain salt, so taste the mixture before adding salt and pepper.

FARRO WITH WILD MUSHROOMS AND BUTTER-TOASTED ALMONDS

The combination is intriguing: the fragrance of the forest in the woodsy mushrooms plus the earthy grain. This side dish would love to share space alongside veal, poultry, or fish.

SERVES 4 TO 6

½ ounce dried porcini mushrooms

⅓ cup hot water

4 tablespoons butter

½ cup sliced almonds

8 ounces mixed fresh wild mushrooms
(a combination of any 3 in season:
hedgehog, cremini, chanterelle,
shiitake)

½ cup finely minced shallots (about
4 ounces)

1 teaspoon finely minced garlic (about
1 large clove)

1 teaspoon fresh thyme leaves

Salt and pepper to taste

½ cup beef broth

⅓ cup Madeira

2 cups cooked farro (see page 236)
(wheat berries or barley can be
substituted)

2 tablespoons finely minced chives

Place the dried mushrooms in a cup and pour the water over them. Let stand for 30 minutes, then drain the liquid and mushrooms through a dampened coffee filter into a cup. Squeeze the filter to extract most of the liquid from the mushrooms and reserve the liquid. Remove the mushrooms, cut them into small pieces, and set aside.

In a 12-inch nonstick skillet, melt 1 tablespoon of butter and add the almonds. Toast for 1 to 2 minutes, until they just begin to color. Remove with a slotted spoon and set aside.

Clean the wild mushrooms, trim and discard the tough stems, and slice them thickly. Set aside. Add another tablespoon of butter to the same skillet and sauté the shallots and garlic over medium heat for 4 to 5 minutes, stirring occasionally, until soft but not browned. Remove to a plate using a slotted spoon and reserve. Melt the remaining 2 tablespoons of butter in the same skillet over medium heat and add the wild mushrooms. Stirring often, sauté for about 4 minutes, then return the shallot-garlic mixture to the skillet along with the thyme, salt, pepper, reserved porcini mushrooms, and the mushroom liquid. Add the beef broth and Madeira, and bring to a boil. Lower the heat, cover the skillet, and simmer for 8 minutes.

Stir in the cooked farro, cover, and continue to simmer until the grain is hot and the sauce is absorbed, about 5 to 8 minutes. When ready to serve, gently mix in the reserved almonds, spoon the mixture into a serving dish, and sprinkle with the chives.

LINGUINE WITH ROQUEFORT, BASIL, AND WHITE TRUFFLE OIL

Mushrooms are closely related to truffles, a delicious, expensive fungus. Truffle oils and butters are a year-round alternative to the costly and brief seasonal Italian white truffles and the black French truffle. The white truffle oil, used here, is more pungent and can be trickled over vegetables, salads, and toasts, and added to mashed potatoes. However, it is particularly good with risottos and pastas.

SERVES 4

1 pound linguine

1 tablespoon olive oil

1 teaspoon coarsely chopped garlic (about 1 large clove)

⅔ cup diced roasted sweet red pepper (about 1 large)

2 tablespoons white truffle oil

5 ounces Roquefort cheese, diced

1½ cups coarsely torn basil leaves

Salt and pepper to taste

In a large pot of salted water, cook the linguine until one strand tests done. While the pasta is cooking, heat the olive oil in a 12-inch nonstick skillet over medium heat. When the oil is hot, quickly add the garlic and sauté, stirring, for 1 to 2 minutes, just until it begins to color. Add the red pepper and cook, stirring, for 1 minute. Turn off the heat under the skillet, and when the pasta is cooked, drain and add to the skillet and toss. Add the truffle oil and toss again. Add the cheese, basil, salt, and pepper, and toss once more to combine. Serve hot.

Add truffle oil or truffle butters to hot foods last. *Do not cook with them because their flavor diminishes with high heat.*

CHICKEN BREASTS WITH MORELS, ASPARAGUS, PEAS, AND MARJORAM

Fresh crenelated, cone-shaped morels and spears of the greenest asparagus and tiny sweet peas sauce the quickly grilled chicken breasts. The dish is the epitome of springtime.

SERVES 4

8 ounces asparagus, trimmed and cut diagonally into 1-inch lengths
½ cup tiny frozen peas
4 tablespoons butter
4 chicken breast halves, boned, skinned, trimmed, and pounded (about 2 pounds)
Salt and pepper to taste
Flour for dredging
½ cup Madeira

3 large shallots, cut lengthwise into quarters
4 ounces fresh morels, cleaned (see page 104) and stems trimmed (if morels are large, cut into ¼-inch strips; if small, cut in half lengthwise)
¾ cup chicken stock
2 teaspoons fresh marjoram leaves
⅔ cup crème fraîche

In a 1½-quart saucepan, boil salted water over medium heat and add the asparagus. Cook for 4 minutes, or until tender and crisp. Add the peas for the last 2 minutes. Drain and set aside.

In a 12-inch nonstick skillet, melt 2 tablespoons of the butter over medium-high heat until it begins to bubble. Season the chicken with salt and pepper, and dredge lightly with flour. Sauté the chicken for 7 or 8 minutes, turning once, until the breasts are slightly soft in the center (since you will complete the cooking later on). Remove the breasts and set aside on a platter.

Pour the Madeira into the same skillet. Cook and stir to reduce it to ¼ cup. Pour off into a cup and set aside. Wipe out the skillet and add the remaining 2 tablespoons of butter over medium heat. Add the shallots and sauté gently, stirring frequently, until they are soft but not brown. Add the morels and continue to cook, sliding the pan over the burner for 2 to 3 minutes. Add any accumulated juices from the chicken breasts and Madeira reduction, chicken stock, and half of the marjoram. Cover the pan to braise the mushrooms over medium heat for about 10 minutes.

Add the crème fraîche a little at a time, stirring gently after each addition. Add the reserved chicken breasts, cover the pan, and continue to cook 3 minutes more, until the chicken is cooked through. Scatter the reserved vegetables over all and cook 1 more minute, or until the vegetables are heated. Transfer to a warm serving platter and scatter the rest of the marjoram on the surface.

ENOKI MUSHROOM SALAD WITH RADICCHIO, WATERCRESS, AND SESAME SEEDS

These tiny white mushrooms, the size and shape of carpenter's nails, are delightful in this salad with an Asian accent.

SERVES 4

DRESSING (MAKES ½ CUP):
1 tablespoon lime juice
  (½ medium lime)
2 tablespoons rice wine vinegar
1 tablespoon bottled nuoc mom sauce
  (see page 292)

1 tablespoon sugar
⅛ to ¼ teaspoon red hot chile flakes
3 tablespoons canola oil

SALAD:
4 cups watercress, coarse stems
  trimmed (1 large bunch)
½ small head radicchio (about
  2 ounces), cut into fine shreds

3½-ounce package enoki mushrooms
2 teaspoons toasted sesame seeds

Make the dressing first: In a small bowl, combine all the ingredients with a whisk, then set aside.

To make the salad: Place the watercress and shredded radicchio in a large bowl. Rinse the mushrooms and dry them very well on paper towels. Cut 1½ inches off the root base that keeps them attached, separate them, and scatter over the top of the salad.

Whisk the dressing and pour ¼ cup over the salad. Toss lightly to combine and sprinkle the surface with the sesame seeds.

Tiptoe Through the Tubers

Provence Potatoes with Onions and Anchovies

Warm Lyonnaise Potato and Sausage Salad with Six Fresh Herbs

Irish Colcannon

Potato and Arugula Soup

Sautéed Potatoes with Red Onions, Thyme, and Vinegar

Garnet Yams with Pears, Dried Figs, and Crystallized Ginger

The potato has played a fascinating role in agricultural history. Native to South America, where more than twenty-seven varieties of potatoes have been cultivated for over eight thousand years in the Bolivian and Peruvian Andes, it was yet another of the crops encountered by the Spanish invaders in the sixteenth century. After it was introduced to Europe, it fell under suspicion that it was poisonous—similar to rumors about the tomato and eggplant, also members of the nightshade family.

It was probably Sir Walter Raleigh who finally debunked the poison myth of the potato in England and also introduced the potato into Ireland. The Irish potato blight of 1845 through 1851 and the resultant famine caused the deaths of an estimated one to two million people and was responsible for countless others to emigrate.

Potatoes have appeared on the tables of both kings and peasants in a hundred different guises and languages: as *pommes de terre*, *papas*, *kartoffel*, or spuds. You can eat them baked, fried, boiled, mashed, hashed, riced, chipped, scalloped, gratinéed, pancaked, or croquetted; for breakfast, lunch, dinner, or snack. In 1998, according to the Idaho Potato Commission, 13.5 billion pounds were consumed in the United States—over *142 pounds per person.*

These days there are numerous potato varieties available, but many markets continue to identify them only under their generic names or uses—such as baking potatoes, boiling potatoes, or all-purpose potatoes. What you really need to know is the starch content of a particular potato variety, for that is the prime element that dictates the most suitable cooking method.

Potatoes can be grouped into three major categories: high starch–low moisture, medium starch, and low starch–high moisture.

High Starch–Low Moisture

Long, large, and oval-shaped, these are often called baking potatoes. Choose russets, a California summer potato, or russet/Burbank, or Idahos, named after the state with the largest production. They have thickened, nettled, rough brown skin and are harvested in the autumn. They store well, giving them year-round availability.

These are the mealy potatoes, best for baking, but they fall apart when boiled too long. They make the fluffiest mashed potatoes because they soak up milk and butter well. They are also best for French fries and for potato pancakes.

Each one weighs between 8 and 12 ounces.

Medium Starch

These are the long whites from California and the round whites with thin tan skins and white flesh that usually hail from Maine. They are sometimes called Irish potatoes or all-purpose potatoes. The medium starch, yellow-fleshed, newly popular Yukon Gold potatoes are round with thin tan skins and golden buttery texture. They are the ones to use if you prefer creamier, moist mashed potatoes. They're also great for roasting, in a gratin, scalloped, or in chowders.

The imported French heirloom potato, *la ratte*, which is also grown in Oregon, is in this category, too, as are the novelty purple and blue Peruvian potatoes.

Ten to twelve small potatoes = 1 pound.

Low Starch–High Moisture

Round whites and round reds, commonly referred to as boiling potatoes, include varieties known as *red bliss*, *red creamer*, and new potatoes. Creamer potatoes are less than one inch in diameter. They can either be new or just small, immature potatoes. Thus, new potatoes are *not* a separate grouping but rather just a description of young small or medium-size potatoes of any variety. They are usually harvested in late spring or early summer before their sugar content has been fully converted to starch. They have thin, crisp, waxy skins and are best cooked with the skins intact. The round whites hail from the Northeast, and the round reds from the Northwest. They retain their shapes well after being cooked, are good for boiling, steaming, or roasting, and are the preferred variety for potato salad.

Some of the specialty potatoes, such as the yellow-fleshed yellow finns and the *fingerlings*, have a good, deep flavor and fall into this category. Recognized by their long fingerlike shapes, they are usually about one inch thick and up to three inches long. You'll find them sold under such names as Russian Banana and Ruby Crescent.

SHOP SMART

- As a rule, when selecting any potato variety, buy firm, heavy, unblemished ones without spongy spots or sprouted "eyes," or those that are shriveled or cracked.
- Sometimes there is a green tinge under the potato skin, indicating the presence of the alkaloid solanin, which is toxic in large quantities. Cut the green parts away; the remaining sections are okay.
- Buy potatoes loose, not in bags, so you can make your own selection.
- Store them for no more than a few weeks, away from the light and in a well-ventilated place but *not* in the refrigerator. Refrigeration converts the starch to sugar and gives the potatoes an "off" taste.
- In storage at home, some potatoes will begin to sprout. As long as the potato is still firm and not soft or wrinkled, it is okay; just cut out the sprouts and cook the rest.

Notes for the Cook

ON BOILING POTATOES . . .

- Scrub all unpeeled potatoes but keep the skins on. The potatoes will be more flavorful and will absorb less water. They stay intact and, once cooked, are easier to peel. An attractive way to serve the small whole red is to cut a strip of peel from the center, leaving a white strip around it.
- If a recipe says to "peel before cooking," briefly place the peeled potatoes in a bowl of cold water with a few squeezes of lemon juice to prevent discoloration while you prepare them.
- Cook potatoes in salted water. They tend to taste flat when salt is added afterward.
- For potato salads, chill the potatoes before slicing or dicing.
- When mashing boiled potatoes, don't use a food processor. The excessive starch released will change the taste, and the texture will become "library paste." The best tool to use is a potato ricer or an old-fashioned potato masher. After adding warm liquids or room-temperature butter or oil, finish whipping with a balloon whisk to get rid of any lumps and to incorporate some air for lightness.

ON BAKING POTATOES . . .

◆ Our ideal baked potato is a high starch one with a crisp, papery skin and a light, fluffy center. Scrub the potato and bake on a rack in the oven. Halfway through the baking time, pierce the potato with the tines of a fork to allow the steam to escape. If you prefer a more pliable skin, however, brush the potato lightly with a bit of oil or butter before putting it in the oven.

◆ Wrapping a potato in aluminum foil steams it and gives it a damp texture, a yucky flavor, and a soft skin.

◆ The Idaho Potato Commission recommends baking at 500 degrees for 45 to 60 minutes, depending on the size.

◆ Test the potato for doneness by squeezing it gently while wearing an oven mitt. When done, it will feel soft and give slightly.

◆ Before cutting it open, roll or lightly massage the potato to fluff the interior. Slit the top and push on both ends to plump up the flesh.

◆ Add one of the following: butter, oil, yogurt, milk, cream, salsa, roasted garlic. Or scoop out the flesh, mash the potato, and mix it with, for example, olives, cheese, chives, or bacon, and return it to its jacket, mounding the mixture. Then bake it again for fifteen minutes in a 375-degree preheated oven. These twice-baked potatoes are perfect if you don't plan to serve them immediately.

THE GREAT SWEET POTATO CONTROVERSY

The battle has been ongoing, resurfacing every year when it's time to stock the larder for Thanksgiving dinner. Yams or sweet potatoes? Are they the same? Does it, in fact, really make any difference?

True yams, found mostly in Hispanic markets, are the oddly shaped, scaly-surfaced, very long tubers—sometimes up to three feet long—that are grown in the tropics.

In many markets "yam" refers to a certain variety of sweet potato that is sheathed in a skin of rose, purple, or copper, with a twisted or chubby to tapered shape. Its flesh is bright orange, has the most consistently moist and buttery texture, and is very sweet when cooked. These tubers are sometimes labeled by their variety, such as Jewel, Garnet, or Beauregard, and they hail from Louisiana and North Carolina. "Sweet Potatoes" are lighter-skinned and drier in texture, with yellow- to cream-colored flesh.

SHOP SMART

- Sweet potatoes and yams are available sporadically throughout the year, but they are at their best in winter.
- Choose a medium size that has a smooth, unbruised skin. These tubers are fragile and do not store well unless the environment is right. Don't refrigerate them. They like it dry, dark, and about 55 degrees, and they should be used within a week of purchase.

About 2 pounds = four servings.

Notes for the Cook

ON YAMS AND SWEET POTATOES . . .

- Rather than boiling, slow roasting brings out the sweetness of the orange-fleshed yams, with the added bonus of a very seductive scent that permeates the kitchen.
- When using the dark orange fleshed yams (rather than sweet potatoes), less liquid and butter are needed for purees since they are naturally buttery.

PROVENCE POTATOES WITH
ONIONS AND ANCHOVIES

This cheeseless gratin borrows its lusty palette of flavors directly from the south of France.

SERVES 4

1 tablespoon olive oil

2 medium onions, thinly sliced (about 2 cups)

½ teaspoon black pepper

Salt to taste

4 tablespoons soft butter

1½ pounds russet potatoes, unpeeled and sliced paper-thin (about 2 large potatoes)

4 or 5 flat anchovies, rinsed, dried, and coarsely chopped

3 tablespoons finely chopped parsley

2 teaspoons grated lemon zest (1 medium lemon)

3 tablespoons lemon juice (about ½ large lemon)

⅔ cup whole milk

Heat the oil in a 12-inch nonstick pan. Add the onions and sauté over medium heat, stirring occasionally, until transluscent but not brown, about 4 to 5 minutes. Season with pepper and salt. Spread 1 tablespoon of the butter on the bottom of a 1½-quart tempered glass or ceramic baking dish. Layer overlapping slices of potatoes on the bottom, then half of the onions. Combine the anchovies, parsley, and lemon zest together and place half of this mixture over the onions. Dot with butter and repeat the process, ending with a top layer of potatoes and butter. Pour lemon juice over all and then the milk.

Cover with aluminum foil and bake in a preheated 400-degree oven for 1 hour 10 minutes. Remove the foil, raise the heat, and slip the pan under the broiler for 2 or 3 minutes, or until the surface is dappled with brown.

WARM LYONNAISE POTATO AND SAUSAGE SALAD WITH SIX FRESH HERBS

This hearty whole meal, a warm potato salad flavored with garlicky sausage and fresh herbs, has become a favorite spring and summer treat, just when all the fresh herbs are at their prime.

SERVES 4 TO 6

2 pounds small ("new") waxy red or white potatoes, unpeeled but with a center peel slice removed

1 pound kielbasa, cut in ½-inch-thick slices

Bouquet garni: 2 sprigs thyme, 1 bay leaf, 5 sprigs parsley, 2 leek leaves

1 teaspoon whole black peppercorns, tied into a cheesecloth bag for easy removal

¾ teaspoon coarse salt, or to taste

4 large shallots, coarsely chopped (about ⅓ cup)

4 teaspoons balsamic vinegar

8 teaspoons olive oil

2 sprigs tarragon, minced

¼ cup snipped chives

2 tablespoons finely minced parsley

1½ teaspoons thyme leaves

1 teaspoon finely minced marjoram

1 tablespoon finely minced chervil

In a 5-quart Dutch oven, place the potatoes, kielbasa, bouquet garni, peppercorns, and salt. Cover with water by 1 inch and bring to a boil over medium heat. Lower the heat and simmer for about 15 minutes, or until the potatoes are tender. Remove the bouquet garni and the peppercorn bag and discard them. Drain the potatoes and sausage, and transfer to a large bowl.

Add the shallots, vinegar, and oil, and toss the potatoes and sausage in the mixture while still warm. Add the fresh herbs and toss again to cover. Serve at room temperature with a good, sharp mustard if you wish.

IRISH COLCANNON

A classic Irish potato dish that is wonderful with roasted ham or grilled fennel pork sausages. A nice change from the ubiquitous garlic mashed potatoes that have appeared on almost every restaurant menu for the past few years.

SERVES 6

2 pounds medium starch potatoes,
   such as Yukon Gold, or round white,
   peeled and cut into 2-inch chunks
4 tablespoons butter, cut into 1 equal
   pieces
⅔ cup finely chopped onion
   (1 medium onion)
1 pound Savoy cabbage, quartered,
   cored, and thinly sliced (about
   6 cups)

¼ cup water
Salt and pepper to taste
⅓ cup buttermilk
¼ cup milk
⅛ teaspoon ground mace
¼ cup diagonally and thinly sliced
   scallions (2 scallions), green
   part only

Place the potatoes in a 3-quart saucepan with salted water to cover. Cook over medium-high heat, covered, until the potatoes come to a boil. Put the pot lid ajar to prevent boilovers and cook about 20 to 30 minutes after they come to a boil. Test the center of the potatoes with a thin knife point to see if they are cooked through. If not, continue to cook until they are tender.

While the potatoes are cooking, heat 1 tablespoon of the butter in a 10-inch skillet over medium-high heat. Add the onion and sauté, stirring, for 1 or 2 minutes. Stir in the cabbage. Add the water and season with salt and pepper. Cover the skillet, lower the heat, and braise for 5 minutes, stirring once or twice.

When the potatoes are cooked, drain and return them to the same pot over very low heat to evaporate any moisture. Then transfer them to a bowl.

Mash the potatoes with a hand masher, adding the remaining butter one piece at a time. Do not mash them too smoothly. Leave some texture. Add the buttermilk and milk, and combine with a wooden spoon or whisk. Stir in additional salt and pepper if you wish, then the mace and braised cabbage. Beat just to combine. Transfer to a serving dish and scatter the scallion greens over the surface.

Note: Colcannon can be reheated in a 350-degree oven for 10 to 15 minutes. Leftovers can also be formed into cakes, dipped in flour, and fried in bacon fat until crisp and sublime. (In Ireland they're called *farls*.)

THE MANY WAYS OF MASHED POTATOES
ADD ANY OF THE FOLLOWING:

olive paste
chipotle peppers in Adobe sauce
wasabi (Japanese mustard)
horseradish
sage and sautéed onions
herb cheese

POTATO AND ARUGULA SOUP

We tend to think of arugula only as a fresh, zappy salad green. But wilting it in a nutmeg-and-ginger-spiced potato soup mellows its edge and gives it an unexpected mildness.

SERVES 4

3 tablespoons butter

2 medium onions, coarsely diced
    (about 2 cups)

2 thin leeks, trimmed, halved
    lengthwise, washed well, and
    coarsely sliced (about ¾ cup)

2 large cloves garlic, sliced (about
    1 tablespoon)

Salt and pepper to taste

1 pound low-starch potatoes such as
    large red or Yellow Finn, peeled and
    quartered

4 cups chicken broth

½ cup milk

¼ teaspoon ground ginger

¼ teaspoon grated nutmeg

2 bunches arugula leaves, trimmed and
    coarsely shredded (about
    4 cups tightly packed)

Melt 2 tablespoons of the butter in a 5-quart pot. Add the onions, leeks, garlic, salt, and pepper. Stir once, cover, and cook over medium-low heat for about 15 minutes, stirring occasionally, until the vegetables have softened. Add the potatoes and broth, raise the heat, and bring the mixture to the boiling point. Lower the heat and simmer, covered, until the potatoes are tender, about 30 minutes.

Remove all the potatoes with a slotted spoon and puree in a food mill or potato ricer until smooth. Return them to the pot along with the milk, ginger, and nutmeg. Bring to a boil, and if the soup is too thick, thin it with additional milk. The recipe can be prepared in advance up to this point.

When ready to serve, scatter the arugula over the surface of the boiling soup, cover the pot, and cook until the leaves have wilted, about 2 minutes. Stir and taste for additional salt and pepper. Swirl in the remaining tablespoon of butter and serve.

SAUTÉED POTATOES WITH RED ONIONS, THYME, AND VINEGAR

Fresh thyme and red wine vinegar bring these simply sautéed potatoes into another dimension.

SERVES 4

2 or 3 large long white (medium starch) thin-skinned potatoes (about 1½ pounds)
2 large red onions (about 1 pound)
2 tablespoons olive oil

Salt to taste
¼ teaspoon black pepper
1 tablespoon red wine vinegar
1 tablespoon fresh thyme leaves or 1 teaspoon dried thyme

Peel the potatoes, halve them lengthwise, and then cut them into semicircular slices crosswise about ¼ inch thick. Do the same with the red onions.

In a 12-inch nonstick skillet, heat the oil over medium heat. Add the potatoes, onions, salt, and pepper, and stir to coat. Sauté for 1 minute, then cover the skillet, lower the heat, and cook until the onions are wilted and the potatoes are tender, about 10 minutes.

Uncover the skillet, raise the heat to high, and cook, stirring gently and frequently, until the potatoes begin to brown, about 10 minutes more. Stir in the vinegar and thyme, and transfer to a warm serving dish.

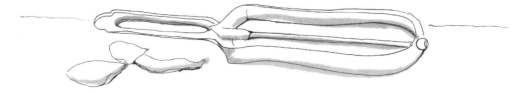

GARNET YAMS WITH PEARS, DRIED FIGS, AND CRYSTALLIZED GINGER

Crunchy crystallized ginger and succulent cubes of fresh pears are added to creamy mashed yams, along with figs soaked in balsamic vinegar for a tart, sweet edge. Serve it with your next Thanksgiving turkey or a roasted chicken or pork. It has always been a hit at our home.

SERVES 6

3 pounds medium-size garnet yams (about 6)

12 dried black figs (or Calymyrna figs), stemmed and quartered

2 teaspoons balsamic vinegar

1½ pounds ripe Bartlett pears (about 3), peeled, cored, and cut into ¾-inch cubes

1 teaspoon lemon juice

4 tablespoons butter

⅛ teaspoon freshly grated nutmeg

⅛ teaspoon ground cloves

3 tablespoons crystallized ginger in ¼-inch cubes

Salt and pepper to taste

Preheat the oven to 400 degrees. Place the yams on a rack in a 9 x 12 x 3-inch roasting pan and roast for about 1 hour, or until the yams can be pierced easily with a knife and are very soft. While the yams are roasting, soak the figs in the vinegar for 15 to 20 minutes, stirring once.

When the yams are done and are cool enough to handle, peel them and put them through a potato ricer.

Fill a bowl with water, add the pears and lemon juice, and set aside.

In a small saucepan over low heat, heat the butter until it browns slightly and smells nutty, then stir in the nutmeg and cloves. Pour this mixture over the riced yams. Stir in the figs and vinegar and the ginger. Drain the pears and add them. Season with salt and pepper and transfer to a 2½-quart buttered oven-to-table baking dish.

When ready to serve, bake in a 350-degree oven for 20 minutes, or until hot.

The Squash Cornucopia

HARD-SKINNED OR WINTER SQUASH

Baked Maple Butternut Squash with Prunes, Walnuts, and Cardamom

Candied Acorn Squash with Mace, Honey, and Toasted Hazelnuts

Roasted Sweet Dumpling Squash with Apples, Chutney, and Cloves

Pumpkin Rum Mascarpone Tart with an Almond Crust

SOFT-SKINNED OR SUMMER SQUASH

Cold Curried Golden Zucchini Bisque

Baked Yellow Squash Filled with Spinach and Gruyère Cheese

Zucchini and Summer Squash Flan with Dill and Feta Cheese

The word "squash" is adapted from the Native American word *asquash* (or asku-tasquash), meaning gourd. It is one of the few vegetables indigenous to the Americas; archaeologists have discovered seeds dating as far back as 2000 B.C.

Squash can be classified into two groups:

1. Hard-skinned winter squash, which are trailing vine types and are picked fully matured.
2. Soft-skinned summer squash or "Bush" varieties, which are harvested when they are young and tender, before the first frosts kill them.

Both kinds are now cultivated throughout the world, and numerous new hybrid varieties from Asia, Latin America, and the Mediterranean are constantly being introduced to the marketplace.

HARD-SKINNED OR WINTER SQUASH

ACORN: It is the size of a small melon and deeply ridged, which makes peeling quite difficult. The skin, which is dark green and splashed with dark yellow or all yellow, helps retain the shape while cooking.

BUTTERCUP: This squat, drum-shaped squash has a turbanlike top growth. The dark green color is streaked with gray, and the orange flesh is very sweet.

BUTTERNUT: Light tan in color—the color of coffee with lots of cream—8 to 10 inches, and with an elongated pear shape, it has a fat, bulbous bottom that harbors the seed cavity. The flesh is moist, orange, and finely grained.

DELICATA: This looks like a large, fat cucumber or a small watermelon and has orange and yellow stripes. It is similar in color and flavor to the Sweet Dumpling but is not quite as sweet.

HUBBARD: Rough, hard, warty, gray-greenish blue, this one is very large, often weighing twelve pounds or more. The flesh is drier and stringier than many other winter squash, but it is very good when steamed.

KOBOCHA: Also called "Sweet Mama," this Japanese import resembles a flattened greenish gray globe. The flesh is golden and has an intense "squash" flavor.

PUMPKIN: The jack-o'-lantern ornamentals are large—some weighing over one hundred pounds! The ones that we eat are called *sugar pumpkins*, and they have a deep, rich flavor and an orange color. They weigh between three and five pounds. Don't forget the cutie-pie miniature *jack-be-little* that can fit into the palm of your hand and is best used as a container for pumpkin custard since it has only a small amount of edible flesh.

SWEET DUMPLING: The orange flesh of this Asian hybrid is dense and very flavorful. It is squat and small enough for single servings, and the skin is creamy white with green stripes. As the season progresses, the stripes become more yellow and the squash sweeter.

TURBAN: A very ornamental squash, it comes in various shapes and colors, always topped with a hat 6 to 10 inches in diameter. It is very bland in flavor.

 ## SHOP SMART

Buy heavy squash that has a tough, hard, unblemished skin. Avoid those with decay spots or deep scars. Store them in a dry place for up to two months if whole. Once cut, wrap them in plastic and refrigerate for up to one week.

Notes for the Cook

ON WINTER SQUASH . . .

- ◆ Most of these squash are cooked with the skin on and thus the skin acts as a protective container to prevent the pulp from falling apart.
- ◆ They all have large, removable seeds and stringy, fibrous centers that can be removed and discarded by scraping them out with a spoon before baking or steaming.

THIN-SKINNED OR SUMMER SQUASH

MINIATURE SQUASH: These may be harvested at an early developmental stage or may be genetic hybrids that are raised to be perfectly formed miniature replicas of their full-size cousins: minuscule zucchini, yellow squash, or button-size pattypan.

PATTYPAN: Also called custard marrow or button squash, cymling or bush scallop, these are 2 to 4 inches in diameter, have round, scalloped edges, and are pale green or yellow. They can be cooked and eaten whole when small. Scallop squash is a larger version of the pattypan.

SCALLOPINI: This squash looks like a pattypan but is not quite as scalloped. It is harvested when larger and is speckled green.

YELLOW SQUASH: There are two kinds—the slightly narrow, curve-necked, pebbly-skinned crookneck and the smooth-skinned, cylindrical straightneck. Both are banana yellow in color inside and out. They have tender, edible skins and are best when 5 to 8 inches in length. The flesh is delicate and succulent.

ZUCCHINI: This is also called *marrow* in England and *courgette* in France. Although thought of as an Italian squash, it is an American native that has adapted beautifully to Mediterranean growing conditions. It now comes in a range of colors—pale gray, yellow, and the familiar mottled green—with smooth and shiny cylinders. Choose ones that are 4 to 6 inches long; the large ones are less flavorful and have larger seeds and watery flesh.

SHOP SMART

All varieties peak between July and September, and many are available year-round. Buy squash that are under 8 inches, unbruised, firm, with glossy skins. Refrigerate them in a plastic bag for four to five days.

Allow 1 pound for two servings.

Notes for the Cook

ON SUMMER SQUASH . . .

◆ The tender skins are edible. Just scrub them gently and trim the ends.

◆ They can be eaten raw and should be cooked only until crisp/tender, or they will be mushy and watery.

BAKED MAPLE BUTTERNUT SQUASH WITH PRUNES, WALNUTS, AND CARDAMOM

Butternut is a winter squash. The flavor and color of the flesh are reminiscent of yams, but they are not as filling and have a lighter, moister texture.

SERVES 4 TO 6

3-pound butternut squash, peeled and strings and seeds removed and cut into 1-inch chunks

¼ cup maple syrup

½ teaspoon ground cardamom

1 tablespoon butter, softened

⅓ cup coarsely chopped toasted walnuts

8 pitted prunes, cut into quarters

1 teaspoon grated orange zest

Salt and pepper to taste

Steam the squash in a steamer basket until tender, about 30 minutes. Butter a 2- or 2½-quart shallow baking dish and set it aside.

Preheat the oven to 350 degrees. When the squash is tender, mash it in a large bowl using a potato masher. There should be about 3 cups. Combine all the remaining ingredients with the squash and spoon into the prepared baking dish. When ready to serve, bake for 15 minutes. Serve hot.

CANDIED ACORN SQUASH WITH MACE, HONEY, AND TOASTED HAZELNUTS

Acorn squash are usually halved or cut into wedges or thick horizontal slices and then baked to bring out their sweetness.

SERVES 4

Four 12-ounce acorn squash, green or
    golden or a combination
Salt to taste
2 tablespoons butter
3 tablespoons acacia or other pale
    honey

Ground mace to taste
4 ounces hazelnuts, toasted, skinned,
    and finely chopped in a food
    processor (about ½ cup)

Preheat the oven to 350 degrees. Line an 11 x 16 x 2-inch pan with aluminum foil and butter the foil. Cut each squash in half vertically and with a spoon scrape out the seeds and fibrous matter. Place on the prepared pan and sprinkle with salt.

In a small saucepan over low heat, melt the butter and add the honey to warm. Brush the insides of the squash liberally with this mixture, using all of it. Sprinkle with mace.

Bake for 45 minutes to 1 hour. Baste a few times with a brush, using the mixture that has settled in the squash cavities. Test the flesh with the point of a knife for tenderness. Transfer the squash to a serving platter and sprinkle the chopped nuts over all.

ROASTED SWEET DUMPLING SQUASH WITH APPLES, CHUTNEY, AND CLOVES

Sweet Dumplings are adorable and ideal for single servings. Highly spiced chutney, tart apples, and cloves add contrast to its natural sweetness.

SERVES 4

4 small Sweet Dumpling squash (about 12 ounces each) or 1 large 2½-pound Dumpling or Carnival squash
Salt to taste
½ cup bottled chutney such as Major Grey or Mrs. H. S. Ball's

1 medium Golden Delicious or Fuji apple, peeled, cored, and finely diced (about 1½ cups)
⅛ teaspoon ground cloves
1 tablespoon butter, cut into small pieces
Boiling water

Preheat the oven to 350 degrees. Cut each squash ⅓ down from the top. Set aside the tops, to be baked alongside the squash bowls. If using large squash, quarter them. Scrape out the seeds and fibrous matter from the centers using a spoon and discard them.

Place the squash on a rack in a 9 x 12 x 3-inch roasting pan and place the tops alongside them. Sprinkle the squash with salt and brush the cut surfaces with some of the chutney. Combine the apples and chutney, and spoon into the squash cavities. Sprinkle with the cloves and dot the cavities with butter. Pour boiling water into the bottom of the pan to keep the squash moist while roasting. Roast about 1 hour 30 minutes. Test with a knife point for tenderness.

Serve individual small squash with the cap leaning against it or serve a wedge for each person if the squash is large.

PUMPKIN RUM MASCARPONE TART WITH AN ALMOND CRUST

"What moistens the lip and brightens the eye? What calls back the past like a rich pumpkin pie?" Thanks to John Greenleaf Whittier and other poets, pumpkin pie is synonymous with holidays and nostalgia. This is a contemporary version, but it will brighten the eye nonetheless.

MAKES ONE 10-INCH TART

ALMOND CRUST:

⅔ cup whole almonds with skin, toasted

3 tablespoons sugar

1¼ cups flour

½ teaspoon salt

8 tablespoons (1 stick) butter, cut into small pieces

1 egg yolk

1 tablespoon water

¼ teaspoon almond extract

PUMPKIN FILLING:

3 eggs

½ cup light brown sugar

2 tablespoons mild light honey

8 ounces mascarpone cheese, at room temperature

1½ cups pumpkin puree (canned is fine)

¾ teaspoon ground ginger

½ teaspoon salt

1 teaspoon ground cinnamon

¼ teaspoon freshly grated nutmeg

2 tablespoons dark rum

1 cup half-and-half or light cream

A few thinly sliced almonds (optional)

Preheat the oven to 350 degrees. To make the crust: In the bowl of a food processor, grind the almonds until fine. Add the sugar and process a few seconds more. Add the flour and salt, and process again until combined. Add the butter and process until the texture is coarse and mealy.

In a small cup, whisk the egg yolk with the tablespoon of water and the almond extract. Add it to the food processor and process only until the mixture just sticks together.

Press the mixture evenly into the sides first and then the bottom of a 10½ x 1½-inch-deep tart pan with a removable base. Bake for 15 minutes, or until the crust is just beginning to color. If the bottom puffs up after 5 minutes, pierce the bubbles with the point of a knife to deflate. Remove from the oven to cool and prepare the filling.

To make the filling: In a food processor, beat the eggs. Add the brown sugar and honey, and process until combined. Add the cheese and process until incorporated. Add the pumpkin puree and process for a few strokes. Add the ginger, salt, cinnamon, and nutmeg, and process to combine. Add the rum and half-and-half, and process until smooth.

Pour into the prebaked crust and bake in the preheated oven for about 40 minutes, or until firm except for a small central area about the size of a quarter. (It firms up as it cools.) Cool on a wire rack. Place the sliced almonds in a circular pattern in the center if you wish. Transfer to a serving plate, remove the rim of the pan, but keep the tart on the base. Whipped cream is optional.

COLD CURRIED GOLDEN ZUCCHINI BISQUE

Zucchini, no matter what their color, are notoriously prolific. When your recipe repertoire is exhausted by a zucchini bonanza, try this favorite: a cheerful, mellow, yellow bisque.

SERVES 4

3 tablespoons butter
¾ cup coarsely chopped onion
 (1 medium)
2 teaspoons coarsely chopped garlic
 (2 medium cloves)
3 pounds golden zucchini, cut into
 1-inch chunks (can substitute yellow
 squash)
1 cup thickly sliced carrots (2 thin
 carrots)

2 teaspoons curry powder
2 cups chicken broth
Salt and pepper to taste
½ cup heavy cream
⅛ teaspoon Tabasco
Cayenne pepper for garnish
4 small cilantro sprigs for garnish

Melt the butter in a 5-quart Dutch oven over medium heat. Add the onion, garlic, golden zucchini, and carrots. Sprinkle the curry powder over the vegetables and sauté, stirring frequently, for about 15 minutes, until tender. Add the broth, bring to the boiling point, then lower the heat and simmer for 10 minutes to blend the flavors. Season with salt and pepper.

Let cool slightly and then whirl in a blender, a few batches at a time. Stir in the cream, taste for additional salt, add the Tabasco, and chill until very cold.

Taste and readjust the salt and pepper. Serve garnished with cayenne and a cilantro sprig.

BAKED YELLOW SQUASH FILLED WITH SPINACH AND GRUYÈRE CHEESE

A colorful vegetable dish that would delight any vegetarian.

SERVES 4

2 yellow squash, about 12 ounces each
1 pound spinach, trimmed, or one
   10-ounce package frozen chopped
   spinach
Salt and pepper to taste
2 teaspoons butter

¼ cup finely minced scallions (about
   2 medium)
⅓ cup sour cream
¼ cup coarse bread crumbs
¼ cup shredded Gruyère cheese

Cut the squash in half lengthwise and scoop out and discard the seeds in the center, leaving a ¾-inch shell. In a 6-quart Dutch oven, bring salted water to a boil over high heat. Add the squash shells, lower the heat to medium, and cook until slightly crisp, about 6 minutes. Remove the squash with a slotted spoon and drain upside-down on paper towels.

Steam the fresh spinach in a steaming basket until wilted (or cook the frozen spinach as directed on the package). Drain by pressing out the excess liquid with the back of a spoon against a sieve. Chop the spinach coarsely and place in a bowl. Add salt, pepper, butter, scallions, and sour cream.

Preheat the oven to 350 degrees and butter an oven-to-table baking dish large enough to accommodate the squash in 1 layer. Fill the shells with the spinach mixture and sprinkle with bread crumbs and cheese. Bake for 15 to 20 minutes, until the crumbs are brown and the squash is tender.

ZUCCHINI AND SUMMER SQUASH FLAN WITH DILL AND FETA CHEESE

This light summer luncheon dish is a custard-based flan or a crustless quiche—any way you choose to see it.

SERVES 4

8 ounces green zucchini

8 ounces yellow summer squash

1 teaspoon salt

1 cup grated Feta cheese

⅓ cup finely minced scallions (about 2 scallions)

1¼ cups half-and-half

2 large eggs

⅛ teaspoon cayenne pepper

¼ cup snipped dill

Black pepper to taste

Grate the squash on the large holes of a box grater or the shredder blade of a food processor. Place in a large bowl, stir in the salt, and let sit for 30 minutes. Drain in a strainer, pressing out the excess liquid. Place on paper towels and pat completely dry. Wipe out the bowl, return the squash, and mix in the Feta cheese and scallions.

Preheat the oven to 375 degrees. Butter a 9 x 1½-inch round quiche pan made of tempered glass or ceramic and spread the mixture evenly in the pan. Wipe out the bowl again. Add the half-and-half, eggs, cayenne, dill, and pepper, and whisk to combine. Gently pour the mixture over the squash and bake in the middle of the oven for about 30 to 35 minutes, or until 2 inches of the center still quivers when jiggled slightly. Remove and let cool on a wire rack for 15 to 20 minutes. Serve warm.

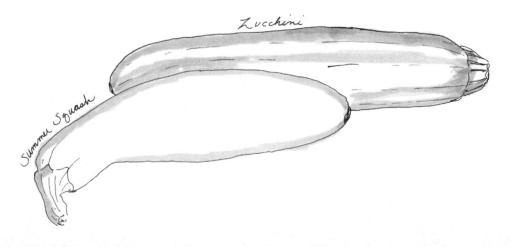

Eggplant: Power to the Purple

Asian Eggplants with Ginger, Garlic, and Toasted Sesame Seeds

Roasted Eggplant and Green Pepper Salad with Cucumber and Tomatoes

Eggplant Sicilian Style with Black Olives and Pine Nuts

Grilled Eggplant Marinated with Fresh Herbs

It was first grown for food in Southeast Asia; was transported by cargo ships to the Middle East, where eggplant then became a staple vegetable that could be cooked a different way on each of a thousand and one nights; and then went on to Europe and the New World. Its biological origin was the deadly nightshade family, as are tobacco, tomatoes, and potatoes.

No longer saddled with a bad reputation, it is probably among the most versatile of all vegetables, for no matter how you slice it, dice it, roast it, stew it, sauté it, or fry it, it is a satisfying and filling repast that takes well to a range of robust flavors. It is rightly called "the meat of vegetarians."

There are a great many varieties from which to choose, and they come in a tempting chromatic color scale that ranges from white to lavender, striped to deep purple, in shapes that are long and slender to plump, and in sizes that vary from the smallest egg to a full 24 inches in length.

BABY EGGPLANT: These are young versions of all the others mentioned. Their youth assures a more delicate flavor, and they are usually available in 2-inch cylindrical shapes that weigh about 4 ounces each. The skin is tender, so cook and serve them whole.

BLACK JAPANESE: Also known as Nasu or Italian eggplant, this one is thinner than the Long Chinese and longer, about 5 to 7 inches. It has dark purple skin with tender flesh and a sweet, mild flavor. Try it fried, sautéed, or grilled.

COMMON EUROPEAN: The most familiar of the family—dark purple and globular or round, or an elongated cylindrical shape with a shiny, sleek, smooth, tough skin. (See "To Peel or Not to Peel," page 143.) It holds its shape well when roasted and has lots of seeds. The flesh is creamy and soft, making it excellent for purées, dips, salads, soups, and stuffed or baked.

LONG CHINESE: This can be a solid lavender color, striped with lavender and white, or solid purple. Small, thin, and gently curved, it has few seeds, a sweet flavor, and holds its shape well when cooked. Try it in vegetable stews such as ratatouille or roasted for salads.

WHITE EGGPLANT: Mostly egg-shaped and sometimes with lavender stripes, these have very few seeds and the texture is pulpy. The flavor is very delicate. The skins are tough, and they need to be peeled before eating.

Allow about 1 1/2 to 2 pounds of any variety for four servings.

 ## SHOP SMART

- ◆ Whichever eggplant you choose, make sure that the skin is sleek, unblemished, and not shriveled. It should be taut and shiny.
- ◆ Although they are available year-round for the most part, they are best and more abundant in the late summer (or earlier in the hotter parts of the country).

Notes for the Cook

ON EGGPLANT . . .

- ◆ To salt or not to salt, that is the question. The answer depends on three factors: the variety of eggplant, your personal taste preference, and the cooking method.
- ◆ *Unsalted* eggplants tend to drink up more oil than presalted and drained ones. Therefore, when frying, sautéeing, or grilling—all quick-cooking methods that can use lots of oil as well as concentrating any bitter flavors—we salt and drain first. With longer cooking, such as in stews, the bitterness usually evaporates, and so there is no need to salt.
- ◆ For salting and draining: Cut the eggplant into the desired shape: cubes, slices, or halves. Place in a stainless-steel or plastic strainer or colander, never aluminum. Place a bowl underneath to catch the draining liquid. Sprinkle all sides of the eggplant generously with coarse salt and let it stand for 30 minutes, weighted down to help release the liquids. Rinse off the salt under cold running water, dry thoroughly on paper towels, and proceed with the recipe.

To peel or not to peel?
- ◆ When baking, stuffing, or roasting, keep the edible skins on to maintain the shape of the eggplant.

♦ Shorter cooking time, such as grilling and broiling, needs the skin in order to keep the eggplant intact.

♦ For sautéeing or stews, if you don't like skins, peel the eggplant beforehand.

ASIAN EGGPLANTS WITH GINGER, GARLIC, AND TOASTED SESAME SEEDS

Here the slim Asian eggplants are split and marinated before baking. Serve them at room temperature for a first course or as a side dish. Double the recipe for a buffet. It can be made well in advance, and it keeps well for hours.

SERVES 4

2 tablespoons cilantro leaves

2 medium cloves garlic, peeled, crushed, and minced (about 1 tablespoon)

½ inch peeled ginger root, sliced

1 cup light soy sauce

½ cup mirin (sweet rice wine)

⅛ teaspoon Tabasco

2 teaspoons Asian sesame oil

4 slim Asian eggplants (Nasu), about 6 to 8 ounces each

1 tablespoon rice wine vinegar

2 teaspoons toasted sesame seeds

In a blender, place the cilantro, garlic, and ginger root, and chop finely. Add the soy sauce, mirin, Tabasco, and sesame oil, and puree until smooth. Prick the eggplant skins all over with a fork and then cut them in half lengthwise. Place them side by side in 1 layer on an oven-to-table baking pan, flesh side up. Make 3 diagonal slashes in each eggplant and spoon about 1 tablespoon of the sauce onto the surface, rubbing it into the slashes. Turn the eggplants skin side up and spoon the remaining sauce over them. Marinate for 45 minutes.

Preheat the oven to 350 degrees. Turn the eggplants over again, skin side down, and bake for 40 to 45 minutes, or until the eggplants are tender. Baste several times and add some water if necessary.

Transfer the eggplants to a large serving platter and trickle any remaining sauce along with the rice wine vinegar over them. Scatter ¼ teaspoon of sesame seeds over each eggplant and serve hot or at room temperature.

ROASTED EGGPLANT AND GREEN PEPPER SALAD WITH CUCUMBER AND TOMATOES

Called patlagele *in Romanian, this smoky-tasting, refreshing salad is perfect with lamb. It also holds its own when served by itself and accompanied by a good, warm flat bread.*

MAKES 3 CUPS

2 pounds common purple eggplant, cut in half lengthwise

2 large green peppers, cut in half lengthwise

1 medium-size Kirby cucumber, cut in ¾-inch cubes (about ¾ cup)

2 to 3 large plum tomatoes, cut in ¾-inch cubes

2 tablespoons olive oil

1 tablespoon red wine vinegar

1 small onion, finely chopped (about ⅓ cup)

Salt and pepper to taste

2 tablespoons finely chopped parsley

Lettuce leaves

4 black olives (preferably Kalamata) for garnish

Place the eggplant and peppers, skin side up, on an aluminum-foil-lined jelly roll pan that has been coated with olive oil spray. Place the pan on the lowest rack of an oven broiler. When the skins have been charred, carefully turn the vegetables over and broil the other side. The peppers will be cooked first, in about 10 to 12 minutes, so remove them first. When the eggplant is soft and the surface has darkened (about 15 to 20 minutes), remove the pan from the broiler and pierce the blackened skins with the point of a knife at several points and sprinkle them lightly with coarse salt. Let the eggplant cool completely, then drain off and discard any accumulated liquid. Peel off the charred skin and cut the eggplant into ¾-inch cubes or coarsely mash the flesh with a fork. Transfer to a medium-size bowl.

Peel off the blistered skins of the peppers and cut them into ½-inch cubes. Add to the eggplant along with the cucumber, tomatoes, oil, vinegar, onion, salt, and pepper to taste. Stir in the parsley and spoon the mixture on lettuce leaves to serve. Top each serving with an olive.

EGGPLANT SICILIAN STYLE WITH BLACK OLIVES AND PINE NUTS

As earthy and rustic as the Sicilian countryside, this can be served as a salad spooned over Romaine lettuce and with tomato wedges, or it can be used as an hors d'oeuvre on bread or crackers.

MAKES 4 TO 5 CUPS

3 pounds eggplants (about 4 to 6), preferably Asian, long lavender, or purple

2 tablespoons plus 1 teaspoon olive oil

2 tablespoons coarsely chopped garlic or rocambole (see Note) (3 to 4 medium cloves)

½ cup coarsely chopped onion (about 4 ounces)

½ cup coarsely chopped Dutch sweet red pepper (about ½ large)

½ cup balsamic vinegar

½ cup pitted and coarsely chopped black olives (such as Kalamata)

Salt and pepper to taste

¼ teaspoon hot pepper sauce (such as Tabasco)

4 tablespoons toasted pine nuts

2 tablespoons coarsely chopped parsley

Preheat the oven to 400 degrees. Line a 12 x 18-inch jelly roll pan with aluminum foil. Pierce the eggplants all over in several places using the point of a sharp knife. Place in the pan and bake for 45 to 60 minutes (depending on size). The eggplants will collapse when roasted through.

Cut off the stem ends, place on paper towels, split in half lengthwise, and let them cool and drain. When they are cool enough to handle, strip off the skin and cut the flesh into strips about ½ x 2 inches. There should be about 4 cups. Set aside.

While the eggplants are roasting, heat 2 tablespoons of olive oil in a 10-inch nonstick skillet over medium heat. Add the garlic and stir for 20 seconds. Add the onion and red pepper, and sauté, stirring frequently, for 5 minutes, until the onions are translucent but not brown. Add the vinegar and cook about 5 minutes, stirring occasionally, until the vinegar is slightly reduced and syrupy. Stir in the olives, reserved eggplant, salt, and pepper, and cook for 1 minute. Stir in the Tabasco and pine nuts, and cook 1 minute more.

Transfer to a serving platter. Trickle the remaining teaspoon of olive oil over the surface and scatter the parsley over the top. Serve at room temperature.

Note: Rocambole is freshly harvested garlic that is more delicate, more moist, and crisper in texture than regular garlic (see page 13).

GRILLED EGGPLANT MARINATED WITH FRESH HERBS

Delicate white eggplant—the one that has the fewest seeds—takes beautifully to grilling indoors or outdoors, doused with your best olive oil and sherry vinegar, and showered with bright fresh herbs and then marinated.

SERVES 4

1½ pounds white eggplants
Salt and pepper to taste
¼ cup olive oil
1½ tablespoons sherry or balsamic
  vinegar

1 tablespoon coarsely chopped garlic
  (about 2 large cloves)
2 tablespoons finely shredded mint
1 tablespoon finely shredded basil
1 tablespoon coarsely chopped parsley

Preheat the oven to 325 degrees. Trim the green stems of the eggplants. Peel and slice them into 1-inch-thick rounds. Line a 12 x 18-inch jelly roll pan with aluminum foil and coat the surface with an olive oil spray. Spread the eggplant rounds on the foil and coat the slices with the olive oil spray. Season with salt and pepper, and bake for 20 minutes (see Note). Turn the slices over and bake about 15 to 20 minutes more, until the eggplant is cooked through and golden brown.

Transfer to a flat serving dish with sides. In a small bowl, combine the olive oil, vinegar, and garlic. Spoon the mixture over the eggplant. Scatter the mint, basil, and parsley over all and let stand for at least 4 hours at room temperature, tilting the dish and spooning the sauce over the eggplant occasionally. Serve at room temperature.

Note: You can grill the eggplant outdoors over wood or charcoal on a rack that is about 6 inches from the source of heat. Turn occasionally so they cook through slowly without burning.

A Panoply of Peppers, Sweet and Hot

Cucumber and Mixed Sweet Pepper Salad with Dill

Cold Roasted Red Pepper Soup with Corn and Chives

Flounder Seviche with Hot and Sweet Pepper Confetti and Kiwi

Hot Green Chile Grits

Archaeological diggings in the Western Hemisphere suggest that as far back as seven thousand years before the birth of Christ, chiles—along with squash, beans, and maize—were part of the diet of the pre-Columbian Mayans, Incas, and Aztecs. They were the base, as they are now, of South American and Mexican cuisines. When Columbus and other explorers from Spain and Portugal made their famous navigational errors while seeking a sea route to find the peppercorns of the Far East, they called the newfound plant *peppers* anyhow, bringing chile seeds back to their mother countries. From there they found their way into the world's trade routes, influencing the flavors and cuisines of Africa, India, and the Orient. Today, three-quarters of the peoples around the world grow and eat chiles.

Here in the United States, the ever-growing constituency of chile lovers has contributed to our melting pot cuisines. Immigration patterns have changed, and the dominant groups entering the country today are Asian, Caribbean, African, Indian, Pakistani, Mexican, and South American—all requesting the "real thing" when it comes to food, and, for the most part, that means *hot*! The folks in the South and Southwest have been aficionados for centuries.

All peppers begin as green and then turn color—bright red or yellow—as they ripen. They grow easily, and they are cross-pollinated just as easily by the winds and birds. So, while some experts claim that there are two hundred varieties, others contend that there may be as many as one thousand, with almost seventy varieties grown in Mexico alone and new ones being deliberately crossbred every day.

They can be smooth, rough-skinned, or wrinkled, and are sold fresh, dried, frozen, canned, and powdered. They vary in color and texture, but most of all they range across the scale in terms of *heat*. A pharmacist by the name of Wilbur Scoville devised a scientific method of measuring the heat in what is now known as the Scoville Unit Rating. Ratings range from as low as fifty to the stratosphere, with anything over five thousand being considered super hot.

There is some disagreement, however, about the spelling—chili, chilli, chile—but the ultimate area of confusion for those who really love hot chiles is that the names may change depending on where they're grown: the *pasilla* of California is actually the *poblano*, but others know the pasilla as the dried form of the *chilaca*. The *Colorado* (which is really the *Anaheim*) can either be mild or hot. And the *Roumanian* can either be sweet or hot.

We have listed below the most common of both the sweet peppers and the chile peppers. You'll find that their level of hotness, their complexity of flavors, and their versatility will help open a new world of experience in seasoning—everything from sauces to condiments to soups, meats, and even seafood. The whole enchilada, so to speak!

THE SWEET PEPPER FAMILY

Sweet bell peppers can be harvested as green or left on the vine to turn various shades of yellow or red. The Dutch have developed a thick-walled version that doesn't collapse when filled and baked, and the range of colors is a virtual artist's palette: pale blond, orange, deep purple, and even an almost chocolate brown. They are available year-round, but the prices may vary somewhat depending on whether they've been grown domestically or have been shipped from the Netherlands or Israel.

The *pimiento*, usually available from late summer into the fall, is another popular sweet pepper. Heart shaped, a bright scarlet, and about 3 to 4 inches in length, it is flavorful and aromatic—even more so than the red bell pepper. The pimiento (or pimento) is generally used in its powdered form for paprika, with the best coming from Hungary and Spain. Whole pimientos can also be found in jars and cans.

Also from central Europe is the Hungarian sweet chile, about 5 inches long, deep crimson, with a broad top and rounded tip, and a very sweet flavor. Others found in various areas of the country from summer through early fall are the tapered light green Italian or frying pepper, the red or yellow Cubanelle, the slightly hot Japanese, and the tapered *lamayo*. The handpicked *piquillo* peppers from northern Spain, which are slow-roasted over wood fires and peeled and packed whole in jars, are perfect for a range of dishes from chile rellenos to soups, salads, and bruschetta.

All of them are versatile and can be eaten raw, baked, grilled, stuffed, or steamed. For the health conscious, they are loaded with vitamin C, vitamin A, and minerals.

THE CHILE PEPPERS: MILD TO WILD

Some of them are hot enough to be used in the sprays developed to ward off muggers and other perpetrators, and one concoction is designed to drive away grizzly bears! Others are quite mild, and all of their "heat ratings" are dependent on the amount they contain of a highly pungent alkaloid called "capsaicin." The seeds and ribs are the hottest part of the chile. Thus, removing the very top of the chile plus the seeds and ribs will modify the heat level a bit.

We strongly recommend asking your greengrocer for advice if you're in doubt, though what he or she considers mild, you may relate to electroshock therapy! Here are some popular varieties arranged in what we think is an order that goes from mild to wild:

ANAHEIM: Also known as New Mexico or California, this is either green or red. One of the best chiles for stuffing, it is also used for stews and sauces. The powdered red anaheim is available as *chile colorado*. Mild to medium hot.

GUAJILLO: A long, tapering, shiny, dark chile, it is dried and used in many stews, soups, and sauces. Its flavor has been described as tangy and citruslike, while others call its flavor almost like green tea and a bit tannic. Mild to medium hot.

POBLANO: Green and (when ripe) red, this green chile is adored all over Mexico for rellenos and other stuffed chile dishes. It is fairly large, about 5 inches long, and is never eaten raw. It has a full, earthy, smoky flavor. The ancho is a dried green poblano. Medium hot.

PASILLA: Dark brown and long, it is not found fresh here. It is also called "chile negro" or "little raisin," and it is actually a dried chilaca, which is used extensively (along with the ancho and mulato) in the Mexican mole. Medium hot.

MULATO: A dried poblano (as is the ancho), it is dark brown, and its smoky flavors have been compared to tobacco, dried cherry, and even licorice—another example of personal "chile taste." It is used widely for mole and other sauces. Medium hot.

ANCHO: This is the dried green poblano, and it is one of the sweetest of the dried chile family. Though medium hot, its flavor is quite mild. It derives its fame for being one of what has been called the "holy trinity" (along with the mulato and pasilla) of the mole sauce.

CASCABEL: The word means "rattle" since the seeds do just that when the dried chile is shaken. They're very small and shaped like tiny plump pillows. They have a rich, smoky, almost woodsy flavor, and they're used in sauces, soups, stews, and salsas. Chile mavens rate them from medium to quite hot.

JALAPEÑO: Sold fresh, and both green and red, this is possibly one of the most popular of chiles mostly because of its versatility. About 2 inches long, it can be used raw, roasted, or pickled in cans and jars. It can be included in a range of recipes from soups to salsas, with fish or meat, and in sauces. Medium hot to hot.

CHIPOTLE: This is a dried, smoked red jalapeños. Available for the most part in Latin American markets, it has a smoky sweet flavor. It can also be found canned and packed in adobe sauce. Hot.

KOREAN GREEN AND THAI: The Thai is about 1½ inches long, and its Korean cousin is twice as large. Both are frequently used in the dishes of their native countries, such as in *kim chee* in Korea, and are now available in specialty stores. Both are *hot*; some say the Thai is hotter.

SERRANO: It is arguably one of the hottest chiles available, and the Mexicans love it in salsas or pickled in escabeche. This green or red chile becomes a bit milder when roasted.

TÉPIN: This is one of the tiniest chiles, but oh my! It is only about ¼ inch in diameter, but it runs a close race for heat with the champion of them all: the habañero.

HABAÑERO: Closely related to the Scotch Bonnet and the Jamaican hot, it looks like a little paper lantern. The colors vary from dark green to orange and red, and it has been described as from fifty to one thousand times hotter than the popular jalapeño. Treat it with respect (and wear rubber gloves when handling it), since it is the all-time Scoville unit champion at somewhere around 326,000! It is generally used in salsas and is a favorite for the super-hot bottled sauces sold commercially through mail order.

HOW TO PUT OUT THE FIRE

There are times when an innocent-looking dish arrives and you blithely dig in. Suddenly, your lips smolder, your eyes water, your tongue numbs, and the top of your head turns red and becomes bathed in perspiration. If you open your mouth, only the Fire Department could extinguish the flame. Take heart, for there are various methods around the world that they "claim" can cool the victim.

First of all, cold water or beer should never be used; they cool only for an instant. The Chinese eat rice to absorb some of the heat, while the Vietnamese drink very hot tea, which burns at first and then cools the mouth (they say). Indians accompany a hot curry meal with a yogurt drink, *lhassi*, or *raita*, a condiment of yogurt, mint, and coriander. The North African *harissa*, a fiery chile paste served with couscous, is moderated by sweet raisins. In Mexico, the natives dip a wet finger into the sugar bowl and lick it clean. Whatever works!

SHOP SMART

- Sweet or hot, look for tight, shiny skins with firm flesh. They should not be bruised or wrinkled.
- When shopping, if you're in doubt as to the heat of a chile, a general rule is that the smaller the pepper, the hotter it will be.
- There is a difference between *chili powder* and *powdered chiles*. The former will be a mix that can include everything from garlic to oregano to cumin, but generally it has very few real chiles. Buy powdered chile that is pure ground dried chiles and has a rich color and an intense aroma.
- Dried chiles keep well in an airtight container in a cool, dry place for four to six months. Remember that dried chiles will be hotter ounce for ounce than the fresh varieties and that some chiles can only be found in their dried state.

Notes for the Cook

ON ROASTING FRESH SWEET PEPPERS OR CHILES . . .

- *Warning!* In handling hot chiles, we strongly recommend wearing rubber gloves. The seeds and ribs are the hottest parts of the chile—the flavor is in the outside shell—and they can actually burn your hands. Also, don't touch your eyes after handling hot chiles.
- When sweet peppers or chiles are split lengthwise and the stem ends, ribs, and seeds are removed before broiling, they can be placed skin side up and do not need to be turned to char the skins for easy removal. You can also grill them whole under a broiler flame or outdoors over wood or charcoal, turning them to char evenly and removing the seeds and skin after they cool.
- When roasting several peppers, a good method to use is to line a cookie sheet with aluminum foil. After the skin is charred, the foil can be used to enclose the peppers so that they steam, and the skins will loosen as they cool.
- Or place two or three peppers or chiles on a wire cake rack (so the small ones don't fall through) directly on top of a gas burner. Tiny chiles such as serrano can be slipped on an ice pick, and the handle can be turned slowly over the flame to char the skin evenly. Then enclose in aluminum foil to steam and cool.

ON DRIED CHILES . . .

- If the recipe calls for reconstituting *dried* chiles, tear them into small pieces, cover them with boiling water, and soak them for 30 minutes before using.
- When using whole dried chiles, remember to retrieve and discard them before serving the dish. We make sure we can find them again by tying them in a piece of cheesecloth before adding them to the pot.

CUCUMBER AND MIXED SWEET PEPPER SALAD WITH DILL

This lovely cucumber and mixed sweet and hot pepper salad keeps for two weeks in the refrigerator and is perfect with seafood.

SERVES 4 TO 6

3 long English or Kirby cucumbers (about 1½ pounds), thinly sliced on the diagonal (about 3 cups)
½ each large red, green, and yellow peppers, finely diced (about ½ cup each)
1 tablespoon seeded and finely minced jalapeño chile (about 1 medium)

1 medium red onion, thinly sliced (about ⅔ cup)
1 tablespoon kosher or coarse salt
1 teaspoon celery seed
¼ teaspoon black pepper
½ cup distilled white vinegar
¾ cup sugar
2 tablespoons coarsely chopped fresh dill

Add the sliced cucumbers to a medium-size bowl along with the red, green, and yellow peppers, jalapeño, red onion, salt, celery seed, and black pepper. Stir to combine and let sit for 1 hour.

Meanwhile, stir the vinegar and sugar together in a cup until the sugar dissolves. After an hour, drain the pepper mixture in a strainer, return it to a bowl, and add the vinegar-sugar mixture. Cover with plastic wrap and refrigerate for 2 to 3 hours or overnight. When serving, use a slotted spoon to drain some of the liquid and scatter dill over the surface.

COLD ROASTED RED PEPPER SOUP WITH CORN AND CHIVES

A lively, vibrantly colored, chilled soup with the crunch of yellow corn kernels and tiny bits of green chives.

SERVES 4

2 pounds large red peppers (about 4 or 5), roasted to make 3 cups puree (see page 154)

3 tablespoons olive oil

1 tablespoon minced garlic (2 medium cloves)

3 cups chicken or vegetable broth

2½ tablespoons red wine vinegar

2 tablespoons coarsely chopped parsley

Salt and pepper to taste

1 cup cooked corn kernels

4 teaspoons snipped chives

After roasting the peppers, seed and cut them roughly and set aside. In a small skillet, heat the olive oil over medium-high heat. Add the garlic and stir for 30 seconds, then turn the heat off under the skillet. The garlic is cooked just to remove the raw garlic taste; do not let it brown, or it will be bitter.

Using a blender or food processor, puree the peppers in several batches along with the oil, garlic, broth, vinegar, parsley, salt, and pepper. Transfer to a bowl and stir in the corn. Chill for at least 2 hours. Sprinkle with the chives just before serving.

red Peppers

FLOUNDER SEVICHE WITH HOT AND SWEET PEPPER CONFETTI AND KIWI

Seviche makes a lovely first course or a light summer luncheon. This one is particularly attractive, with pale green kiwi forming a core for diamond-sliced flounder arranged in a star-shaped pattern and showered with a colorful confetti of hot and sweet peppers.

SERVES 4

1 pound flounder (or fluke or other flat fish) fillets, skinned and cut into 1-inch diamond shapes

½ cup lime juice (about 3 to 4 limes) plus shredded lime zest for garnish

¼ teaspoon ground cumin

Salt and pepper to taste

3 tablespoons very thin diagonally sliced scallion (1 or 2 scallions), green part only

¼ cup finely diced (¼ inch) red sweet pepper (¼ large pepper)

¼ cup finely diced (¼ inch) green sweet pepper (¼ large)

2 teaspoons finely minced and seeded jalapeño pepper (1 medium)

2 tablespoons coarsely chopped cilantro leaves

1 tablespoon rice wine vinegar

3 tablespoons orange juice (½ large orange)

2 kiwis, peeled and cut horizontally into ¼-inch slices

Alfalfa sprouts

Place the fish in a glass or ceramic bowl. Combine the lime juice, cumin, salt, and pepper, and pour the mixture over the fish. Cover the bowl with plastic wrap and marinate in the refrigerator for at least 6 hours or up to 12 hours.

About 2 hours before serving, drain the fish, discarding the marinade. In a small bowl, mix the scallions, sweet peppers, jalapeño, cilantro, and additional salt and pepper if you wish. Add the vinegar and orange juice. Finely dice 4 slices of kiwi, add to the bowl, and mix gently. Place the alfalfa sprouts on the outer borders of 4 serving plates. Place a slice of kiwi in the center of each plate and arrange the slices of fish around the kiwi to form a star shape. Spoon the peppers mixture in a thin circle over the fish, trickling any remaining liquid over all.

Serve at room temperature or cover with plastic wrap and chill in the refrigerator. Return it to room temperature before serving and garnish with the shredded zest.

HOT GREEN CHILE GRITS

Large, thick-fleshed poblano chiles range from medium to hot, and the small serrano chile packs a bit more heat—perfect foils for intensely corn-flavored stone-ground grits.

SERVES 4 TO 6

¾ cup cilantro leaves

2 large cloves garlic, peeled and
 roughly cut

2 large shallots, peeled and
 roughly cut

2 fresh poblano chiles (about
 6 ounces), roasted, peeled, seeded,
 and roughly chopped

1 fresh serrano chile, stemmed and
 seeded

½ cup water

3 cups milk

1 cup chicken broth

Salt to taste

1 cup stone-ground grits

1 tablespoon butter

Pepper to taste

⅔ cup shredded sharp cheddar cheese
 (about 3 ounces)

Sour cream (optional)

Place the cilantro, garlic, and shallots in the bowl of a food processor and process until fine. Add the prepared chiles and water, and process again until fairly smooth. Scrape out the contents and set aside. There should be about 1 cup.

In a 3-quart nonstick saucepan, bring the milk, broth, and some salt to a boil over medium heat. Slowly stir in the grits. Turn the heat to very low and simmer, covered, for 20 minutes, stirring frequently. Add the reserved chile mixture and continue to cook, stirring frequently, about 10 minutes more. Stir in the butter, season with salt and pepper, and transfer to a buttered shallow 1½-quart baking dish. Sprinkle with the cheese. Slip the dish under a preheated broiler until the cheese melts and is dappled with brown, about 3 minutes.

To serve, make a well with the back of a tablespoon in each portion and fill it with a heaping teaspoon of sour cream if you wish.

It's Tomato/Tomahto Time!

*Yellow and Red Cherry Tomatoes and Ciliegine Salad with
Four-Herb Vinaigrette*

*Mixed Tomatoes, Red Onion, and Arugula Salad with
Tomato Cumin Vinaigrette*

Warm Summer Pasta with Fresh Uncooked Tomatoes and Herbs

Cold Moroccan Tomato Soup

There are early girls, big girls, big boys, beefsteaks, pear, cherry, plum, and sweet 100 tomatoes, as well as the many heirloom varieties almost lost forever, such as Pink Brandywine, White Wonder, Green Zebra, Yellow Ruffles, and Purple Cherokee. An estimated three thousand varieties have existed in horticultural history, and many are being revived and appearing once again. Not only do they run the spectrum of bright, inviting, sunny colors—yellow, red, green, and orange—but their sizes run the gamut from thumbnail to huge misshapen orbs weighing well over 2 pounds. Although tomatoes have year-round availability, the true lover of that glorious fruit looks forward to the summertime orgy of vine-ripened, sun-flavored varieties when they are at their flavorful best.

It was the sixteenth-century Portuguese and Spanish explorers who first took the seeds of the Aztec *xitomatles* and brought them back to the Mediterranean area to grow.

In the beginning, the skeptics thought them to be ornamental, not edible, and even poisonous. But obviously someone took a bite out of a tempting red globe, called it a "pomme d'amour," and promptly placed it under suspicion of being an aphrodisiac! Then it went from being shunned to being totally embraced with ardor.

Some remarkable results come from very simple tomato recipes, such as a Catalan specialty of a perfectly ripe tomato rubbed into a slice of rustic bread *(pa amb tomàquet)* and the popular Italian *bruschetta*—a tomato chopped with basil, a sprinkling of olive oil, and coarse salt that tops a garlic-rubbed fire-toasted peasant bread. Best of all, every fresh herb loves tomatoes—oregano, basil, rosemary, thyme, mint—and summer vegetables such as eggplant, corn, and zucchini cry out to be mated with the lush tomato. It's a sexy fruit that bursts with flavor and juices, so much so that "Whadda tomato!" was a very Damon Runyonesque thing to say in the '40s, when referring to a sensual woman.

SHOP SMART

- ◆ Select ripe, firm, unblemished, and brilliantly colored tomatoes.
- ◆ Taste differences among tomatoes are caused by different balances of acidity and sugars, not by color. Many heirlooms, for example, are not red but are grown for better flavor.
- ◆ When you get them home, never refrigerate them; it ruins their taste. Keep them at room temperature for one to two days for ripening and even more flavor.

Notes for the Cook

ON TOMATOES . . .

- ◆ To ripen green tomatoes, place them, stem down, on a double thickness of newspapers in a cool, dry place. In a few days check the state of ripeness.
- ◆ Skinning and seeding are a matter of personal choice and depend on the recipe to be used. When the skins are very tough, it is better to remove them for salads. For soups, puree them in a food mill, and the seeds and skin will be left behind.
- ◆ To skin tomatoes, cut a small shallow X on the bottom, submerge in boiling water for 30 to 40 seconds, and plunge into cold water. The skins will slip off easily. You can then cut them crosswise and gently squeeze out the seeds; however, we prefer keeping the seeds to add a bit of crunch.
- ◆ For stuffed tomatoes, hollow out the centers and turn upside down to drain for an hour to prevent the liquid from diluting the flavor of the filling.
- ◆ Try baking stuffed tomatoes in an oiled muffin pan; they are held upright and retain their shape.
- ◆ Cherry tomatoes may seem perfect for skewering and grilling, but their skins are tough and, when heated, get watery inside. Use larger, ripe tomatoes and insert two bamboo skewers in each to hold them firmly for turning on the grill.
- ◆ Overripe tomatoes make full-bodied sauces and soups. Don't throw them away.
- ◆ A bit of grated carrot or sugar added to tomato sauces can remove their acidic edge.

YELLOW AND RED CHERRY TOMATOES AND CILIEGINE SALAD WITH FOUR-HERB VINAIGRETTE

Tiny creamy-colored mozzarella mouthfuls mix with yellow and red cherry tomatoes on a bed of sharp peppery greens dressed with the bounty of summer herbs.

SERVES 4

FOUR-HERB VINAIGRETTE:
1 tablespoon each roughly chopped
   basil and parsley
1 teaspoon each oregano and mint
   leaves
1 small clove garlic, peeled and
   crushed
Salt and pepper to taste
2 tablespoons lemon juice
¼ cup olive oil

SALAD:
Sharp salad greens such as mizuna,
   young red mustard, or frisée (about
   4 cups)
12 yellow cherry tomatoes
16 red cherry tomatoes
12 ciliegine (sometimes called
   boccancini or mozzarella balls)
Freshly ground black pepper
Toasted triangles of black olive bread
   (optional)

To make the vinaigrette: In a blender, place the herbs, garlic, salt, pepper, and lemon juice, and pulse until the herbs are very fine. Add the olive oil and pulse again. Transfer to a cup using a rubber spatula. There should be ¼ cup of dressing. Set aside.

To make the salad: On 4 chilled plates place the greens toward the outside edges. Place 3 yellow, 4 red, and 3 ciliegine in the center of each plate. Grind the pepper over the mozzarella only. Trickle 1 tablespoon of vinaigrette over the tomatoes and greens on each plate. Tuck in grilled triangles of black olive bread if you wish.

MIXED TOMATOES, RED ONION, AND ARUGULA SALAD WITH TOMATO CUMIN VINAIGRETTE

This very attractive presentation shows off all the sizes and shapes of fresh tomatoes when they are at their most flavorful summer peak. The dressing has a strong Spanish accent and is just minimally trickled over them as a flavor contrast.

SERVES 4

TOMATO CUMIN VINAIGRETTE (MAKES ⅓ CUP):

1 tablespoon sherry vinegar
Salt and pepper to taste
¼ teaspoon ground cumin
⅛ teaspoon paprika
1 teaspoon minced garlic (1 medium clove)
1 teaspoon tomato paste
2 drops Tabasco
3 tablespoons olive oil

SALAD:

2 cups arugula leaves (about 20 to 30)
1 large yellow tomato (about 8 ounces), thinly sliced
1 large red tomato (about 8 ounces), thinly sliced
¾ cup small yellow pear tomatoes and small red currant tomatoes
1 small red onion, thinly sliced (about ½ cup)

To make the vinaigrette: In a small bowl, place the vinegar, salt, pepper, cumin, paprika, garlic, tomato paste, and Tabasco. Whisk to combine. Slowly add the olive oil while whisking until it is incorporated. Set aside.

To make the salad: Arrange the arugula around the outside rim of a large platter. Alternate red and yellow tomato slices on the arugula, slightly overlapping toward the center of the platter. Scatter small tomatoes over the slices. Separate the onion slices and scatter them over the tomatoes. Whisk the dressing after it has been standing and trickle a little over all.

WARM SUMMER PASTA WITH FRESH UNCOOKED TOMATOES AND HERBS

We usually prepare the sauce well in advance to blend the flavors. The pasta takes only minutes to cook and is equally as good served at room temperature.

SERVES 4 TO 6

2½ pounds ripe tomatoes, skinned

½ cup olive oil

2 teaspoons finely minced garlic (about 2 medium cloves)

2 tablespoons finely chopped shallots (about 3 large)

3 flat anchovies, rinsed

12 black Kalamata olives, pitted and sliced lengthwise

1 tablespoon nonpareil capers, rinsed

1 teaspoon grated lemon zest

1 teaspoon dried oregano, preferably Greek

1 tablespoon thyme leaves

2 tablespoons coarsely chopped parsley

6 to 8 basil leaves, chopped

⅛ teaspoon (or more to taste) hot pepper flakes

¼ teaspoon black pepper

Salt to taste

1 tablespoon red wine vinegar

1 pound fusilli, freshly cooked

Grated Parmesan cheese

Cut the tomatoes into 1-inch pieces and place in a colander to drain for 30 minutes. Heat 4 tablespoons of the oil in a 12-inch skillet over medium heat. Add the garlic and shallots, and sauté for 1 to 2 minutes, stirring.

Remove the skillet from the heat and add the anchovies, olives, capers, drained tomatoes, and all the remaining ingredients except the pasta and cheese.

When the pasta is cooked, drain it and, while hot, stir in the sauce. The hot pasta will release all the flavors of the herbs and tomatoes. Transfer to a serving platter and pass the Parmesan cheese and a pepper mill.

COLD MOROCCAN TOMATO SOUP

A favorite cold, fresh tomato soup—Morocco's answer to Spanish gazpacho. It is spicy enough to perk up waning hot-weather appetites, and it is easy on the cook.

SERVES 4

2 tablespoons olive oil

4 to 5 large cloves garlic, peeled, smashed, and minced

1½ teaspoons ground cumin

2½ teaspoons sweet paprika

⅛ to ¼ teaspoon cayenne pepper

2½ pounds ripe tomatoes

1 tablespoon white wine vinegar

2 tablespoons cold water

2 tablespoons lemon juice (½ large lemon)

Salt liberally to taste

¾ cup finely diced celery (about 3 or 4 stalks)

3 tablespoons coarsely chopped cilantro plus 1 tablespoon whole leaves for garnish

Heat the olive oil in a 1-quart saucepan over low heat. Add the garlic and sauté, stirring, for 1 minute. Add the cumin, paprika, and cayenne, and continue to cook, stirring constantly so that the garlic doesn't burn, 2 minutes more. Remove from the heat and set aside.

Puree the tomatoes in a food mill, using a disk with large holes, until coarsely textured. (The seeds and skin left behind should be discarded.) Or puree the tomatoes in a food processor; if you choose this method, the skins should be removed and the tomatoes cored beforehand.

Transfer the tomatoes to a bowl. Stir in the garlic-spice mix, vinegar, water, lemon juice, salt, and celery plus the chopped cilantro. Refrigerate for at least 1 hour, until cold. Taste to adjust the seasoning, then ladle it into bowls. Sprinkle with the cilantro leaves. An ice cube added to each bowl will keep the soup cold on a hot day.

Corn: Now Ear This!

Corn, Okra, Tomatoes, and Black-Eyed Peas

A Casserole of Corn, Chorizo, Tomatoes,
and Peppers with Cheddar Cheese

Corn Flan with Chives

Asian Corn and Tofu Soup with Scallions and Baby Corn

Chilean Sea Bass with Corn-Lemongrass Cream

Corn is uniquely American—both North and South American. As wheat, rye, and barley are to Europe or rice to Asia, corn was born and nurtured here by the Aztecs, Mayans, and Native Americans, who called it "the provider of life" and who introduced it to the Pilgrims, who then called it "Indian corn." Transported to Europe by Columbus and the conquistadors who followed some years later, its name was changed to "maize," and was fed to pigs and cattle. Only recently, with the introduction of Mexican and Tex-Mex restaurants on the European continent, have they begun to discover what Americans on both continents have known and enjoyed for over six thousand years.

Today corn still epitomizes the American experience more than almost any other food. Any backyard barbecue, clambake, or picnic, any summer outdoor family gathering carries with it a picture of piles of steaming hot corn. It is a major ingredient in soufflés, chowders, fritters, relishes, and muffins.

SHOP SMART

- The most popular varieties are the yellow, white, and "butter and egg" variety that has both white and yellow kernels. There is also tender and tasty baby corn, with an edible cob along with the kernels.
- Local corn is available in the summer months, and it is a good idea to buy it fresh picked when possible. Look for ears with moist, grassy green, tightly wrapped husks with just a bit of dry, brown tassel peeking from the tips. Peel a bit of the husk back and look for decay or worms, and make certain that the kernels are plump and evenly spaced. Pierce one kernel with a fingernail, and a fresh corn will squirt a milky juice. No juice? The corn is "over the hill."

◆ Try not to store corn for more than two days. Put them unhusked in a plastic bag in the refrigerator. If you husk them before you're ready to cook them, the corn will convert its natural sugar to starch very quickly. While on the stalk, the sugars are constantly replenished, but once pulled, the sugar replacement stops and the kernels begin to toughen and lose flavor.

Notes for the Cook

ABOUT CORN . . .

BOILING:

◆ Remove and discard the husks (called shucking). If an ear has an imperfect end, cut or break it off. Rinse the ears in cold running water and rub with paper towels to remove the residual silk.

◆ Drop the corn into a large pot of vigorously boiling water. Allow the water to return to a boil, then cover the pot and turn off the heat. Let the corn remain in the water for nine to ten minutes. Remove with tongs and serve at once. Using this method, the corn can remain in the water for 10 to 15 minutes longer, staying hot while not damaging the flavor.

ROASTING OR GRILLING:

◆ Peel back the husks and leave them attached while removing the silks. Then rewrap the husks and tie them crosswise around each ear by using a folded strand of corn husk. Soak the ears in cool water for twenty minutes. Grill them 4 to 5 inches over the hot coals for fifteen to twenty minutes, or until tender. Turn frequently so that the ears roast evenly.

◆ *Oven Roasting* requires the same preparation as above. Butter and salt the ears after the silks are removed or shuck completely and then butter and wrap in aluminum foil. Roast at 425 degrees for the same amount of time as when roasting over hot coals.

I large ear or 2 medium-size ears = I cup kernels.

CORN, OKRA, TOMATOES, AND BLACK-EYED PEAS

All you need to complete this southern vegetable ragout with its hint of smoky bacon is hot buttermilk cornbread baked in an iron skillet.

SERVES 6

1 cup dried black-eyed peas, soaked overnight and drained

4 cups water

1 whole dried hot chile (such as Japonés)

1 large bay leaf

1 small whole onion, peeled

Salt to taste

2 to 3 strips bacon, finely diced (about ⅓ cup)

½ cup coarsely chopped onion (1 medium onion)

28-ounce can Italian plum tomatoes, cut into large chunks (about 2 cups), drained, and liquid reserved

2 cups very small whole fresh okra pods (⅛ inch of stem trimmed)

1 cup fresh or frozen corn kernels (1 or 2 small ears)

Freshly ground black pepper to taste

In a 3-quart saucepan, bring the beans and water to a boil. Skim off and discard any surface foam. Lower the heat and add the chile, bay leaf, and whole onion. Cover the saucepan, and simmer for 30 minutes or more, until the beans are tender. Add salt during the last few minutes of cooking.

Meanwhile, place the diced bacon in a 12-inch skillet and fry until crisp. Remove the bacon with a slotted spoon to paper towels to drain. Pour off all but 1 tablespoon of the bacon fat left in the skillet. Over medium heat, add the chopped onion and stir for 3 or 4 minutes without browning. Add the drained tomatoes and simmer for 10 minutes over medium-low heat. Stir in the okra, corn, salt, and pepper, cover the skillet, and simmer 5 minutes more.

When the beans are cooked, remove the bay leaf, whole onion, and chile, and discard. Drain the beans and add them to the skillet along with ½ cup of the reserved tomato liquid. Cover the skillet and simmer 5 more minutes. Check the seasoning and add additional salt, if needed, and pepper.

Transfer to a serving dish and scatter the crisped, diced bacon over the surface.

A CASSEROLE OF CORN, CHORIZO, TOMATOES, AND PEPPERS WITH CHEDDAR CHEESE

Some of the corn kernels are pureed to form a custard for the chorizo and vegetables in this satisfying, very flavorful casserole.

SERVES 4 TO 6

8 ounces chorizo sausage, diced

1¼ cups coarsely chopped onion (1 large onion)

1 cup coarsely chopped green pepper (1 medium pepper)

1 teaspoon finely minced jalapeño chile

½ teaspoon dried oregano

1 teaspoon ground cumin

Salt and pepper to taste

3 cups fresh corn kernels (about 4 medium ears)

1½ cups diced plum tomatoes (about 8 ounces)

2 eggs

½ cup sour cream

1 cup grated sharp cheddar cheese (about 4 ounces)

3 tablespoons coarsely chopped cilantro

In a 12-inch nonstick skillet, sauté the chorizo over medium-high heat, stirring frequently, until the sausage begins to brown. Remove with a slotted spoon to drain on paper towels and set aside.

Add the onion to the skillet with whatever fat remains in the skillet (about 1 or 2 tablespoons) and stir frequently for 1 minute. Add the green pepper, chile, oregano, cumin, salt, and pepper, and sauté for about 4 minutes. Add 2 cups of the corn kernels, return the chorizo to the pan, and continue to cook 1 or 2 minutes more. Add the tomatoes, remove the skillet from the heat, and set aside to cool slightly.

Heat the oven to 400 degrees. Butter a 2½-quart oven-to-table baking dish. In the bowl of a food processor, beat the eggs along with the remaining cup of corn kernels until pureed. Add the sour cream and ½ cup of the cheddar cheese, and pulse until combined. Stir in the cilantro and add additional salt and pepper if needed.

Transfer the vegetables to the prepared baking dish and pour the egg mixture over them. Sprinkle the remaining cheese over the top and bake for about 25 minutes, or until the cheese is melted and slightly golden. Serve hot.

CORN FLAN WITH CHIVES

A sunny yellow corn custard flecked with tiny green chives, it can be eaten with simply grilled shrimp or chicken.

SERVES 4

3 medium ears of corn, shucked
3 tablespoons butter
1 medium onion (about 6 ounces),
    thinly sliced
3 eggs
1 cup milk
½ cup heavy cream

½ teaspoon nutmeg
⅛ teaspoon cayenne pepper
Salt to taste
¼ teaspoon white pepper
1 teaspoon sugar
⅓ cup finely snipped chives

Cut the kernels from the cobs; there should be about 2 cups. Set aside. In a small skillet, heat 2 tablespoons of the butter and sauté the onion over medium-low heat until transparent and just beginning to color, about 5 or 6 minutes.

Preheat the oven to 350 degrees. Butter a 1-quart soufflé dish or other deep-sided pan and set it aside. In the bowl of a food processor, place 1 cup of the corn kernels and process to a puree. Add the sautéed onion and process again. Add the eggs, milk, cream, nutmeg, cayenne, salt, pepper, and sugar, and process until well combined. Stir in the remaining corn kernels and chives. Pour into the prepared dish and dot with pieces of the remaining tablespoon of butter.

Place the dish in a larger pan and pour boiling water in the pan until it reaches halfway up the sides of the soufflé dish. Bake for 55 minutes to 1 hour, or until the custard is set when tested with the point of a knife. Serve hot.

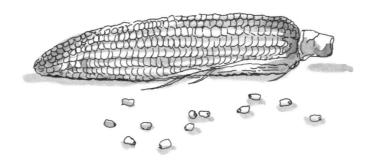

ASIAN CORN AND TOFU SOUP WITH SCALLIONS AND BABY CORN

Corn is used liberally in Chinese cuisine with vegetable and fish dishes. This light and easy soup, intensely corn flavored, has tiny cubes of tofu, miniature corn, and scallions floating on top. It is wonderful and healthful for a summer luncheon when appetites wane.

SERVES 6

1 tablespoon plus 1 teaspoon
  Asian sesame oil
½ cup thinly sliced scallions, white
  part only (about 7 medium
  scallions)
1 cup thinly sliced scallions, green part
  only (the 7 scallions above)
6 cups chicken broth, homemade or
  canned

4 cups fresh corn kernels (about
  6 medium ears); reserve the cobs
12 ounces firm tofu, cut into ½-inch
  cubes
1 tablespoon finely sliced red hot chile,
  or to taste
Salt and white pepper to taste
12 whole baby corn, canned or fresh
  and husked

In a 5-quart Dutch oven, heat the tablespoon of sesame oil over moderately low heat. Add the white part of the scallion, reserving the green part for later. Stir constantly until soft, about 2 minutes. Add the broth, then break the corn cobs in half and add to the pot. Bring to a boil over medium heat. Lower the heat and simmer for 10 minutes. Remove the cobs with tongs and discard them. Add the corn kernels to the pot and simmer about 8 to 10 minutes, until the corn is very tender.

In a blender, puree the mixture in batches and strain into a bowl through a fine sieve, stirring and pressing hard on the solids with a wooden spoon. Discard the solids, return the soup to the pot, and bring to a simmer over moderate heat. Add the tofu, chile, salt, pepper, baby corn, and the green parts of the scallions. Cook over moderate heat for 2 or 3 minutes. Trickle the teaspoon of sesame oil over the soup and serve. Allow 2 baby corn per bowl.

CHILEAN SEA BASS WITH CORN-LEMONGRASS CREAM

Fresh corn kernels and delicate lemongrass, with its evasively mysterious flavor, enhance a creamy, reduced sauce for the firm-fleshed, giant-flaked, plump Chilean sea bass in a winsome pairing.

SERVES 4

SAUCE (MAKES ABOUT 1¼ CUPS):

1½ cups fresh corn kernels (about 2 ears)

3 stalks lemongrass, inner part of bulb only (about 4 inches long), pounded with a mallet and minced (about ½ cup) (see page 8)

1 tablespoon coarsely chopped garlic (about 2 medium cloves)

1 cup fish stock

1 cup heavy cream

Salt and white pepper to taste

1 tablespoon very finely diced (⅛ inch) sweet red pepper (about ¼ small pepper) for garnish

FISH:

Four 6-ounce Chilean sea bass, striped bass, or red snapper fillets

1 tablespoon butter, melted

Salt to taste

To make the sauce: In a 2-quart nonstick saucepan, combine the corn kernels, lemongrass, garlic, fish stock, and cream, and bring to a boil over medium-low heat. Cook at a low boil about 20 minutes to reduce the sauce. Transfer to a blender, puree until smooth, then pour through a fine sieve over a small bowl, extracting as much sauce as possible by pressing and stirring the solids against the sieve. Discard the solids and season the sauce with salt and pepper. Return the sauce to the saucepan and keep it warm while the fish is baking.

Preheat the oven to 400 degrees. To make the fish: Pour the butter into the bottom of an oven-to-table baking pan large enough so that the fish fillets are not crowded. Season the fish with salt and turn the fillets over in the butter to coat both sides. Bake for 15 to 20 minutes, basting occasionally. Test with the point of a knife to see that the fillets are cooked through.

When ready to serve, spoon the sauce over and around the fish. Scatter the diced red pepper over the surface and serve.

Saladarity

Vinaigrette with Garlic and Anchovy

Roasted Red Pepper Vinaigrette with Cumin

Tomato and Basil Vinaigrette

Double Walnut Vinaigrette with Shallots

In fourteenth-century medieval England, recipes for "sallets" contained all sorts of herbs, leeks, onions, garlic, watercress, and purslane, mixed with "oil of raw olives" and a "laying on of salt and vinegar."

By the sixteenth century, vegetables and meats were included in salads, much like our contemporary composed salads, and they were called "salmagundis." Between the 1920s and 1950s, a wedge of iceberg lettuce with Russian dressing, made with a combination of commercial mayonnaise and ketchup, prevailed.

In the '40s and '50s, gelatin salads appeared, usually green and made with bottled ginger ale, pieces of canned fruit, and marshmallows. These were followed by cold, undressed pasta salads accompanied mostly by stale-tasting leftovers and ambivalent fruit salads that just didn't know whether they should be salads or desserts. Along came the ubiquitous do-it-yourself salad bars and take-out delis, and then the popular contemporary vegetarian's delight: grain salads—bulgur, barley, quinoa, or rice, mixed with herbs and raw or cooked vegetables, and set over dressed greens.

Today, chefs across the country have been redefining the role of the salad in this health-conscious age and have basically returned to the old-fashioned one-dish meal or the dinner salad. As a result, markets today are resplendent with creative salad options, rich in contrasting colors, flavors, and textures. When mixed and matched with a complementary dressing made with the finest oils and vinegars, the effect can be stunning both visually and gastronomically.

Most salads fall into distinct groups, with some overlapping:

RAW SALADS: These can include all sorts of raw vegetables with the greens—radishes, cucumbers, carrots, celery, fennel, cauliflower, broccoli, sweet peppers, and tomatoes, for example.

MIXED GREEN SALADS: Mesclun mixes and various improvisations might include endive, watercress, frisée, arugula, romaine, mâche, or radicchio. The Italian *tricolore* salad, composed of Belgian endive, radicchio, and arugula, is almost considered a holy trinity of salads.

COOKED SALADS: Cooked beans, grains, and/or root vegetables such as potatoes, beets, asparagus, and artichokes, make up this group.

COMPOSED SALADS: Any combination of the above can be included and also fish, poultry, or meat. These are light whole-meal salads as entrées for lunch or dinner.

Essentially, the ultimate well-balanced salad should be composed of contrasting textures, flavors, colors, and leaf shapes.

A GLOSSARY OF GREENS

Loose-Leaved Lettuce

They are identified by sprawling and loosely joined long leaves in various shades of green—some plain edged, some ruffled—and occasionally all red or edged in red. Their flavors run the gamut from mild to slightly bitter, and they combine well as accent greens or can be served alone.

OAK LEAF. Shaped as its name implies, this fragile, mild leaf is either green or edged in red.

MÂCHE. Also known as corn salad, lamb's lettuce, or field salad, it is extremely delicate and dainty, and has small, rounded, velvety emerald green leaves.

BROAD LEAF ENDIVE. Also known as Batavian and escarole, the central heart contains the tender, succulent blanched leaves that are used raw in salads. The wide dark green outer leaves are coarse, bitter, and more suitable for sautéeing or in soups.

CURLY LEAF ENDIVE. Also known as frisée, it has fine, narrow-notched, and somewhat curly leaves. It is a mildly bittersweet variety with a loosely tangled crisp heart of yellowish-white leaves tipped with pale green ends. French bistros favor frisée dressed with a hearty red wine vinegar and hot bacon fat.

ARUGULA. Also known as rocket and rugola, it has peppery, long, bright green leaves. In spring the leaves are very tender, but the fall crop produces stronger texture and flavor. Arugula, alone or mixed with tomatoes, or as an accent to a milder leaf lettuce, is wonderful simply dressed with good olive oil, balsamic vinegar, and some roasted garlic.

Head Lettuce

Rather than the splayed-out leaves of the loose-leaved variety, the leaves here curl inward, forming a tightly dense, crisp head, with some softer leaves loosely defining a head shape.

ICEBERG. Also known as crisp head, this lettuce has pale, very mild, crisp leaves that form a sturdy head. It is usually cut into wedges and served with a thick, creamy dressing such as Russian or Roquefort.

ROMAINE. Also known as cos, it has long, large, slightly crenelated leaves and succulent, crisp whitish yellow heart leaves that are tipped with dark green. Its very sweet flavor mixes well with peppery arugula and watercress. It is the popular "Caesar salad" lettuce that can support a robust red wine vinaigrette with a touch of anchovy and garlic.

BUTTERHEAD. Also known as Boston and butter lettuce, it has slightly flattened, loosely formed heads of pale, yellowish, buttery-textured, mild-flavored leaves. The small, oval, sweet, bright green heads of Bibb lettuce are also a part of this group. Use light lemony or other citrus dressings and a dusting of fresh herbs such as tarragon or chervil to allow its delicacy to shine through.

RADICCHIO. Developed in the Veneto region of Italy from various local chicory varieties, each variety of radicchio takes its name from a different village. *Rosa di Chioggia* is a cranberry red compact head of thickish leathery leaves lined with white. Verona has an egg-shaped head with looser red leaves. Treviso is a flavorful, elongated, red leaf head that is also treated as a vegetable and is sometimes grilled whole. Use the slightly bitter radicchio leaves sparingly with other sweeter leaves such as romaine. They hold up well with nut oils—hazelnut and walnut—plus lemon juice and salty components such as capers and anchovies.

BELGIAN ENDIVE. Also known as witloof and chicon, a Belgian endive has a 4- to 5-inch-long pointed, compact, crunchy, white head with pale yellow tips and a bittersweet flavor. The whiter the head, the sweeter the flavor. Separate the leaves from the core or slice it into rounds and serve with darker pungent greens such as watercress and a fresh herb vinaigrette.

The following additions have the ability to punctuate a salad in a most unique way. And don't overlook a moderate dose of scallions, sweet red onions, and chives for additional punch:

You can add mild spinach, young Swiss chard, and beet greens, or peppery watercress. Or try the lemony arrow-shaped leaf called sorrel; slender, pleasantly bitter, saw-toothed dandelion leaves; or long, spiky-leafed, mustardy Japanese mizuna. Red mustard with oval green leaves veined with red will jolt the palette with only a few added leaves. Slivered raw cabbage, red, green, sweet Napa, and michihli (or celery cabbage) add unique flavor and texture to a salad. Or consider sprouts (radish, bean, or broccoli), fresh herbs (mint, basil, or parsley), edible blossoms (tangy nasturtium or arugula, as well as oniony purple chive blossoms or cucumber-flavored borage blossoms).

Mesclun

Mesclun is an eye-appealing, colorful assortment of an ever-changing seasonal selection of various vegetable and lettuce seedlings, sometimes including Asian greens. These are now ubiquitous on most restaurant menus all across the country. At times, mesclun is also strewn with fresh herbs and edible blossoms.

Mesclun is grown organically on any number of farms throughout the country. The Gourmet Garage stores sell something like fifteen hundred pounds of mesclun a week to their busy customers, who appreciate the convenience of buying a premixed salad. But be forewarned. There is no consistency. Some mesclun mixes are delightful, while others are tasteless and bland.

SHOP SMART

- ◆ It is obvious: Buy the freshest, crispiest salad greens, head or loose leaved. Avoid droopy, browning, or wilted leaves. At home, always try to clean them at once. That way they're cleaned and ready to use whenever you crave a salad or are in a typical rush before the guests arrive.
- ◆ As with most produce, the best way to choose the freshest greens is to use your eyes and nose. If the leaves are beginning to turn yellow or you detect even the beginning of a foul smell, the mesclun is not fresh and some rot has probably set in.

Allow 8 cups of loosely packed greens for four people.
For mesclun, allow about 2 ounces per person; 8 ounces should
serve four.

Notes for the Cook

ON SALADS . . .

- Trim and discard tough stems and all imperfect bits of green. Fill the sink or a large bowl with cold water and swish the greens around. Discard the water and any dirt, and repeat the process, rinsing any particularly dirty leaves under cold running water. Remember that curly leaves harbor more grit.
- After cleaning, remove and drain the greens in a salad spinner basket. Add only small amounts at a time and spin until dry, repeating until all the leaves are clean.
- We usually wrap them in layers of paper towels to get rid of excess moisture that might dilute the flavor of the dressing. Then we loosely roll the greens in dry paper towels, place them in a plastic bag, and store them in the vegetable crisper of the refrigerator.
- Dense or coarse greens such as head lettuce, frisée, and escarole keep longer (about four to five days). Mesclun and fragile loose-leaved varieties such as Boston should be eaten within two or three days.

SALAD DRESSING SAVVY

In its simplest form, a salad dressing is usually a vinaigrette consisting of oil and vinegar or some other acid such as lemon juice, plus salt and pepper. Sometimes an emulsifier such as mustard is added to bind them. With the further addition of an egg yolk, also an emulsifier, vinaigrette becomes mayonnaise. And from mayonnaise, sauces such as aioli, remoulade, and tartar can be compounded.

But all vinegars are not compatible with all oils. The best full-flavored extra-virgin olive oil, for example, may overwhelm a delicate fruit raspberry vinegar. On the other hand, the very same oil will sing when married to a mellow red wine or aged sherry vinegar. The ingredients for salad dressings are few and very simple—just oil, acid, mustard, salt, and pepper. Yet making a vinaigrette has always seemed to be part chemistry and part alchemy, for the permutations are infinite.

OILS

We usually categorize oils as either salad oils or cooking oils. At times, however, there is a crossover, and some oils are used for both purposes.

OLIVE OIL. The preferred oil for most salads, olive oil is produced from over fifty different olive varieties. The local conditions of soil and sun will affect the quality of the olive, but more particularly, how the oil is extracted and processed has a great deal to do with the final product—its color, flavor, and aroma.

EXTRA-VIRGIN OLIVE OIL. This is made from the first pressing of top-quality olives, picked at the peak of ripeness; the best are produced entirely by hand by small producers. The olives are crushed into a thick paste and pressed in a manually operated cold stone press. It is then filtered but kept unrefined. Extra-virgin is clear and has a range of greenish tones, with the deeper colors more intensely flavored. It can be full and fruity with a peppery edge.

VIRGIN AND PURE OLIVE OILS. These are two lesser grades, both containing a higher percentage of acidity than the extra-virgin. They are the result of extractions of damaged olives and sometimes represent a second or third pressing of the same olives. In addition, high-powered machinery is used, and the olives are frequently treated with heat or chemicals, impairing their quality and diluting their flavor. Since they are cheaper to produce, they sell for less than extra-virgin. Olive oil labeled *pure* has a high smoking point—the temperature at which the oil breaks down chemically and begins to smoke over high heat—and thus is quite acceptable for sautéeing and frying.

SHOP SMART

Some very fine extra-virgin olive oil comes from Spain, which is the world's largest producer. Italy has promoted their oil so aggressively that we tend to seek out the Italian oils while overlooking the wonderful ones from both Spain and Greece. A label that reads "Imported from Italy" only means it was shipped from that country but might well be Spanish or Greek in origin. "Produced in" or "Product of" denotes that it was made and imported from that country.

NUT OILS. The best nut oils for salads are the costly, lightly toasted virgin hazelnut and walnut oils, which are cold-pressed and unrefined. They are very flavorful and can be used in combination with more neutral flavored oils such as canola and safflower. Peanut oil is produced and sold in two ways: unrefined, to be used for salads, and as a mass-produced refined cooking oil with a good (400-degree) smoking point. Try nut oils with pungent or slightly bitter greens such as mizuna and arugula.

SEED AND VEGETABLE OILS. Safflower, sunflower, sesame seed, pumpkin seed, grape seed, and canola (rape) seed are the oils that range from very light and neutral in flavor (canola and safflower) to heavier, with very distinct flavor (sesame, sunflower, and pumpkin seed). They are used for both salads and for cooking. Sesame oil can be overpowering unless used judiciously. It can be very distinctive in salad dressings, however, when about one teaspoon is added to a bland oil such as canola.

Other products labeled "vegetable oil" may be one oil or a blend of several. Check the labels.

Notes for the Cook

ON OILS . . .

- ◆ Keep all oils in a cool, dark place in a closed bottle. If kept on the kitchen counter, it should be in a dark bottle since light fades the color.
- ◆ Refrigerate oils only if you live in a very hot climate or if it is in an open bottle. The cloudiness that occurs during refrigeration will dissipate when the oil is brought to room temperature.

VERSATILE VINEGARS

Vin-aigre is French for sour wine, but it is not only wine that sours into vinegar. All sorts of fermented liquids—from grains, from fruits such as raspberries and apples, from molasses, and even from ale and beer—can be turned into vinegars by the activity of "good" bacteria that turn the liquid into a solution called acetic acid. It is the percent of this acid that denotes the sourness of the vinegar.

Primary fermentation results in an alcohol product such as Spanish sherry. After the second fermentation, the alcohol magically disappears and the result becomes sherry vinegar. The flavors of vinegar are infinite, and good vinegars, like wine, can be used fresh and young or aged, full, and round. Vinegar is an essential ingredient for vinaigrettes, pickles, marinades, numerous sweet-and-sour dishes, and mustard.

WINE VINEGAR: This can be made from fermented red and white wines as well as from champagne and sherry. Sherry vinegar, which is aged in wooden casks, possesses the most character of this class, becoming smoother the longer it ages. Red and white vinegars vary greatly in intensity and degree of sharpness; the reds seem rougher, although their degree of acidity is the same as the white. Champagne vinegars, to our taste, are very delicate but too costly for what they offer in the way of flavor.

VERJUS: The pressed juice obtained from red or white unripe grapes has been used for hundreds of years by cooks in the Middle East and Europe. Unlike vinegar, it is sweet, slightly tart, and very mildly acidic. It is perfect for anyone allergic to anything fermented.

BALSAMIC VINEGAR: Created from the juice of the Trebbiano grape, boiled down to a dark brown, syrupy consistency, and aged in a series of barrels made from different kinds of wood, the best balsamic vinegar is produced in Modena, Italy. By law it must be aged at least ten years, but we have been told that some rare balsamics have been aged as much as one hundred years. They cost a substantial amount and are treasured as much as fine vintage wines. For the average consumer, however, there are two grades of balsamic vinegar:

1 *Tradizionale* bears the *consorzio's* seal and is a highly concentrated, tart-sweet, mellow vinegar that must be used in very small amounts. Try a splash over ripe strawberries as the Italians do.

2. *Industriale* grade is produced like a speeded-up movie version of the real thing. It is quickly produced and then aged for five to twenty years. It is a lot less costly and is quite acceptable for sauces and salads. It can be used liberally.

DISTILLED WHITE VINEGAR: This harsh, colorless, acidic product is used for pickling.

APPLE CIDER VINEGAR: A tart, pale caramel–colored vinegar with a haunting apple taste, apple cider vinegar is particularly good with cabbage slaws and salads with smoked meats. It is also used as a base for flavored vinegars with the addition of berries, herbs, or garlic.

ASIAN RICE VINEGAR: A clean, mild, mellow, slightly sweet vinegar made from either fermented rice or rice wine in a range of colors from clear to dark, it's usually diluted with water and is an excellent gentle vinegar for salads when great olive oil is to be the star attraction.

CITRUS: Fresh citrus juices—lemon, orange, grapefruit, and lime—are being used increasingly in place of vinegars. They can be combined with vinegar for another taste dimension.

CUTTING THE MUSTARD

The great Greek physician Hippocrates gave lavish praise to the power of mustard back in 460 B.C. It was probably because a strong mustard can make your eyes run and clear your sinuses. Today it is the most popular condiment on the shelves of the market, available in both prepared and powder form.

When the mustard seed is crushed, the intense flavors of the volatile essential oils are released and then mixed with a liquid such as water, verjus, wine, or vinegar to tame their intensity.

The chart on page 185 should help you Shop Smart for some major culinary fireworks.

Notes for the Cook

ON SALAD DRESSINGS . . .

- We use only the finest extra-virgin olive oil and French unrefined walnut oil in our vinaigrettes.
- If the dressing is to be used immediately, a whisking of the ingredients to form an emulsified vinaigrette is fine. However, most vinaigrettes will have to be rewhisked before spooning them on the salad.
- We prefer using an electric blender, which results in a more stable emulsion with the consistency of a thin mayonnaise. It also takes less effort.
- We usually refrigerate vinaigrette; it keeps nicely for a week to ten days. If anything, the flavors will mellow in a day or two. If fresh herbs are used in the vinaigrette, use it within three or four days and bring it to room temperature before using.
- Allow about 1½ tablespoons of dressing per person—or a bit more or less to your own taste. Add just a little at first, taste a leaf of lettuce, and then adjust the amount until it pleases you.

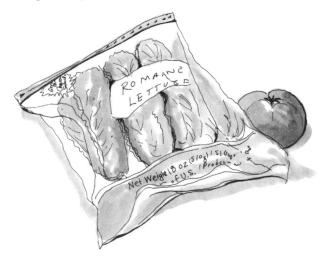

CUTTING THE MUSTARD

TYPE	DESCRIPTION	USES
AMERICAN STYLE ◆ Hot Dog ◆ Delicatessen	"Hot dog," the classic bright yellow mustard, is colored with turmeric. Smooth, mild, and sweet. Delicatessen mustard is coarser in texture and somewhat spicier. Both are made from ground seeds, vinegar, sugar, and spices.	Hot dogs (naturally) and sandwiches
DIJON AND DIJON STYLE	Authentic type produced only in Dijon, France, with laws strictly regulating use of only black or brown seeds. Made from ground seeds, vinegar, white wine, and herbs and range from mild to hot. Some are flavored with tarragon, green peppercorns, and a variety of other ingredients. Other mustards are called "Dijon Style" and contain other additives.	Most versatile of the mustards. Used in vinaigrettes and with steak, beef, and charcuterie.
ENGLISH (Powder)	Smooth, pasty, hot, and, to the nose, tweaking hot. Made with powder and hulls, flour and spices, and can be blended to your own instructions. Add tepid water to powder, stir, and let sit 10 minutes. You can also add wine or vinegar.	For deviled eggs, salad dressings, and cold roast beef.

TYPE	DESCRIPTION	USES
GERMAN STYLE ◆ BAVARIAN ◆ DUSSELDORF	Bavarian is a dark, sweet, mild mustard containing a few seeds and some husks. Dusseldorf is creamy with a flavor range of savory mild to sharp.	With smoked meats, sausages, and ham.
GRAINY MUSTARD	An ancient variety, dating back to Roman times. Sometimes sold as *moutarde de Meaux*. Made from coarsely bruised and crushed seeds with hulls mixed with verjus or vinegar. Texture and spiciness vary according to the procedure.	For flavor and texture in sauces, sausages, and sandwiches.
ASIAN	Prepared from a variety of black seeds called *Juncia L.* and best made fresh from powder (as with English mustard). Fiery, hot, potent, and smooth. It gets tamer as it ages.	With Asian foods.
SWEET MUSTARDS ◆ SWEDISH ◆ BAVARIAN ◆ HONEY MUSTARD	The Swedish and Bavarian styles are sweetened with sugar, corn syrup, or honey. Along with the newly popular honey mustard, they have the consistency of honey. Some are overly sweet; some are labeled "sweet-hot."	Excellent with smoked meats such as ham. Or added to salad dressings.

VINAIGRETTE WITH GARLIC AND ANCHOVY

This basic vinaigrette has just a touch of anchovy, and cheese makes a nice addition.

MAKES ⅔ CUP

> **Try with:**
>
> 1. **Romaine, tomatoes, cucumber, scallions, black olives, oregano, and mint with feta cheese.**
> 2. **Arugula and endive with diced apples and walnuts and Gorgonzola**
> 3. **Radicchio, sliced and grilled Portobello mushrooms with shaved Parmesan**

2 tablespoons red wine vinegar
1 tablespoon dry white wine
1 medium clove garlic, roughly cut
½ teaspoon Dijon mustard
4 flat anchovies, rinsed, dried, and
    chopped coarsely

Pinch of sugar
Pepper to taste
¼ cup olive oil
Salt if necessary

In a blender, combine the vinegar, wine, garlic, mustard, anchovies, sugar, and pepper, and blend until smooth. Add the olive oil and blend until an emulsion forms. Taste for salt and add if necessary.

Note: Add 2 ounces of crumbled Gorgonzola or Feta, or shaved
Parmesan if you wish just before serving.

ROASTED RED PEPPER VINAIGRETTE WITH CUMIN

A gorgeous, deep salmon–colored vinaigrette that looks smashing trickled over some of the salads we've listed below.

MAKES 1⅓ CUPS

Try with:

1. **Endive, watercress, and hearts of palm over green frilled lettuce.**
2. **Blanched asparagus and chopped hard-cooked egg on Bibb lettuce.**
3. **Torn romaine topped with grilled chorizo and shaved Spanish manchego cheese.**

---

1 large shallot, roughly cut
1 medium clove garlic
6½-ounce jar roasted red peppers or
   pimiento, drained
2 tablespoons white wine vinegar
1 tablespoon lemon juice
   (½ small lemon)

⅛ teaspoon cayenne pepper or
   to taste
1½ teaspoons ground cumin
Salt and pepper to taste
⅓ cup olive oil

Place the shallot, garlic, and red peppers in an electric blender and blend well. Add the vinegar, lemon juice, cayenne, cumin, salt, and pepper, and blend again. Add the olive oil and blend until an emulsion forms. Scrape out with a rubber spatula into a container and let stand for 30 minutes before using to allow the flavors to blend. If necessary, whisk just before using. Will keep about 7 to 10 days.

TOMATO AND BASIL VINAIGRETTE

A lovely, pale pink dressing that is fragrant with fresh basil.

MAKES 1 CUP

> **Try with:**
>
> 1. **Arugula, red onion, white beans, and shrimp.**
> 2. **Sliced mozzarella and roasted yellow peppers over mesclun. Top with a few additional basil leaves.**
> 3. ***Haricots verts* and wheat berry salad on a bed of frisée.**

¾ cup diced tomato (1 large) or
   ¾ cup tomato juice
½ cup roughly torn and loosely packed
   basil leaves
1 tablespoon aged sherry vinegar

1 tablespoon lemon juice
   (½ small lemon)
A few drops of Tabasco
Salt and pepper to taste
⅓ cup olive oil

In an electric blender, blend the tomato and add the basil or puree the tomato juice and basil. Add the vinegar, lemon juice, Tabasco, salt, and pepper, and blend. Add the olive oil and blend until emulsified.

DOUBLE WALNUT VINAIGRETTE
WITH SHALLOTS

The intensity of the walnut oil is tamed a bit with neutral-tasting canola oil. Crunchy, toasted walnuts pick up the flavor again in a different manner.

MAKES ABOUT ¾ CUP

Try with:

1. **Mesclun greens and Bibb or Boston lettuce.**
2. **Radicchio, endive, and shredded pears.**
3. **Mizuna, red mustard leaves, and shredded romaine with crumbled Roquefort cheese.**

½ cup walnuts
2 teaspoons finely minced shallot
   (1 medium)
2 tablespoons aged sherry vinegar
1 tablespoon lemon juice (about
   ½ lemon)

1 heaping teaspoon Dijon mustard
Salt and pepper to taste
4 tablespoons French walnut oil
4 tablespoons canola oil

Preheat the oven to 425 degrees and toast the walnuts for 5 minutes. When cool, break them coarsely and set aside. Place the shallot, vinegar, lemon juice, mustard, salt, and pepper in an electric blender and combine (or use a whisk). Add both oils and blend again. After adding the dressing to the salad, top with the walnuts.

Fresh Legumes:
Peas and Beans, Green and Gorgeous

FRESH PEAS

Piselli con Orecchietti

Sugar Snap Peas, Sweet, Hot, and Crisp

Snow Peas, Tofu, and Chinese Mushrooms in a Ginger-Cilantro Broth

FRESH BEANS

Stewed Yellow Wax Beans with Tomatoes, Garlic, and Mint (Greek Style)

Haricots Verts with Shiitake Mushrooms and Shallots

Fresh Cranberry Beans with Rosemary, Tomatoes, and Prosciutto

Fresh Fava Beans, Baby Artichokes, and Peas

Fresh Lima Beans with Whole Hominy (A Different Kind of Succotash)

FRESH PEAS

Many Americans are completely unfamiliar with the incomparably delicious sweet flavor of the fresh garden pea in its own pod. Because the season is fleeting and shelling peas takes time, we have become used to eating frozen, canned, or dried peas. And yet there are few tasks as rewarding as the pleasantly time-consuming one of shelling fresh peas.

Peas and beans are part of the legume family; legumes are nothing more than a bean or a pea in a pod in various stages of maturity or immaturity. The ancients grew peas, beans, and lentils to full maturity, then harvested and dried them to survive both winters and long periods of famine. We still do the same today, though perhaps not for the same reasons. In the 1500s, tender varieties of fresh garden shelling peas were developed by the Italians after they arrived in Venice via the Chinese silk route. They were then taken to France where the status of the humble pea rose considerably as the French court of Louis XIV popularized fresh peas in eating orgies.

Thomas Jefferson is said to have grown fifty varieties of peas, all with their own special qualities, but in the United States today they are mostly grown for canning and freezing. Many lovely fresh-in-the-pod varieties were deemed unsuitable for processing and have been phased out.

SHOP SMART

There are two major categories of peas: shelling peas and edible pod peas:

1. *Shelling peas* are also known as garden peas, English peas, and green peas. French *petit pois* are baby peas (which are also available frozen). Canned Peas are *ugh!*
   - It's best to buy them in their pods. Buy pods that are bright, light green, shiny, and amply filled. They can be large or small depending on the variety.
   - Peas are highly perishable since their high sugar content begins to turn to starch from the moment they are picked, very much like corn.
   - Sample the contents of one pod to judge its freshness and maturity. The best ones are sweet and tender. Do not buy flat, dark green pods—they're immature—or pods that are crammed to the bursting point since they are usually tough and too large. The latter can be used for purees.

   One pound of whole garden peas = 4 cups and will yield about 1 cup of shelled peas (depending on size).

2. *Edible pod peas* are also known as *mange tout.*
   - *Snow peas* (Chinese snow peas). These are the flat, slightly limp, dull green pods that contain very immature "embryo" peas. They are eaten before the peas grow and swell. They're available year-round, but the best are in the market in the fall and spring.

   Eight ounces is a generous amount for four. Usually only a few pods are added to stir-fry dishes.

   - *Sugar Snap Peas.* This variety was developed only about ten years ago. With full, round, fully edible pods, they are bright green and plump but not quite ready to pop.

Notes for the Cook

ON SHELLING PEAS . . .

- Ideally, use shelling peas immediately. If you must store them, keep them in their pods in a plastic bag to retain their moisture and shell them just before cooking.
- To shell, twist the stem, pry open, and run your finger down the inside of the pod's spine. The peas will pop out.

◆ Fresh peas should be cooked in only enough boiling salted water to cover for about 5 minutes. Some cooks add a pinch of sugar and a pat of butter while cooking.

SHOP SMART

Buy bright green, small pods for sweetness. Some varieties are stringless, so test one first. Snip off the stem ends and zip off the string if it has one. They are best when crisp.

Notes for the Cook

ON EDIBLE POD PEAS . . .

◆ With snow peas, strings must be removed after washing. Just pull off the stem end and zip off the string. They are best blanched in boiling water for 2 minutes.

◆ Try wrapping a blanched snow pea around a scallop or shrimp for an hors d'oeuvre.

◆ Sugar snap peas are blanched the same as snow peas—for about 2 minutes in boiling water. Or you can eat them raw—they're great!

◆ For a quick, salty-sweet treat, wind a string of Syrian string cheese around a blanched sugar snap pea.

FRESH BEANS

Growers have developed many varieties of beans—some to be consumed young and fresh, others to be grown to maturity, dried, and stored. As with peas, there are two basic categories for fresh beans: snap beans, to be eaten whole (such as string bean), and shell beans (such as lima or fava).

Snap Beans

GREEN BEAN: (Also known as snap bean, string bean, or green bean). These are the common everyday green string beans, although now there are varieties that are mostly stringless. The young, slender green bean, called *haricot vert*, has become the darling of chefs and home cooks because of its sweetness and elegance on the plate.

YELLOW WAX BEAN: A bright, lemony yellow bean, it is preferred in the eastern and southern United States as well as in the Mediterranean area. It has a less grassy, more delicate taste than the green bean, but it looks lovely when mixed with its green cousin.

PURPLE PODDED BEAN: Similar in flavor to the green bean, it has either a purple or mottled green-purple color that gets lost when cooked. It is best to buy these young and serve them raw in salads so that the color remains.

ITALIAN SNAP BEAN: (Also known as Romano beans). These beans need stringing. They're broader and rather flatter than the others, and they come in yellow or green. They have an excellent flavor.

YARD-LONG BEAN: These are indeed almost three feet long. They're narrow and very dark green, and they're popular in Asia, where they are usually diced and added to stir-fry dishes. The taste is intense and elusive.

SHOP SMART

- Buy crisp, bright, unblemished beans the year round, although peak season is between May and August.
- Store them in plastic bags in the refrigerator for no more than three or four days.

One pound of untrimmed beans = 4 cups.

Notes for the Cook

ON SNAP BEANS . . .

- Trim and slice them diagonally for an attractive appearance and cook them minimally to retain their color and slight crisp texture. It takes about 3 minutes in boiling salted water or 2 to 3 minutes for steaming.

Fresh Shell Beans

These are the beans that have dual uses: They can be shelled and eaten fresh and young, or they can be left on the vine to mature. They are then dried, stored, and reconstituted in water before cooking. Although there are virtually thousands of different dried varieties, there are three popular and easily attainable shell beans, starting in late spring and running into the fall.

CRANBERRY BEAN: (Also known as shell bean or shellout.) A gorgeous bean with a mottled cream and cranberry shell, once opened it reveals the same color bean within. It is a popular and delicate, buttery-textured bean that is used extensively in Mediterranean cuisines.

FAVA BEAN: (Also known as horse bean and broad bean.) This ancient bean has been found dried in archaeological sites in the lake area of Switzerland, giving evidence that it was one of the earliest cultivated European beans. It is still favored in Europe as a spring harbinger. The young beans are shelled, skinned, and eaten raw as a snack, dipped in salt or olive oil.

Fava beans are quite large, anywhere from 5 to 8 inches long, and have shiny, bright green pods.

Two and one-half pounds in the shell = 3 cups of shelled beans with
their skins on—or 1¾ cups of skinned beans.

LIMA BEAN: (Also known as butter bean.) Sometimes called "summer beans" because they are available locally only in late summer or a little earlier when grown in a hot climate, they are originally from Peru and got their name from the capital city. They grow on bushes and vines, and the beans, when shelled, vary greatly in size. The large fresh ones are usually called *fordhook limas*; the smaller ones are sometimes called *butter beans* in certain regions of the country. The pods are lumpy, flat, pliable, and pale smoky green. It is easy to remove the bean from the pod—just snap off the stem end and pull down the string to open it.

When lima beans are young, they are delicate, sweet, have a buttery texture, and can be quickly cooked. When they are past their prime, they're mealy and starchy and require longer cooking time. They are also sold shelled and frozen as both "baby" limas and "large" limas to stretch the short season. (They are also sold canned; once again: *ugh!*)

One and one-half pounds = 1 cup shelled beans.

SHOP SMART

As with snap beans, buy shell beans that are bright and unblemished, and keep them in a plastic bag in the refrigerator for no more than 3 or 4 days.

Notes for the Cook

ON FAVA BEANS . . .

◆ Double-shell the beans by opening the pod to remove the bean and then slit the skin with a fingernail and peel off the pale skin, revealing a bright green, meaty treasure. The skins are bitter, though some people eat them. We prefer the beans skinned. Just add the beans to boiling salted water, and when the water returns to a boil, the beans need only 5 to 10 minutes of cooking (depending on size). Bite-test one for desired doneness.

◆ We sometimes prefer them raw on a languid summer day, peeled right at the table and accompanied by a glass of white wine.

Fava Beans

PISELLI CON ORECCHIETTI

In Italy the peas are harvested very early—when they are at their smallest and sweetest and called piselli, *the equivalent of the French* petits pois. *Here they are frozen when still that small, thus becoming a time-saving year-round treat. Many times these quick-frozen peas are actually much sweeter than the older fresh peas still in their pods in the supermarket.*

SERVES 4

12 ounces dried orecchietti or
    conchigliette pasta
2 ounces finely diced prosciutto
2 tablespoons olive oil
⅔ cup finely chopped onion
    (1 medium onion)
1 teaspoon finely minced garlic
    (1 large clove)
1 cup chicken broth

2 pounds shelled fresh green peas
    (about 2 cups shelled) or one and
    one-half 10-ounce packages tiny
    frozen peas, thawed
1 tablespoon butter
2 teaspoons finely minced fresh mint
2 tablespoons finely minced parsley
Salt and pepper to taste
⅓ cup freshly grated Parmesan

Bring a large pot of salted water to a boil. Add the pasta and cook until slightly al dente. In a 12-inch skillet, sauté the prosciutto and olive oil over medium heat, stirring, for 1 or 2 minutes. Add the onion and garlic, and sauté until wilted, stirring occasionally. Add the chicken broth and bring to a boil. Add the peas, lower the heat, and cover the pan. Cook for 2 or 3 minutes for frozen peas, about 5 minutes for fresh peas—or only until tender. Don't overcook.

Drain the pasta when cooked and toss it with the butter, then add it to the peas. Sprinkle with mint and parsley. Season to taste, adding lots of black pepper, and toss it again. Transfer to a large serving platter and sprinkle with the cheese. Toss again at the table just before serving.

SUGAR SNAP PEAS, SWEET, HOT, AND CRISP

This lively, refreshing salad mixture is marvelous with curry or grilled fish.

SERVES 4

1 cup sugar snap peas (about
   4 ounces)
2 small Kirby cucumbers (about
   8 ounces)
2 cups cubed fresh pineapple, cut into
   ¾-inch cubes (see page 390 on how
   to peel)
2 tablespoons lemon juice
   (1 medium lemon)

3 tablespoons rice wine vinegar
1 tablespoon plus 1 teaspoon sugar
½ teaspoon hot red pepper flakes
Salt to taste
4 large leaves radicchio or red frilled
   lettuce
1 tablespoon coarsely chopped mint
   leaves

String the sugar snap peas and blanch in boiling water for 1 minute. Drain and refrigerate. They will be added just before serving so they maintain their color. Trim the ends of the cucumbers, cut them lengthwise, and then lengthwise again. Cut into ¼-inch slices. Place in a nonreactive bowl and add the pineapple.

In a small cup, mix together the lemon juice, vinegar, sugar, hot pepper flakes, and salt. Pour over the cucumber mixture, stir, and let stand at room temperature for 1 hour. Just before serving, line a serving platter with the lettuce. Stir the sugar snap peas into the lemon juice mixture and spoon in the center of the platter. Scatter the mint on the surface.

SNOW PEAS, TOFU, AND CHINESE MUSHROOMS IN A GINGER-CILANTRO BROTH

Smoky, succulent mushrooms, tiny cubes of tofu, and jade green snow peas float in a rich cilantro broth spiked with fresh ginger. Although the mushrooms must soak for forty-five minutes or more, the soup takes only minutes to cook.

SERVES 4

8 large dried Chinese mushrooms (black forest shiitake) (about 2 ounces)

4 cups chicken broth

8 cilantro stems, tied up for easy removal

1 teaspoon light soy sauce

2 thin slices peeled ginger (the size of a quarter), thinly slivered (1 teaspoon)

4 ounces firm tofu, cut into ¼-inch dice

12 snow peas, strings removed

2 large scallions, green parts only, sliced diagonally in ½-inch pieces

1 to 2 tablespoons cilantro leaves

Rinse the mushrooms well and place in a small bowl. Bring 1 cup of the broth to a boil, and pour it over the mushrooms. Let them steep for 45 minutes, until the mushrooms are pliable. Remove the mushrooms and reserve the broth. Cut off and discard the stems and slice the caps thickly.

In a 3-quart saucepan, place the reserved mushroom broth and the remaining chicken broth. Add the mushrooms, cilantro stems, soy sauce, ginger, tofu, and snow peas. Simmer over low heat for about 1 or 2 minutes. Discard the cilantro stems. Ladle the soup into 4 bowls, add some scallions and cilantro leaves to each bowl, and serve.

STEWED YELLOW WAX BEANS WITH TOMATOES, GARLIC, AND MINT (GREEK STYLE)

In the traditional Greek way of preparing snap beans, they are simmered for a long time and are not colored as brightly as quickly cooked snap beans. But replacing the loss of color, the long cooking time revealed a new flavor depth. Using a heavy pot will prevent them from getting mushy and will give just a little bit of snap to the texture.

SERVES 4 TO 6

1 pound yellow wax beans or green snap beans
3 tablespoons olive oil
⅔ cup coarsely chopped onion (1 medium onion)
1 tablespoon coarsely chopped garlic (2 large cloves)
1 cup diced plum tomatoes (about 8 ounces)

1 tablespoon tomato paste
1 cup water
½ teaspoon dried oregano
Salt and pepper to taste
8 black pitted Kalamata olives or 2 ounces crumbled Feta cheese
1 tablespoon finely shredded mint leaves

Trim the ends of the beans and cut them diagonally into 1½- to 2-inch pieces (about 3 or 4 cups). In a heavy 5- to 6-quart Dutch oven, heat the oil over medium-low heat. Add the onion and garlic, and sauté for 4 or 5 minutes, stirring occasionally, until wilted but not brown. Add the beans and stir, then raise the heat to medium. Add the tomatoes, tomato paste, water, oregano, salt, and pepper, and bring to a boil. Turn the heat to low and simmer, uncovered, stirring occasionally, until the sauce has evaporated a bit and the beans are tender, about 25 minutes.

Spoon into a serving dish and scatter the olives or cheese and mint over the surface.

HARICOTS VERTS WITH
SHIITAKE MUSHROOMS AND SHALLOTS

Woodsy mushrooms and fragrant truffle-scented oil are in keeping with these slim, crisp, elegant beans.

SERVES 4 TO 6

1½ pounds *haricots verts,* stem ends trimmed diagonally and beans left whole with tiny tail intact

Salt and pepper to taste

2 tablespoons truffle oil

1 tablespoon butter

2 large shallots, thinly sliced crosswise and separated into rings

8 to 10 shiitake mushrooms (about 4 ounces), cleaned, stems discarded, and cut into halves

Large lemon wedge

In a 2½-quart saucepan, bring salted water to boil. Add the *haricots verts* and cook for 3 minutes, until crisp-tender. Drain and place on a serving platter. Season with salt and pepper, trickle truffle oil over, and toss to coat. Cover with aluminum foil to keep warm.

In a small skillet, melt the butter over medium heat. Add the shallots and mushrooms, and sauté, stirring constantly, until they just begin to color. Season with salt and pepper. Scatter over the beans, squeeze lemon juice over all, and serve.

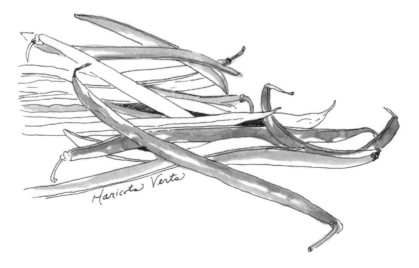

Haricots Verts

FRESH CRANBERRY BEANS WITH ROSEMARY, TOMATOES, AND PROSCIUTTO

When fresh cream-colored cranberry beans, veined with red, are in season, they provide the makings of this special classic Italian dish. We always cook some extra, and the next day we tuck in some grilled Italian sausage to serve over green fusilli pasta.

SERVES 6 TO 8

2 pounds fresh shelled cranberry beans
  (about 2½ cups)
6 cups water
Salt to taste
3 tablespoons olive oil
4 ounces prosciutto di Parma, cut into
  ¼-inch cubes
1 tablespoon coarsely chopped
  rosemary leaves (2 large sprigs)
1 tablespoon coarsely chopped garlic
  (2 or 3 large cloves)
3 tablespoons coarsely chopped
  shallots (3 large)

⅓ cup coarsely chopped onion
  (1 small onion)
½ cup coarsely diced celery
  (1 large stalk)
1 whole red dried hot chile such as
  Japonés
Black pepper to taste
¼ cup coarsely chopped parsley
¾ cup dry white wine
2 cups canned imported Italian plum
  tomatoes, cut in half (including
  liquid)

In a 3-quart saucepan, bring the beans and water to a boil over medium heat. Cover the pot, leaving the lid slightly ajar, turn the heat to low, and simmer until the beans are tender, about 40 minutes. Add salt to taste in the last 5 minutes of cooking.

While the beans are cooking, heat the oil in a 12-inch skillet over medium heat. Add the prosciutto and half of the rosemary, and cook, stirring, for 30 seconds. Add the garlic, shallots, onion, celery, chile, salt, pepper, and half of the parsley. Cook over medium-low heat, stirring occasionally, for 15 minutes. Raise the heat to medium-high, add the wine, bring to a boil, and cook for about 3 minutes. Add the tomatoes and liquid, and bring to a boil. Turn the heat to low and simmer for 15 minutes.

Keep the mixture in the skillet until the beans are tender, then drain the beans and add them to the tomato mixture. Stir in the remaining rosemary and parsley. Taste and add additional salt and pepper if you wish, remove the chile, and serve the beans hot.

FRESH FAVA BEANS, BABY ARTICHOKES, AND PEAS

In early March when spring begins in Italy, the market stalls are filled with artichokes, fava beans, and small fresh peas. Italy is not alone, for similar springtime dishes using these ingredients are found in Spain and Greece as well. What a way to celebrate the season!

SERVES 6

2 tablespoons olive oil

2 ounces prosciutto, cut in ¼-inch dice (about ⅓ cup)

6 medium scallions, white parts sliced crosswise (⅓ cup) and green parts cut diagonally in ¼-inch pieces (about 1 cup)

1 pound baby artichokes, 2 to 3 inches (about 12); see page 29 for preparation

1 tablespoon lemon juice (½ lemon)

Salt and pepper to taste

1 cup chicken broth

2½ pounds fresh fava beans, shelled and skinned (about 1¾ cups); see page 197

1 tablespoon fresh summer savory or 1 teaspoon dried

1 pound fresh shelling peas (about 1 cup), shelled, or 1 cup frozen defrosted peas

Heat the oil in a 5-quart Dutch oven over medium heat. When the oil is hot, add the prosciutto and sauté, stirring, for 1 minute. Add the white parts of the scallions and stir and sauté for 2 minutes. Add the artichoke hearts, lemon juice, salt, and pepper, and stir for 30 seconds to coat with oil. Add the chicken broth and bring to a boil. Add the fava beans, cover the pot, and turn the heat to medium-low. Cook for 12 to 15 minutes, until the artichoke hearts and the beans are tender.

Stir in the summer savory and peas, and simmer 3 to 5 minutes more. Stir in the green parts of the scallions, taste and add additional salt if you wish, and transfer to a serving dish.

FRESH LIMA BEANS WITH WHOLE HOMINY

(A Different Kind of Succotash)

This is not the traditional succotash of field corn and beans. Here, the intense corn flavor of hominy is combined with tender melt-in-the-mouth lima beans, mellowed with a bit of cream and perked with Tabasco.

SERVES 4 TO 6

About 2 cups shelled, fresh lima beans
   (2½ to 3 pounds in pod) or one
   10-ounce package frozen baby
   lima beans
1-pound can whole white or yellow
   hominy, rinsed and drained
3 tablespoons butter

¾ cup finely chopped onion
   (1 medium onion)
¾ cup finely chopped green pepper
   (1 medium)
⅔ cup heavy cream
⅛ to ¼ teaspoon Tabasco
Salt and pepper to taste

Place the beans in a 3-quart saucepan with salted water to cover and boil until tender. (Follow directions if frozen beans are used.) Drain and set the beans aside in a bowl, along with the hominy. Melt the butter slowly in a 10-inch skillet over medium heat. Add the onion and sauté for 2 minutes. Stir in the green pepper and cook, stirring occasionally, for 8 to 10 minutes, until wilted. Turn the heat to low, add the cream and Tabasco, and heat slowly until the cream bubbles around the edges. Do not boil. Season with salt and pepper, and stir in the reserved hominy and lima beans. Stir gently, cover, and warm over low heat for 5 to 8 minutes, stirring occasionally to coat the beans. Transfer to a shallow serving dish and serve hot.

Dried Beans: Legumes for All Seasons

Curried Red Lentil Soup with Yogurt and Mint

French Lentil Salad with Garlic Sausage

Cannellini Bean Gratin with Prosciutto and Gruyère Cheese

Flageolet Summer Soup with Fresh Herbs and Lemon

*Great Northern Beans and Tuna with Arugula,
Gingered Orange, and Red Onion*

Lima Beans and Mustard Greens

Although once considered a peasant food staple, the last few years have seen a renaissance of beans. This is partly due to the swing away from eating large amounts of meat and substituting healthful fiber-rich beans, grains, herbs, and vegetables.

Nearly every culture in the world offers basic dishes that take advantage of bean and grain combinations for a complete protein substitute: the rice and beans of the Caribbean, Mexico, and Latin America; the lentil and rice dishes of India; the pasta and beans of Italy, Greece, Spain, and Portugal; and the tofu (soybeans) and rice in Asia.

Beans have a versatility that is hampered only by lack of imagination, for they can be made into hors d'oeuvres and used in pancakes, gratins, soups, stews, and side dishes. They come in a kaleidoscopic range of colors, sizes, shapes, and patterns. Best of all, almost every type of bean is now on either supermarket or specialty shop shelves. Not only are the old-time standards available, but many "lost" heirloom beans are now appearing—old-fashioned varieties grown for generations on small family farms and particularly prized for their flavor. And many "hybrid" beans have now surfaced; some have been bred to resist disease and insects, or have been raised only for their individual beauty or flavor, such as calypso and appaloosa beans.

The imports have also burgeoned, such as the Greek *gigandes*; the *ful*, small Egyptian fava beans; as well as the *pardina*, tiny green lentils of Spain. The choice is really quite overwhelming, and what follows is but a mere sampling.

DRIED BEAN CHART

BEAN	CHARACTERISTICS	TRADITIONAL USES	AVAILABILITY
DRIED PEAS (WHOLE) (SPLIT)	Small, about 1/4 inch, with wrinkled skin. Round and greenish gray. Green and yellow. Yellow has a more intense flavor. Do not keep shape when cooked.	An acceptable substitute for fresh shell peas; has an earthier flavor. They are the "pease porridge" of the nursery rhyme. Dating to about 6000 B.C. the green is popular here as well as in Europe and Asia. The yellow is more popular with the Dutch, Germans, and Scandanavians. The flavors blend well with smoked ham and in soups.	Available everywhere.
BLACK AKA FRIJOLE NEGROS, TURTLE BEANS	Medium size, oval, matte black with small white line on ridge. Flavor is earthy and sweet, with a hint of mushrooms.	Basis for Brazil's national dish, feijoada, and Cuban black bean soup; also found in many Mexican dishes.	Dried and canned.
BLACK-EYED PEAS AKA BLACK-EYED SUZIES, SOUTHERN PEAS, CROWDER PEAS	Medium size, creamy white, kidney shaped, plump with dark purple circle on ridge. Robust with earthy, sweet flavor and buttery texture.	African and Indian dishes as well as southern U.S. and Caribbean. Hopping John of the South is a famous black-eyed pea and rice dish; it is eaten for luck on New Year's Day. The Maine yellow eye sometimes alternates with the black-eyed pea.	Dried and fresh in pod in summer. Also frozen and canned.

BEAN	CHARACTERISTICS	TRADITIONAL USES	AVAILABILITY
CHICKPEAS *AKA* GARBANZOS, CECI	Medium size, plump, and hard; looks like a fat baby chick. Full-bodied, nutty, rich flavor, reminiscent of chestnuts.	Widely used in India and the Middle East, ground into flour or pureed into *hummus*, a spread made with sesame paste, garlic, and lemon, or *falafel*, made of ground chick peas and spices and then fried like a fritter.	Dried and canned in various sizes.
CRANBERRY *AKA* ROMANS, BORLOTTI, OCTOBER BEANS, TONGUES OF FIRE; ALSO SHELLOUTS OR SHELLY BEANS	About ½ inch with dappled markings, similar to the *pinto* bean. Dark tan, plump, with wine stripes on tan background. Sweeter and more delicate than the pinto.	Used in New England for succotash and in the Middle East cooked with sweet spices, nutmeg, and cinnamon. In Italy they're eaten fresh from the pod or dried and used in many pastas, side dishes, and soups.	Dried and seasonally fresh in pods.
FAVA *AKA* BROAD BEANS, HORSE BEANS, WINDSOR BEANS, DAFFA BEANS, FUL (EGYPT)	Large oval shape, thicker on bottom. Light brown. Creamy texture and nutty flavor.	Dried variety used primarily by ethnic cooks—Middle Eastern, Italian, Spanish, Portuguese. The British, Italians, and increasingly more Americans eat them fresh.	Dried whole in skins or peeled and split. Fresh in pods in season. Also in cans and jars.

Name	Description	Use / History	Availability
LENTILS	Many varieties. Vary from flat, disk-shaped to plump. Green, brown, salmon, bright red or orange, and olive green. All are small and lens-shaped.	The recipes vary from continent to continent, with India being the champion, growing over 50 varieties. A common staple for 8,000 years: The first Roman cookbook, by Apicius, included a recipe with lentils and mussels or chestnuts or spices, herbs, and vinegar. It has been known as the "poor man's meat."	Dried, found in supermarkets, specialty stores, and ethnic markets in a wide range of colors. We lean toward the French green Le Puy.
LIMA *AKA* BURMA, RANGOON, MADAGASCAR, CHRISTMAS LIMAS, GRANDMA BEANS	3/4 to 1 inch long, creamy white with green tint. Christmas lima is slightly larger with maroon pattern on a cream background.	Used extensively in Africa, Central and South America. It was also a favorite of Native Americans who combined it with corn, becoming the popular colonial "succotash."	Fresh in pod, frozen, canned, and dried. Found everywhere.
BABY LIMAS *AKA* BUTTER BEANS, DIXIE SPECKLED, CALICO BEANS	About 1/2 inch, flat, thinner than large limas. It is not just a smaller version but comes from a separate category.	Used extensively in Africa, Central and South America. It was also a favorite of Native Americans who combined it with corn, becoming the popular colonial "succotash."	Fresh in pod, frozen, canned, and dried. Found everywhere.
PIGEON PEAS *AKA* GANDULES, GUNGA, LONGO, CONGO	1/4 inch long, plump, looks like a purse with an elongated eye on the flat cotyledon. Gray-yellow in color.	Used mostly in rice dishes in Hispanic communities.	Dried, canned, and fresh in pod when locally grown. Found in most supermarkets and ethnic stores.

BEAN	CHARACTERISTICS	TRADITIONAL USES	AVAILABILITY
PINK BEANS *AKA* PINQUITO	Smaller than pinto; resembles red bean	Used in most dishes that call for the pinto or small red bean, especially in the cuisines of the Southwest and Louisiana.	Dried or canned.
PINTO *AKA* APPALOOSA, RATTLESNAKE	Slightly smaller than kidney (about 1 inch); square or oval with a light buff background and a pink freckled pattern. Appaloosa are creamy white with black diagonal splotches. Rattlesnake are almost identical in color and shape to the pinto.	Native to South America, it is the staple ingredient in the cuisines of most Spanish-speaking countries as well as in our own Southwest. They turn pink when cooked and can be used as substitutes for the pink bean or kidney bean.	Pintos are found almost everywhere. Rattlesnake and appaloosa are hybrids and can be found in specialty stores and through mail order.
RED KIDNEY *AKA* MEXICAN, *HARICOTS ROUGES*, SPANISH *TOLASANAS*	Elongated, medium size. Gets its name from the kidney shape. Comes in deep reddish brown and light red. (See also the white kidney bean, called a *cannellini*, on page 213.)	Used for a great many Spanish and Mexican dishes. In the West Indies it is cooked with coconut milk, hot chile, and herbs.	Usually found dried or in cans. Available almost everywhere.

THE WHITE BEAN FAMILY

All the so-called white beans are from the New World and, along with pinto beans, red kidneys, lima beans, and black beans, were growing in the Western Hemisphere long before the conquistadores and other adventurers arrived. All of them sent back samples that would change the culinary habits of Europe. White kidney beans were brought to Italy in the sixteenth century and became an important crop in Tuscany. All the beans listed below are sometimes called haricot beans, derived from the mispronounced Aztec word ayacotl. They are available dried, fresh in the pod, or frozen. Most are carried in supermarkets or ethnic specialty stores.

BEAN	CHARACTERISTICS
ANASAZI	Closely resembling Jacob's cattle bean (see below) and believed to be its direct descendants, they are about ½ inch long and more plump than their relatives. The patterns are quite similar, but the anasazi has no freckles. They are still popular with the Indians of the Southwest and Mexico.
CALYPSO	A dramatic hybrid bean, round, plump, and about ½ inch long. Half white, half black, with one polka dot for emphasis, it could almost pass for the traditional Chinese yin and yang symbol.
CANNELLINI *AKA* WHITE KIDNEY, *HARICOTS BLANCS,* FAGIOLI	Kidney shaped, white, and with a tough seed coat. Though originally from South America, it is generally used in Europe. Has a robust flavor and creamy, rich texture. Also available in cans.

BEAN	CHARACTERISTICS
FLAGEOLETS	Probably the most expensive of all beans, they are cultivated mostly in Italy and France and then shipped back to us, where they originally came from (and thus are called the "Rolls-Royce of Beans"). Medium size, kidney shaped, and a pale green, they are actually the pod beans that have been harvested before maturity.
GREAT NORTHERN	Medium size, flattish, with a slight kidney shape and a bright white color.
JACOB'S CATTLE *AKA* COACH DOG, DALMATIAN	Heirloom beans that have been grown in New England since Colonial days. They are long (about 5/8 inch), slim, creamy white, and have a dark maroon-colored splotch and tiny freckles of the same color.
NAVY	Small (about 1/4 inch), plump, oval white beans. Also available in cans.
PEA *AKA* CALIFORNIA, SMALL WHITES	Very small, about half the size of the navy bean and can be used interchangeably in recipes. Also available in cans.
SOLDIER *AKA* RED EYE	An heirloom variety, many of them grown in Maine. There are splashes of color in the shape of a soldier's silhouette at the eye of the bean. Kidney shaped, chalk white, they are about 5/8 inch long.
STEUBEN YELLOW-EYES	Probably the original bean used for Boston baked beans. They're white with an amber eye that covers almost half the surface of the bean.

AND FINALLY: THE SOYBEAN

Perhaps one of the most versatile of the entire family, soybeans were cultivated by the Chinese as far back as 2800 B.C. However, they are generally not used whole partly because they require a minimum of twelve hours of soaking plus another four for cooking. And they are difficult to digest. But the range of processed soybean foods is quite overwhelming, many of them on our kitchen shelves: Chinese soy sauce, shoyu, tamari, miso, tofu, tempeh, milk, flour, oil, and sprouts. We even find soy listed as an ingredient in veggie burgers, imitation cheese, and margarine.

SHOP SMART

- ◆ Buy dried beans where the turnover of stock is continuous, which is the best way to ensure freshness. Beans planted in the spring and harvested, dried, and sold the same year are called current crop. They are the brightest-colored, freshest-tasting beans that have the most moisture and thus have the shortest soaking and cooking time.
- ◆ Buy see-through packages that allow you to see the beans' bright colors. Packages are not dated. If the color is dull, the beans are probably old, and even after long soaking and cooking, they will probably remain tough.
- ◆ Use beans within a few months. Store them in airtight containers to prevent additional loss of moisture.
- ◆ Beans should be uniform in size for best timing when cooking. And they should not be shriveled, cracked, or broken.
- ◆ Beans bought in bulk from burlap sacks may contain more field debris and foreign matter such as twigs and pebbles.
- ◆ The convenience of cooked, canned, and processed beans cannot be overlooked as a time saver. Brands vary, so experiment until you find one you prefer. Remember to drain and rinse the canned beans before using.

BEAN MATH

When using cooked or canned beans, and the recipe is given in dry weight or measurement, use this formula for adjustment:

One pound of dried beans = 2¼ cups, or 5 to 6 cups cooked.
One cup dried beans = 2½ to 3 cups cooked.

One 15-ounce can of cooked beans = 1¾ cups.
Two 15-ounce cans = 3½ cups cooked or the equivalent of a bit more
than 1 cup of dried beans. Either will serve about four to six people.

Notes for the Cook

ON BEANS . . .

◆ Before cooking, spread the beans out on a jelly roll pan and carefully look them over. Discard any broken bits, small pebbles, or other debris. Rinse and soak them to return the moisture lost through drying. After soaking and cooking, dried beans will double in weight and volume. Soaking shortens the cooking time, prevents the skins from bursting before they become tender enough to eat, and helps break down and leach out the indigestible complex sugars called oligosaccharides that may cause intestinal rumblings.

◆ During soaking, some beans called "floaters" may rise to the surface and should be skimmed off.

◆ Split peas and lentils do not require soaking before cooking.

◆ Standard instructions call for soaking overnight, but experience tells us that a 4- to 8-hour soak is acceptable. The short-soak method is also a time saver. Put the picked-over, washed beans in a large saucepan, add tepid water to cover the beans by 2 to 3 inches, and bring slowly to a boil over medium-high heat. Lower the heat to a simmer for two minutes, then turn it off, cover the pan, and let the beans soak for 1 hour. When using either the long or short method, discard the soaking water when done.

◆ For stove-top cooking (after soaking) add fresh tepid water to the beans—about 6 to 8 cups per pound—and make sure they are always covered by 2 inches of water during cooking. Add more boiling water as needed. Use a heavy pot, bring slowly to a boil, then reduce the heat and let the beans simmer, covered (or with pot lid ajar to prevent boilovers), until tender. Size, variety of bean, and how you plan to use them will determine the length of cooking time—anywhere from 20 to 90 minutes. As a rule, the longest cooking time (1 to 1½ hours) will be required for Great Northern beans, pinto beans, and chick peas; the shortest time (20 minutes) will be needed for lentils and split peas; and about 30 minutes will be fine for thin-skinned beans such as black-eyed peas.

◆ Salt and acidic ingredients—such as tomatoes, wine, molasses, vinegar, and lemon juice—will inhibit water penetration; if added at the beginning of the cooking time, the beans may toughen. Add these ingredients when the beans are already tender, toward the last part of the cooking time. Bite one for tenderness, adjust the seasoning as needed, and let them sit off the heat for the flavors to meld. Beans improve in both flavor and texture when cooked one day in advance.

◆ Of course, beans can be baked in the oven, precooked on the stove and then baked, or prepared in a pressure cooker. There are several books on pressure cooking that cover the subject in detail.

CURRIED RED LENTIL SOUP WITH YOGURT AND MINT

A mildly spiced, silky soup the color of saffron and very quick to prepare.

SERVES 4 TO 6

1 cup dried, peeled, and split red lentils, picked over and washed

3 cups water

2 tablespoons olive oil

1 teaspoon coarsely chopped garlic (1 large clove)

¾ cup coarsely chopped onion (1 medium onion)

1 teaspoon each ground cumin, ground coriander, and ground turmeric

¼ teaspoon each ground cardamom, cayenne pepper, and ground cinnamon

⅛ teaspoon ground cloves

Salt and pepper to taste

3 cups chicken or vegetable broth

1 cup plain yogurt

2 tablespoons coarsely chopped mint

In a 2-quart saucepan, bring the lentils and water to a boil over medium-high heat. Turn the heat to low and simmer for 10 minutes. Set aside.

In an 8-inch skillet, heat the oil and sauté the garlic and onion over medium heat, stirring frequently, for about 5 minutes. Combine all the dry spices in a small bowl and add them to the onion mixture. Continue to sauté, stirring, for 1 minute, then add this mixture to the lentils. Transfer to a blender and puree. Add the puree to a 5-quart Dutch oven along with the broth. Bring to a simmer over low heat and simmer for 5 minutes. Taste to adjust the seasoning. Ladle into bowls and top with a dollop of yogurt and some mint.

FRENCH LENTIL SALAD WITH GARLIC SAUSAGE

The delicious, mottled dark green French lentils have a slightly natural spicy flavor. With the addition of vegetables, a bit of garlic sausage, and some chèvre, this typical French bistro classic is great picnic fare and perfect for a buffet since it doesn't go limp or wilt.

SERVES 6 TO 8

1 ¼ cups dried French green lentils, picked over and washed
1 small onion, stuck with 1 whole clove
1 small carrot
1 small stalk celery
Bouquet garni: 3 sprigs parsley, 3 sprigs thyme, 1 bay leaf, 4 whole black peppercorns
Salt to taste
2 tablespoons olive oil
1 teaspoon finely minced garlic (1 small clove)
⅔ cup finely minced onion (1 small onion)
½ cup finely chopped celery (1 stalk)

½ cup finely chopped carrot (1 medium carrot)
1 tablespoon lemon juice (½ medium lemon)
Black pepper to taste
2 tablespoons red wine vinegar
6 tablespoons walnut oil
4 ounces kielbasa or andouille sausage, cut into ½-inch dice (about 1 cup)
Red frilled lettuce leaves
4 ounces chèvre cheese, crumbled
2 tablespoons finely minced parsley
½ cup small black olives, such as Niçoise or nyons

In a 5-quart Dutch oven, place the lentils, onion, carrot, and celery stalk. Cover with cold water and bring to a boil over medium-high heat. Add the bouquet garni, lower the heat, and simmer for 20 to 30 minutes, or until the lentils are tender but still maintain their shape. Add salt during the last 10 minutes of cooking.

Remove the vegetables and bouquet garni with tongs and discard. Drain the lentils well, transfer to a large bowl, and set aside.

While the lentils are simmering, heat the olive oil in a 10-inch nonstick skillet over medium heat. Add the garlic, onion, celery, and carrot. Sauté for 5 minutes, stirring frequently. Season with salt and pepper, then stir into the cooked and drained lentils.

Place the lemon juice and vinegar in a small bowl and slowly whisk in the walnut oil. Pour the mixture over the lentils and vegetables while they are still warm. Taste for additional salt and pepper, and stir gently to combine. Cover tightly with plastic wrap and let stand for 30 minutes. Add the kielbasa and adjust the seasoning if needed. Line serving plates with a few lettuce leaves. Spoon the lentils on and garnish each with some chèvre, parsley, and black olives. Serve at room temperature.

CANNELLINI BEAN GRATIN WITH PROSCIUTTO AND GRUYÈRE CHEESE

SERVES 6

5 tablespoons olive oil

½ cup finely chopped onion
(1 small onion)

⅓ cup finely diced carrot (1 small carrot)

¼ cup finely diced celery (1 small stalk)

5 whole peeled garlic cloves

4 sprigs thyme, tied together

1 cup dried cannellini beans, soaked and drained

4 cups water

Salt and pepper to taste

1 cup diced plum tomatoes (about 3 large tomatoes)

2 ounces prosciutto, cut into ½-inch dice (about ¼ cup)

¼ cup finely chopped parsley

1 cup freshly made coarse bread crumbs (preferably sourdough)

½ cup grated Gruyère cheese

Heat 2 tablespoons of the olive oil in a 3-quart oven-to-table casserole. Add the onion, carrot, celery, and garlic, and cook, stirring frequently, over medium-low heat for 5 minutes, until the vegetables are wilted but not brown. Add the thyme, soaked beans, and water, raise the heat to medium, and bring to a boil. Then turn the heat to low, cover with a lid, leaving it slightly ajar, and simmer for about 40 minutes, or until the beans are tender. Add salt during the last 5 minutes of cooking.

Remove the thyme bundle and discard. Season the beans with additional salt and pepper. The liquid in which the beans were cooked should be rather thick and syrupy. If not, drain the beans, return them to the same casserole, and reduce by boiling the liquid separately for 5 to 8 minutes, until it is the right consistency. Return this liquid to the casserole along with the tomatoes, prosciutto, and 1 tablespoon of the parsley.

Preheat the oven to 350 degrees. Combine the remaining parsley and the bread crumbs in a small bowl along with the cheese and the remaining olive oil. Spread this mixture evenly over the beans and bake, uncovered, for about 30 minutes, or until the top is evenly brown and bubbly around the edges. Serve hot directly from the baking dish.

FLAGEOLET SUMMER SOUP WITH FRESH HERBS AND LEMON

This light French bean soup belies the cliché that bean soups are hearty winter fare. This one can even be served chilled if you prefer.

SERVES 6

5 tablespoons butter
½ cup finely sliced leek (1 small leek with 1 inch green part)
1 cup coarsely chopped onion (1 large onion)
1 cup thinly sliced celery (2 stalks)
6 cups chicken broth
1 cup dried flageolets, soaked and drained
1 bay leaf
2 large peeled garlic cloves
Salt to taste
½ cup half-and-half or light cream

1 egg yolk
1 teaspoon grated lemon zest (½ large lemon)
3 tablespoons lemon juice (1 large lemon)
Coarsely chopped mixed fresh herbs: 2 tablespoons parsley, 1 tablespoon basil, 2 tablespoons summer savory, 1 teaspoon tarragon
Black pepper to taste
⅛ teaspoon nutmeg
Paper-thin lemon slices for garnish

In a 5-quart Dutch oven, melt 3 tablespoons of the butter over low heat. Add the leek, onion, and celery, and sauté, stirring occasionally, until the vegetables are soft but not brown, about 6 to 8 minutes. Add the broth, flageolets, bay leaf, and garlic, and bring to a boil over medium heat. Lower the heat, and with the pot lid slightly ajar, cook for 1 hour and 20 minutes, or until the beans are very tender. Add salt toward the end of the cooking time.

Remove and discard the bay leaf and drain the beans and vegetables into a bowl, reserving the broth. Puree the bean mixture in a food processor along with a ladleful of the broth, blending until smooth. Return this mixture to the Dutch oven.

In the same unwashed bowl of the food processor, place the half-and-half, egg yolk, and the remaining butter cut up into small pieces, and the remaining warm broth. Process until combined. Add this mixture to the bean-vegetable puree in the Dutch oven and bring slowly to a simmer over low heat, stirring occasionally. Simmer for 10 minutes, until hot.

Remove the pot from the heat and stir in the lemon zest, lemon juice, mixed herbs, pepper, and nutmeg. Taste to correct the seasoning. Ladle into bowls and float a lemon slice on the surface of each serving.

GREAT NORTHERN BEANS AND TUNA WITH ARUGULA, GINGERED ORANGE, AND RED ONION

Marinated large white beans tossed with tuna sit on a bed of dark green peppery arugula, cooled with refreshing oranges and tinged with hot pepper and candied ginger. Tart, sweet, hot, satisfying, and refreshing, it's perfect for luncheon or a light summer dinner salad supreme.

SERVES 6

2½ cups cooked and drained Great Northern or cannellini beans (see Note)

½ cup finely sliced scallions (2 or 3 scallions)

2 teaspoons finely minced garlic (1 large clove)

Salt and pepper to taste

2 tablespoons lemon juice (½ large lemon)

1 tablespoon balsamic vinegar

2 teaspoons coarse grain mustard

6 tablespoons olive oil

4 cups loosely packed and trimmed arugula leaves

Two 6-ounce cans water-packed tuna, drained

3 large navel oranges, peel and pith removed and cut into bite-size segments

¼ teaspoon hot pepper flakes

1 tablespoon finely minced crystallized ginger

1 small red onion, very thinly sliced and separated into rings

Place the cooked warm beans and scallions in a large bowl and set aside. In a small bowl, place the garlic, salt, pepper, lemon juice, vinegar, and mustard, and whisk to combine. Slowly whisk in the olive oil. Add ¼ cup of the vinaigrette to the warm beans (reserving the remaining ¼ cup), toss well, and set aside to marinate for several hours. (This can be done the day before if you prefer.)

When ready to serve, put the arugula in a large bowl and toss with the remaining vinaigrette. Distribute among 6 serving plates. Break up the tuna into large flakes, add to the beans, and combine. Spoon 3 or 4 tablespoons of the mixture in the center of the arugula-lined plates. Combine the orange segments with the hot pepper flakes and ginger, and tuck them in around the beans. Scatter the red onion rings over the surface.

Note: Canned cannellini beans, drained and rinsed, can be substituted.

LIMA BEANS AND MUSTARD GREENS

Creamy-textured lima beans and slightly bitter mustard greens perked with a touch of balsamic vinegar form an amalgam of palate-pleasing flavors.

SERVES 6 TO 8

1 cup small dried lima beans, soaked and drained

1 bay leaf

6 whole black peppercorns, tied in cheesecloth

3 strips bacon

1 pound trimmed mustard greens, well washed (do not drain) and coarsely chopped (about 12 cups)

⅛ teaspoon hot pepper flakes

1 cup finely diced onion (1 large onion)

1 cup finely diced green pepper (1 medium pepper)

1 cup finely diced celery (about 3 stalks)

1 teaspoon sugar

¾ cup coarsely diced plum tomatoes (about 2 tomatoes)

Salt and pepper to taste

Balsamic vinegar

Place the beans, bay leaf, and peppercorns in a 3-quart saucepan with water to cover. Bring to a boil over medium heat, then turn the heat to medium-low and simmer, uncovered, for 50 to 60 minutes. Add boiling water if necessary to keep the beans covered as they cook.

About 15 minutes before the beans are finished, fry the bacon slowly in a 10-inch nonstick skillet, turning it frequently until brown and crisp. Remove the bacon from the skillet with tongs and drain on paper towels, then crumble and reserve. Pour off most of the bacon fat and reserve.

Return 2 tablespoons of the bacon fat to the skillet and turn the heat to medium-high. Add the mustard greens, stir, and add the hot pepper flakes. Cover the skillet and steam for 8 to 10 minutes. Remove the greens to a bowl and set aside.

Wipe out the skillet, add 1 tablespoon of the bacon fat, and heat over medium heat. Add the onion, pepper, and celery, and sauté for 5 to 8 minutes, stirring occasionally, until the vegetables begin to brown. Stir in the sugar, tomatoes, salt, and pepper. Cover the skillet and simmer for 5 minutes. When the beans are tender, drain, add salt if needed, and add to the vegetables in the skillet. Taste once again to adjust the seasoning, then transfer to a large shallow oven-to-table casserole. Arrange the greens around the rim of the casserole and scatter the crumbled bacon over all.

Slip the casserole into a 375-degree preheated oven for 5 to 10 minutes just before serving to reheat. Sprinkle a few drops of balsamic vinegar over the greens just before serving.

Glorious Grains

Barley, Onion, and Mushroom Pilaf with Chicken Livers and Sage

Whole Kasha with Chicken, Dried Fruit, and Walnuts

Polenta with Fresh Corn and Sage

Fresh Herbs and Tomatoes with Millet

Toasted Oats and Fresh Tomato Soup with Basil and Orange Zest

Quinoa Pilaf with Hazelnuts, Apples, and Thyme

Springtime Risotto with Morels, Artichoke Hearts, Asparagus, and Peas

Long-Grain Rice Pilaf with Corn, Black Beans, and Peppers

Wild Rice and Mushroom Soup with Madeira

Wheat Berries (Farro) with Bitter Salad Greens, Peas, Walnuts, and Dried Cranberries

Bulgur and Couscous with Mixed Vegetables

As far back as 9000 B.C., as hunters began to settle into smaller and smaller areas, tiny crop yields of spelt or barley or oats were the buffers against starvation. The Sudanese were harvesting wheat, barley, and millet five hundred years before the birth of Christ. Roman soldiers brought grains to the British Isles; their daily allowance of two pounds a day was roasted or boiled, cooled, and hardened into a kind of porridge. The excavations of Mayan cities have uncovered maize. The Aztecs cultivated amaranth, the Incas quinoa, and the Chinese rice. No major culture has ever evolved without growing a basic grain.

But until a few years ago in the United States, our familiarity with grains was generally limited to those used as part of other products—bread or cereals. A major portion of the American crop is either exported or used to feed the animals, with as little as one pound of whole grains per year consumed by the public—as compared with one hundred pounds of sugar!

We probably can thank the people who began to frequent the health food stores for "discovering" what culinary history might have told us had we bothered to read. We not only began to find new names such as triticale, amaranth, and teff, but we also began to realize that whole grains are rich in vitamins and minerals, and are a primary source of fiber. Sprouted grains are rich in enzymes, protein, minerals, fat, and vitamins.

As we demystify the huge field of whole grains, we can begin to shift the balance in our diet, using more grains and adding small portions of meat only as a condiment—a painless and delicious way to reduce saturated fat and cholesterol.

COOKING THE GLORIOUS GRAINS

(Note: All grains were tested in a 3-quart nonstick saucepan unless otherwise noted.)

GRAIN	DESCRIPTION	COOKING METHOD AND YIELD	COMMENTS
AMARANTH	Quite tiny, about the size of millet. Ranges in color from buff yellow to purple and black. Chewy texture and nutty, almost peppery flavor.	Add 3 cups of water to 1 cup of grain. Combine, bring to a boil, and cook 25 minutes. Do not wash or soak before cooking. Yield: 2½ cups.	Use immediately. Grain congeals if left standing. Add salt after cooking.
BARLEY (Pearled)	When hulled, some vitamin B is lost, but protein is high. Can be cooked unground, added to soups and casseroles, or used as a whole-grain cereal.	Add 3½ cups of salted water to 1 cup of grain. Wash and rinse several times until water is clear. Boil, add grain, and simmer, covered, for 30 to 35 minutes. Yield: 3¼ cups.	After cooking, slip a paper towel under the lid to absorb moisture and let stand 10 minutes. Fork-fluff after standing.
BUCKWHEAT (Roasted—Kasha)	Strong, nutty aroma; may be an acquired taste. Comes in four forms: fine, medium, coarse, and whole grain.	Use a 10-inch nonstick skillet. Mix 1 cup of grain with a lightly beaten egg. Toast 3 minutes to coat. Add 2 cups of boiling salted water or stock and 1 teaspoon of butter. Will splutter up. Cover, lower the heat, and simmer: whole, for 10 to 20 minutes; coarse, for 10 to 15 minutes; medium, for 8 to 10 minutes; fine, for 5 to 6 minutes. Yield: 4 cups.	After cooking, slip a paper towel under the lid and let stand 5 minutes. Fork-fluff after standing.

GRAIN	DESCRIPTION	COOKING METHOD AND YIELD	COMMENTS
BULGUR	Made from either red or white wheat, so kernels will vary from pale golden to a fairly dark color. Comes in 4 granulations: fine, medium, coarse, and whole.	For fine or medium, use 1 cup of grain to 2½ cups of water. For coarse and whole, use 1 cup of grain to 3 cups. Pour boiling water over the grain and steep. *Do not cook.* Let fine stand 15 minutes; medium, 30 minutes; coarse and whole, 60 minutes. All yield 3 cups.	After letting grain stand, line a colander with a man's handkerchief, gather up the ends and squeeze the excess water out of the grain. Place in a bowl, fluff with a fork, and season with salt.
	Note: In spite of articles to the contrary, bulgur is not cracked wheat. Bulgur has been steamed; cracked wheat is uncooked.		
CORN: (CORNMEAL)	Made from whole dried corn kernels—white, yellow, or blue, and usually of medium-fine consistency.	(Also for polenta, see page 241): Add 4 cups of water to 1 cup of grain. Boil 3 cups salted water and whisk 1 cup of cold water into the cornmeal. Add slowly to the boiling water and whisk constantly. Lower the heat and cook, uncovered, stirring frequently, for 10 minutes. Yield: 3¼ cups.	This is a "no-lump" method of cooking.

(WHOLE HOMINY) *AKA* MOTÉ, POSOLE, SAMP, AND MIXTAMAL	Comes in yellow or white. Also canned. Whole corn kernels are treated with slaked lime or a combination of unslaked lime, calcium carbonate, lye, and wood ash.	Add 6 cups of water to 3 cups of grain, plus additional boiling water as needed. Soak grain overnight, then drain. In a 5-quart saucepan, combine the grain and unsalted water. Bring to a boil, lower the heat, and simmer, covered, for 2½ to 3 hours. Yield: 8 cups.	Add salt 15 minutes before the end of the cooking time. Grain bursts open when tender. Three and one-half 1-pound cans drained and rinsed will yield 6 cups.
(HOMINY GRITS)	Made from coarsely ground (preferably stone-ground) corn. Now come in white or yellow and in fine, medium, coarse, and instant forms.	Add 5 cups of water to 1 cup of grits. Bring salted water to a boil and slowly add the grits, stirring. When the mixture boils, lower the heat to a simmer and cook, stirring occasionally, for 25 to 30 minutes. Let stand for 10 minutes. Yield: 4 cups.	We prefer coarse stone-ground grits, and the recipe is for that grind. For other grinds see instructions on the box; our friends in the South cringe at quick-cooking grits!
MILLET **(WHOLE GRAIN)**	Tiny golden grains, always hulled. One of the most nutritious of grains, easy to digest, and rich in vitamins and minerals.	Add 2½ cups of water to 1 cup of grain. In a saucepan, add 2 teaspoons of butter and toast the grain 2 to 3 minutes, stirring constantly. When you hear a crackling sound, add boiling salted water. Return to a boil, then cook over low heat, covered, for 25 to 30 minutes. Yield: 4 cups.	Let stand for 10 minutes after cooking. This method makes a drier, fluffier grain. For stickier texture, eliminate the toasting and cook in boiling salted water same amount of time. Let stand 10 minutes.

GRAIN	DESCRIPTION	COOKING METHOD AND YIELD	COMMENTS
OATS: (STEEL-CUT) *AKA* SCOTTISH OR IRISH OATS	Natural, unrefined oat groats that have been cut into 2 or 3 small pieces. Tasty and chewy.	To cut cooking time, whirl the oats in a food processor, then toast in a 350-degree oven for 20 minutes. Add 1 cup of oats in 3½ cups of salted water. Bring to a boil, lower the heat, cook for 15 minutes, and let stand for 5 minutes. Yield: 3 cups. Without toasting, oats take 45 minutes and do not have a nutty flavor.	Also available as oat bran and oat flour, perfect for thickening soups or for breads, pancakes, muffins, granolas, pilafs, and meuslis.
(OLD-FASHIONED rolled oats)	Large, separate flakes that have been steamed and flattened. The "quick" or "instant" have been further processed and thus have less nutrition than the "old-fashioned."	Add 2¾ cups of salted water to 1 cup of oats. Bring water to a boil, stir in the oats, cover, and cook over low heat for 5 minutes. Yield: 2½ cups.	Usually used as a cereal and also in cookies, cakes, breads, and toppings for fruit crisps.

QUINOA
(KEEN-WAH)

Used by the Incas, it is not really a cereal grain but the fruit of an herb in the goosefoot family, related to beets, spinach, and chard. Ranges across the color wheel, and the taste is delicious—but descriptions vary from rice through millet to mustard!

Pick over and discard black seeds. Toast quinoa in a nonstick saucepan, stirring over medium heat for 5 minutes. Add 2 cups of boiling salted water; grain will sputter. Lower the heat, cover, and simmer 10 to 12 minutes. It is cooked when a transparent "halo" forms around each grain. Turn off the heat, let stand 5 minutes, and fluff with a fork. Yield: 3½ cups.

Do not soak or wash even though some packages give instructions to wash first to remove the saponin, a natural insect repellent. The taste is quite satisfactory without washing. Use quinoa as a side dish in place of rice or for stuffings, casseroles, and even puddings and desserts. It is a nutritional powerhouse!

RICE

Although the past few years have witnessed a remarkable proliferation of varieties of rice here in the United States, the average American consumes only about 10 pounds a year, whereas Asians consume up to 400 pounds per person annually. Although we grow less than 1 percent of the world's crop, we export up to 10 million pounds, or about 70 percent of what we grow. Rice is composed mostly of carbohydrates, but when combined with other ingredients such as beans, it becomes a remarkably economical and nutritious addition to our diet. Here are just a few of the most popular varieties.

GRAIN	DESCRIPTION	COOKING METHOD AND YIELD	COMMENTS
WHITE LONG GRAIN (CAROLINA BRAND)	Thin, long kernels with hull, bran, and germ removed. Has a bland, mild flavor.	Add 2 cups of salted water to 1 cup of rice. Add 1/4 to 1/2 teaspoon of salt, and 1 teaspoon of butter (optional). Bring water to a boil, stir in the rice, return to a boil, lower the heat, and simmer 15 minutes, covered. Yield: 3 1/4 cups.	Let stand 5 minutes, then fluff with a fork. Good for pilafs, side dishes, casseroles, and salads. For converted rice, such as Uncle Ben's, follow the package instructions.
(JASMINE)	Louisiana rice, sometimes called "popcorn rice" because of the way it smells while cooking. Very flavorful, soft, white, and delicately mild.	Add 2 cups of salted water to 1 cup of rice, with butter optional. Follow the cooking instructions for Carolina brand (above). Yield: 4 cups.	Excellent white rice. Our favorite for pilafs, salads, casseroles, and side dishes.
(BASMATI)	An aromatic rice from India, Pakistan, and our own Texas. Long, slender, opaque grain. When cooked, results in firm, long, white, fluffy grains.	Pick over and remove broken grains. Wash well and rinse several times. Add 1 3/4 cups of salted water to 1 cup of rice (butter optional). Follow the instructions for long-grain white rice. Cook 18 to 20 minutes and let stand 5 minutes. Yield: 3 1/2 cups.	For use with Middle Eastern and Indian cuisines. Also an excellent rice for pilafs. Domestic basmati has a milder flavor than the imported.

Type	Description	Cooking	Notes
BROWN LONG GRAIN	Hulled with bran and germ intact. When cooked, has chewier texture with nuttier, more intense flavor than white, but fluffier than short-grain brown.	Add 2½ cups of salted water to 1 cup of rice. Bring to a boil, add the rice, lower heat to a simmer, and cook for 30 to 45 minutes, covered. Let stand 10 minutes. Fluff with a fork. Yield: 3¼ cups.	Preferred by vegetarians, along with short-grain brown. More nutritious than white, it can be used in all the dishes mentioned above.
WHITE SHORT GRAIN	These include the Italian arborio, vialone nano, and tesori, used for risottos, as well as the Spanish Valencia, preferred for paellas. See pages 245–246 for recipe instructions.		
MEDIUM GRAIN (WHITE)	Size is midway between the short and long grain. After cooking, consistency is not quite as sticky as the short grain.	Rinse this grain. Add 2½ cups of salted water to 1 cup of rice. Cook over low heat for 18 to 20 minutes, covered. Let stand for 5 minutes. Yield: 3¼ cups.	This is the all-purpose sushi rice. Can also be used for dishes that require stickier quality, such as puddings and molded desserts.
MEDIUM GRAIN (BROWN)	Same size as white but buff colored. After cooking, grains are slightly sticky and have a nutty flavor.	Rinse this grain. Add 3 cups of salted water to 1 cup of rice. Will require longer cooking, up to 40 minutes. Let stand for 10 minutes. Yield: 3¼ cups.	More intensely flavored than white, with a better cohesive quality.

GRAIN	DESCRIPTION	COOKING METHOD AND YIELD	COMMENTS
Black Japonica *aka* Thai black rice	Long, slightly plump, with blunt ends and shaded from black to russet. Color of rice leaches into the water and food. Smells like grassy new-mown hay; good flavor, toothsome, and slightly glutinous.	Pick over, clean, and wash before cooking. Add 1¼ cups of water to 1 cup of rice. Cook for 25 minutes, let stand for 10 minutes, and salt after cooking. Yield: 2 cups.	In Asia it is usually combined with coconut cream or shredded coconut for desserts. Also makes a novelty rice pudding because of the color.
Bhutan Red *aka* Christmas rice	A russet brown rice variety with bran and germ intact. Has unusual wild mushroom flavor and chewy texture.	Rinse first. Add 3 cups of boiling water to 1 cup of rice. Cook for 45 minutes, covered, let stand for 10 minutes, and salt after cooking. Yield: 3 cups.	Good for side dish with game such as venison or pheasant. Also good in salads.
Wehani	A California hybrid in the brown rice family, crossed with Indian basmati. Very nutty flavor, with sticky, toothsome texture.	Rinse well. Add 3 cups of water to 1 cup of rice. Cook for 40 minutes, let stand for 10 minutes, and salt after cooking. Yield: 2⅔ cups.	Can be used in salads for texture and color and a flavor reminiscent of wild rice.

WILD RICE

Actually, not a rice but an aquatic grass seed. It is a true American crop, harvested in the upper Midwest and originally a staple of the Native Americans in the Great Lakes region. It is the most expensive of all the grains since it is not only difficult to grow but also tedious and time-consuming to harvest. It has a chewy, nutty, smoky flavor, making it perfect for a side dish as well as for soups, salads, and stuffings. It can also be "stretched" by blending it with other forms of rice or with vegetables, poultry, nuts, and fruits. There are three major forms:

GIANT (LONG)	The super deluxe of wild rice, each grain is about 1 inch long. It is also the most expensive.	Pick over and rinse. Add 4 cups of boiling salted water for 6 ounces of rice. Simmer, covered, for 50 to 60 minutes, drain excess water, then let stand for 10 minutes. Yield: 3 cups.	When rice is tender, some grains will "bloom" or burst open. Bite-test a few before draining.
EXTRA-FANCY (MEDIUM)	Most popular grade. Grains are of equal size and quality.	Same as above. Cook for 45 to 50 minutes. Let stand for 10 minutes. Yield: 3 cups.	Generally used for salads, side dishes, and stuffings. Can be used interchangeably with giant rice.
SELECT (SHORT)	Some grains may be broken and not of uniform size or length. If appearance is not important, this grade will do well. It is also the least expensive.	Same as above. Cook for 45 to 50 minutes. Let stand for 10 minutes. Yield: 3 cups.	Best used for baked goods such as muffins or in pancakes, soups, or stuffings.
WHEAT	Although almost all of the wheat grown in North America goes into the milling of flour—mostly white flour—informed home cooks have increased their repertoires with the multiple forms of the grain: whole grain berries, peeled wheat berries, cracked wheat and bulgur, wheat germ, wheat grits, puffed wheat, bran flakes, and even wheat grass. The more wheat is processed, the more benefits are removed.		

GRAIN	DESCRIPTION	COOKING METHOD AND YIELD	COMMENTS
WHOLE GRAIN BERRIES	The whole grain of the wheat, including the bran, endosperm, and germ. Its most nutritious form.	Pick over and toast unwashed berries until they begin to pop. Transfer to a bowl, wash, and soak overnight. Drain and add 3½ cups of liquid to 1 cup of grain. Simmer, covered, for 50 to 60 minutes. Drain excess liquid and let stand for 10 minutes. Do not add salt until cooked. Yield: 3 cups.	Can be used for pilafs, stews, or home-baked breads. When sprouted, can be made into croquettes or added to salads and baked goods.
WHOLE PEELED WHEAT BERRIES *AKA* FRUMENTO OR GRANO IN ITALIAN	Pale golden color with only the outer hull removed. Shorter and plumper than spelt, with a line down one center. Generally milled for pastry flour.	Rinse and soak overnight. Drain and add 3½ cups of salted water to 1 cup of grain. Bring to a boil, lower the heat to a simmer, and cook, covered, for 50 to 60 minutes. Let stand for 10 minutes. Yield: 3 cups.	They have a slightly chewy, sweet taste. They're somewhat gelatinous, a desirable quality for desserts and soups.
FARRO (FAHR-OH) *AKA* EMMER	An Italian import, called *emmer* in English. Long, slim, light tan, mottled surface with a line on one side of the grain.	Soak one hour and drain. Add 3 cups of water to 1 cup of farro plus salt to taste. Bring to a boil, then simmer, covered, for 15 to 20 minutes. Yield: 2¼ cups.	After cooking, grain has a whitish bloom, a very mild flavor, and a soft texture.

		When cooked, has a slightly gelatinous surface texture and a more delicate flavor than spelt.

KAMUT
(KAH-MOOT)

It's the Egyptian word for wheat and called "King Tut's Wheat." Large, slim, elongated grain; pale golden tan with a hairline traced on one side.

Soak overnight and drain. Add 4 cups of water to 1 cup of kamut. Do not salt while cooking; it will lengthen the cooking time and toughen the grain. Simmer, covered, for 80 or 90 minutes. Yield: 2 cups.

When cooked, has a slight snappy crunch and a pleasant nutty flavor.

SPELT

Tawny tan, oval, and plump, with slight point at the tip and a hairline split down the center of one side. Similar to whole pearled barley.

Soak overnight and drain. Add 3 cups of water to 1 cup of spelt and salt to taste. Bring to a boil, lower the heat, and cook at a vigorous simmer with the pot lid ajar to prevent boilovers. Cook for 55 to 60 minutes, checking occasionally to see if additional boiling water is needed. Let stand 5 minutes, then drain the excess liquid. Yield: 2½ cups.

SHOP SMART

- Whether you buy your whole grains prepackaged or in bulk, the best way to ensure freshness is to shop where you know there is a large turnover. Purchase your grains in small amounts.
- If you buy in a store that sells in bulk from burlap sacks (as do many health food stores), make sure the air is dry and not foul or humid. Whole grains can develop mold under damp conditions.
- When buying packaged grains, the word "natural" does not mean much. After all, both sugar and salt are natural. Just keep in mind that any grain that has been processed has probably lost a good part of its nutritional value.
- Before you store them (see Notes for the Cook), don't wash them. They stick together when they're wet, and they'll get moldy rather quickly. Store them dry.
- There are also white and wild rice mixtures and some that are parboiled or precooked. The best way to check size and quality is to look through the plastic bag.

Notes for the Cook

ON GRAINS . . .

- Whole grains should be stored in a dry, cool place such as a refrigerator or freezer. Properly stored, grains can last an incredibly long time, as witness the grains found in the tombs of Egypt.
- When cooking whole grains, remember that most of them will double or even triple in size, so plan the pot size carefully. (Our recipes have all been tested with a 3-quart nonstick saucepan, generally using 1 cup of grain.)
- While cooking grains, don't stir and keep the pot tightly covered. Grains bruise easily and get sticky when stirred. Don't peek! After a while, bite-test a grain to see if it is done.
- After cooking the grain, it is a good idea to insert a piece of paper towel between the pot and the lid to absorb any excess moisture. Let it stand for 5 to 10 minutes and then fluff the grains with a fork to separate them.

BARLEY, ONION, AND MUSHROOM PILAF WITH CHICKEN LIVERS AND SAGE

A delightful side dish and perfect companion for any sort of roasted poultry.

SERVES 6 TO 8

4 cups chicken broth

1 cup whole pearled barley, washed
until the water is clear

4 tablespoons olive oil

2 large onions, thinly sliced and
separated into rings

8 ounces cremini mushrooms, cleaned
and thickly sliced

1 tablespoon lemon juice (½ lemon)

Salt and pepper to taste

2 tablespoons finely minced parsley

8 chicken livers, cut into small pieces

2 tablespoons finely minced sage leaves
(about 4 or 5 large leaves)

In a 3-quart saucepan, bring the broth to a boil over medium-high heat. Stir in the barley and return to a boil. Lower the heat and simmer for 30 minutes, or until the barley is tender and the liquid is absorbed. Remove from the heat, let stand for 10 to 15 minutes to allow the grains to separate a bit, then fluff with a fork. Keep the barley in the pan.

Meanwhile, heat 2 tablespoons of the olive oil in a 12-inch nonstick skillet over medium-high heat. Add the onions and cook, stirring occasionally, for 15 to 20 minutes, or until the onions are soft and dark in color. Remove with a slotted spoon and stir the onions into the barley.

In the same skillet, heat 1 tablespoon of olive oil. Add the mushrooms and sauté, stirring, for 5 to 8 minutes. Stir in the lemon juice, salt, pepper, and parsley, then add them to the pilaf. In the same skillet, heat the remaining tablespoon of olive oil. Add the chicken livers and sauté, stirring, for 3 to 4 minutes over medium heat. Season with salt, pepper, and sage, and stir into the pilaf.

Rewarm the pilaf over low heat just until hot, then transfer to a serving dish and serve.

WHOLE KASHA WITH CHICKEN, DRIED FRUIT, AND WALNUTS

If you decide to try this recipe without the chicken, this warm grain, fruit, and nut dish can be used as an unusual stuffing for a crown roast of pork or for duck or goose.

SERVES 6

2 tablespoons corn oil or canola oil

1 cup finely chopped onion
  (1 large onion)

1½ cups finely chopped celery with leaves (about 3 or 4 stalks)

2 tablespoons fresh thyme leaves

2 tablespoons finely minced sage leaves
  (about 4 to 6 large leaves)

Salt and pepper to taste

1 teaspoon grated lemon zest

4 cups cooked whole kasha (see chart, page 227, for instructions)

1 cup diced mixed dried fruit

½ cup coarsely broken and toasted walnuts

One 6- to 8-ounce cooked chicken breast, sliced into thin julienne

In a 12-inch skillet, heat the oil, add the onion, and sauté, stirring occasionally, until wilted, about 3 or 4 minutes. Add the celery, thyme, sage, salt, and pepper, and cook, stirring, 5 to 8 minutes more. Add the lemon zest and combine with the cooked kasha. Place the dried fruits in a vegetable steamer and steam to soften them, about 5 minutes. Combine with the kasha mixture along with the walnuts. Transfer to a serving platter and scatter the julienned chicken over all. Serve warm.

POLENTA WITH FRESH CORN AND SAGE

Crunchy bits of fresh corn add a surprise texture as well as intensify the flavor of this dish. Fresh corn is so American. Polenta and sage are so Italian. A very happy international marriage.

SERVES 6

3 cups chicken broth
¾ cup polenta (coarse grain, not instant)
1½ cups uncooked corn kernels (about 2 ears corn)
Salt and pepper to taste

2 tablespoons grated Parmesan cheese
1 tablespoon finely minced fresh sage plus 6 leaves for garnish
3 tablespoons soft, sweet butter plus additional to coat a dish

In a heavy 3-quart nonstick saucepan, bring the broth to a simmer over medium-high heat. Slowly add the polenta. Stir constantly or use a whisk to prevent lumping and cook for 10 minutes. Fold in the corn, salt, pepper, and 2 tablespoons of the butter. Continue to cook 8 to 10 minutes more, stirring occasionally, until quite thick.

Butter an 8¼ x 8¼ x 2-inch tempered glass or ceramic dish. Transfer the polenta to the dish and smooth the surface. Cool at room temperature, covered with plastic wrap, for at least 1 hour or cool longer in the refrigerator until thick. (If refrigerated, bring to room temperature again.)

When ready to serve, melt the remaining tablespoon of butter and trickle it over the surface. Sprinkle with Parmesan cheese and slip under a preheated broiler for 4 to 5 minutes, or until the top is crusty and golden. Cut into 6 squares, top each with a sage leaf, and serve hot.

FRESH HERBS AND TOMATOES WITH MILLET

A verdant, warm grain salad with the taste of summer in every forkful. It relies on the freshest, most aromatic herbs and the most flavorful ripe tomato for its sprightly taste.

SERVES 8

4 cups cooked toasted millet (see
   chart, page 229, for instructions)
¼ cup finely minced parsley
⅓ cup finely minced basil
⅓ cup finely snipped chives
2 teaspoons finely minced marjoram
Salt and pepper to taste

2 tablespoons lemon juice
   (½ large lemon)
4 tablespoons olive oil
½ ripe skinned and diced tomato
   (about 1 pound)
Black olives for garnish

While the millet is hot, transfer it to a large bowl and combine it with the parsley, basil, chives, marjoram, salt, and pepper. Add the lemon juice and oil, and stir. Gently stir in the tomato. Transfer to a serving platter, garnish with the olives, and serve at room temperature.

TOASTED OATS AND FRESH TOMATO SOUP WITH BASIL AND ORANGE ZEST

Toasted oats thicken this basil-scented fresh tomato soup with an elusive hint of orange zest. A lightly cooked soup, it depends on the most luscious summer harvest of tomatoes.

SERVES 6

1 cup rolled oats

4 tablespoons butter

1 cup coarsely chopped onion
   (1 large onion)

1 tablespoon finely chopped garlic
   (3 large cloves)

5 cups skinned and coarsely diced ripe
   tomatoes (about 2 pounds)

5 cups chicken broth

2 teaspoons finely minced orange zest

⅓ cup basil leaves, finely shredded

Salt and pepper to taste

2 tablespoons finely minced parsley

Place the oats in a heavy iron 8-inch skillet and toast over medium-low heat, stirring frequently, until they begin to turn color, about 5 to 8 minutes. Set aside.

In a 7-quart Dutch oven, melt the butter over medium-high heat. Add the onion and garlic, and sauté, stirring, until the onion is wilted, about 5 minutes. Stir in the tomatoes and cook 2 minutes more. Add the broth and orange zest, and bring to the boiling point. Turn the heat to medium-low and add the reserved oats and the basil, salt, and pepper. Cover and cook for 8 minutes. Adjust the seasoning and serve hot, sprinkled with parsley.

QUINOA PILAF WITH HAZELNUTS, APPLES, AND THYME

Fluffy, tiny grain quinoa, the staple grain of the Incas, is teamed with toasted hazelnuts, tender morsels of apple, and a touch of thyme. A lovely change from rice and a winner with any kind of pork.

SERVES 8

3½ cups cooked whole quinoa (see chart, page 231, for instructions)

1 large red delicious apple, cored and cut into ¼-inch dice

1 teaspoon lemon juice (1 lemon wedge)

4 tablespoons butter

1 cup scallions, sliced diagonally in ½-inch strips (about 5 or 6)

1 teaspoon dried thyme

Salt and pepper to taste

5 ounces hazelnuts, toasted, skinned, and coarsely chopped (about 1 cup)

Put the cooked quinoa in a large bowl and set aside. Combine the apple and lemon juice in a small bowl and set aside. In a 12-inch nonstick skillet, melt the butter over medium-high heat. Add the scallions, thyme, salt, and pepper, and sauté, stirring constantly, for 2 minutes. Stir in the nuts and diced apple, and continue to cook, stirring, for 4 or 5 minutes. The apples should be tender but still maintain their shape. Stir in the quinoa and turn the heat to low. Cook, stirring occasionally, until hot. Transfer to a serving dish and serve hot.

SPRINGTIME RISOTTO WITH MORELS, ARTICHOKE HEARTS, ASPARAGUS, AND PEAS

When spring beckons, we crave a celebratory risotto using all these welcome vegetables to herald the season.

SERVES 4 TO 6

2 cups salted water

1 lemon wedge

5 baby artichokes (about 8 ounces), trimmed to hearts only and cut into quarters

1 cup medium-size asparagus (about 8 ounces or 10 spears), trimmed and sliced diagonally

1/3 cup frozen or fresh tiny peas

1 1/2 ounces dried morels, soaked in warm water for 30 or 40 minutes

Chicken broth

4 tablespoons butter

1/3 cup finely minced shallots (2 or 3 large)

1 1/2 cups short-grain rice (arborio or vialone)

1/3 cup dry white wine

Salt and pepper to taste

1/3 cup grated Parmesan cheese

In a 3-quart nonstick saucepan, place the salted water, squeeze in a wedge of lemon, and then add the wedge to the pot. Bring it to a boil over medium heat. Add the artichoke hearts and simmer for about 6 minutes. Add the asparagus and peas, and cook until the asparagus are tender/crisp and the peas are cooked, about 3 or 4 minutes. Drain through a sieve, reserving both the vegetables and the vegetable broth (about 1 1/2 cups of broth). Discard the lemon wedge.

Strain the morels after they are pliable, pressing them against a sieve and reserving the mushroom liquid. Set the mushrooms aside and strain the liquid through a dampened paper coffee filter. Add it to the vegetable broth. Transfer the liquid to a 2-quart saucepan and add enough chicken broth to make 5 cups total. Bring the liquid to a simmer and keep it warm.

Wipe out the saucepan, add 3 tablespoons of the butter, and melt over medium heat. Add the shallots and stir and cook for 3 minutes. Add the rice and stir to coat with the butter mixture, about 1 or 2 minutes. Add the wine and stir until absorbed. Add a ladleful of simmering liquid to the rice and stir until absorbed. Repeat the process, adding simmering liquid and stirring frequently until absorbed. Stir in the reserved mushrooms and continue to add liquid, a little at a time, until absorbed.

After about 18 minutes, start bite-testing a grain of rice. When the rice is tender, add the reserved vegetables and continue to cook, stirring gently, 2 to 3 minutes more, adding more liquid as needed until the rice is creamy. Stir in the remaining tablespoon of butter, season with salt and pepper, and stir in the cheese. Serve at once.

LONG-GRAIN RICE PILAF WITH CORN, BLACK BEANS, AND PEPPERS

A delightfully colorful rice dish we find ourselves making frequently. Everyone loves it, and it can be prepared ahead of time and rewarmed. A wonderful accompaniment for seafood, poultry, or meat.

SERVES 8

2 cups chicken broth

1 teaspoon butter

1 cup long-grain white rice (preferably jasmine)

3 tablespoons olive oil

1 cup scallions, sliced in ½-inch diagonals (about 6 to 8)

1 teaspoon finely minced garlic (1 clove)

1½ cups finely diced sweet peppers, ½ each of green, yellow, and red, seeded

Salt and pepper to taste

1 teaspoon ground cumin

½ teaspoon dried oregano, preferably Greek

1 cup corn kernels, scraped from 1 or 2 ears of corn

15-ounce can black beans, rinsed and drained

2½ tablespoons finely minced parsley

In a 2-quart saucepan, bring the broth and butter to a boil over medium heat. Add the rice and bring to a boil again, then lower the heat and simmer, covered, for 15 minutes. Fluff with a fork and set aside.

While the rice is cooking, heat the olive oil in a 12-inch nonstick skillet and sauté the scallions, garlic, and peppers over medium-high heat, stirring frequently, for 3 minutes. Add the salt, pepper, cumin, oregano, and corn, and sauté 2 minutes more. Add the reserved rice and the drained beans, and continue to simmer on low heat, stirring occasionally, until heated through. Stir in the parsley, transfer to a 2½-quart serving dish, and serve hot.

WILD RICE AND MUSHROOM SOUP
WITH MADEIRA

We are wild, wild, wild about our most festive, favorite, elegant soup! On holidays and other special occasions, it always receives compliments.

SERVES 8

1½ cups warm water

1 ounce dried shiitake or porcini mushrooms, cleaned and trimmed

1 pound fresh cremini mushrooms

4 tablespoons butter

⅓ cup coarsely chopped shallots (2 ounces)

1 small carrot

1 large celery stalk

4 ounces Idaho potato

¾ teaspoon dried thyme

½ teaspoon dried marjoram

2 cups cooked wild rice (see chart, page 234, for instructions)

4 cups chicken broth

Salt and pepper to taste

1 tablespoon tomato paste

1 cup light cream or half-and-half

⅛ teaspoon Tabasco or more to taste

3 tablespoons Madeira wine

Snipped chives for garnish

In a small bowl, combine the water and dried mushrooms, weighing them down so that they're completely submerged, and soak for 30 minutes. Cut off and discard any tough stems. Squeeze the mushrooms, forcing the excess liquid back into the soaking liquid. Strain the liquid through a dampened paper coffee filter into a cup to get rid of any fine grit. Reserve both the liquid and the mushrooms. Trim the stems, slice the cremini mushrooms thickly, and set aside.

In a 7-quart Dutch oven, melt the butter and sauté the shallots over medium heat, stirring frequently, for 2 minutes. Place the carrot, celery, and potato in a food processor and process until coarsely chopped. Add the vegetables to the pot along with the thyme and marjoram, and sauté 2 minutes more. Add both of the mushrooms and sauté, stirring, for 5 minutes. Add the cooked rice along with the reserved mushroom liquid and the chicken broth and bring to a boil. Turn the heat to low, season with salt and pepper, and add the tomato paste. Cover the pot and simmer for 30 minutes.

Puree the soup in several batches in a blender or food processor. It should not be too smooth. Return the pureed soup to the same pot. Stir in the cream and reheat over low heat. Stir in the Tabasco and Madeira. Taste to adjust the seasoning and serve hot, topped with some of the snipped chives.

WHEAT BERRIES (FARRO) WITH BITTER SALAD GREENS, PEAS, WALNUTS, AND DRIED CRANBERRIES

The ancient/new crunchy whole grain, Italian farro (or wheat berries), plays sweet green peas and slightly tart dried cranberries against the sharply biting salad greens in an orchestra of flavors.

SERVES 4

1½ cups cooked Italian farro (see chart, page 236, for instructions) or cooked whole wheat berries (page 236)

2 tablespoons finely minced shallots (2 large shallots)

1 cup cooked tiny peas (¾ of a 10-ounce package frozen peas)

4 teaspoons dried cranberries

2 tablespoons balsamic vinegar

1 tablespoon lemon juice

Salt and pepper to taste

1 teaspoon grainy mustard

⅓ cup walnut oil

8 cups mixed bitter salad greens such as arugula, mizuna, frisée, escarole, endive, radicchio, and red mustard

¼ cup coarsely broken toasted walnuts

In a medium-size bowl, combine the farro with the shallots, peas, and cranberries, and set aside. In a small bowl, whisk together the vinegar, lemon juice, salt, pepper, and mustard until smooth. Very slowly whisk in the walnut oil. Remove 2 tablespoons of this vinaigrette and add it to the grain mixture. Place the remaining vinaigrette in the bottom of a large bowl, add the greens, and toss lightly.

Distribute the greens among 4 plates. Place some of the grain mixture in the center of the greens and scatter a few walnuts over each portion.

BULGUR AND COUSCOUS WITH MIXED VEGETABLES

A side dish that couldn't be easier to prepare. Bulgur and couscous need only a good soak in a flavorful chicken broth and then are combined with lightly sautéed vegetables and chives. (See Note.)

SERVES 8

¾ cup #2 medium bulgur

2 cups quick-cooking medium-grain couscous

4½ cups boiling chicken broth

4 tablespoons softened butter

2 cups coarsely chopped leeks, white part plus 1 inch pale green (4 or 5 thin leeks)

2 cups coarsely chopped carrots (6 medium carrots)

1 small turnip, coarsely chopped

1 small yellow squash, coarsely chopped

1 small zucchini, coarsely chopped

1 cup cooked tiny frozen green peas

Salt and black pepper to taste

3 tablespoons finely snipped chives

Place the bulgur in a small bowl and the couscous in a larger bowl. Pour 1 cup of the boiling broth over the bulgur and let stand for 15 or 20 minutes, or until the liquid is absorbed. Add 2 tablespoons of soft butter to the remaining broth, then pour it over the couscous and let stand for 30 minutes, or until the pellets swell and the liquid is totally absorbed. (Disregard the box instructions that read 5 minutes.) Fluff the couscous with a fork and combine it with the bulgur. Fluff again and set aside.

In a 12-inch nonstick skillet, melt the remaining 2 tablespoons of butter over medium heat. Add the leeks, carrots, turnip, squash, and zucchini, and sauté for 5 to 8 minutes, stirring frequently, until the leeks are wilted but not brown. Add the vegetables to the couscous mixture and combine. Stir in the cooked peas. Add salt and a liberal amount of pepper. Stir in the chives and toss the mixture with 2 forks to lighten and combine. Transfer to a serving dish and serve warm. If prepared in advance, cover with aluminum foil and place in a preheated low oven until ready to serve.

Note: The leeks, carrots, turnip, squash, and zucchini can be coarsely chopped together in a food processor.

Pasta Perfect

Linguine with Sea Scallops, Sugar Snap Peas, and Red Salmon Caviar

Penne with Veal Ragu, Sage, and Peas

Farfalle with Leeks, Asparagus, and Fennel Sausage

Vietnamese Rice Noodle and Chicken Salad with Lemongrass and Ginger

Couscous with Summer Vegetables and Clams

Orzo with Vegetables, Black Olives, and Arugula

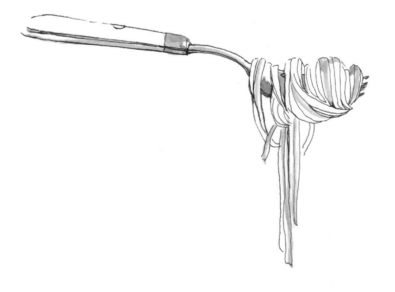

Although most of us associate pasta with Italy, it really is an important part of cuisines around the globe: the German *spaetzle*, Polish *pirogi*, Japanese *udon*, and Greek *orzo*, to name a very few. And the story of Marco Polo bringing it back from China, where it had been eaten for over two thousand years, was finally discredited when archaeologists discovered that ravioli was a favorite dish of Rome twenty years before the explorers left for the East.

Considering that pasta is merely flour and water and, occasionally, egg, it is amazing how many different shapes, recipes, and uses we can find for the simple combination of ingredients. Look at the shelves of our supermarkets—the shapes and sizes astound.

And then there are the names. The Italian list rolls off the tongue like the libretto of an opera: *ditalini, fettuccine, tripolini, tortellini,* and on and on. Certainly charming and whimsical, but so many can make choosing them confusing. Nevertheless, the vast array can be separated into categories, and many can be used interchangeably with the same sauces. Moreover, the basic shapes and sizes of pasta are beautifully designed to determine just which sauces are best to use with each category. There is actually a method to this Italian madness.

THE LANGUAGE OF PASTA

There are several common denominators:

- *Length.* Long or short. The Italian verb *tagliare* (to cut) is often used to indicate short-cut pastas such as *ziti tagliati* (cut ziti).
- *Surface Texture.* Smooth or grooved. The latter holds the sauce better. *Rigati* denotes grooves, such as *ziti rigati*.

- *Shape.* Some have curled edges, and some are flat and usually in ribbons or sheets, such as *ricci: lasagna ricci* (curly-edged lasagna).
- *Size.* The thickness of strings, the diameter of a tube, or the width of a ribbon pasta. In the United States, numbers are used to differentiate sizes. In Italy a more poetic solution describes size by a diminutive or superlative ending being placed on the basic pasta name: large size is *oni* (*rigatoni,* a large-sized grooved pasta); small size is *-ini, -ine, -ette,* or *-ina* (spaghetti and spaghett*ini,* and fettuce and *fettuccine.*

THE BASIC FORMS

STRINGS: These are extruded by machine in many sizes—spaghettini (thinnest), spaghetti (medium), and spaghettoni (thickest). There are also such thin pastas as vermicelli (small worms), cappelini (hair), fusilli (twists), and linguine (thin tongues).

TUBES: Extruded hollow tube forms in countless variations. There are long tubular pastas such as ziti (bridegrooms). Short tubular pastas include tubetti (little tubes), ditali (thimbles), the familiar macaroni and cannelloni (large reeds), and more unusually named pastas such as *occhi di lupo* (wolves' eyes) and *denti di cavallo* (horses' teeth).

The short tubular pastas are also made with diagonally cut ends, penne (quills) and manicotti (muffs), or they are curved into elbows that range from thick to thin: *cavatappi* (elbow twists), *capelli di galli* (cockscombs), and a favorite of ours, *capelli di prete* (priests' hats).

SHEETS: Called *sfoglia* in Italian, these are usually available only fresh or homemade.

RIBBONS: These range from the thin trenette and fettuccine through the wider tagliatelle, the 1-inch-wide pappardelle, and the familiar broad ribbon, lasagna.

CUT-OUT SHAPES: *Farfalle* (butterflies) are wide ribbons cut with a pastry wheel and twisted into shapes.

SPECIALTY PASTAS: *Conchiglie* (shells), *orecchiette* (little ears), and the grooved cavatelli, as well as the spiked cartwheel (*ruoti*), are designed to hold sauce.

FILLED PASTAS: Variations of filled fresh sheet pastas, these are made in three basic shapes: squares such as ravioli, circles that include tortellini, *cappelletti* (stuffed hats), and *angoletti* (fat little lambs), and triangles such as *pansotti* (potbellies).

SOUP PASTAS: Usually small, some are unique to soups and come from every category previously described: orzo, alphabet, *stellette* (stars), *conchigliette* (tiny shells), and *anelli* (rings).

> ### ◆ About Pasta Sauces ◆
>
> *There are probably as many pasta sauces as there are pasta shapes. Each region of Italy boasts its own special recipe, modified by every mother and grandmother in each village. We have only a few suggestions when it comes to the sauces:*

- ◆ We don't believe in the storied eight-hour slow cooking on the stove. We think that pasta sauces should be light and quickly done.
- ◆ If the pasta has a shape—shell, spiral, tubular—that will catch and hold the sauce (and thick sauces are perfect), this is a chance to use meat and/or vegetables.
- ◆ If the pasta is thin and long, such as linguine, capellini, and spaghettini, a thin sauce made with olive oil or a seafood base should be used.
- ◆ Use about half a cup of sauce for each 4 ounces of pasta.

Notes for the Cook

ON PASTA . . .

- ◆ Use a very large pot and a large amount of water. Too little water, and the pasta will turn out gummy.
- ◆ Make sure the water is at full boil, then add lots of salt—2 teaspoons to 1 tablespoon per pound of pasta—or the pasta will taste flat. Add the pasta in small amounts, stirring with a long-handled wooden fork in order to distribute the pasta evenly.
- ◆ If the water stops boiling when the pasta is added, cover the pot partway until it boils again, then cook the pasta uncovered.
- ◆ Timing depends, of course, on the pasta. We frankly never believe the package instructions and generally add some time. It also depends on how you like your pasta, *al dente* ("to the tooth") or much softer. Fresh, soft pasta cooks much faster than the dried packaged variety.
- ◆ Pasta loves company. Italians insist that you do not leave the kitchen when cooking pasta. After five to seven minutes, remove a piece and bite-test it. For fresh pasta, test after two or three minutes.
- ◆ If you're using the pasta in a dish that will be baked later on, undercook it a bit.
- ◆ We find the best way to mix the sauce and the pasta is to leave the sauce in the large pan in which it was made and then drain the pasta in a colander. The steam

gives us what we have always called a "Sophia Loren facial." We then put the pasta right into the pan with the sauce, stirring as we do so.

◆ Serve the pasta on hot plates—and remember that the pasta should not wait for the guests. Let the guests wait for the pasta!

◆ And, finally, remember that pasta loves pepper! So pass a pepper mill around.

LINGUINE WITH SEA SCALLOPS, SUGAR SNAP PEAS, AND RED SALMON CAVIAR

Sea scallops and crisp jade green sugar snap peas, paired with briny orange caviar eggs and tempered with refreshing mint along with tiny bursts of hot chile flakes, make a quick, colorful, and delicately balanced pasta dish. It can be prepared in just under fifteen minutes.

SERVES 4

12 ounces thin linguine

3 tablespoons butter

12 ounces sea scallops (if large, cut in half horizontally)

1 teaspoon grated lemon zest

2 tablespoons lemon juice (about ½ large lemon)

⅛ teaspoon hot pepper flakes

4 ounces sugar snap peas, strings removed

Salt and pepper to taste

2 ounces salmon roe caviar

3 tablespoons grated Parmesan cheese

1 tablespoon coarsely chopped mint

Cook the linguine in a large amount of boiling salted water until tender, about 13 minutes. In a 12-inch nonstick skillet, heat the butter over medium-high heat. When hot, add the scallops and sauté about 1 minute on each side. Turn off the heat under the skillet, add the lemon zest, juice, and hot pepper flakes, and stir to combine.

In a small bowl, pour boiling water over the peas and let stand for 2 minutes. Drain, add the peas to the skillet, and season with salt and pepper.

When the linguine is cooked, remove ½ cup of the pasta water and set aside. Drain the pasta in a colander and add the pasta to the skillet. Transfer to a warm serving dish, add the ½ cup of pasta water, and combine gently. Scatter the caviar, cheese, and mint on the surface. Combine gently again just before serving.

PENNE WITH VEAL RAGU, SAGE, AND PEAS

Sprightly, tiny, sweet green peas are added to a robust sauce of veal and sage and combined with penne (or the smaller pennette). It is a totally irresistible medley of flavors.

SERVES 6

1 medium red onion

1 medium carrot

2 tablespoons coarsely chopped parsley

3 ounces prosciutto, cut into fine dice

1 tablespoon olive oil

1 pound ground lean veal

10 fresh sage leaves, coarsely chopped

1 cup dry white wine

3 cups chicken stock

Salt and pepper to taste

1 pound penne

10-ounce package frozen petit peas, defrosted

2 tablespoons freshly grated Parmesan cheese

Place the onion and carrot in the bowl of a food processor along with a handful of the parsley leaves and process until coarsely chopped. Add the prosciutto, combine with 2 or 3 strokes, and set aside.

In a 12-inch sauté pan, heat the oil over medium-high heat. Add the veal and stir until it begins to brown. Add the prosciutto-vegetable mixture and sauté for 1 minute, stirring constantly. Raise the heat to high, add the sage and wine, and cook until the liquid evaporates, about 15 minutes.

Add the stock, turn the heat to low, and simmer, uncovered, for about 45 minutes. Add salt and pepper to taste.

About 15 minutes before the sauce is finished, cook the penne. Stir the peas into the sauce and cook for 1 minute. Drain and add the pasta to the sauce. Transfer to a large serving dish and scatter the remaining tablespoon of chopped parsley on the surface along with the cheese.

FARFALLE WITH LEEKS, ASPARAGUS, AND FENNEL SAUSAGE

Fresh asparagus with just a touch of tomato and fennel sausage flavor this quickly prepared pasta dish.

SERVES 6

1 pound farfalle

3 tablespoons olive oil

2 teaspoons finely chopped garlic
  (1 large clove)

1½ cups thinly sliced leeks, white part
  plus 1 inch of green (about 2 or
  3 thin leeks)

8 ounces fennel sausage, removed
  from its casings and crumbled

½ cup dry white wine

½ teaspoon crushed fennel seeds

1½ cups diced plum tomatoes (about
  3 large)

1 pound asparagus, trimmed and sliced
  diagonally in 1-inch pieces

⅔ cup chicken broth

Salt and pepper to taste

½ cup grated Parmesan cheese

2 tablespoons coarsely chopped
  parsley

Bring a large pot of salted water to a boil and cook the pasta until tender. While the pasta is cooking, prepare the sauce. In a 12-inch sauté pan, heat the olive oil over medium heat. Add the garlic and leeks, and sauté, stirring, for about 3 minutes, or until the leeks wilt. Add the crumbled sausage and sauté 1 or 2 minutes more, until the meat loses its pink color. Add the wine and fennel seeds, and bring to a boil. Stir in the tomatoes, asparagus, and broth, and bring to a boil again. Lower the heat and simmer just until the asparagus tests tender/crisp with the point of a knife, about 4 to 5 minutes.

Season with salt and pepper. Drain the pasta and add it to the sauce, combining well. Transfer to a large serving platter or bowl, sprinkle with the cheese and parsley, and toss at the table before serving. Pass a pepper mill and more cheese.

VIETNAMESE RICE NOODLE AND CHICKEN SALAD WITH LEMONGRASS AND GINGER

A pasta dish with panache and sprightly contrasting flavors and textures. Every forkful is an adventure.

SERVES 6

DRESSING:

2 tablespoons white rice wine vinegar

1 tablespoon shredded lime zest

2 tablespoons lime juice (1 large lime)

1 tablespoon Vietnamese fish sauce (*nuoc mam*) (see page 292)

2 teaspoons sugar

Salt and pepper to taste

2 tablespoons Asian sesame oil

1 tablespoon finely minced red cayenne chile or ½ teaspoon hot pepper flakes

1 tablespoon very finely minced lemongrass made from the bottom ⅓ of 1 or 2 inner tender stalks

2 teaspoons peeled and finely minced ginger root

2 tablespoons water

SALAD:

1½ pounds boned and skinned chicken breasts

2 tablespoons coarsely chopped garlic (2 large cloves)

3 tablespoons coarsely chopped shallots (2 large)

1 tablespoon corn oil

Salt and pepper to taste

6 ounces rice stick vermicelli (*mei-fun* or *bun*) noodles (see Note)

1½ cups julienne-cut cucumbers (2 or 3 small Kirby)

⅓ cup julienne-cut carrot (about 1 carrot)

⅔ cup diagonally sliced scallions (2 or 3 thin scallions)

3 cups finely shredded romaine lettuce

¼ cup whole cilantro leaves

¼ cup whole mint leaves

2 tablespoons basil leaves, roughly torn if large

½ cup coarsely chopped toasted cashew nuts

Make the dressing first: Combine all the ingredient in a small bowl and let stand until ready to use.

In a bowl, combine the chicken breasts, garlic, shallots, corn oil, salt, and pepper, and marinate for 30 minutes, turning the breasts once.

While the chicken marinates, put the noodles in a large bowl, cover with warm water, and let stand for 20 minutes. Heat a pot of water to boiling, drain the soaked noodles, and add them to the boiling water. Cook for 2 minutes. When tender, drain and rinse the noodles in cold water. Add the reserved dressing to the noodles and combine.

Remove the garlic and shallots from the chicken marinade and discard. Grill or broil the breasts about 4 or 5 minutes on each side, or until just cooked through. When cool enough to handle, cut or tear the breasts into bite-size pieces and add them to the noodles. Stir in the cucumbers, carrot, and scallions, and toss gently.

Line a large platter with the shredded lettuce and transfer the noodle salad to the platter. Scatter the cilantro, mint, and basil leaves over the surface and top with the nuts. Serve at room temperature.

Note: Rice stick vermicelli—or *mei-fun* or *bun*—are as thin as angel hair pasta.

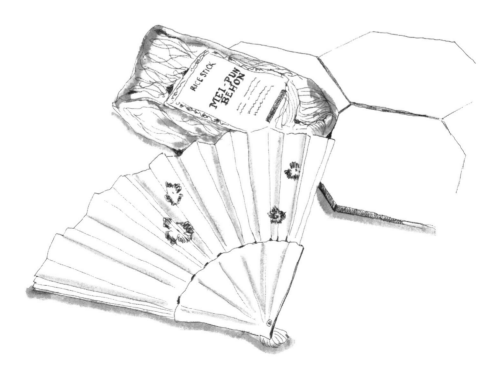

COUSCOUS WITH SUMMER VEGETABLES AND CLAMS

Couscous and seafood are a combination long enjoyed in Sicily. Our version of the famous Sicilian cuscusu *is steeped in clam broth, tossed with fresh summer vegetables and herbs, and then studded with tender clam morsels.*

SERVES 4

24 cherrystone clams, well scrubbed

2 tablespoons butter

1 teaspoon finely minced garlic
  (1 medium clove)

4 sprigs parsley

1 cup quick-cooking couscous, medium
  granulation

8 ounces small zucchini, shredded

12 ounces plum tomatoes, quartered
  (about 4 tomatoes)

1 teaspoon finely grated lemon zest

3 tablespoons lemon juice (2 medium
  lemons)

3 tablespoons finely shredded basil
  leaves

⅛ teaspoon cayenne pepper

Black pepper to taste

Salt to taste

In a 5-quart Dutch oven, place 2½ cups cold water and the clams in one layer. Cover the pot tightly and bring to a boil over medium-high heat. Steam for 5 to 8 minutes, or until the clams open, sliding the pot back and forth a few times during cooking. Remove the clams with a slotted spoon. Discard any that remain closed. Cool and remove the meat from the shells and set aside.

Strain the clam broth through a strainer lined with a man's cotton handkerchief. Measure the broth and add enough water to make 3 cups of liquid. In a 3-quart saucepan, melt 1 tablespoon of the butter over low heat. Add the garlic and sauté until soft, about 1 or 2 minutes. Add the reserved clam broth and sprigs of parsley, and bring to a boil over medium heat. Slowly add the couscous, lower the heat, and cook, covered, for 5 minutes. Remove the pot from the heat and let the couscous stand, covered, for 30 minutes. (See Note.) Remove and discard the parsley and fluff the couscous with a fork to separate the grains.

Stir in the remaining butter, the shredded zucchini, tomatoes, lemon zest and juice, basil, cayenne, black pepper, and the reserved clams. Taste for additional salt; since the clam broth is naturally salty, you may need no salt or very little. Transfer to a serving dish and serve at room temperature.

> Note: Prepackaged quick-cooking couscous usually has instructions for cooking right on the box; they generally allow 5 minutes of cooking time and 5 minutes of standing time, using 1 cup of dry couscous to 1½ cups of liquid. *Ignore these instructions,* for experience has taught us that if we use 1 cup of dry couscous, double the liquid to 3 cups, and allow 30 minutes of standing time, the grains will absorb more liquid in the pot and *not* in the gut. (This might account for the possibility of stomach rumblings for some people.)

◆ The Couscous Connection ◆

Although most people think of couscous as a whole grain, it is not. It's a pasta, usually made of semolina flour and water and then turned into pellets of various sizes. All across North Africa—Algeria, Morocco, Tunisia—and up through Sicily, Sardinia, Israel, and the Middle East, couscous is the pasta dish of choice. It is used as a base for many kinds of dishes, sparked with vegetables, spices, fruits, fish, and meats.

ORZO WITH VEGETABLES, BLACK OLIVES, AND ARUGULA

A light, warm pasta dish that could easily serve four for lunch, be part of a buffet, or serve six as a salad.

SERVES 4 TO 6

1 medium zucchini (about 8 ounces), cut into ½-inch dice

1 cup small broccoli florets or asparation (broccolini)

4 tablespoons olive oil

1 tablespoon finely minced garlic (2 medium cloves)

⅔ cup finely sliced scallions (about 3 medium)

3 plum tomatoes, cut into ½-inch dice

1 medium yellow sweet pepper, cut into ½-inch dice

12 black Kalamata olives, pitted and cut into slivers

2 teaspoons fresh thyme leaves
1 tablespoon grated lemon zest
2 tablespoons lemon juice
⅔ cup orzo

Salt and pepper to taste
3 cups stemmed and coarsely torn
  arugula

Blanch the zucchini and broccoli florets in boiling salted water for 2 minutes. Drain in a sieve and refresh under cold running water. Drain, dry well, and put in a large bowl.

In a small skillet, heat 1 tablespoon of the olive oil. Add the garlic and sauté over medium heat, stirring, for 1 minute. Add the garlic to the bowl, then add the scallions, tomatoes, yellow pepper, olives, thyme, lemon zest and juice, and combine.

Cook the orzo in 3 cups of boiling salted water until tender, about 10 minutes, then drain. Add the orzo to the bowl and combine. Season liberally with salt and pepper. Add the arugula and toss with the remaining olive oil.

Divide among 4 to 6 serving plates and serve.

Finfish: Casting a Wider Net

Salmon with Pickled Cocktail Onions, Cucumber, and Dill

Tuna Tartare with Pickled Ginger and Cucumber

Red Snapper with a Mussel, Tomato, and Saffron Cream Sauce

Cod with Manila Clams in a Garlic and Parsley Sauce

Flounder Sandwiches Filled with Tiny Shrimp in a Tomato Basil Sauce

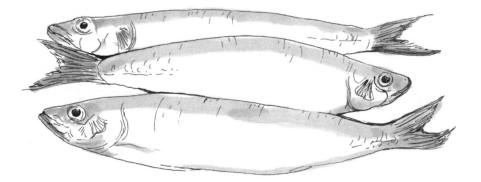

It's no longer the same kettle of fish. Not long ago, those of us who were "hooked" on fish could guarantee a really fresh selection of seafood only if we lived near the sea or if we fished for the seasonal catch ourselves. Even then the selection was usually quite limited to a few standards such as flounder and fluke. But as the industry developed more efficient methods of flash freezing aboard the fishing boats, and air transportation guaranteed speedy delivery, we began to see the proliferation of "day" boats, with skippers who went out at night and returned in the early morning, sending the catch right to the marketplace, truly fresh and unfrozen.

On the other hand, technology has also created the problem of efficient gill and drag nets some miles long that have been responsible for the overfishing of the popular species. In addition, fish caught in these traps naturally struggle to free themselves and become bruised. Fish that are caught early on stay in the nets much longer and become mushier in texture. Pollution has also taken its toll around the world, not only limiting the catch of popular fish but creating an environmental problem in every part of the seafood world. Fortunately, much of the gap is being closed by aquaculture—for salmon, trout, and shellfish such as mussels.

An increase in consumer interest in nutrition and the eating of more seafood has meant that former junk fish such as skate, monkfish, talapia, opah, Arctic char, and Chilean sea bass have become popular and accepted by both home cooks and restaurant chefs.

We have always had one rule in our household when it comes to buying seafood: *Find a fishmonger you can trust.* It takes questioning, investigation, and close inspection of the samples that are neatly laid out—always on ice. But essentially it all comes down to the man or woman behind the counter who says, "Try this one. It's fresh."

SHOP SMART

WHOLE FISH . . .

◆ Whole fish are probably the best bet for choosing fin fish. Make your selection and have the fishmonger prepare it for the recipe you've chosen—fillet, steak, or whole and gutted.

◆ Eyes should be bright and gleaming. If they're gray or clouded or sunken into the socket, pass it up. (Grouper is one exception. Cloudy eyes are due to pressure changes going from deep sea to the surface.)

◆ The gills should look bright red and healthy. As a fish ages, the gills fade to grayish pink and then brownish green.

◆ Scales should be shiny and tightly attached to the skin. For fish without scales, such as catfish, the same rule still holds: bright, shiny, and glistening.

◆ The texture of the flesh should be firm and elastic to the touch. Poke it; the flesh should spring back without leaving an indentation. Some fishmongers will not let you touch the fish. Watch him or her carefully as the fish is picked up. The same rule holds.

◆ Above all, *odor*. A fresh fish smells of the sea, briny and tempting. A fish odor probably means that it has been lying around too long or has been stored at too high a temperature. We also feel this way about the fishmarket itself; if we can smell it on the street, we pass it by.

When buying whole fish: a 5-pound fish = 2 pounds of fillets for
4 people.

PRECUT FISH . . .

◆ The same rule about smell applies to precut fish, fillets or steaks. The flesh should be shiny and have no bruised, brown, or yellow edges. The texture should be firm.

◆ If possible, use fish that are displayed on crushed ice and preferably are not prewrapped.

When buying fillets, figure 6 to 8 ounces per portion.

SUBSTITUTING FISH . . .

You go to the fish counter, a recipe clutched tightly in your hands. The sole (or salmon or tilefish or swordfish) looks dry or the fish you want is out of season or a new kind of fish looks interesting and tempting. Our philosophy has always been to find the best-looking specimen, buy it, take it home, and then find a recipe for it. There are more than six hundred species of fish; certainly you can find one to suit you.

In choosing a substitute, here is a guide:

- Fillets or steaks from lean, mild-flavored fish can be interchangeable: cod, scrod, haddock, pollack, whiting, all bass.
- Monkfish, turbot, halibut, and mahimahi can be used for the same recipe.
- Snappers, rockfish, sea bass, tilefish, and grouper are interchangeable.
- Flatfish (sole, fluke, and flounder) are similar to halibut and turbot. The latter two can be cut as steaks.
- Stronger fish can be substituted for each other: bluefish, mackerel, mako, swordfish, and tuna. However, they cannot be used in soups or stews.

Notes for the Cook

ON FINFISH . . .

- Refrigerate it immediately in the coldest part of your refrigerator.
- Cook it the same day or, at most, a day later.
- If you have bought a whole fish and the fishmonger has cut it into fillets for you, ask for the bones and the head. You can use them to make a fish stock that will keep in the freezer for future use when poaching fish or shellfish.
- If you have been lucky enough to receive a fresh line-caught fish from a neighbor and you'd like to freeze it for future use, rinse it in cold running water and keep it wet. Then wrap it tightly in aluminum foil, making sure all the air is squeezed out, and label with the name of the fish and the date. Wrap each fish or fillet separately; don't combine them or they'll stick together. Keep frozen and use within three months.
- When thawing frozen fish, run the packet under cold water until thawed. Don't thaw at room temperature or under warm water. And never refreeze fish once it has been thawed.

SALMON WITH PICKLED COCKTAIL ONIONS, CUCUMBER, AND DILL

Quickly sautéed, fresh fish is indeed a fast food. This salmon dish, easy to prepare and elegant to serve, proves our point.

SERVES 4

1 tablespoon olive oil

3 tablespoons butter

4 salmon fillets (about 6 ounces each), with skin on

Salt to taste

2 tablespoons pickled cocktail onions, including 1 teaspoon of pickling liquid

¼ cup finely julienned cucumber with skin (thin English cucumbers and Kirbys can be used)

1 tablespoon freshly snipped dill

Heat the oil and 1 tablespoon of the butter in a 12-inch nonstick skillet over medium-high heat until hot and bubbly. Dry the salmon well on paper towels, season with salt, and add to the skillet in 1 layer, skin side down. Sauté for about 4 minutes on each side, depending on the thickness of the fish.

Meanwhile, melt the remaining butter in a small saucepan over medium-low heat. Add the onions, pickling liquid, and cucumber, and cook over very low heat while the fish is cooking. Transfer the fish to serving plates, spoon the sauce over the fish, and sprinkle with dill.

TUNA TARTARE WITH PICKLED GINGER AND CUCUMBER

An appetizer that will delight any sashimi lover and possibly may convert those who say they don't like raw fish.

SERVES 4 TO 6

12 ounces fresh tuna in 1 chunk (preferably the marbled flesh from the tuna belly, called *toro* in Japanese

2 tablespoons pickled Japanese ginger, drained and cut into fine julienne (see Note)

2 small Kirby cucumbers (about 6 ounces), cut into ¼-inch dice

2 tablespoons green part of scallion, finely sliced on the diagonal (1 scallion)

⅓ cup tamari

2 tablespoons rice vinegar

1 teaspoon sugar

1 teaspoon (or more to taste) wasabi paste (Japanese mustard) (see Note)

Paper-thin slices of lemon for garnish

Trim the tuna of any dark flesh and cut into ¼-inch dice, removing and discarding any whitish membrane you may come across. Place the tuna in a medium-size bowl and add the ginger, cucumbers, and scallion, and combine.

Place the tamari, vinegar, sugar, and half of the wasabi paste in a small cup. Taste and add the remaining wasabi a bit at a time until there is a sharp pungency. Pour over the tuna mixture and combine lightly. Transfer the mixture with a slotted spoon to chilled serving plates. (It looks lovely on clear glass.) Slash each lemon slice halfway across, twist, and use to garnish each plate.

Note: Japanese pickled ginger is available in jars either thinly sliced or precut into juilienne. Wasabi comes in paste form and powder. The powder needs a bit of water to make it into a thick paste.

RED SNAPPER WITH A MUSSEL, TOMATO, AND SAFFRON CREAM SAUCE

The sweet and meaty red snapper, with its deep red and silver mottled skin, is a fish with a huge extended family of other snapper varieties all over the world. Here we have broiled it quickly and covered it with a gorgeous, colorful sauce of black mussels in a golden saffron cream sauce studded with tiny dots of tomato.

SERVES 4

SAUCE:

1 pound small blue mussels

2 sprigs fresh thyme

½ cup dry white wine

½ teaspoon loosely packed and crushed saffron threads

⅓ cup finely minced shallots (about 2 or 3 large)

1 cup heavy cream

⅛ teaspoon cayenne pepper

1 tablespoon soft butter

1 medium plum tomato, peeled, seeded, and cut into ¼-inch dice (about ¼ cup)

Salt to taste, if necessary

FISH:

1 tablespoon olive oil

1½ pounds red snapper fillets (or black sea bass, grouper, or tilefish), scaled but with skin intact and cut into 6-ounce portions

Salt to taste

1 tablespoon lemon juice (about ½ lemon)

Prepare the sauce first: Scrub the mussels with a nylon scrub pad and rinse in several changes of cold water. Pull off the "beards" if they are still on. Place the mussels in a 10-inch sauté pan along with the thyme and wine. Cover the pan and cook over high heat for 3 to 5 minutes, sliding the pan back and forth a few times over the burner while cooking. When the mussels have opened, remove them with a slotted spoon to a bowl to cool, discarding any that remain closed.

Strain the pan liquid through a dampened paper coffee filter that has been set in a strainer over a bowl. Add the saffron to this broth and let steep for 10 minutes.

In a 2-quart saucepan, combine the shallots and cream and add the mussel broth. Cook, uncovered, over medium heat for about 10 to 12 minutes, or until slightly thickened and reduced. While the sauce is cooking, remove the mussel meat from their shells. When the sauce has been reduced, remove it from the heat. Finish the sauce while broiling the fish.

Stir in the cayenne, butter, mussels, and tomato, and cook for about 1 minute to heat the sauce and melt the butter. Taste to see if salt is needed and add if necessary.

To prepare the fish: Preheat the broiler. Add the olive oil to an oven-to-table baking pan large enough to accommodate the fish in 1 layer. Add the fish and turn to coat both sides with the oil. Season with salt and lemon juice, and broil for 8 to 10 minutes, or until fish is opaque and cooked through when tested with the point of a knife.

Spoon the sauce over the cooked fish and serve.

COD WITH MANILA CLAMS IN A GARLIC AND PARSLEY SAUCE

Tiny clams and a beautifully balanced heavenly sauce, redolent of garlic and tempered by verdant parsley, cover the large moist flakes of the snowy white-fleshed cod. Serve with white rice.

SERVES 4

1 ½ pounds cod or scrod fillets, pin
    bones removed and cut into
    4 portions
3 cups flat Italian parsley leaves
⅓ cup olive oil
2 tablespoons coarsely chopped garlic
    (4 large cloves)
2 tablespoons all-purpose flour

1 cup fish stock
⅓ cup dry white wine
¼ teaspoon hot pepper flakes
Salt and pepper to taste
36 Manila clams (or cockles or small
    hard-shelled littleneck clams),
    scrubbed

Rinse the fish and place on paper towels to drain. In a food processor, coarsely chop the parsley and set aside. In a 12-inch skillet with a tight-fitting lid, heat the oil over medium-high heat. Add the garlic and sauté for 30 seconds, stirring constantly. Do not let the garlic burn, or it will be bitter. While stirring, quickly sift the flour lightly over the garlic and stir in 1 cup of the parsley. Add the fish stock, wine, hot pepper flakes, salt, and pepper, and bring to a boil. Lower the heat to medium, add the fish, and baste with some sauce. Cover tightly and cook for 5 minutes. Add the clams, hinge side down, cover the skillet again, and cook 2 or 3 minutes more, or until the fish flakes easily when tested with the point of a knife. Transfer the fish to a serving platter, stir in the remaining parsley, cover, and finish cooking the clams, sliding the skillet back and forth over the burner anywhere from 1 to 3 minutes more, depending on the size of the clams.

Spoon the clams and sauce over the fish and serve with rice to absorb the wonderful sauce.

FLOUNDER SANDWICHES FILLED WITH TINY SHRIMP IN A TOMATO BASIL SAUCE

In the winter this delicate, lean fish is called a "winter flounder," and in the summer it is called a "fluke" or "summer flounder." Tiny shrimp fill these fish sandwiches with a bread crumb–thickened sauce to absorb the natural cooking juices that form from the filling.

SERVES 4

4 skinned flounder fillets (about
   6 ounces each)
Salt and pepper to taste
1 tablespoon Dijon mustard
1 tablespoon mayonnaise
⅛ teaspoon cayenne pepper
1 tablespoon finely minced shallot
   (1 small shallot)
3 tablespoons soft butter

8 ounces small shrimp, shelled and
   deveined if necessary
2 large fresh tomatoes, peeled and cut
   in quarters
2 tablespoons finely shredded basil plus
   4 small whole fresh leaves for
   garnish
2 tablespoons melted butter
½ cup fine soft bread crumbs

Preheat the oven to 350 degrees. Oil a large oven-to-table baking pan. Place 2 fillets in the pan and season with salt and pepper. In a small bowl, place the mustard, mayonnaise, cayenne, shallot, and 2 tablespoons of the soft butter, and whisk together. Spread half of this mixture on the fillets and top with shrimp arranged in one direction. Spread the remaining mustard mixture on the other 2 fish fillets and place them, spread side down, on the shrimp, like a sandwich.

Surround the fish with the tomato quarters and basil. Mix the melted butter and bread crumbs together and sprinkle over all. Spread a piece of aluminum foil the size of the baking pan with the remaining tablespoon of soft butter and place it, butter side down, over the fish. Bake for 20 minutes.

After 15 minutes, remove the foil, baste, and test the fish. Return it to the oven uncovered for any additional cooking.

To serve, cut each "sandwich" crosswise to make 4 portions. Transfer to 4 plates, spoon the sauce and tomatoes over the fish, and garnish with the basil leaves.

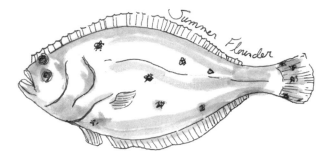

The Shell Game:
Crustaceans and Mollusks

Cold Poached Lobster Tails in a Seven Greens Sauce

Double Citrus Squid and Monkfish Salad with Celery and Parsley

Vietnamese Shrimp Salad with Jicama Slaw, Frisóo, and Mint

Littleneck Clams and Linguiça Sausage, Portuguese Style

Herbed Mussels with Orange Zest, Fennel, and Sweet Red Peppers

Seared Sea Scallops with Julienned Leeks and Ginger Cream

Crab Cakes with Chipotle Mayonnaise

LOBSTER

Lobsters have been around for somewhere near two million years, and the very best can be found along the northeast coast all the way up to Canada, especially in the State of Maine. There is nothing to compare with its sweet flavor when its dark green to black hard shell magically turns to bright red when it's cooked. And there is nothing quite like the festive atmosphere around the table as diners devour them section by section.

We love eating them, but we confess that we have great difficulty in dispatching a feisty live lobster into the pot, particularly when it looks up at us with its black hatpin eyes. "Experts" claim the lobster feels no pain; unfortunately, we do!

Americans consume about sixty-five thousand tons of lobsters every year. The claw-less variety, also known as the spiny or rock lobster, is the species that provides lobster tails; they are sold mostly frozen and uncooked from the warmer waters of the world. In terms of taste, we think there is no comparison: The lobsters of the Northeast win claws down.

SHOP SMART

In spite of what you may have read, we think that size does not matter. We have prepared 1½ pounders and 5 pounders, and we even had an out-of-body experience in Cape Cod with a 20 pounder. Also, we're convinced that male and female lobsters taste exactly the same.

◆ Lobsters should be vitally alive and kicking when you pick them up. The tail and claws should move energetically. The sluggish ones have probably been sitting around in pens for too long.

◆ Look for lobsters with the hardest shells to assure the best flavor. They're at their best before they molt, and if they're from the coldest waters of Maine and Canada, usually from October through late December. If the shells are soft (usually at the end of summer), it indicates that the lobster is molting and the flesh will be soft and delicate.

◆ If you're buying lobster tails, try to get them unfrozen. The flesh will be less stringy and more tender.

Notes for the Cook

ON LOBSTERS . . .

◆ Lobsters are versatile. They can be steamed, boiled, grilled, broiled, or baked with stuffing.

STEAMING: Our preferred method. It takes just a few inches of salted water at the bottom of a steamer. Bring to a boil, put the lobsters in with tongs, cover, and steam for 14 minutes for 1½ pounds, 18 minutes for 2 pounds.

BOILING: You'll need a large pot and a lot of water, enough to cover the lobsters completely. Use seawater or water with kosher salt; bring to a boil, immerse the lobsters carefully, cover, and cook 12 minutes for 1½ pounds, 14 to 15 minutes for 2 pounds.

GRILLING: Use lobsters up to 2 pounds since large ones will dry out on the grill. Split the live lobster down through the stomach and tail, remove the head sac and intestine, and crack the claws on the side away from the coals. Place the lobster on a rack over the coals and baste the meat with butter or oil. Cover with a large pan and do not turn the lobsters. Grill for 8 to 10 minutes for a 1½ pounder. The meat should be opaque and firm to the touch.

BROILING: Split the lobster as in grilling. Baste the lobster with butter, oil, or a sauce. Place on a rack about 6 to 8 inches below a preheated broiler for about 5 minutes. Remove, baste, and return the lobster 5 more minutes for a 1½ pounder, 3 to 4 more for a 2 pounder.

BAKING: Split and clean the lobster as in grilling. Add a seafood stuffing of shrimp, crab, and scallops along with bread crumbs and fresh herbs. Brush with butter or oil and bake at 425 degrees for 17 minutes for a 1½ pounder, about 22 to 24 minutes for a 2 pounder.

SQUID

Squid is not overly popular in the United States. However, Mediterranean and Asian people devour most of the world's catch in a range of dishes that can make your head spin. Now we too have begun to see it and eat it more frequently, especially in restaurants.

SHOP SMART

Fishmongers now sell precleaned squid for just pennies more than uncleaned squid—and without a loss in quality.

- ◆ Make certain to get equal amounts of body sacs and tentacles. They should be creamy white and have a glossy surface and a fresh sea aroma.
- ◆ Larger squid, 2 or 3 per pound, are usually good for stuffing or grilling. The smaller baby squid, about 6 ounces each and 2 inches long, are sweeter and more tender.

Large or small, allow 1½ pounds to serve four.

Notes for the Cook

ON SQUID . . .

- ◆ Depending on the recipe, the body sac can be left whole and stuffed with the tentacles, bread crumbs, cheese, and herbs, and then quickly grilled over charcoal.
- ◆ Squid sacs can be sliced into rings or slit open and then scored with a crisscross diamond pattern to pick up sauce and prevent the flesh from curling. The same holds true if you cut the sacs into strips—score the surface first. It also gives the squid an attractive look in a dish, and it is particularly pretty in a mixed seafood salad.
- ◆ *Don't cook squid too long!* If it has been cut into rings and fried or sautéed, all it needs is 1 to 2 minutes over medium-high heat to get from chewy to fork tender. Overcooking will take it from tender to rubbery.
- ◆ If squid is being cooked in a sauce on top of the stove, 5 to 8 minutes over medium heat should be sufficient. If you overcook it by accident, the only way to save it and bring it back to tenderness again is *slow* cooking for over an hour or so.

SHRIMP

Possibly one of the best examples of a fast food, shrimp require very little cooking to make them table ready. They are caught and marketed throughout the world from the tropics to the polar regions—in bays, estuaries, and the open sea. There are several hundred species, in rainbow hues that range from white to pink, blue-gray, green, brown, and tiger striped.

The northern varieties are usually firmer and more delicate than their tropical cousins, although 80 percent of the shrimp we eat comes from tropical waters off the coasts of South America, Australia, Asia, and from the Gulf of Mexico. Modern methods of flash freezing usually result in excellent quality at the marketplace, and almost all the shrimp we see neatly laid out on ice has been frozen and thawed.

 ## SHOP SMART

- Make sure the shrimp were recently defrosted. Use your nose and hands. They should smell like a sea breeze—briny and pleasant. The flesh should feel firm between your fingers, not soft.
- The shells should be filled with the flesh and should not be broken or loose. Shrimp should be glossy. As they age, the shine goes. Yellowed shells are also a sign of age.
- Shrimp can be kept on ice, covered with damp paper towels, for twenty-four hours, but it is best to eat them on the day you buy them.
- A generous amount for four shrimp lovers would be about 2 pounds of headless shrimp in shells, which will yield about 1 ½ pounds of peeled shrimp. If you are buying shrimp with heads on, allow an additional half pound.

SHRIMP MATH

Larger shrimp are the most expensive. Bigger is also the most popular, since shelling the larger ones takes less time than shelling smaller, less expensive ones. The size of shrimp depends on the approximate count per pound:

COUNT PER POUND

Small	40 to 60
Medium	30 to 40
Large	20 to 30
Jumbo	16 to 20 or more

Note: Large shrimp are sometimes referred to as "prawns," depending on where you live. Dublin Bay prawns and scampi are not shrimp at all but another related species of the saltwater lobster.

Notes for the Cook

ON SHRIMP . . .

- *To devein or not to devein:* The black vein on the back of the shrimp is not harmful and may not even be in every shrimp. If you find it esthetically displeasing, cut ¼ inch down the shelled shrimp and lift out the vein with the point of a knife.
- The shells are filled with flavor, so we suggest cooking the shrimp in their shells before peeling.
- The biggest mistake you can make is overcooking shrimp. A good rule is to let the shrimp turn from translucent to opaque, just a very few minutes.

CLAMS

The clam, a bivalve in the mollusk family—as are oysters, scallops, and mussels—is essentially an American culinary specialty. The tidal sands and bays of both the East and West coasts of the United States give us a diverse harvest: quahogs and steamers in the East, and razor clams and geoducks in the West.

Almost all the illnesses caused by eating seafood comes from raw oysters or clams; this is a result of the pollution problems almost everywhere in the world. We therefore have a very personal cardinal rule in our family: We don't eat bivalves raw.

Most areas where bivalves are harvested now require that the supplier tag and certify the catch, stating that it has been harvested from safe waters. If in doubt, ask to see the certification tag, and then cook them.

Hard-Shell Clams

QUAHOGS: Many times quahogs are labeled and sold by their size, with the market names corresponding to the size of the clams. Littlenecks are the smallest, about 1½ inches long, and most tender. Cherrystones are a bit longer, about 2 inches in length, and similar to the littlenecks in flavor. The largest are the chowder clams, which are much tougher and usually chopped for chowder or fritters.

OCEAN QUAHOGS: These are 3 to 4 inches long and are sometimes referred to as black clams or mahogany clams, which describes their shell color. It is a deep-sea clam harvested commercially, and it is usually chopped for freezing, canning, and chowders.

SURFS: Also known as bar or sea clams, these are the big ones, from 4 to 7 inches, and found right on the beach. They're the ones that the seagulls fight over. They're edible but usually very sandy, and only the two adductor muscles are eaten while the clam body is discarded.

COCKLES: Although there are many varieties around the world, and many travelers have tried them first in Europe, we import most of them from New Zealand. They can be prepared in the same manner as hard-shelled clams. They're distinguished by their tiny size, ridged shells, and, we think, a tendency to be sandy.

MANILAS: A hard-shell Pacific clam that is small—about 1¼ to 1½ inches in length—and very round with light brown striated ridges. Their size makes them very easy to use since they all open at the same time when cooked. They can be used in a variety of dishes: pastas, soups, stews, risottos.

Soft-Shell Clams

STEAMERS: Also known as long neck, belly, or pisser clams, they are small—about 2 to 3 inches—and have a soft white shell and a dark "handle." Usually they are steamed open, swished around in natural broth, and then the handle (a bit tougher than the belly but edible) is stripped of its dark gray skin; the whole clam is dipped in melted butter and lemon juice. They can also be batter-dipped and fried, New England style.

RAZORS: These have fragile shells, are in the shape of an old-fashioned sharp razor, and are about 4 to 10 inches long. Asian and other specialty markets stock them occasionally.

 *SHOP SMART*

Clams, oysters, and mussels are purchased live in their shells.

♦ When they're alive, the shells are tightly closed; they open only after they are cooked. Make sure they are lying on a bed of ice and that the shells are closed. The exceptions are soft-shell clams, razor clams, and geoducks (gooey-duck), which keep their shells agape naturally.

◆ When you get them home, take them out of the plastic bag or container and put them in a bowl with layers of ice cubes. Cover with damp paper towels and keep refrigerated. Check from time to time for melted ice and pour off the water.

◆ Before cooking, tap any clams that are agape. If the shells close, they're okay. Discard any that will not close.

Notes for the Cook

ON CLAMS . . .

◆ *Cleaning and shucking:* Unless you harvest your own, clams need only a thorough scrub under cold running water, using a non-soapy nylon pad.

◆ If the recipe calls for shucking (opening) the clam and removing the body, the easy way to do it is to steam the clams until they pop partly open, pry them fully open, and remove the clam from the shell. They can then be used for baking on the half shell or in chowders, pastas, and sauces, where they will be cooked further.

◆ *When cooking clams in the shell:* If some don't open at all, discard them. There are times when some will be laggards and open after the others have been removed and you continue the cooking. If they still don't open, throw them away.

MUSSELS

Mussels that grow naturally in the wild are briny and sweet, but they come with a price: diamond-hard barnacles and beards (byssus) that make for a time-consuming, labor-intensive few hours of pulling, scraping, and scrubbing.

Europeans seem to love mussels more than we do and have been the leaders in growing them on rope ladders that hang in their bays and estuaries. American cultivated mussels are now widely available neatly packaged in netting—grit-free, debearded, and uniform in size in their dark blue patent-leather shells.

SHOP SMART

- Cultured mussels, usually in 2-pound net bags, are ready to be cooked. All they need is a rinse under cold running water.
- A good, healthy mussel should be alive, with its shell tightly closed. Don't buy or use any that won't close, or if they open *before* cooking, discard them.
- Blue mussels range in size from 1 to 3 inches. The meat of the male is ivory color, the female deep orange. The flavor is the same.

Allow 4 pounds to serve four people.

- New Zealand greenlips are larger than the blue mussels, with a more pronounced flavor and a shell color that ranges from brown to green. The aquacultured Prince Edward mussels from Nova Scotia in Canada are smaller and have a more delicate flavor.
- If they have been put in a plastic bag, remove them when you get home. If they're in a net bag, keep them that way until ready to cook. Place them in a bowl surrounded by ice cubes, cover loosely with a damp paper towel, and put in the refrigerator.
- Like all raw shellfish, mussels should ideally be cooked the day you buy them, but keep them for no more than one or two days in the refrigerator.

Notes for the Cook

ON MUSSELS . . .

- If your mussels come from the wild, before cooking them you should fill a bowl in the sink with cold water and swish the mussels around well. Drain in a colander and then rinse again under cold running water. Remove any wiry beards by grasping them and pulling them off right before cooking. Even if the shells seem clean, give them a once-over with a non-soapy nylon pad under cold running water. If some stubborn barnacles still cling, scrape them off with a clam knife.
- Mussels are usually steamed open in wine or water, and they are done very quickly. They can be fried, grilled, stuffed, or roasted, and they are eaten whole. Don't chop them. They'll turn to mush. Store cooked mussel meat in some of the cooking broth so it doesn't dry up or shrivel.
- As with clams, if some don't open when they are cooked, discard them.

SCALLOPS

If you have ever watched the dredging of scallops or have done it yourself, you have been blessed with one of the most amusing sights in the world of mollusks. Dragged from the bottom, they snap their shells like a symphony of castanets, opening and closing with loud pops several times a second.

Scallops are very active swimmers, and this snapping movement speeds them along the ocean floor, developing their adductor muscles (called the "eye") at the same time. In the United States this is the only part of the scallop that we get to see, for they are shucked out at sea; in most of the world, especially in Europe, the entire scallop including the orange roe is consumed. As a result, the scallops sold in Europe are still alive, just like clams and mussels, and obviously they are the freshest you can buy.

Scallop shells have been an inspiration for painters throughout the centuries—made famous by Botticelli's Venus perched on a scallop shell. Although there are somewhere around four hundred varieties of scallops around the world, for the most part only three are popular here in the United States.

BAY SCALLOPS: The very sweetest of them all, they are found only on inshore saltwater bays and ponds off the Atlantic Coast, with top quality coming from Massachusetts and Long Island. The supply is limited due to the problem of the brown tide algae, which destroys the beds. When available, their season is fall through early spring. Their flesh varies in color from creamy white to pale salmon, and they range in weight from 50 to 100 per pound.

CALICO SCALLOPS: These are the most popular substitute for bay scallops. They are harvested in warm waters along the Carolina coast and down to Florida, and on the Gulf coast. Whiter in color than the bays, they are slightly smaller and are less expensive and also less flavorful.

SEA SCALLOPS: Harvested from the sea, they are the largest variety and range in size from 1 to 2 inches. They are sometimes large enough to be cut in half before cooking. Firmer in texture than the smaller scallops, they have a creamy translucency. They average about 28 to 30 per pound.

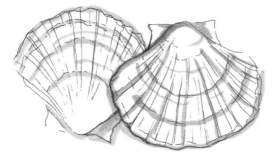

SHOP SMART

Since sea-shucked scallops are no longer alive, they are highly perishable, so use your nose and ask your trusted fishmonger about your purchase.

- Generally, all scallops should be firm, smell fresh, and look like shiny jewels.
- They should be cream, beige, or pink and have a translucent look. If they are too white, they may have been soaked in a phosphate bath to lengthen their shelf life or steam-blasted open on the boats to make the adductors easier to remove. The steam can also partially cook the scallops, making them less flavorful.
- When you get them home, take them out of their wrapping or bag and refrigerate immediately. Use them the same day you buy them if possible, but no later than the next day.

For any variety, allow 6 ounces per person.

CRAB

We have eaten crab all over the world on our travels through the years: the giant Queensland Mud Crab in Australia, the Hairy Crab chosen live from a holding tank in Hong Kong, and the Spider Crab in Vietnam. Happily, North America is the largest provider of edible crabs in the world, so we have also happily enjoyed the mouth-tingling hot chile boiled Blue Claws in Baltimore, the finger-lickin', butter drippin' Stone Crabs of Florida, and the springtime delicacy of soft-shell crabs in the New York area.

BLUE: Their shells can vary from brownish green to dark green with a white underbelly. Males are distinguished by blue claw tips, while females boast orange-tipped claws. They turn bright red after cooking, and since they have a 3-inch body, the picking can be labor intensive but very relaxing and worthwhile once you taste their flavor.

Blue Crabs molt about twenty times a year, are harvested before they grow to the next size, and are kept alive for only a few days out of water. They are eaten whole at this soft-shell stage. Your fishmonger will kill and clean them for you, but cook them as soon as possible.

We allow one to three of the tiniest soft shells per person—the 3- to 3½-inch "hotel" or 3- to 4-inch "prime" crabs.

DUNGENESS: These West Coast answers to the East Coast blue crabs are giants, sometimes 6 inches across. Since they are large, they are easier to pick at, but we feel their meat is not quite as sweet as the blues. They are usually sold in holding tanks and sold live or already cooked or frozen.

KING: An Alaskan miracle, with the average size up to 10 pounds. The large, meaty legs are usually cooked and frozen right on site in Alaska and then shipped to the marketplace. They are among the easiest to prepare, taking only a few minutes of steaming to thaw them since they are already cooked.

STONE: Although originating in Florida, where they are a popular menu item, they are also available from the Carolinas to Texas. The stone crab might be called a "recycled species." When they are caught, one claw is twisted off and cooked right aboard the ship. The rest of the crab is returned to the sea where it regenerates its lost claw. They are traditionally served with a butter or mustard sauce.

SNOW: Part of the spider crab family, they hail from the North Pacific. Smaller than the king crab, they average about 3 pounds each. They are usually found already cooked and in frozen clusters of legs and claws or packaged frozen as crabmeat.

SHOP SMART

Live crabs, frozen crabs, and crabmeat are available year-round.

COOKED CRABMEAT: Freshly cooked and already picked from the shell, it is available in various grades and prices. Buy only a recently packed container since crabmeat is highly perishable.

- *Lump meat* are large chunks of picked-over crabmeat from the body, with no waste. Considered the Rolls-Royce of crabmeat and, naturally, the most expensive.
- *Backfin* is just as good for most recipes, such as crab cakes. It has smaller chunks, some of them broken, and is less expensive than lump meat.
- *Flaked* usually has very small pieces that come from various body parts.
- *Combinations* are flake and lump mixed together. These are sometimes marketed as "special" or "mixed crabmeat." Read the labels carefully.
- *Pasteurized crabmeat* has been steamed, picked over, and immersed in a hot water bath. It usually comes in cans rather than plastic containers. We think

pasteurization alters the flavor in the same way that heavy cream that is "sterilized" doesn't taste the same as unsterilized cream.

◆ *Frozen crab* is available in almost all varieties, fully cooked and frozen.

◆ *Surimi* is, we think, unacceptable imitation crab. Usually made from a fish, Alaskan pollack, it is chopped into paste with all sorts of additives and then partially dyed to imitate crab.

COLD POACHED LOBSTER TAILS IN A SEVEN GREENS SAUCE

A verdant, versatile uncooked sauce, the color of pistachio ice cream, this is particularly good with lobster or lobster tails. We have also used it with poached monkfish, crab, and salmon with equally good results.

SERVES 4 TO 6

SAUCE (MAKES 2⅓ CUPS):
½ cup loosely packed fresh dill fronds
½ cup loosely packed parsley leaves
½ cup stemmed watercress leaves
½ cup stemmed spinach leaves
½ cup celery leaves
1 tablespoon fresh tarragon leaves
2 medium scallions, roughly chopped
1 small clove garlic
¼ cup finely snipped fresh chives
1 teaspoon finely grated lemon zest

2 tablespoons lemon juice
   (1 medium lemon)
1 cup mayonnaise
2 tablespoons sour cream
2 teaspoons Dijon mustard
1 hard-boiled egg, roughly chopped
Salt and pepper to taste
¼ teaspoon sugar
5 or 6 stemmed sorrel leaves with
   center rib stems removed (optional)

LOBSTER TAILS:
Four 6-ounce lobster tails in the shell
1 cup cold water
1 cup dry white wine

¼ cup roughly cut shallots (2 to
   3 large)
Salt to taste
10 black peppercorns

Prepare the sauce first: Wash all the greens: dill, parsley, watercress, spinach, celery, tarragon, and scallion. Drain in a sieve and then blot up the excess water well using paper towels. Place the greens in the bowl of a food processor, add the garlic and chives, and process until coarsely chopped. Add the lemon zest and juice, and continue to process until all the ingredients are finely chopped. Add the mayonnaise, sour cream, mustard, and egg, and process again until well combined. Season with salt, pepper, and sugar, and combine. Transfer to a serving bowl, cover with plastic wrap, and refrigerate for at least 2 hours. Taste the sauce just before serving for additional seasoning and add if necessary. Also add the sorrel leaves, if available.

To prepare the lobster: If the lobster tails are frozen, thaw them quickly by running cold water over the backs of the shells. In a 3-quart saucepan, bring the water, wine, shallots, and salt to a rolling boil over high heat. Add the lobster tails and return to a boil. Turn the heat to medium-low, cover the pot, and simmer for about 8 minutes, or until the flesh is opaque and just cooked through. Remove with tongs and let cool.

When they are cool, split them down the underside of the tail and break each tail open like a book to remove the meat. Cut into large chunks and arrange on a plate (preferably glass). Serve the sauce on the side in a large scallop shell or spoon over the lobster in a striped design. Add extra cold shrimp or salmon if you wish; you'll have lots of extra sauce.

Cold Poached Lobster tails in a Seven Greens Sauce

DOUBLE CITRUS SQUID AND MONKFISH SALAD WITH CELERY AND PARSLEY

We usually prepare this seafood salad the night before, letting it marinate in its light lemony dressing, along with the bite-size pieces of sweet orange, the salty black olives, and the crisp celery. It's a lovely light luncheon dish and a favorite first course for dinner.

SERVES 4 TO 6

1 pound monkfish

1 ½ pounds small squid, cleaned and
    with tentacles reserved

1 cup dry white wine

1 cup fish stock

2 sprigs thyme

½ cup thinly sliced scallions (about
    2 medium)

½ cup thinly sliced celery (1 rib)

1 large navel orange

1 teaspoon finely grated lemon zest

2 tablespoons lemon juice

1 tablespoon white wine vinegar

Pinch of sugar

⅛ teaspoon Tabasco

Salt and pepper to taste

6 tablespoons light olive oil or
    canola oil

3 tablespoons finely minced parsley

6 cups roughly torn red frilled lettuce
    leaves

10 pitted black Kalamata olives, cut
    in half

Pull off the membrane from the monkfish and cut the fish into ¾-inch cubes. Cut the squid bodies into ¼-inch rings. Leave the tentacles whole if the squid are small and halve them if they are larger.

In a 3-quart saucepan, bring the wine, fish stock, and thyme to a boil over medium heat. Add the monkfish, turn the heat to low, and simmer for 2 minutes. Add the squid and continue to simmer 1 minute more, until both are opaque. Remove and discard the thyme and strain the seafood, reserving and freezing the liquid for another use (such as poaching fish). Place the seafood in a medium-size nonreactive bowl to cool slightly. Add the scallions and celery, and toss lightly.

Working over a bowl, cut the peel and pith from the orange and discard them. Cut the flesh of the orange into segments, slicing between the membranes. Cut the flesh into bite-size pieces and add them to the bowl. Add the lemon zest and juice, vinegar, sugar, Tabasco, salt, and pepper. Slowly whisk in the oil. Pour the mixture over the seafood, add 2 tablespoons of the parsley, and combine. Cover the bowl with plastic and chill in the refrigerator for at least 6 hours or overnight.

When ready to serve, taste and correct the seasoning. Divide the lettuce among the serving plates and mound the seafood salad in the center. Scatter the remaining tablespoon of parsley and a few olive halves over each portion.

VIETNAMESE SHRIMP SALAD WITH JICAMA SLAW, FRISÉE, AND MINT

A tart, sweet, crisp, and cool salad, all blended and balanced with refreshing clementines and slightly bitter French frisée. Definitely a French-Vietnamese connection for shrimp lovers.

SERVES 4

½ teaspoon finely minced garlic
   (1 small clove)

1 small serrano chile, seeded and
   minced

1 tablespoon each lemon and
   lime juice

2 tablespoons *nuoc mam* bottled sauce
   (see Note)

2 tablespoons rice vinegar

1 tablespoon sugar

3 tablespoons corn oil or canola oil

½ pound jicama, peeled and cut into
   fine julienne

1 Kirby cucumber (about 8 ounces),
   cut into fine julienne

2 thin carrots (about 4 ounces), cut
   into fine julienne

⅓ cup finely chopped red onion
   (½ medium onion)

8 ounces frisée (curly endive), torn
   into bite-size pieces (about 3 to
   4 cups)

2 clementines, peeled and segmented

6 sprigs mint, leaves only, with one
   whole sprig reserved for garnish

3 cups cold water

6 whole black peppercorns

1 bay leaf

Coarse salt to taste

1½ pounds shrimp, in shells

In a small bowl, whisk together the garlic, chile, lemon and lime juice, *nuoc nam* sauce, vinegar, sugar, and oil, and set aside.

In a large bowl, place the jicama, cucumber, carrots, onion, frisée, clementines, and mint leaves, and toss lightly.

In a 3-quart saucepan, add the water, peppercorns, bay leaf, salt, and shrimp, and bring to a boil over medium-high heat. Cook for 1 or 2 minutes, or until the shrimp are opaque, then drain and cool the shrimp slightly. Peel the shrimp and add them to the large bowl. Pour the reserved dressing over all, season with coarse salt to taste, and toss to combine. Transfer to a large flat platter and garnish with the reserved mint sprig.

Note: *Nuoc mam* is Vietnamese fish sauce. It comes bottled and is available in most well-stocked supermarkets. The Thai version is called *nam pla* and can be substituted.

LITTLENECK CLAMS AND LINGUIÇA SAUSAGE, PORTUGUESE STYLE

Small briny clams are cooked in a spicy tomato and onion sauce with tiny chunks of garlicky sausage. It is a traditional Portuguese dish that hails from the southern Algarve province, where we first tasted it and fell in love with the lusty flavors.

SERVES 4

¼ cup olive oil

2 cups coarsely chopped onions (2 to 3 large onions)

1 tablespoon finely chopped garlic (3 to 4 cloves)

1 tablespoon sweet paprika

¼ teaspoon cayenne pepper

8 ounces sweet Portuguese linguiça sausage or sweet Spanish chorizo, cut in ¾-inch pieces

¾ cup dry white wine

1 pound plum tomatoes, skinned and diced (4 to 5 tomatoes)

1 bay leaf

⅛ teaspoon ground cloves

¼ teaspoon black pepper

24 small littleneck clams, well scrubbed, or 36 Manila clams (see Note)

2 tablespoons coarsely chopped parsley

Lemon wedges

Sourdough bread cut into thick slices

In a 12-inch skillet with a tight-fitting lid, heat the olive oil over medium heat. Add the onions and sauté slowly, stirring occasionally, for about 10 to 12 minutes, until the onions are tender and just becoming golden. Add the garlic, paprika, and cayenne, and cook, stirring, for 1 minute. Add the sausage and cook 3 minutes more. Stir in the wine, tomatoes, bay leaf, cloves, and black pepper. (Do not add the salt until just before serving, since the clams will be salty.) Bring the sauce to a boil, then turn the heat to low and simmer for 15 minutes. Raise the heat to medium-high. Add the clams, placing them in the sauce bottom side down in 1 layer. Cover tightly and cook for 5 to 6 minutes, sliding the pan back and forth over the burner a few times during the cooking, until the clams open. Discard any clams that do not open. Remove and discard the bay leaf. Taste for salt and add if needed.

Spoon into large, warmed bowls and sprinkle with parsley. Tuck a wedge of lemon into each bowl, to be squeezed over the dish at the table. Serve with warm thick slices of sourdough bread to mop up the sauce.

Note: Manila clams are tiny, and if you use them, they may need less than 5 minutes to steam open.

HERBED MUSSELS WITH ORANGE ZEST, FENNEL, AND SWEET RED PEPPERS

It is not difficult to understand our growing infatuation with the Belgian national dish: mussels. They are light, satisfying, and quickly prepared— and have all the prerequisites for today's interest in healthful eating.

SERVES 4 TO 6

4 pounds medium-size mussels, rinsed in cold water and scrubbed with a nylon pad

1 navel orange, zest cut in 2- to 3-inch strips plus ¼ cup squeezed orange juice

½ teaspoon saffron threads

3 tablespoons olive oil

4 to 5 large shallots, thickly sliced (about ¾ cup)

1 tablespoon finely minced garlic (2 to 3 cloves)

½ small fennel bulb (about 8 ounces), cored and roughly chopped (about 1 cup)

1 large sweet red pepper (about 8 ounces), cored, seeds and inner ribs removed, and cut into thin julienne (about 1½ cups)

1 cup crushed canned Italian tomatoes

⅛ teaspoon hot pepper flakes

½ cup dry white wine

4 sprigs fresh thyme or 2 teaspoons dried

1 small bay leaf

Salt and pepper to taste

2 tablespoons finely shredded basil plus 1 tablespoon for garnish

Sourdough toasts

If the mussels are from the wild, you will need to wash them in several changes of water until the water runs clear. Scrub and debeard them and rinse again. Set aside.

Reserve the orange zest strips. In a small cup, combine the orange juice with the saffron and set aside.

In a 5- to 6-quart Dutch oven with a tight-fitting lid, heat the oil over medium-low heat. Add the shallots and garlic, and stir for 1 or 2 minutes. Add the fennel and red pepper, and sauté, stirring frequently, until the vegetables are wilted, about 5 to 8 minutes. Add the tomatoes, reserved orange zest, hot pepper flakes, wine, reserved orange juice and saffron mixture, thyme, bay leaf, salt, and pepper. Raise the heat to medium and bring to a boil, then turn the heat to low and simmer for 2 minutes.

Add the mussels and basil, and stir once. Raise the heat to high, cover tightly, and cook for about 4 or 5 minutes, sliding the pot back and forth a few times over the burner. Remove the pot from the heat, let it sit for 1 minute, then open the cover and discard any closed mussels. Taste the broth and adjust for salt and pepper. Remove the bay leaf and thyme sprigs with tongs and discard.

To serve, divide the mussels and sauce among large bowls. Scatter a bit of the basil on the surface and serve with a basket of sourdough toasts to sop up the sauce.

SEARED SEA SCALLOPS WITH JULIENNED LEEKS AND GINGER CREAM

Quickly seared large scallops are a boon to the home cook who is pressed for time. Here they are paired with perky ginger root, tamed with a bit of cream and julienned leeks.

SERVES 4

1½ pounds medium-size sea scallops (about 26 to 28), picked over for bits of shell
5 tablespoons butter
1 cup julienned leeks, white parts only, plus 2 tablespoons finely minced leeks

1 tablespoon plus 1 teaspoon peeled and finely minced ginger
⅓ cup dry vermouth
1 tablespoon fresh lime juice
⅔ cup heavy cream
Salt and white pepper to taste

Dry the scallops on paper towels. Heat a 12-inch nonstick skillet until very hot and almost smoking. Add 1 tablespoon of the butter, swirl it around in the pan, and add the scallops in 1 layer. Sear for 2 to 3 minutes on each side, until the scallops are brown on the top and bottom, and the centers just cooked through. Transfer to a plate and set aside, keeping them warm by covering the plate with aluminum foil.

Wipe out the pan and return it to the stove. Add 2 tablespoons of the butter and the julienned leeks, and cook over medium heat, stirring, for 4 or 5 minutes, until the leeks begin to color. Transfer to another plate with a slotted spoon and set aside.

Return the same skillet to the stove once again and melt the remaining 2 tablespoons of butter over medium heat. Add the minced leeks and stir for 30 seconds. Add the ginger, vermouth, lime juice, and any accumulated juices from the scallops. Cook to reduce the liquid to half the amount. Stir in the cream and cook, swirling the skillet, for 3 or 4 minutes, or until the sauce is slightly thickened. Taste for salt and add the pepper.

Arrange the scallops in a circle on 4 warm plates. Spoon the sauce around the scallops and top with the reserved julienned leeks.

CRAB CAKES WITH CHIPOTLE MAYONNAISE

There are as many versions of crab cakes as there are cooks who make them. Some are thickened with bread crumbs, bound with eggs, or laced with mayonnaise. Our favorite recipe is this one, bound with a piquant béchamel sauce and created by a generous, talented chef who would never use flaked *crab but only the best lump crabmeat. Thank you, Jim Reed.*

MAKES 10 TO 12 CRAB CAKES

CRAB CAKES:
4 tablespoons butter
5 tablespoons flour
1 cup hot milk
¼ teaspoon Tabasco
1 tablespoon Dijon mustard
¼ teaspoon white pepper
Salt to taste

½ cup very finely minced scallion, green part only (about 3 large scallions)
¼ cup very finely minced parsley
1 pound lump or backfin crabmeat, picked over to remove any bits of shell or cartilege

CHIPOTLE MAYONNAISE

(MAKES I CUP):

7-ounce can chipotle chiles in
   adobe sauce

I cup commercial mayonnaise

I teaspoon finely minced garlic
   (I medium clove)

I tablespoon lime juice (½ lime)

2 teaspoons finely minced shallot
   (about I medium)

Salt to taste

FLOUR FOR DREDGING:

I large egg, lightly beaten

I cup fine dry bread crumbs

Corn oil for frying

To make the crab cakes: In a 3-quart nonstick saucepan, melt the butter over low heat. As soon as the butter is melted, quickly whisk in the flour and whisk just until smooth. Gradually add the hot milk, whisking constantly to prevent lumps. Use a wooden spoon and beat the mixture for 2 or 3 minutes, until very thick and the sauce leaves the sides of the pan. Remove from the heat and beat in the Tabasco, mustard, pepper, and salt. Let cool slightly and then stir in the scallions and parsley. Gently fold in the crab, leaving the lumps as whole as possible.

Divide the mixture into 10 or 12 equal portions and shape into slightly flattened patties. Place on a waxed paper–lined plate, cover tightly with plastic wrap, and chill in the refrigerator for at least 3 hours.

While the crab cakes are chilling, prepare the mayonnaise: Remove the chipotle chiles from the can with a fork, leaving the adobe sauce that clings to the chiles. Puree the chiles in a food processor. It will make about ½ cup of puree. Put 2 tablespoons aside for use in the recipe and the balance in a covered container in the refrigerator, where it will keep for several weeks for use in other recipes.

In a small bowl, combine the mayonnaise, garlic, lime juice, shallot, the 2 tablespoons of puree, and salt. Cover with plastic wrap and chill until the crab cakes are ready.

When ready to cook, place 2 pieces of aluminum foil on the work surface. Place the flour on one and the bread crumbs on the other. Place the beaten egg in a pie plate. Dip each cake lightly in the flour first, then in the egg, and then in the bread crumbs.

In a 12-inch nonstick skillet, slowly heat the oil over moderate heat until hot but not smoking. Add as many cakes as will fit in 1 layer without crowding and fry for about 2 or 3 minutes on each side, until the cakes are golden brown. Drain on paper towels and serve with the sauce on the side.

Chicken: Home on the Free Range

Poussin with Fresh Herbs

Drunken Chicken Ashiya with Pearl Onions and Red and Green Peppers

Asian Chicken Salad with Cilantro and Ginger Dressing

Chicken Breasts with Taleggio Cheese and Olivada on Tomato Concasse

*Chicken with Italian Fennel Sausage and
Pickled Peperoncini (Pollo Scarpariello)*

"A Chicken In Every Pot"

Chicken is now the number one "white meat" in the country, with a per capita consumption of more than seventy pounds a year. This is a far cry from the time when chicken was an expensive luxury and Herbert Hoover, campaigning for the presidency during the Great Depression, promised Americans "a chicken in every pot."

But over the years, the mass production of poultry has meant raising fowl in confined spaces, feeding them a diet based on the cheapest rather than the best, and having chickens gain weight rapidly by injecting them with growth hormones and antibiotics to reduce the spread of diseases that close quarters promoted. In addition, mass-produced chickens are tasteless and rubbery, and many health-conscious consumers began to object. We demanded better processing, the use of organic feed instead of growth stimulants, and more room for the birds to be truly "free-ranged" instead of being cooped up. But some confusing new terminology has remained, and though the Department of Agriculture has tried to solve the problem, there is still no consensus between the breeders and the marketers.

Here are some of the new terms: *Free range* merely means that the bird has access to the outdoors. *All natural* does not mean antibiotics were not used but only that preservatives were not. And, technically, if antibiotics were removed from the feed one or two weeks before the chickens' demise, they are *antibiotic free*. The word "organic" has never been fully defined, but poultry are generally considered *organic* when the feed contains no pesticides. And *fresh farm raised* means exactly what it says: "Fresh" denotes that they have been stored and transported at temperatures ranging from zero to 34 degrees; "farm raised" means the fowl have not been raised on a city rooftop!

SHOP SMART

- ◆ Purchase local or regional premium brands if possible.
- ◆ Big is not necessarily better. Specialty brands from smaller companies offer birds that have been allowed to grow naturally, up to nine weeks rather than the hormone-boosted six to seven weeks.
- ◆ Check the "sell dates," which indicate the shelf life of the bird. Buy only one or two days after processing and keep no more than one or two more days.
- ◆ We prefer to buy whole chickens rather than parts since we don't know if the rest of the chicken was bruised or damaged. We also prefer the whole chicken because we've learned that the reason for a successful relationship is that one partner likes the white meat while the other prefers the dark.

A GUIDE TO CHICKEN TERMINOLOGY

CORNISH HENS OR ROCK CORNISH GAME HENS: These are about thirty-five days old. It is a cross between two breeds of chicken that produces a 1- to 1½-pound chicken, the smallest size. Sold whole, it is large enough for one serving, perfect for quick-roasting at high heat or braising.

POUSSIN: This is also a very young (at thirty-five days old), small (under 1½ pounds) bird. The fact that it has a French cachet raises the price. We find them worth it, since the flavor is better than that of the Cornish hens.

BROILER: Usually under 2 pounds (at forty days old) and generally sold whole, it is tender and good for quick cooking under high heat.

FRYER: Between 2 and 4 pounds (at forty-five days old), it is usually sold whole or in parts. Both broilers and fryers respond well to grilling, roasting, sautéeing, and braising.

YOUNG ROASTER: About 4 to 5 pounds (at fifty days old), it is usually sold whole and referred to as a *pullet* by butchers. A *roaster* weighs between 5 and 8 pounds (at 60 days) and is sold whole. Both types are best roasted at moderate heat.

CAPON: This large-breasted, castrated rooster is very tender (at 75 days old), weighing between 8 and 12 pounds. They are sold whole and are best when roasted slowly at low heat.

Notes for the Cook

ON POULTRY . . .

Improper handling of poultry by either the producers or the consumer can cause food poisoning. Producers are monitored by public health officials, but you must play safe by following a few rules when handling poultry.

- ◆ Loosen tight store wrapping before refrigerating. Rewrap loosely in waxed paper and store in the coldest part of the refrigerator until ready to cook.
- ◆ Wash your hands before and after handling the bird.
- ◆ After washing your hands, rinse the sink and wash all utensils and cutting surfaces with a mixture of water and household bleach, then hot, soapy water, followed by a thorough rinse with clear water. And remember, wooden cutting boards are porous and can harbor bacteria better than other nonporous surfaces.
- ◆ If the bird is frozen, thaw and marinate only in the refrigerator, *never* at room temperature.
- ◆ If roasting a whole bird, cook to an internal temperature of 180 degrees.
- ◆ Don't keep leftovers at room temperature. Refrigerate them as soon as possible.

POUSSIN WITH FRESH HERBS

About ten years ago you had to have a garden if you wanted fresh herbs, but now they're available year-round almost anywhere in the country. So this poultry dish is easy to make no matter where you live.

SERVES 2

Two 1-pound poussins or
　　Cornish hens
Coarse salt to taste
¼ teaspoon Tabasco
3 tablespoons olive oil
1⅓ cups fresh, coarse bread crumbs,
　　prepared in a food processor

2 tablespoons finely minced chives
1 tablespoon finely minced parsley
1 teaspoon whole thyme leaves
2 teaspoons finely minced marjoram

Split the poultry up the backs. Trim the wings to the first joint and discard. Insert fingers under the skin and pull off as much skin as possible, leaving the skin only on the wings. Press the breast bone down so that the birds lie flat. Sprinkle lightly with coarse salt, ¼ teaspoon of Tabasco, and ½ teaspoon of olive oil on each bird. Place on an aluminum foil–lined baking sheet. Cover with foil and refrigerate until ready to bake, a minimum of 1 hour.

Preheat the oven to 400 degrees. In a small bowl, combine the bread crumbs and all the herbs. Stir in the remaining 2 teaspoons of olive oil. Press approximately ⅔ cup of the herbed bread crumbs over each poussin. Bake for 30 to 35 minutes. Remove from the oven and let rest, covered loosely with aluminum foil, for 10 minutes before serving.

DRUNKEN CHICKEN ASHIYA WITH PEARL ONIONS AND RED AND GREEN PEPPERS

We first ate this dish in a Kyoto restaurant called Ashiya Steakhouse, and we loved it. After prevailing upon the chef to give us the recipe, we were enthralled by its ease of preparation. A long marinating time in sake seems to be the secret of its unique flavor. Serve with rice.

SERVES 4

1 ½ pounds chicken breasts, boned, skinned, and cut into 1-inch squares
¾ cup sake (Japanese rice wine)
2 tablespoons shoyu or tamari soy sauce plus 2 additional teaspoons
2 teaspoons peeled and grated ginger root

1 small clove garlic, smashed
16 whole tiny white pearl onions
1 large red pepper (about 8 ounces)
1 large green pepper (about 8 ounces)
2 tablespoons corn oil
⅛ teaspoon cayenne pepper

Place the chicken in a nonreactive bowl (glass, ceramic, or stainless steel). In a cup, combine the sake, 2 tablespoons of soy sauce, ginger, and garlic, and pour the mixture over the chicken. Stir to combine, cover with plastic wrap, and refrigerate for 8 hours.

When ready to cook, pour off and discard all but 2 tablespoons of the marinade. Blanch the onions in boiling water for 3 or 4 minutes. Drain and cut off a thin slice from the root end of each onion and slip the skins off. Set aside.

Remove the seeds and membranes from the inside of the peppers and cut the peppers into 1-inch squares. In a 12-inch nonstick skillet or wok, heat the oil over medium-high heat. Add the onions and sauté them for 5 minutes, stirring frequently, until the onions just begin to color. Add the peppers and continue to stir and sauté 3 or 4 minutes more, or until tender/crisp. Raise the heat, add the drained chicken, and stir constantly until the chicken becomes opaque. The chicken should have a slight resilience at this point.

Combine the reserved marinade with the 2 teaspoons of soy sauce and cayenne and add to the skillet. Stir once or twice while the chicken quickly cooks through. Do not overcook. Remove from the heat and serve at once.

ASIAN CHICKEN SALAD WITH CILANTRO AND GINGER DRESSING

For those who like their salads hot, tart, zippy, sweet, and satisfying, this chicken salad with roots in the Far East is just the ticket.

SERVES 4

SALAD:

8 ounces boneless and skinned chicken breast, poached and cut into long, thin strips (about 1½ cups)

1 medium carrot, sliced into thin shreds with a vegetable peeler

3 scallions, cut diagonally into 1-inch pieces

1 to 2 cucumbers, preferably Kirby (about ½ pound), halved lengthwise, seeded, and sliced into thin crescent shapes

5 to 6 leaves young mustard greens or Chinese cabbage

2 teaspoons toasted sesame seeds

1 tablespoon slivered almonds, toasted

2 tablespoons whole fresh cilantro leaves

DRESSING:

1½ tablespoons light soy sauce or tamari

1½ tablespoons rice vinegar

1½ tablespoons corn oil

1 teaspoon Asian sesame oil

1 teaspoon hot chile oil

½ teaspoon light honey

¼ teaspoon fennel seeds, crushed lightly

1 scant tablespoon finely minced and peeled ginger root

To make the salad: Arrange the chicken, carrot, scallions, cucumbers, and greens on a large serving platter. Sprinkle the sesame seeds and almonds over the salad. Scatter cilantro leaves over all and chill while preparing the dressing.

To make the dressing: Combine all the ingredients and spoon them evenly over the salad. Toss and serve at the table.

CHICKEN BREASTS WITH TALEGGIO CHEESE AND OLIVADA ON TOMATO CONCASSE

In Italy, we fell in love with the deep, aromatic flavor of Taleggio cheese, named after a small town near Bergamo. It melts beautifully, mixing with olive paste spiked with a bit of oregano to form a quick and lovely sauce for a sautéed chicken breast.

SERVES 4

TOMATO CONCASSE:

4 large plum tomatoes (about
  ¾ pound), skinned and cut into
  ½-inch pieces
1 tablespoon olive oil
1 teaspoon sherry wine vinegar

1 teaspoon finely minced shallot
  (1 small shallot)
Salt and pepper to taste
2 or 3 basil leaves, finely shredded into
  tiny strips

CHICKEN:

4 skinned and boned chicken breasts
  (about 1½ pounds)
Salt and pepper to taste
Flour
3 tablespoons butter
8 ounces Taleggio cheese, at room
  temperature

4 tablespoons black olivada
  (olive paste)
2 teaspoons olive oil
¼ teaspoon crushed dried oregano,
  preferably Greek

To make the concasse: Combine all the ingredients in a small bowl and set aside.

Preheat the broiler until hot. Pound the chicken breast lightly between sheets of plastic wrap. If one part is too thick, cut and fold back part of the breast to flatten evenly before pounding. Season with salt and pepper. Place the flour in a plastic bag, add the chicken breasts, and shake to coat them with flour. Melt the butter in a 12-inch nonstick skillet over medium-high heat. When the butter is hot, shake off the excess flour from the chicken breasts and add them to the skillet. Sauté for 1 or 2 minutes, then turn them over and sauté 2 minutes more. The chicken should not be completely cooked through, and it should be resilient to the touch. It will finish cooking under the broiler.

Transfer the chicken breasts to a baking pan and place slices of the cheese over them. In a small bowl, combine the olive paste, olive oil, and oregano, and spoon 1 tablespoon over the cheese. Slip the pan 2 or 3 inches under the source of the heat and broil until the cheese is melted and starts to brown and the olive paste becomes a part of the cheese sauce, about 4 minutes. The chicken should be cooked through as well.

Ring the tomato concasse around the rim of 4 warm plates, leaving the center empty. Transfer each chicken breast to the center of the plates and serve at once.

CHICKEN WITH ITALIAN FENNEL SAUSAGE AND PICKLED PEPERONCINI (POLLO SCARPARIELLO)

Why this dish is called "chicken with little shoes" is a mystery to us and to our Italian friends. But the recipe is an old one from our kitchen card file, stained and dog-eared, so we have obviously used it a lot.

SERVES 4

One 3- to 3½-pound chicken, cut into
   8 pieces, bone and skin on
Salt and pepper to taste
4 tablespoons light olive oil
8 ounces Italian fennel sausage, cut into
   1-inch pieces
5 large garlic cloves, peeled,
   crushed, and minced (about
   2 tablespoons)
1 medium red onion (about
   8 ounces), thinly sliced (about
   1½ cups)

1 medium red pepper (about
   8 ounces), stemmed, seeded, and
   cut into ½-inch-thick strips (about
   1½ cups)
6 pickled peperoncini from a jar,
   seeded and cut in half (see Note)
3 tablespoons peperoncini liquid (from
   the jar)
¼ cup dry white wine
1 cup chicken broth
3 tablespoons coarsely chopped
   parsley

Make sure the chicken is dried very well so it doesn't splatter when cooking. Season liberally with salt and pepper. Heat the olive oil in a 12-inch sauté pan over medium-high heat. Add the chicken, skin side down, and sauté, turning once, until both sides are crisp and golden brown. Transfer to paper towels to drain and then set aside.

Pour off all but 1 tablespoon of oil, add the sausage to the skillet, and sauté until browned. Transfer the sausages to paper towels to drain and set aside. Pour off all but 2 tablespoons of the fat in the skillet, add the garlic and onion, and sauté for 1 minute, scraping up any brown bits in the pan as you do so. Stir in the pepper and peperoncini, and sauté, stirring, for 2 minutes. Add the peperoncini liquid, white wine, and broth, and bring to a boil.

Return the chicken and sausage to the skillet, cover, lower the heat, and simmer for about 25 minutes, or until the chicken is tender but moist. Transfer the chicken and sausage to a serving platter and keep warm while reducing the sauce over medium-high heat for about 3 minutes.

Pour the sauce over the chicken and sausage, sprinkle with the parsley, and serve hot.

> Note: Pickled peperoncini are sometimes labeled Tuscan peppers. They
> may be medium to medium hot. Wash your hands well after handling
> them or wear rubber gloves, just as you would with hot chiles.

Meat: Please Ring for the Butcher

Pan-Grilled Steak with a Parsley and Red Wine Sauce

Lamb and White Bean Stew with Spinach, Parsley, and Dill

Roasted Pork Tenderloin with Ginger, Orange, and Campari

Oven-Poached Lettuce Bundles Filled with Veal and Mushrooms

Many years ago there were small butcher shops in every neighborhood, and we knew the butcher's name and he knew ours. We could rely on his expertise and count on his advice. Unfortunately, only a few of these personal, face-to-face shops still exist; they have mostly been replaced by prepackaged self-service stores, leaving many home cooks very much in the dark about an almost limitless subject.

But possibly once again, hearing the plaintive voice of the confused consumer, both supermarkets and specialty shops such as Gourmet Garage are making their butchers available to answer our questions by installing real live employees either outside or inside their own counters or behind see-through glass enclosures with a handy bell with which to call them to ask for advice or for special cuts.

We therefore will never need to know the difference between pinbone sirloin, flat bone sirloin, round bone sirloin, wedge bone sirloin, top or bottom sirloin. On the next trip to the market, we can ring the bell for the butcher and ask.

PAN-GRILLED STEAK WITH A PARSLEY AND RED WINE SAUCE

Aged top loin New York strip steak is one of the greats for tenderness—robust and satisfying, pan-grilled to a rich brown, yet so very tender that the touch of a knife reveals a rosy inner succulence. A simple red wine reduction spiked with aromatic herbs is just the right sauce to honor this cut of beef.

SERVES 4

SAUCE:

2 tablespoons olive oil

¼ cup finely minced shallots (about 3 or 4 large)

1 teaspoon finely minced garlic (about 1 medium clove)

1 teaspoon fresh thyme leaves

1 cup dry red wine

¼ cup red wine vinegar

3 to 4 drops Tabasco

1 tablespoon butter

2 tablespoons finely chopped parsley

STEAK:

2 boneless top loin New York strip steaks (about 12 ounces each), cut 1 inch thick

Salt and freshly ground pepper to taste

1 teaspoon corn oil

Heat the olive oil in an 8-inch nonstick skillet over medium heat. When hot, add the shallots and cook, stirring, for 30 seconds. Add the garlic and thyme, and cook 1 minute more, until wilted but not brown. Add the wine, bring to a boil, and cook until reduced by half, about 7 to 8 minutes. Add the vinegar and continue to boil until the mixture is slightly thickened, about 4 minutes. At this point prepare the steaks: Dry the meat well on paper towels and season liberally with salt and pepper. Heat the corn oil in a 12-inch heavy skillet such as black cast iron over medium-high heat. When the oil is hot, add the steaks in 1 layer so they do not touch. Cook about 5 minutes on one side, until thoroughly browned. Turn the steaks over with tongs (not a fork or the juices will leak out) and continue cooking about 4 or 5 minutes more for medium with a slight pink center. Remove the steaks and let them rest on a plate, covered with aluminum foil, for 5 minutes. Cut into 4 serving pieces.

Rewarm the sauce, adding any accumulated juices from the resting steaks plus the Tabasco. Swirl in the butter and parsley, spoon over the steaks, and serve.

LAMB AND WHITE BEAN STEW WITH SPINACH, PARSLEY, AND DILL

This unusual Iranian stew is served hot at the table from the casserole in which it has been cooked. The lid is lifted, and the delicious aromas of rich tender lamb, fresh herbs, spinach, and beans fill the room. Serve with rice or orzo.

SERVES 4

2 tablespoons butter

2 tablespoons olive oil

⅔ cup finely chopped leek, white part only (about 1 medium leek)

1¼ cups thinly sliced scallions (about 5 or 6 large scallions)

2 teaspoons finely minced garlic (2 large cloves)

2 pounds fresh crinkly leaf spinach, stems trimmed, or two 10-ounce packages or 1¼ pounds frozen spinach

2 cups coarsely chopped fresh parsley (about 4 ounces)

2 tablespoons coarsely snipped fresh dill

1 pound lean lamb, cut into ¾-inch cubes and dried on paper towels

Salt and pepper to taste

1 tablespoon ground turmeric

1¼ cups chicken broth

2 tablespoons lemon juice (about ½ large lemon)

1 teaspoon finely grated lemon zest

2 cups cooked white cannellini beans (about 4 ounces dried beans cooked or one 19-ounce can, rinsed and drained)

In a 5-quart heavy-duty Dutch oven, heat 1 tablespoon of the butter and 1 tablespoon of the oil over medium heat. Add the leek, scallions, and garlic, and sauté, stirring occasionally, until just tender, about 5 minutes. Add the spinach, parsley, and dill, and stir constantly until the greens are just wilted. Remove the Dutch oven from the heat and set it aside.

In a 10-inch skillet over medium-high heat, add the remaining butter and olive oil.

When hot, add the lamb, a few pieces at a time, and brown on all sides. Season with salt and pepper, and transfer the lamb to the Dutch oven with the greens. The meat may be seared in 2 batches.

Add the turmeric to the same skillet and stir for a few seconds. Add the chicken broth, scraping up any brown bits, and bring to a boil. Pour over the meat and greens mixture. Cover the Dutch oven, bring to a boil over medium heat, then turn the heat to low. Add the lemon juice and zest and simmer for 1 hour.

Stir in the cooked beans and continue to simmer 10 to 15 minutes more, until the beans are hot and the meat is tender. Spoon over a bed of orzo or rice if you wish.

ROASTED PORK TENDERLOIN WITH GINGER, ORANGE, AND CAMPARI

Pork tenderloin is the leanest and most tender cut of the whole hog. No bones, little waste, and a dieter's delight because it is roasted without any additional fat.

SERVES 4

1 pound pork tenderloin
⅛ teaspoon cayenne pepper
½ teaspoon paprika
½ teaspoon ground coriander
1 teaspoon finely minced garlic
    (1 medium clove)
1 teaspoon ground cumin
Salt and pepper to taste

½ cup frozen orange juice concentrate,
    defrosted
1 tablespoon orange marmalade
1 teaspoon peeled and finely minced
    ginger root (about a 1-inch piece)
¼ cup Campari
2 teaspoons finely minced mint plus
    1 teaspoon minced for garnish

Dry the pork with paper towels. In a small bowl, combine the cayenne, paprika, coriander, garlic, cumin, salt, and pepper. Rub the mixture all over the meat, enclose it in aluminum foil, and refrigerate for at least 1 hour.

When ready to cook, preheat the oven to 400 degrees and prepare the sauce. In a small bowl, combine the orange juice, marmalade, ginger, Campari, and mint. Place the meat, still in the foil, in an 8 x 12 x 1½-inch roasting pan. Open the foil completely so that it acts as a pan liner. Roast the meat for 10 minutes, then turn it over with tongs and roast 5 minutes more. Spoon the sauce over the meat and roast 10 minutes more, basting frequently. Remove it from the oven, cover with aluminum foil to keep it warm, and let it rest for 5 minutes.

Slice the pork crosswise into ½-inch-thick slices and transfer to warm plates. Spoon a bit of the sauce over the slices and scatter some minced mint over all.

OVEN-POACHED LETTUCE BUNDLES FILLED WITH VEAL AND MUSHROOMS

A specialty of Genoa that is usually served at Easter time. It's a light, delicate dish with just a touch of tomato and enough sauce to spoon over some orzo or other tiny pasta.

SERVES 4

½ ounce dried porcini mushrooms

1 pound ground lean veal

1 tablespoon olive oil

¼ cup finely minced onion
(1 small onion)

½ teaspoon finely minced garlic
(1 small clove)

1 teaspoon grated lemon zest
(1 lemon)

Salt and freshly ground black pepper
to taste

¼ teaspoon freshly ground nutmeg

¼ cup finely minced parsley

1 egg, lightly beaten

2 large heads Boston or butter lettuce

⅔ cup chicken broth

½ cup skinned and coarsely diced plum
tomatoes (1 or 2 large) or canned
Italian plum tomatoes

¼ teaspoon dried oregano,
preferably Greek

1 tablespoon butter, cut into small
pieces

¼ cup grated Parmesan cheese

Soak the mushrooms in warm water to cover for 30 minutes, then squeeze dry and mince finely. Set aside. Meanwhile, put the veal into a medium-size bowl. Heat 1 tablespoon of olive oil in a 6-inch skillet over low heat. Add the onion and garlic, and sauté, stirring occasionally, until wilted. Stir in the minced mushrooms and sauté 1 minute more. Remove from the heat, let the mixture cool slightly, and then add it to the veal along with the lemon zest, salt, pepper, nutmeg, parsley, and egg. Combine well with a wooden spoon. Form the mixture into twenty-four 1-inch balls and set aside on a sheet of waxed paper.

Peel off the large outer leaves from both heads of lettuce. Carefully shave a thin slice along the center stem of the leaves (so that they stay flat) and steam the leaves in a steamer over boiling water for 1 or 2 minutes, or just until they are wilted. Carefully remove the leaves to paper towels to drain, patting the surfaces gently to blot up any excess moisture.

Preheat the oven to 400 degrees and butter a shallow 3-quart baking dish. Place 1 veal ball on each leaf of wilted lettuce and form small bundles by folding the top and bottom and then the sides. Place in the prepared dish in 1 layer, folded side down. Carefully pour the broth around them and scatter the diced tomato and oregano on top. Dot with butter, cover with aluminum foil, and bake for 10 minutes. Remove the foil, baste, and bake 5 minutes more. Spoon some of the juices over and sprinkle with cheese and some additional pepper. Serve hot or at room temperature.

Comfort Me with Apples

Baked Apples Filled with Almond Paste and a Caramel Almond Sauce

Maple Apple Hasty Pudding

Apple Fool with Calvados

Apple Sour Cream Rum Raisin Pie

Basic Cream Cheese Pie Pastry

Beginning with the Song of Solomon in the Bible and through the earliest times in history, apples have been a part of lore, history, art, and politics—from the classic Greek myths to contemporary popular culture: Adam and Eve, Johnny Appleseed, Sir Isaac Newton, William Tell, up to the New York City nickname and the popular swing dance of the '40s, "the Big Apple."

Today, commercial growers select varieties that ship and keep well, thus making a range of apples available throughout most of the year. In addition, local growers, usually small farmers, have revived many of the heirloom varieties grown for complexity of flavor and texture. Many are organically grown, more fragile to ship, and with a shorter season of availability.

At one time the only way to find these wonderful and unusual varieties was to either live near an orchard or grow your own. Today specialty markets and greenmarkets, and even many supermarkets, are alive with fine-flavored apples as soon as we begin to detect a nip in the air.

Incredibly there are twenty-five hundred varieties grown around the world; the major varieties are distinguished by color, size, flavor, approximate time of ripening, and suggested uses.

THE APPLE ORCHARD

VARIETY AND SEASON	DESCRIPTION	USE
	Mild Flavors	
GOLDEN DELICIOUS SEPTEMBER–JUNE	Pale to bright yellow. Fine-grained flesh, crisp, flowery, and sweet. Resists discoloring when sliced.	Retains shape well when baked in tarts. Not good for applesauce.
MCINTOSH SEPTEMBER–MARCH	Thin-skinned. Reddish in color, blushed with green. Tender, very juicy flesh.	Excellent for applesauce when mixed with other varieties. They compress when baked in pies, so overfill the crust.
RED DELICIOUS YEAR-ROUND	Most popular eating apple. Bright red, shiny. Five knobs at base of characteristically elongated shape. Crunchy and sweet.	Best eaten raw. Not particularly good for cooking.
	Sweet/Tart Flavors	
BRAEBURN IMPORTED: MARCH/APRIL LOCAL: OCTOBER–APRIL	Originally from New Zealand, now grown in New York State. Firm, crisp, very juicy. Creamy yellow flesh and complex flavor.	Excellent for eating raw and for salads, crisps, and pies.
CORTLAND SEPTEMBER THROUGH EARLY SPRING	Large, red with purple undertones. Smooth, wide, and shiny. Snow-white flesh. Tender and resists discoloration when exposed to air.	Good eating apple. Excellent for baking, poaching, or in pies or salads.

VARIETY AND SEASON	DESCRIPTION	USE
EMPIRE OCTOBER–FEBRUARY	Hybrid cross between McIntosh and Red Delicious, resembling former. Bright red with tiny yellow dots and yellow-red stripes. Has better eating quality than both parents.	Good for eating raw and for applesauce. Not the very best for pies.
FUJI OCTOBER–FEBRUARY	Also popular in New Zealand and Japan where they originated. Red with golden-dotted skin. Boxy shape with distinctive crisp, sweet flavor.	Can be used well in tarts and pies since it holds its shape.
GALA OCTOBER–FEBRUARY	Similar to the Fuji but juicier. Softer than the Braeburn and more tart than the McIntosh.	Good for eating and for tarts.
GRAVENSTEIN AUGUST/SEPTEMBER	Popular West Coast apple, with skin streaked in shades of red. Crisp and juicy.	Makes good applesauce.
JONAGOLD OCTOBER–APRIL	A cross between Golden Delicious and Jonathan. Grown all over the U.S. Large, yellowish, with minute green dots and reddish stripes. Creamy-colored flesh is more sweet than tart.	A good all-purpose apple. Try it sautéed with butter and cinnamon.
JONATHAN OCTOBER/NOVEMBER	Grown all over the U.S. Bright red with tiny yellow surface dots and yellow stripes. Rich, lively flavor.	Texture causes "meltdown" when baked in pies. Makes good pink applesauce.

MACOUN / OCTOBER/NOVEMBER	A high-quality McIntosh hybrid. Small, red, with a smoky purple cast and light green top. Aromatic, with crisp, white flesh.	Best for eating raw. If you like "Macs," you'll love these more flavorful versions. Try some with cheese.
MUTSU / *AKA* CRISPIN / OCTOBER/NOVEMBER	A Golden Delicious hybrid with Japanese origins. Large, yellow-green with red dot blush. White flesh is crispy, juicy, and just slightly tart.	Our personal favorite eating apple.
NORTHERN SPY / NOVEMBER–MAY	A large apple with pale red skin that appears to be striped yellow-green. Crisp, very juicy, with a fine, firm texture and aromatic yellowish flesh.	An excellent all-purpose apple.
ROME BEAUTY / OCTOBER TO EARLY SUMMER	Grown in all regions. Large, firm, with solid, light red skin and tiny green dots. Fairly dry in texture.	Good for eating and all-purpose cooking. Especially suited for baking whole since it holds its shape well.
RUSSET / OCTOBER–DECEMBER	A preholiday apple that dares to be different. Medium-size. Rough ochre skin over a yellow-green base. Within lies a creamy, crisp, complex tart-sweet flavor. Not overly juicy. A good dense texture.	Try it in pies.
STAYMAN / (LARGE WINESAP) / OCTOBER–APRIL	An improved heirloom descendant of the Winesap. Dark, intense red with pale green blush and dots. (The Winesap is smaller and very juicy.)	A good keeper. Excellent for eating raw or for pies and tarts.

VARIETY AND SEASON	DESCRIPTION	USE
	Tart Flavors	
BALDWIN OCTOBER–MARCH	An heirloom first grafted in the 1700s. Large, light yellow-green blushed with red and marked with tiny green dots. Mildly sweet, hard, and juicy with lots of pectin and perfume.	Good for eating and excellent for cooking.
GRANNY SMITH YEAR-ROUND	Yes, there actually was a Granny Smith, an Aussie grandma who grew these in her back-yard. Solid green in color. Tart with not too distinct flavor.	An excellent keeper and good for pies.
GREENING *AKA* RHODE ISLAND GREENING OCTOBER–FEBRUARY	Flattish shape with waxy grass green color and light yellow dots. Not too juicy.	Great for pies but needs sugar. Eat it out of hand *only* if you love tart apples!
IDA RED OCTOBER/NOVEMBER	Cross between Jonathan and Wagener, both known for distinctive flavor. Medium-large with cranberry red color blushed with light green near stem. Slightly sweet-tart. Rich, crisp, juicy flesh.	Excellent for both eating raw and for cooking.

SHOP SMART

Big, shiny red apples that have been polished to a fare-thee-well are not necessarily better. For example, when you can find them, the small, ugly, grainy-skinned russet apple (or the rare Cox's orange pippin) usually has an exquisite flavor.

For sprightly balanced flavor, try mixing several varieties when making applesauce or baking pies—just as cider makers do.

Choose with your senses:

◆ Smell them. They should be flowery and sweet.

◆ Touch them. The flesh should be hard, with no give when pressed. The skin should be tight, with no bruises or rust marks at the stem.

◆ Listen to them. Tap an apple with your knuckle up close to your ear. It should sound hollow and resonant, not dull.

◆ Taste them before cooking, so that you can adjust the sweeteners and the cooking time to suit the flavor and texture.

◆ Keep them in the crisper bin of the refrigerator in a plastic bag. Wash them right before using.

◆ Remember that taste is a very personal thing. Next time at the market, make an effort to find some of the more unusual varieties—some that you've never tried before. It is worth the small effort.

APPLE MATH

One pound = 4 small or 3 medium or 2 large.

One pound = 3 cups diced or sliced.

Two medium = I cup grated.

Three pounds = generous amount for 9-inch pie.

BAKED APPLES FILLED WITH ALMOND PASTE AND A CARAMEL ALMOND SAUCE

A perfect, compatible marriage—a sweet apple and a nut.

SERVES 4

APPLES:

4 Rome, Cortland, or Ida Red apples
  (about 2 pounds)
1 tablespoon lemon juice (about
  ½ large lemon)

3 ounces almond paste
4 tablespoons light brown sugar
½ teaspoon ground cinnamon
4 teaspoons butter, cut into pieces
1 cup white wine or apple juice

CARAMEL ALMOND SAUCE:

1 tablespoon butter
4 tablespoons light brown sugar

½ cup heavy cream
4 teaspoons sliced almonds

Preheat the oven to 350 degrees. Core the apples and cut the peel to about ¾ to 1 inch from the top. Trickle lemon juice over the exposed surface. Combine the almond paste, sugar, cinnamon, and butter, and fill the center of each apple with the mixture.

Place the apples in a baking pan and pour the wine on the bottom. Bake for 1 hour, basting every 15 to 20 minutes.

Prepare the sauce just before apples are finished baking. In a small saucepan, melt the butter and sugar over low heat, stirring until the sugar is melted. Add the cream and bring to a boil. Cook for 1 or 2 minutes, until slightly thick. To serve, pour the sauce around the base of each apple and scatter the sliced almonds over the sauce. Serve warm.

MAPLE APPLE HASTY PUDDING

Maple syrup moistens and sweetens this simple all-American dessert. It can be put together very quickly, hence its name.

SERVES 4 TO 6

3 tart/sweet apples (about 1 pound) such as Northern Spy or Ida Red, peeled, cored, and thinly sliced
2 teaspoons lemon juice (½ small lemon)
¼ cup dark raisins
Soft butter for baking dish
1 cup flour
1½ teaspoons baking powder
½ teaspoon salt

3 tablespoons light brown sugar
½ cup milk
1 teaspoon vanilla extract
1 tablespoons melted butter
¼ cup coarsely broken pecans
¾ cup maple syrup (Grade B cooking maple can be used)
½ cup water
Whipped cream or vanilla frozen yogurt (optional)

In a medium-size bowl, mix the apples with the lemon juice and set aside. Soak the raisins in water for 15 minutes. Butter a 1½-quart baking dish and preheat the oven to 350 degrees.

In another bowl, whisk together the flour, baking powder, salt, and sugar until combined. In a cup, mix the milk, vanilla extract, and melted butter. Add all at once to the dry ingredients and whisk until smooth. Scrape this rather thick batter into the prepared dish. Scatter apple slices over the surface and then scatter the nuts. Drain the raisins and add them.

In a small saucepan, combine the maple syrup with the water and bring to the boiling point over medium-high heat. Pour over all and bake for 35 minutes, or until browned. Serve warm with a dollop of whipped cream or yogurt if you wish.

APPLE FOOL WITH CALVADOS

Jonathan apples, cooked with their skins for extra flavor and color, melt into a thick rosy puree that is spiked with Calvados and a swirl of whipped cream. A festive, light, and airy finale to any meal.

SERVES 6

3 pounds apples, preferably Jonathans, Empire, Macoun, or Macs
⅔ cup sugar
½ cup water
1 teaspoon grated lemon zest (1 medium lemon)
⅛ teaspoon salt

2 tablespoons butter
1-inch piece cinnamon stick plus 4 sticks for garnish
¼ cup Calvados
1 cup heavy cream, chilled
Sprigs of mint for garnish

Core and thickly slice the unpeeled apples. Place in a 3-quart nonstick saucepan. (See Note.) Add the sugar, water, lemon peel, and salt, and stir to combine. Cover the pan and cook over medium heat, stirring once or twice, until the apples are very soft, about 20 to 25 minutes.

Puree the apples in a food mill to remove the skins and return the puree to the same saucepan. Stir in the butter and cinnamon stick, and cook, uncovered, over medium-low heat about 30 minutes, stirring occasionally, until very thick. There should be 2 to 2½ cups of thick puree. Remove and discard the cinnamon stick, transfer the puree to a covered container, and chill for at least 3 hours.

When ready to serve, stir in the Calvados. Whip the cream until thick but *not* with stiff peaks. Fold the cream into the puree with a rubber spatula. Spoon into a footed wide-bowl wineglass. Place a cinnamon stick in the surface at an angle, leaving ¾ of the stick exposed, and add a sprig of mint.

Note: A gadget well worth owning is an apple cutter that both cores and slices apples into wedges with one downward press.

APPLE SOUR CREAM RUM RAISIN PIE

Thinly sliced tart/sweet apples and rum-flavored raisins are baked together with a sour cream custard. The fruit shows through in the center of this partially overlapping pastry.

SERVES 6

PASTRY CRUST:

1 recipe Basic Cream Cheese Pie
   Pastry (page 328)

FILLING:

2 cups dark raisins

2 tablespoons dark rum

2 pounds tart/sweet apples such as
   Fuji, Jonagold, Winesap, or Golden
   Delicious (about 6 or 7)

1 teaspoon lemon juice

1/2 teaspoon ground cinnamon

2 tablespoons flour

1/8 teaspoon salt

1/3 cup light brown sugar

1 tablespoon butter, cut into small
   pieces

1 egg, lightly beaten

1 cup sour cream

1 teaspoon vanilla extract

1 egg yolk mixed with 1 tablespoon
   milk for glaze

Roll out the pastry into a 13-inch circle, 1/8 inch thick. Set aside.

In a small cup, combine the raisins and rum, and set aside. In a large bowl, peel, core, and slice the apples thinly and toss them with the lemon juice and reserved raisins and rum. Combine the cinnamon, flour, salt, sugar, and butter in the bowl of a food processor with a few strokes. Add to the apples. In a small bowl, combine the egg, sour cream, and vanilla, and add to the apples.

Carefully fit the pastry into a 9-inch pie pan, with the 3-inch overlap hanging evenly around the rim of the pan. Fill with the apple mixture and fold the overhanging pastry to partially enclose the fruit, pleating it softly as you do so. Chill in the refrigerator for 20 minutes.

Preheat the oven to 400 degrees and bake the pie for 15 minutes. Lower the oven temperature to 350 degrees and bake for 20 minutes. Remove the pie from the oven and brush the top of the pastry with the glaze. Return to the oven and bake 30 minutes more. Let cool slightly but serve warm.

BASIC CREAM CHEESE PIE PASTRY

This is an old family recipe that handles well. The delicate cheese flavor marries beautifully with fruit fillings. We have tried other recipes for pie crusts, but we always come back to this one.

ENOUGH FOR A 10-INCH DOUBLE CRUST OR A LATTICE-TOP PIE

1 ½ cups flour
⅛ teaspoon salt
2 tablespoons sugar
8 tablespoons (1 stick) cold butter, cut
    into ¼-inch pieces

4 ounces cream cheese
2 tablespoons milk

In the bowl of a food processor, place the flour, salt, and sugar, and pulse a few times to combine. Add the butter and cream cheese, and process only until the texture is crumbly. Trickle the milk over all and process just until the dough begins to form.

Place a large piece of aluminum foil on a work surface. Scrape the dough out of the food processor, gather it together, and then slam it down on the foil to release any bubbles. Wrap the pastry in the aluminum foil and chill for 1 hour, or freeze it if you wish to store it longer. Defrost before rolling, if frozen, but keep the pastry cold.

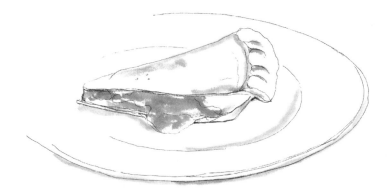

In Praise of Pears

Shredded Pear Flan with Citrus Peels and Mace

German Pear Kuchen

Baked Forelle Pears with Butterscotch Bourbon Sauce and Pecans

*Pears Poached with Saffron and Bay Leaf and Stuffed with
Stilton and Mascarpone Cheese*

Their origins are Asian; they have been gathered in the wild and then cultivated. The earliest cultivated pear is said to have been grown on the peninsula of Peloponnesus in Greece—also called Apia, or "the land of the pear." Today an estimated thirty-five hundred varieties are grown throughout the world.

Pears actually ripen only after picking—from the inside out. They are firm when mature, and unlike many other fruits, they are not tree ripened when harvested.

Here are some popular varieties:

ANJOU—OCTOBER TO MAY: A winter pear, it is quite large and round or heart-shaped. The greenish yellow skin does *not* change color to indicate ripeness. The flesh is creamy colored. The anjou has a juicy, sweet, spicy flavor and some gritty cells near the core.

BARTLETT—JULY TO DECEMBER: Of medium size, they are bell-shaped and thin-skinned. They turn from green to yellow when ripe, and the finely textured flesh is white. They hold their shape well for poaching and baking. Red Bartletts, with their bright crimson skins, are especially attractive in the fruit bowl. Although they are available for five or six months, August through October is their peak season.

BOSC—SEPTEMBER TO MAY: They have an elegant, long, tapering shape and a slightly mottled yellow and russet color. They are very firm. Medium to large pears are good for baking and poaching, since they hold their shape well. When fully ripened, they are sweet, buttery, and juicy.

COMICE—OCTOBER TO MARCH: They have a rather thick, yellow-green skin, often with a red blush. Its broad, chubby bottom and short neck identify this very juicy, aromatic, sweet, and buttery pear. They're best eaten raw since they lose their shape when cooked. For sheer heaven try them with some toasted walnuts, a wedge of Stilton cheese, and a glass of tawny port.

FORELLE—OCTOBER TO FEBRUARY: This variety is small and bell-shaped, and its skin is a bright chartreuse, freckled, and blushed with red. It is tender, sweet, and slightly spicy. Great for snacking.

NELIS—OCTOBER TO MAY: Round, sweet-fleshed, and of medium size. It is a russetted light green, turning more golden when it ripens. It is good for cooking, preserving, and eating raw.

PECKHAM—LATE WINTER (although sometimes it is imported in the spring): Its surface is bumpy, and its green skin turns yellow (like Bartlett) as it ripens. The juicy, mellow flesh is delicious uncooked.

SECKEL—AUGUST TO DECEMBER: The smallest popular variety of pear, they are red or yellow-green with a heavily red-blushed skin. They are well suited for poaching or preserving whole as well as for snacks and pickling.

YALI—WINTER: Pale yellow-green and distinguished by an off-center stem. They are succulent and sweet.

ASIAN—LATE FALL THROUGH WINTER: Not quite a pear and not really an apple, they are instead the result of many crossbreedings between both fruits. They are sometimes called apple-pears or Oriental pears. They are sweet and mellow like a pear, but they have the crispness of an apple. Since they do not soften when ripe (as a pear does), they should be eaten like an apple when hard. These three varieties are the ones that are most commonly found in the marketplace: The *Chojuro* is russet colored and round, and has a slight perfume flavor and aroma. Try them baked or sliced and served with a creamy Brie for a textural contrast. *Hosu* is similar to Chojuro but has a golden brown skin. *Kikusu* have a tart/sweet flavor and a greenish yellow skin.

SHOP SMART

- ◆ Choose pears that are firm but not rock hard. Buy them a few days before you intend to use them; this will allow for ripening time. Leave the pears for two to three days at room temperature or in a brown paper bag. Do not refrigerate them.
- ◆ Pears are ripe when they respond to gentle pressure at the stem end and have a pronounced fragrance. Use at once after ripening for no more than a day. Their moment of perfection is fleeting but well worth it.

SHREDDED PEAR FLAN WITH CITRUS PEELS AND MACE

This dessert is easy to make, and it's so festive and delicious that four guests may well devour the whole recipe—which under normal conditions is designed to serve six!

SERVES 4 TO 6

4 ripe Bartlett pears, peeled
   and cored
5 tablespoons sugar
1 tablespoon grated orange zest
1 teaspoon grated lemon zest
¼ teaspoon ground mace
2 tablespoons butter, cut into small
   pieces

3 eggs
¼ cup milk
¼ cup heavy cream
1 teaspoon vanilla extract
A few berries or slices of fruit and a
   sprig of mint for garnish

Preheat the oven to 350 degrees. Shred the pears in a food processor, using the shredder blade. Transfer the pears to a medium-size bowl and mix with 2 tablespoons of the sugar, orange and lemon zest, and mace. Spoon into a 9-inch nonstick tart or quiche pan and dot with butter. Bake for 10 minutes.

Meanwhile, in a food processor, beat the eggs with the remaining sugar. Add the milk, cream, and vanilla, and process until well blended.

Carefully pour the mixture over the pears and return the pan to the oven. Bake for about 30 minutes, or until the center is almost set.

Let cool in the pan to room temperature. Garnish with the fruit and mint.

GERMAN PEAR KUCHEN

Winter, spring, summer, or fall, this is a fabulous and easy dessert that can change with the arrival of other seasonal fruits. Try it throughout the year—with peaches, nectarines, prune plums, apples, or cherries.

SERVES 8 TO 10

DOUGH:

2 cups unbleached flour

½ cup sugar

2 teaspoons baking powder

½ teaspoon salt

6 tablespoons slightly soft butter, cut into small pieces

½ cup milk

1 teaspoon vanilla extract

1 egg

FRUIT TOPPING:

1½ pounds large Bartlett or Anjou pears, peeled, quartered, cored, and thinly sliced

¾ cup light brown sugar

1 tablespoon unbleached flour

1 teaspoon ground cinnamon

⅛ teaspoon freshly grated nutmeg

1 tablespoon grated lemon zest

2 tablespoons lemon juice (about ½ lemon)

3 tablespoons melted butter

To make the dough: In a large bowl, whisk together the flour, sugar, baking powder, and salt to combine. Using a pastry blender, work the butter into the dry ingredients until the texture is coarse and mealy.

In a small bowl, whisk together the milk, vanilla, and egg to combine. Add to the dry ingredients all at once and mix with floured hands or a wooden spoon until just combined. Do not overmix.

Preheat the oven to 350 degrees. Butter a 14-inch-diameter pizza pan or a 10½ x 15½ x 1½-inch jelly roll pan. Flour your hands and the surface of the dough, and using your fingers, press the dough into the pan. It should cover the pan thinly right up to the edge and have a slight rim.

To make the fruit topping: Arrange the sliced pears on top of the dough, with a slight overlap. In a small bowl, whisk together the sugar, flour, cinnamon, nutmeg, and lemon zest. Drizzle the lemon juice over the pears and then the melted butter. Spoon the brown sugar mixture evenly over the surface. Bake for 30 to 35 minutes. Let cool a bit, then serve warm or at room temperature.

BAKED FORELLE PEARS WITH BUTTERSCOTCH BOURBON SAUCE AND PECANS

An easy autumn dessert with a warm, sweet, rich butterscotch sauce and the contrasting crunch of pecans, this is served with a cold, tart cream for counterpoint.

SERVES 6

1½ pounds Forelle pears (about 6), peeled, halved, and cored (or 4 small Anjou pears)

2 tablespoons lemon juice

3 tablespoons plus 1 teaspoon soft butter

½ cup light brown sugar

½ cup light corn syrup

½ cup heavy cream

½ teaspoon vanilla extract

1 tablespoon bourbon

½ cup coarsely broken toasted pecans

6 teaspoons crème fraîche or sour cream

Preheat the oven to 350 degrees. As they are peeled and cored, drop the pear halves into a bowl of cold water mixed with the lemon juice. Butter a round 10½-inch oven-to-table baking dish using the teaspoon of butter.

Remove the pears with a slotted spoon and arrange them like the spokes of a wheel. Bake the pears for 10 minutes, or until the top of a knife inserted indicates that they are tender. While the pears are baking, prepare the sauce.

In a 1½-quart nonstick saucepan over medium-low heat, combine the remaining butter, brown sugar, and corn syrup, stirring constantly until smooth, about 2 minutes. Add the cream and continue to cook for an additional 3 or 4 minutes, stirring constantly, until bubbles form around the edges. Remove from the heat and add the vanilla, bourbon, and pecans. Spoon the mixture over and around the pears.

Serve the pears warm with generous spoonfuls of sauce and a teaspoon of cold crème fraîche on top.

Note: A melon ball scoop is just the right size to core the pears.

PEARS POACHED WITH SAFFRON AND BAY LEAF AND STUFFED WITH STILTON AND MASCARPONE CHEESE

The pears are poached in a golden syrup fragrant with the touch of sweet spices. Pears, Stilton cheese, and walnuts—a classic combination that should be served with a small glass of tawny port.

SERVES 6

2 cups dry white wine
½ cup sugar
1 bay leaf
2-inch strip of orange zest
¼ teaspoon saffron threads steeped in
    2 tablespoons hot water
6 large, firm, wide-based pears (about
    ½ pound each, either Comice
    or Anjou)

Lemon or orange wedge
3 ounces Stilton cheese, at room
    temperature
1 ounce mascarpone cheese, at room
    temperature
⅔ cup finely chopped toasted walnuts

In a 5-quart, wide-based Dutch oven, combine the wine, sugar, bay leaf, orange zest, and saffron threads steeped with water. Bring to a boil over medium heat, then lower the heat and simmer for 5 minutes. Meanwhile, peel the pears with a vegetable parer, leaving the stems intact. Cut a very thin slice off the bottom of each pear to steady them as they are peeled. Drop them into a bowl of cold water with a squeezed wedge of either lemon or orange.

After all the pears are peeled, transfer gently and upright to the simmering poaching liquid. Baste, cover the pot tightly, and cook over low heat, basting once or twice, for 10 to 15 minutes, or until the pears are tender but firm.

Remove the pears carefully with a slotted spoon and place them on their sides on paper towels to drain and cool. While they cool, bring the poaching liquid to a boil over high heat, then turn the heat to low and cook until reduced to ⅔ cup. Remove from heat. Strain the syrup into a cup, discarding the orange peel, bay leaf, and saffron. Refrigerate the syrup for 20 to 30 minutes, until cold and thickened. When the syrup is chilled, pour it into a small bowl.

While the syrup cools, use a melon ball scoop to make a round cavity in the base of each pear. Mash the softened cheeses together with a fork and place about 1 teaspoon of the mixture into each pear cavity.

Place the chopped nuts on a flat plate. Dip the base of each pear into the syrup, coating it about 1 inch up from the bottom. Carefully roll the pear in the chopped walnuts around the 1-inch circle.

Arrange each dipped pear upright in a serving dish with a lip that will hold the syrup. Brush the top of the pears with some of the syrup and sprinkle a few nuts over them. Spoon any remaining syrup into the serving dish and scatter any remaining nuts in the syrup.

Serve warm or chill until serving time.

Pears Poached with Saffron and Bay Leaf & Stuffed with Stilton and Mascarpone Cheese

The Groovy Grove of Citrus

Orange and Walnut Cake with Cognac

Blood Oranges with Orange Flower Water and Pistachio Nuts

Kumquats Poached in Chinese Star Anise

Whole Clementines Marinated in Honey, Basil, and Lime Syrup

Meyer Lemon Cream

Key Lime Chicken Soup, Mexican Style

Seviche with Lime, Orange, Avocado, and Red Onion

Citrus has an amazing versatility. The multitude of culinary possibilities include the whole fruit—the peel, juice, pulp, and even the blossoms, which are found in orange flower water (now available in specialty and Middle Eastern shops). Citrus marries beautifully with seafood, meat, and poultry. It perks up vegetables, and it can become the very soul of sauces and desserts.

Fall and winter provide the most comprehensive array of citrus from California, Arizona, and Florida as well as the imports of Asia, Morocco, Spain, and Israel. Luckily they travel well, for they ripen only on the tree, and once picked, they stop developing and the flavor does not improve.

The orange is said to date back as far as twenty million years; the Chinese and Japanese discovered and cultivated the mandarin orange thousands of years before they ever appeared on our shores. Portuguese and Spanish explorers first brought oranges to Europe during the Middle Ages, and the conquistadors introduced them here during the sixteenth century.

CITRUS: A SUNSHINE SAMPLER

Oranges

VARIETY AND SEASON	DESCRIPTION	USE
BLOOD ORANGE DECEMBER–APRIL	Round and small to medium size. Thick-skinned, deeper magenta flesh shows a darker blush on the skin surface. *Moro* and *Tarocco* contain red-veined flesh and have an ovoid shape and skin slightly dappled red. *Sanguinelli* has the palest of flesh of the three. Flavors are reminiscent of raspberries and range from slightly tart to sweet.	Produces gorgeous red juice and is beautiful in salads, desserts, and as a garnish.
MURCOTT *AKA* HONEY MURCOTT OR MURCOTT HONEY ORANGE JANUARY–MARCH	A Tangor, which is a cross between an orange and a mandarin. Slightly flattened shape and glossy, smooth, thin peel. More golden than orange with deep-colored floral juice and a complex flavor combination of apricots and mangoes.	Eat raw or use in salads. Cooking ruins the flavor complexity.
NAVEL *AKA* WASHINGTON NAVEL, CALIFORNIA NAVEL OCTOBER–MARCH	Usually large and round. The opposite stem end has a navel (called an open stylar) with what resembles another orange within it. Color is bright orange with thick, bumpy, easily peeled skin and thick pith. Easy to peel and segment, and contains no seeds. Sweet, juicy, and slightly crisp pulp.	Wonderful all-purpose and long-seasoned. Known as the ultimate eating orange. Good in baked goods and for juice and salads.

VARIETY AND SEASON	DESCRIPTION	USE
SEVILLE *AKA* SOUR OR BITTER ORANGE SHORT SEASON: JANUARY–MARCH	One of the earliest oranges grown in the world. It is usually imported from West Africa, Spain, and Sicily. Usually small, with a cosmetically funny-looking thick yellow-green rind, tough membrane, rather dry pulp, and many seeds. Rich in acid and pectin. The skin is rich in oil and very fragrant, as are the blossoms.	Definitely not an orange for eating out of hand. High acid content makes the sour juice perfect for marinades and sauces, such as seviche, French classic Bigarade sauce for duck, or with rich meats like pork or goose. Fragrant blossoms are used for flower water; the skin oils for orange liqueurs such as Cointreau and Grand Marnier; and the skins for marmalades.
TEMPLE JANUARY–MARCH	A Tangor, which is a cross between an orange and a mandarin, but usually called an orange. Called Temple in Florida and Royal Mandarin in California. Medium size, round, with deep orange, slightly bumpy skin that slips off easily. Very juicy with spicy, sweet, tart flavor and slightly seedy, juicy, pale orange flesh.	Good eating orange or for use in salads.
VALENCIA EARLY SPRING: MARCH–JUNE	Various sizes. Pale orange, pebbly, with thin surface skin. Very juicy and sweet, acidic fleshy pulp, with few seeds.	Known primarily as a juice orange since there is less waste because of its thin skin and pith.

Mandarins and Tangerines

Only in the United States are the terms mandarin and tangerine interchangeable. The rest of the world calls them mandarins, with many varieties frequently crossed with other citrus to produce new hybrids. Tangerines originated in Tangiers and technically are just another variety of mandarin. Tangerines have a more flattened shape while mandarins are rounder. With both, the skin does not cling to the fruit and is peelable, and the fruit separates easily into segments.

VARIETY AND SEASON	DESCRIPTION	USE
CLEMENTINE *AKA* "OH-MY-DARLIN'" NOVEMBER–FEBRUARY	A hybrid cross between a mandarin and sour orange. Very small to medium size. Flattened shape with deep orange, puffy, loose, smooth, peelable skin. Segments easily and is virtually seed free. Nectarlike flavor. Many varieties extend the season, with some imported from Spain and others domestically grown.	Can be lightly poached whole or as garnish on tarts and cakes. Kids love them because of size, sweetness, easily peelability, and no seeds.
DANCY TANGERINE	Sweet and mellow tasting, a low-acid fruit with easy-to-remove thin, shiny, vermilion, puffy skin and bright orange pulp with many seeds.	Put one in the toe of the Christmas stocking.

VARIETY AND SEASON	DESCRIPTION	USE
SATSUMA MANDARIN Available very early, September–November	Originally grown and exported from Japan but now grown in California and Florida where they are marketed as Emerald Mandarins. Bright orange, shiny peel zips off easily, revealing a virtually seedless, bright orange pulp that is mild and refreshing yet not too acidic. Breaks apart easily into segments.	Usually eaten out of hand or in fruit salads.

Tangelos

There are several varieties, resulting from a cross between a mandarin orange and a grapefruit.

VARIETY AND SEASON	DESCRIPTION	USE
MINEOLA *aka* Honey Belle December–April	The most popular kind. Distinguished by a circular, raised, nipplelike neck shape on the stem end. Honey-sweet, slightly tart flavor. It has firm, large, smooth, bright orange skin and orange pulp with few seeds. Grown primarily in Florida.	Eat out of hand or in salads.

Ugli Fruit

Basically the same hybrid cross as the tangelo, which favors its mandarin parent, the ugli favors its grapefruit relative. It is much sweeter when grown in the tropics (Jamaica) than in subtropical climates such as New Zealand or South Africa.

SEASON	DESCRIPTION	USE
NOVEMBER–MARCH	Larger than a grapefruit—up to 2 pounds—it has rumpled, light green to light orange skin and succulent, tender, sunny yellow-orange pulp that is zesty but not firm. It is pungent, brightly refreshing, and juicy.	Can be used for juice or halved, cut into segments, and eaten like grapefruit.

Pommelo

The botanical precursor of the grapefruit, the pommelo is an ancient fruit and the largest citrus in the world, weighing from three to twenty pounds. Very hearty, it grows in sheltered, hot, tropical areas near the sea or riverbanks. The pommelo is highly prized for Southeast Asian and Caribbean cuisines.

SEASON	DESCRIPTION	USE
NOVEMBER–MARCH	The only citrus that gets sweeter after it is picked if it is left at room temperature for 10 days. Pale yellow like a grapefruit, this giant has thicker, cushionlike pith and salmon-colored, very juicy pulp. Imported and also grown domestically.	Use in Southeast Asian dishes with seafood or poultry. Can be peeled and segmented for salads or served halved as with grapefruit. The peel can also be candied or used for conserves.

Grapefruit

This is the most recent citrus arrival, an offspring of the pommelo and sweet orange. It's grown throughout the tropical and subtropical regions of the world, with about 70 percent of the total production coming from Florida, Texas, and Arizona.

SEASON	DESCRIPTION	USE
NOVEMBER–MAY	Two types: pale yellow and pink; the latter is usually sweeter and blander in flavor. There are several seedless varieties, including the Florida Marsh Seedless, which is round and has pale yellow skin and pulp, and Pink Marsh, *AKA* Thompson, which has pale pink flesh. The Texas Red Blush, *AKA* Star Ruby, has a pink-blushed skin and coarse, tender, deep-salmon-colored, sweet, juicy flesh with few seeds and very little acid brightness.	For juice or eaten, halved and sectioned. Segment for fruit and vegetable salads and fish dishes. Use the juice for marinades.

Lemons

Although frost sensitive, lemons do not require heat to mature and always have some blossoms; ripening fruit and fully ripe fruit are available year-round. They are rarely marketed under their varietal names, with the exception of the Meyer lemon, the darling of pastry chefs.

SEASON	DESCRIPTION	USE
YEAR-ROUND	They are available in many sizes, mostly oval-shaped with bright yellow skin and a nipple on one end. The large, smooth-skinned, glossy lemon with the fewest seeds and sharp acidic juice is usually the California grown Lisbon. The Meyer lemon, available from December to February, is recognizable by its rounder, fragile, orange-yellow skin. Has lots of sweet, aromatic juice with less "pucker power" and fewer seeds. It has a fleeting season since it is not yet mass produced.	Use the zest or a squeeze to add sprightly flavor to fish, beverages, marinades, sauces, salad dressings, baked goods, preserves, and a wide variety of cuisines.

Limes

They prefer growing in the hotter, damper climates, where they're harvested when small, ripe, and yellow. We choose a variety that is the size of lemons and green through and through.

SEASON	DESCRIPTION	USE
JANUARY–SEPTEMBER	The Persian, the most available, has a thin green skin, seedless pale green flesh, and plentiful peppery, acidic juice. The Key lime is rounded, very small, yellow-green, aromatic, and has a thin skin. It has some seeds and an acid juice that is of more complex character than the Persian. Although harvested year-round, their availability varies from area to area. Always available in Mexico, for example, but in northeast markets only during the winter.	Versatile in both sweet and savory dishes, particularly in the ethnic cuisines of Southeast Asia and Central and South America. Used in marinades (for seviche), soups, drinks, sauces, and salad dressings. Both the zest and the juice are used. Small Key limes are used for its namesake, Key lime pie.

Kumquats

Although the overall harvest of these golden orange miniatures is small, they are always abundantly available in the Chinese communities during the New Year celebrations when they are given as gifts.

SEASON	DESCRIPTION	USE
NOVEMBER–FEBRUARY	About 1½ inches long and usually sold with stems and leaves still attached, packed in small baskets. The only citrus fruit where the peel is sweet and the pulp is sour, so the whole fruit is eaten in spite of several small seeds. Two popular varieties are the oval Nagami and the sweeter Meiwa.	Eat whole, raw, or in citrus or other fruit salads. Poach in syrup or brandy. Add to duck or pork or goose dishes, or puree and seed for sauces and baked goods.

SHOP SMART

- Bright color does not necessarily indicate the best flavor. Some oranges and mandarins are at their peak when green. Colder weather triggers the deep orange color that attracts us, but some become tinged with green as the season progresses.
- When buying grapefruit or oranges, selecting heavy fruits guarantees both freshness and juiciness. With oranges, look for taut skin with a bit of give and no signs of bruising or soft damp spots.
- For mandarins and clementines, very puffy skin means the fruit may be withered inside or they've been kept on the tree too long.
- Lemons and limes should show no soft mold spots.
- Store citrus, uncovered, in your refrigerator for several weeks. Room-temperature storage makes them soften and develop a medicinal taste.

CITRUS MATH

When a recipe calls for the juice or the zest of citrus, this guide gives you the approximate amount of fruit you'll need.

CITRUS	JUICE	ZEST
1 large lemon	about 4 tablespoons	2 teaspoons
1 large lime	about 3 tablespoons	about 1 1/2 teaspoons
1 large orange	about 1/2 cup	about 1 tablespoon
1 large grapefruit	about 1 cup	about 1 1/2 tablespoons

Notes for the Cook

SECTIONING CITRUS THE PROPER WAY

- Slice off both ends of the fruit with a very sharp knife.
- Stand the fruit upright on one flat end and cut off the zest and pith together from top to bottom right down to the pulp.
- Working over a bowl to catch any juice, cut the pulp sections from each side close to the dividing membrane. Work toward the center of the fruit to release the segments into the bowl.
- Squeeze the membranes between your fingers to release any residual juice into the bowl.

A ZEST FOR LIVELINESS

The outer colored part of the citrus peel, called the "zest," is a very important agent for flavoring and garnish.

◆ When removing the zest, the best tool is a swivel blade peeler, allowing you to include only the zest, where the oils are, and not the bitter white pith. Cut the zest into thin julienne or finely mince it.

◆ Another special tool that can be used is a zester, which has small round holes that scrape over the fruit to make very fine, long shreds.

◆ The fine side of a 4-sided box grater can also be used for zest. If you use one, keep turning the fruit as you grate so that no pith is included.

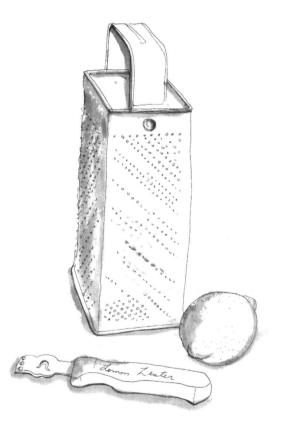

ORANGE AND WALNUT CAKE WITH COGNAC

This family recipe, handed down for two generations, is an ode to the orange—a marriage of whole oranges and crisp nuts in a dense, fruity cake drenched with brandy. And like most of us, it gets better as it gets older!

SERVES 8

CAKE:

¾ cup shelled toasted walnuts (3 or 4 ounces)

2 small navel oranges

8 tablespoons (1 stick) softened butter

1 cup sugar

2 eggs

2 tablespoons boiling water

1 teaspoon baking soda

2 cups flour, sifted

1 cup golden raisins

¼ cup cognac

FROSTING:

4 tablespoons soft butter

¾ cup confectioners' sugar

1 tablespoon heavy cream

½ teaspoon vanilla extract

Shreds of orange zest made with a zester tool and a few walnut halves for garnish

Preheat the oven to 375 degrees. Butter and flour a 9 x 2½-inch springform cake pan. Chop the walnuts finely in a food processor and set aside. Peel the zests of the oranges, finely chop in the food processor, and set aside. Remove and discard the white pith of the oranges, add the pulp to the food processor, and process. Scrape the pulp into a bowl and set aside.

In the same processor, process the butter until soft. Add the sugar and process until light and creamy. Add the eggs, 1 at a time, and process until thoroughly incorporated.

In a cup, mix the boiling water and baking soda together. Add it alternately with the flour, orange pulp, and zest, and process until combined. Add the raisins and reserved walnuts, and pulse a few times, just until combined. Scrape the rather thick batter into the prepared pan and bake for about 50 minutes, or until the center of the cake is baked through when tested with a cake tester.

Cool completely on a wire rack. Remove the sides of the springform pan, invert the cake on a serving plate, and remove the pan bottom. Pierce the surface of the cake in several places with a skewer or ice pick and spoon the cognac over the cake. Wrapped in plastic, it can keep for several hours or overnight.

When ready to serve, prepare the frosting: Process all the ingredients (except the garnish) in a food processor. Frost only the top of the cake. Decorate with orange shreds and walnut halves.

BLOOD ORANGES WITH ORANGE FLOWER WATER AND PISTACHIO NUTS

Whenever we serve this gorgeous color combination, a simple Sicilian dessert, we get ooohs and ahs!

SERVES 4

4 blood oranges, preferably the dark Moro variety
1 teaspoon orange flower water
3 or 4 teaspoons sugar
Ground cinnamon to taste

4 tablespoons toasted, skinned, and very coarsely chopped pistachio nuts (see page 412 for toasting nuts)

With a zester tool, shred the peel of 1 orange for garnish, or if you prefer, peel with a vegetable parer and cut into needle-thin julienne strips, and set aside. Cut a thin slice from the bottom and top of each orange, and with a very sharp knife, cut the peel and pith from the oranges from top to bottom. With a serrated bread knife (so that the juices are not lost), cut each orange into about 5 or 6 thin horizontal slices. Arrange in an overlapping circle on individual serving plates. Sprinkle each orange with a few drops of orange flower water and about 1 teaspoon of sugar. Dust the oranges and part of the plate with cinnamon. Sprinkle 1 tablespoon of pistachio nuts and a few shreds of orange peel over each serving.

KUMQUATS POACHED IN CHINESE STAR ANISE

Serve these tiny, zesty, golden ovals over yogurt or vanilla ice cream for a fast, unusual dessert. The sprightly slight licorice flavor of these poached kumquats will also give a lift to roasted pork or duck, or you can include a few in your next fruit salad.

MAKES I QUART

1 ½ pounds kumquats, rinsed and
   stemmed
Boiling water
1 cup cold water
⅓ cup sugar

3 tablespoons light honey
2 or 3 whole Chinese star anise
  (see Note)
Yogurt or vanilla ice cream

Place the kumquats in a bowl and pour the boiling water over them to cover. Let steep for 30 seconds, then drain. In a 2-quart heavy saucepan, combine the cold water, sugar, and honey. Add the star anise and bring to a boil over medium-low heat. Turn the heat to low and stir in the blanched kumquats. Cook over very low heat for 15 minutes to prevent the kumquats from bursting. Stir occasionally so they are covered with syrup.

Cool and then transfer to a covered container along with the star anise. Refrigerate for 24 hours before using, stirring once or twice during that time. They will keep, refrigerated, for 1 month.

Note: If star anise is difficult to obtain, use a 2-inch piece of
cinnamon stick.

WHOLE CLEMENTINES MARINATED IN HONEY, BASIL, AND LIME SYRUP

These small, sweet, easily peeled, seedless darlings are served in a sweet, tart syrup perfumed by fresh basil.

SERVES 4

1 large lime
1 cup water
⅛ teaspoon cream of tartar
½ cup sugar
1 tablespoon light mild honey

4 large basil leaves plus a few leaves for garnish
2 tablespoons orange liqueur such as Grand Marnier
4 clementines

Using a zester tool, peel long shreds of lime for garnish. Wrap in plastic wrap and set aside. Squeeze the juice from the lime (about 2 tablespoons) and set aside.

In a 1½-quart nonstick saucepan, combine the water, cream of tartar, sugar, honey, and basil leaves. Heat slowly over medium heat to boiling and then boil for 10 minutes. Remove from the heat and stir in the lime juice and liqueur.

Peel the clementines, keeping them whole and removing any clinging bits of thread-like pith, and place in a bowl.

Strain and pour the syrup over the clementines and sprinkle with the shredded lime peel. Cover and refrigerate for several hours, turning the fruit in the syrup occasionally. Serve individual clementines with some syrup spooned over and garnish each serving with a fresh basil leaf.

MEYER LEMON CREAM

A festive cloud of tart-sweet lemon cream takes only five minutes to prepare. Serve it in your best Baccarat or Waterford wine goblets for an elegant finale.

SERVES 4

1 cup cold heavy cream
¼ cup lemon juice (about 1 large lemon), preferably Meyer
¼ cup cold sweetened condensed milk

¼ cup sugar (additional sugar may be needed with other than Meyer lemons)
Lemon roses and mint sprigs for garnish (see Note)

In a chilled mixing bowl, combine the cream, lemon juice, condensed milk, and sugar. Using an electric hand beater, whip the mixture until it is very thick. Spoon about ¾ cup into each of four lovely crystal goblets. Decorate with a lemon rose and a sprig of fresh mint. Chill until serving time.

Note: To make a lemon rose, start at the blossom end of a medium lemon and, using a vegetable parer, pare off the zest in one continuous long strip. Wind the strip around and around to form a rose. Fasten it with a toothpick, which can be hidden by some lemon cream.

Meyer Lemon Cream

KEY LIME CHICKEN SOUP, MEXICAN STYLE

Part of the citrus circuit is the small, tart yellow-green Key lime, similar to the Mexican lime used in the traditional sopa de Lima. *Our version of this beautifully flavor-balanced soup, which can be used as a whole meal, is a reconstruction after a memorable trip to Mexico.*

SERVES 6

2 tablespoons canola oil

2 cups finely chopped red onions
(2 medium onions)

1 teaspoon finely minced garlic
(1 medium clove)

3 tablespoons seeded and finely
minced Serrano chiles

1 teaspoon dried oregano

½ teaspoon dried cumin

⅛ teaspoon ground cloves

⅛ teaspoon ground cinnamon

Salt and pepper to taste

1½ cups skinned and diced plum
tomatoes (12 ounces)

6 cups chicken broth

1¼ pounds chicken cutlets

6 Key limes: 2 juiced for
2 tablespoons juice, 2 cut into
wedges for condiment, 2 thinly
sliced for garnish (see Note)

8 corn tortillas, cut in half and then
crosswise into ½-inch strips

6 to 8 sprigs cilantro. Use leaves for
garnish

1 Haas avocado

In a 5-quart Dutch oven, heat the oil over medium-high heat. Add 1 cup of the onions, garlic, and 1 tablespoon of the chile, and sauté, stirring frequently, for 3 minutes. In a cup, combine the oregano, cumin, cloves, cinnamon, salt, and pepper, and add it to the onion mixture. Cook, stirring, 1 to 2 minutes more. Stir in the tomatoes and continue to cook, stirring occasionally, for 5 minutes. Add the chicken broth and bring to a boil. Add the chicken cutlets, turn the heat to medium-low, and poach the chicken for 8 to 10 minutes, or until just cooked through.

Remove the chicken with tongs and cool just enough to be able to handle them. While the chicken is cooling, stir the lime juice into the soup. Tear the cutlets into shreds and add to the soup. Heat over low heat until the soup is hot enough to serve.

Peel and cut the avocado into ½-inch cubes. To serve, ladle the soup into large bowls, float a slice of lime on top, scatter the cilantro leaves over all, and top with tortilla strips. Pass small bowls of the remaining red onions, the remaining minced Serrano chile, the diced avocado, and the wedges of lime. These can be added as desired.

Note: If Key limes are not available, use 2 to 3 Persian limes.

SEVICHE WITH LIME, ORANGE, AVOCADO, AND RED ONION

Seafood is definitely in the limelight in this colorful seviche.

SERVES 6

12 ounces sea scallops, cut into
½-inch pieces
1 pound halibut or tilefish or Chilean
sea bass, skinned, boned, and cut
into 1-inch cubes
¾ cup lime juice (about 6 large limes)
2 tablespoons lemon juice
(½ large lemon)
½ teaspoon finely minced garlic
(1 small clove)
2 tablespoons finely minced onion
(½ small onion)
1 cup skinned and diced plum
tomatoes (3 to 4 large)
1 large jalapeño chile, seeded and finely
minced (about 1 tablespoon)

1 teaspoon fresh thyme leaves or
½ teaspoon dried thyme
2 teaspoons nonpareil capers, rinsed
Salt and pepper to taste
½ cup coarsely chopped cilantro
(1 medium-size bunch) plus a few
sprigs for garnish
Red or green frilled lettuce leaves
1 small, thinly sliced red onion
1 medium-size navel orange, peeled
and thinly sliced crosswise
1 ripe Haas avocado, peeled and cut
into ½-inch cubes

In a large nonreactive bowl, combine the seafood, lime and lemon juice, garlic, minced onion, tomatoes, jalapeño, thyme, capers, salt, pepper, and chopped cilantro. Cover the bowl with plastic wrap and place in the refrigerator for at least 12 hours, stirring once or twice during that time.

When ready to serve, make a bed of lettuce leaves on a platter. Place overlapping and alternate slices of red onion and orange in a ring over the lettuce leaves. Remove the seafood from the marinade with a slotted spoon and heap it in the center of the platter. Scatter avocado over the seafood and garnish with the cilantro sprigs. Serve at once so that the avocado doesn't darken.

Romancing the Stone Fruits

Cherry Clafouti with Cognac

Peach Slush with Cardamom and Blueberries

Nectarine and Raspberry Upside-Down Cake

Italian Plum and Strawberry Crumble with Kirsch

The lazy days of summer herald the arrival of apricots, peaches, nectarines, plums, and cherries, all members of the rose family. They are the fruits that harbor only a single pit and, when perfectly ripe, are at their most enticing and sensual—fragrant, honey sweet, a slight tart edge, and their succulent juices dripping with each bite.

APRICOTS

A China native cultivated four thousand years ago, the apricot was brought to California by the Spanish missionaries. The season, from late June through July and part of August, is brief, and most of the crop of this fragile (the flesh separates easily from the pit) freestone fruit is canned or dried. Very little is sold fresh, and that small amount is shipped out before they ripen completely, so many of them are either too hard or too dry.

The varieties are: Freestone Royals, which are large and golden orange with a slight indentation on one side and a bit of a blush; and Blenheim, Katy, and Castlebrite, which are all similar in size and color.

SHOP SMART

♦ Try to find apricots that are just beginning to soften and have an apricot scent. Continue ripening for one or two days in a brown paper bag with holes punched in it. They will become more tender but not sweeten like the tree-ripened fruit. Poaching allows them to develop more flavor.

◆ Buy apricots with a perfect appearance and with a uniform golden color. They should be plump and juicy looking, and the velvety skin should yield slightly to gentle pressure.

◆ Avoid greenish, rock-hard, bruised, shriveled, dull, or mushy-looking fruit. They will either be underripe or overripe.

One pound = 10 to 12 medium to large apricots or 2 cups stoned
and halved.

CHERRIES

This fruit has a short-lived harvest of just a few weeks—from late May to early August, with July as the peak. There are two kinds of cherries: sweet and sour. The most popular are the sweet red varieties:

Bing: round and large with mahogany-colored skin.

Burlat: dark red, sweet, and softer to the touch.

Lambert: heart-shaped dark red with a rich, sweet flavor.

Ranier also known as Queen Anne or Royal Anne: large, golden, with a red blush. Firm, very sweet, and the most expensive.

Montmorency: small, tart, bright red. This sour cherry is used for pies, jams, and various spirits such as kirsch (an eau-de-vie), maraschino, and ratafia.

 SHOP SMART

Cherries are highly perishable. Handle them carefully since they bruise easily.

◆ Refrigerate them, unwashed, in one layer on a paper-towel-lined tray and cover loosely with a paper towel for no more than two or three days.

◆ Wash them just before serving or serve them Italian style in a glass bowl of water with an ice cube or two. Swish them around and eat them out of hand.

One pound = about 2¼ cups pitted cherries that will serve four.

PEACHES

In China some twenty-five hundred years ago, the peach was revered as a symbol of immortality and longevity. The peach season runs from late May through October, with early peaches coming from California and the South, and later ones from Michigan and the Atlantic states.

Although hundreds of varieties exist, they are marketed by their place of origin and rarely by their names. Thus, we see peaches labeled California, Georgia, or one of the other thirty states where peaches are grown, but seldom are they labeled as Fay Elberta or White Babcock peaches.

There are two basic categories for peaches: *freestone,* where the flesh separates easily from the pit, and *clingstone,* where the pit clings as the name implies. Some varieties are semi-freestone and have a slightly loose pit.

FREESTONE: This later-season peach is soft, sweet, and usually larger than the cling-stones. Popular varieties are Redhaven (an August peach), Fairtime, Elberta, and Angelus.
CLINGSTONE: An early peach that has good flavor and golden color is the Georgia Bell. Other clingstones include the white-fleshed Japanese Babcock, Sunhaven, Spring, and Maycrest. Some say that clingstone peaches have better flavor and firmer flesh. They are not used for purees.
SEMI-FREESTONE: This early peach is of medium size, and its varieties include June Lady, Desert Gold, and Red Top.

There is also a novelty peach with a good flavor that is being marketed at specialty stores—the flat, doughnut-shaped Saturn.

SHOP SMART

Some of the early season peaches are grown mostly for canning and preserving, so wait for the later-season, tree-ripened, sweet, aromatic peaches.

- A perfectly ripe peach is one that has reached maturity on the tree. It should be soft, with downy skin, a warm summer scent, and a tart sweet flavor, and it should drip juices. Pick one up and sniff it. The flesh at the base should yield to a slight thumb pressure—a sign that it has indeed been tree-ripened.
- Some varieties have varying degrees of blush. If the downy skin is green, the peach is underripe.

- Use ripe peaches as soon as possible or refrigerate them as they ripen. If peaches are not quite ripe, keep them at room temperature. They will soften and get juicier, but they will not sweeten.
- Avoid hard green fruit and peaches that are very soft with flattened bruises or any other sign of decay that starts as a pale tan spot, expands in a circle, and slowly turns darker.

One pound = 3 large or 4 medium whole peaches, which yields about
2 cups, peeled, pitted, and sliced.

Notes for the Cook

ON PEACHES

- Slightly underripe peaches with skins kept on develop better flavor when poached.
- If a recipe calls for peeled peaches, cover them with boiling water, let stand for 1 or 2 minutes, then cool them in cold water. The skins usually will slip off easily.
- When slicing peaches, lemon juice helps keep their color true and prevents browning.

NECTARINES

The Greeks called the drink derived from the fruit *nektar*, the drink of the gods. It has been described as "a peach after it has had a shave," since they are so close botanically. The nectarine is a summer fruit with fuller flavor than the peach. It appears in June and fades in late September. Unlike the fuzzy, thick-skinned peach, it never needs peeling and can usually be used interchangeably in recipes that call for peaches. Among the three most popular varieties are Flamekist, Fantasia, and Firebrite, although there are many others too numerous to mention.

SHOP SMART

The same criteria for selecting peaches also apply to nectarines. They are smaller than peaches, have a blushing orange-red background, and should yield to gentle pressure but not be as soft as a ripe peach.

PLUMS

There are over 150 varieties of plums cultivated in this country alone, with a wide range of shapes, colors, and sizes—from a cherry to a baseball. They can be round, elongated, or heart-shaped, and all are indented deeply on one side. Colors range from pale yellow to green, red, purple, and black, with some mottled colors tossed in for good measure. When at their flavor peak, all have a most desirable tart/sweet balance.

There are two basic types of plums: those of European origin and those that originally hailed from Japan. Most varieties appear in the marketplace in early June and peak in July and August, while others are available into early fall.

Plums are notorious crossbreeders, accounting for dozens of varieties and making some choices a challenge.

Red Skin Varieties with Golden Flesh

Santa Rosa, along with the closely related Red Beauty and Casselman, are fairly juicy and have small pits. They have a characteristic tinge of astringency in their flavor. All are of the clingstone type.

Black Skin or Reddish Black with Golden Flesh

El Dorado, Friar, and Black Amber plums are a bit sweeter than the red-skinned varieties. Elephant Heart, Laroda, and Black Beauty are clingstone red-fleshed black plums.

Green to Gold Skins with Yellow-Tinged Flesh

Kelsey, sometimes mislabeled Green Gage (also known as Reine Claude), which they resemble, are less juicy than other varieties but are sweet. They are one of the freestone varieties. The small, tart baking and preserving Mirabelle plum also has golden skin and flesh.

Purple Skins with Green to Amber Flesh

The Italian Prune plum is the small, oval, purple plum with a smoky bloom and bright green flesh. It is available late in the season and is excellent in baked goods. President and Emily are two others that fit this category of freestone plum. They are used for eating out of hand and baking. The Italian Prune plums and d'Agen plums are also dried as prunes. The Damson plum, small and tart, has purple flesh as well as skin and is used primarily for preserves.

One of the novelties sometimes seen in the marketplace is the Dinosaur Egg plum, recognized by its mottled ochre to burgundy surface color.

SHOP SMART

Whichever variety you choose, they should be plump, slightly soft at the tip, with smooth skin, even color, and a waxy bloom.

- Refrigerate soft ripe fruit at once and let the firmer fruit stand at room temperature to ripen for two or three days. Plums, unlike other stone fruits, can finish ripening off the tree.
- After they ripen, transfer to the crisper in the refrigerator and keep for no more than three days.
- Avoid broken skins, brown spots, bruises, and rock-hard fruit.

One pound = about 6 medium-size plums, depending on variety, or about 2½ cups pitted and sliced.
Smaller plums, such as late-season Italian Prune plums, contain about 14 to 18 plums per pound.

Notes for the Cook

ON PLUMS . . .

- Plums are cooked and eaten unpeeled. The skins have a lot of flavor, and they keep the fruit intact when cooked.
- Many of the clingstone plums are eaten uncooked, but when you want to poach them or use them in tarts, they need to be pitted. To pit: Use a small, sharp knife to cut along the seam all around the pit. Twist the fruit halves in opposite directions to separate and then cut out the pit.
- For cooking, choose firmer plums to retain their texture. Choose fully ripe plums for eating uncooked.

♦ It's the Pits! ♦

Pitting large amounts of cherries can be a daunting and time-consuming job. Since we are gadget freaks and pit lots of cherries and olives, we have invested in a kitchen gadget that does both. Check your local kitchen specialty or major department store or kitchen gadget mail order catalog for the several types available.

The other option when pitting a few at a time is to put a cherry (or olive) on the mouth of a soda pop bottle and push out the pit with the head of a clean bobby pin, hairpin, or opened paper clip. Or make a tiny slash in the cherry with the tip of a knife and remove the pit.

CHERRY CLAFOUTI WITH COGNAC

A true country dessert from the Limousin region of France. Although other fruits such as peaches, pears, and plums can be used, cherries are the traditional fruit of choice.

SERVES 6

4 tablespoons butter, melted

4 cups dark sweet cherries, stemmed and pitted (about 1½ pounds) (see It's the Pits! above)

2 tablespoons cognac (or kirsch)

⅔ cup flour, sifted

¼ teaspoon salt

3 eggs, lightly beaten

½ cup sugar

1 cup milk

½ teaspoon vanilla extract

Confectioners' sugar

Place 2 tablespoons of the melted butter in a 10-inch quiche pan. Arrange the pitted cherries on the bottom of the pan, sprinkle with cognac, and set aside for 20 minutes.

Preheat the oven to 425 degrees. In a small bowl, whisk the flour and salt together, and set aside. In a larger bowl, whisk the eggs with the sugar. Add the milk and vanilla, and whisk until well blended. Add the remaining melted butter and the flour-salt mixture, and whisk again until smooth. Pour the batter slowly and evenly over the cherries so they are not dislodged. Bake for 5 minutes, and then lower the heat to 350 degrees. Bake about 35 to 40 minutes more, or until the clafouti is puffed, firm, and golden brown. Serve warm with confectioners' sugar sifted over the surface.

PEACH SLUSH WITH CARDAMOM AND BLUEBERRIES

One of those refreshing hot summer day treats, easy on the cook. Peaches can be frozen beforehand, and your food processor does the rest in minutes.

SERVES 4

1 pound ripe freestone peaches (about
   3 or 4 large), peeled, pitted, and
   sliced
½ cup sugar
⅓ cup cold water
2 teaspoons lemon juice

1½ teaspoons vanilla extract
¼ to ½ teaspoon cardamom
½ cup sour cream
2 cups blueberries
4 sprigs mint for garnish

Arrange the sliced peaches in a single layer on a jelly roll pan and freeze for 45 minutes. Also chill 4 wineglasses in the freezer.

Place the frozen peaches in the bowl of a food processor. Add the sugar, water, lemon juice, vanilla, and cardamom, and process until slushy. Add the sour cream with the food processor on and process until smooth.

Distribute ⅔ of the blueberries among the 4 chilled wineglasses. Spoon the peach slush over the berries. Scatter the remaining berries on top along with a sprig of mint for each. Serve at once.

NECTARINE AND RASPBERRY UPSIDE-DOWN CAKE

We once baked this cake for a summer charity raffle, and it looked so great that it was sold for $40!

SERVES 4 TO 6

3 tablespoons butter
½ cup light brown sugar
3 to 4 ripe nectarines, pitted and
  thickly sliced
½ pint raspberries
6 tablespoons soft butter
⅔ cup sugar

1 large egg
1 ⅓ cups all-purpose flour
¼ teaspoon salt
1 teaspoon baking powder
1 teaspoon vanilla extract
3 tablespoons cognac
⅓ cup milk

In a round 9-inch nonstick baking pan, melt the butter and brown sugar on top of the stove over low heat, stirring until dissolved. Let cool for 10 minutes and then arrange the sliced nectarines over the sugar in an attractive pattern. Scatter the raspberries among the nectarines and set aside.

Preheat the oven to 350 degrees. In a food processor, cream the butter and sugar until light and fluffy. Add the egg and combine.

In a small bowl, place the flour, salt, and baking powder, and whisk to combine. In a small cup, place the vanilla, cognac, and milk, and combine. Add ⅓ of the flour mixture to the food processor and combine. Add ⅓ of the milk mixture and process. Repeat until both mixtures are used up. The batter should be thick.

Spoon the batter evenly over the fruit. Bake in the middle of the preheated oven for about 35 minutes, or until a skewer inserted in the middle of the cake comes out clean. Cool for 15 to 20 minutes on a wire rack. Loosen the edges of the cake by running a knife inside the edge of the pan. Invert the cake onto a serving plate to cool completely.

ITALIAN PLUM AND STRAWBERRY CRUMBLE WITH KIRSCH

We have always loved the homey American and English fruit desserts with the musical names: grunts, slumps, crumbles, buckles, crisps, and cobblers. This one, with lightly simmered plums and uncooked strawberries, is a summer favorite. Three minutes under the broiler crisps and browns the top.

SERVES 4 TO 5

I cup rolled oats

3 tablespoons butter, cut into small cubes, plus I teaspoon for buttering dish

I cup light brown sugar

2 pounds prune plums, pitted

Scant teaspoon ground cinnamon

I tablespoon kirsch

I cup small strawberries, hulled and left whole

Frozen vanilla yogurt

In the bowl of a food processor, process the oats for a few strokes to break down the flakes. Butter a 4-cup baking dish with the teaspoon of butter. Scatter 3 tablespoons of the oats on the bottom of the baking dish and set aside.

Add ½ cup of the sugar and the 3 tablespoons of butter to the remaining oats in the bowl of the food processor. Pulse until the butter absorbs the sugar and oats. Remove to a bowl and chill while preparing the fruit.

Place the plums in 2 batches in the food processor and pulse only 5 times to coarsely chop them. Transfer to a 3-quart saucepan with the remaining sugar and the cinnamon. Bring the plums to the boiling point over medium heat, then lower the heat to simmer and cook, uncovered, for 10 minutes. Remove from the heat and stir in the kirsch and strawberries.

Spoon the fruit over the prepared pan. Crumble the chilled oats mixture evenly over the surface of the fruit. When ready to serve, preheat the broiler and slip the crumble under the source of heat for 2 or 3 minutes to brown the top. Serve warm topped with frozen yogurt.

The Berry Bounty

Mixed Berry Cobbler

Marsala Cream–Filled Strawberries

Untraditional Hazelnut and Raspberry Pie

Blackberry and Almond Cream Tart with Shortbread and Honey Crust

Cranberry Gratin with Orange Zabaglione

In midsummer the air is filled with the fragrance of fresh berries at their very peak of sweetness; this is also when they are most plentiful. Today when we buy them, they are laid out neatly in flat little baskets in a rainbow of jewel-like colors. But we remember when, as kids, we confronted the brambles, thorns, mosquitoes, poison ivy, ticks, and sunburn to pick our fleeting treasures in spite of the hardships. Popping the first ripe, sun-warmed berry into our mouths made it all worthwhile.

STRAWBERRIES

They are usually the harbingers of every kind of berry that will appear throughout the summer and into the fall months. March is the local strawberry month on the West Coast, while June brings the local crop to the East Coast. Some varieties, such as the Driscoll, are now available almost year-round. Select the brightest, solid red berries that have a lustrous surface and bright green caps. Any trace of white near the cap indicates immaturity.

FRAISES DES BOIS

These tiny, very expensive, aromatic, highly perishable, thimble-size strawberries are now making an occasional appearance in the marketplace. They have a slightly longer growing season than the larger varieties and a very intense taste.

RASPBERRIES

Everybody seems to love them. June through October are peak months with the fall red raspberries, and the wonderfully delicious golden variety, which are a bit larger than the early summer crop. The black raspberries are smaller and less juicy than the others and have more seeds, but they are highly aromatic.

BLACKBERRIES AND THEIR KIN

In addition to the most common, mild-flavored, plump, shiny, deep purplish blackberries, there is a veritable cornucopia of crossover bramble hybrids related to both the raspberry and the blackberry. Here is how to recognize them if they appear in your supermarket, specialty store, or farmer's market:

LOGANBERRY: This is a cross between a raspberry and a blackberry. About 1 inch long and dark red in color, it has a tart and intensely flowery flavor. Use with honey or another sweet berry for contrast. They are generally available at the beginning of summer.

MARIONBERRY: A cross between loganberry and raspberry, they range from deep red to black and are packed with flavor. Their seeds are very fine, making them seem almost seedless.

BOYSENBERRY: This is a big, juicy, deep purple blackberry-loganberry cross.

OLALLIE: A deep maroon variety that has a sweet taste.

DEWBERRY: Bluish gray in color, it has a delicate, nutlike flavor that is quite similar to the blackberry.

BLUEBERRIES

Blueberries are the kin of one of our authentic North American bush-grown fruits: the wild, low-bush huckleberry and the whortleberry, a softer, sweeter berry. Huckleberries are deep smoky blue or purple throughout, the color of unpolished sapphires. They have a slightly tart/sweet and peppery edge and appear in mid to late summer. A goodly supply comes from Maine and Michigan.

Most commercial outlets offer the cultivated high-bush blueberries, which are sweet, soft, and the size of marbles. They are navy blue and have an exterior bloom, a silvery dusting of natural wax that changes as they age and sweeten, going from a powdery blue to a midnight blue. The peak months around the country are from late May through September.

CRANBERRIES

This is another wild native North American berry first cultivated in 1816 in Massachusetts but now also produced in New Jersey, Wisconsin, and Washington. They grow close to the earth in boggy soil, and when the harvest is ready, one of the most wonderful and colorful sights in agriculture is the flooding of the fields to make the cranberries float, covering the water with an undulating blanket of deep red.

Except at Thanksgiving and Christmas, cranberries are no longer offered as a fresh, seasonal autumn treat. They are now frozen, dried, pureed, canned, and made into conserves for year-round use. A 12-ounce bag of the fresh fruit contains about 3¼ cups, and the berries need to be picked over to remove any reluctant lingering stems before cooking them with sugar to temper their tartness.

GOOSEBERRIES

Found growing on thorny bushes, they are glossy and grape green to a blush of red, with the latter being the sweetest. They have striated, slightly downy skins, are crisp and acidic, and have seeds. Also, before using them, they need to be "topped and tailed"—the stem and base ends removed.

These berries have an abundance of pectin, and the British, Germans, and Scandinavians use them in preserves and in many traditional dishes such as Gooseberry Fool.

CURRANTS

Red currants grow on thornless bushes and hang down in clusters—tiny, round, and as clear as red crystal beads. They make a festive garnish. Red currants are tart and contain a center seed, which the French remove with a needle or goose quill when making the extravagantly costly Bar le Duc currant jelly. Black currants are strong and musky tasting, and when they're mixed with brandy, the result is the elegant crème de cassis. White currants are the most scarce, and they appear and disappear in the marketplace in the blink of an eye.

MULBERRIES

They grow on large trees. Some produce blackish red berries while others are milky white and sweeter. In the Middle East, they are dried in the sun like raisins and eaten out of hand as a snack. They are available in the United States both fresh and dried.

SHOP SMART

Since berries in normal commercial distribution can take one to five days to reach us, getting the best of ripe, full-flavored berries takes a little bit of detective work. Berries do not continue to ripen after picking, so they can last only two or three more days at most after we get them home.

- Look for berries that are free of bruises and mold, that are plump to the bursting point, dry, and fully colored. Never buy a box of berries that are soft, leaky, or split. Inspect the berries at the bottom of the container by looking through the slits; you may spot ones that have begun to rot. Mold spreads quickly to other berries in the container, so once you get them home, check them as quickly as possible and discard any that look damaged.
- Don't wash berries until you plan to use them. Store them in the fruit bin of the refrigerator or, if you have the room, spread them out on a tray and place it on the bottom shelf.
- Make sure raspberries are firm, have an intense, lightly smoky color, and are free of mold.
- When buying blackberries, don't select ones that still have their caps attached. Blackberries when ripe, just like raspberries, will pull away from a white core completely, leaving it behind on the bush and the berry with a hollow center.
- The best way to choose berries is to smell them. The aroma should mimic the finest fruity perfume.

Notes for the Cook

ON BERRIES . . .

- Most berries freeze well. Place them in one layer on a baking tray with a rim, put the tray in the freezer for several hours, and then transfer the berries to a plastic container. When you're ready to use them, they'll still be separate, marblelike jewels.

- ◆ When washing strawberries, keep the caps on until the job is done, then cut off the caps. Strawberries will absorb water when they're uncapped.
- ◆ Some delicate berries, such as strawberries, will keep in the refrigerator for only two or three days. Blueberries, however, can be kept for five or six days, and green gooseberries will refrigerate for one to two weeks, gradually ripening and softening to a sweeter pink stage.

MIXED BERRY COBBLER

When all the ripe berries are at peak flavor in the summer, a simple, homey dessert showcases them to perfection in this sweet, quintessential summer finale.

SERVES 4 TO 6

FILLING:

1 pint blueberries, picked over for any stems

1 pint strawberries, caps removed

½ pint raspberries

½ pint blackberries

1 teaspoon lemon juice

1 tablespoon orange-flavored liqueur such as Cointreau or Grand Marnier

¾ cup dark brown sugar

1 tablespoon cornstarch

DOUGH:

1 ½ cups flour

⅓ cup sugar plus 1 tablespoon

2 teaspoons baking powder

1 teaspoon baking soda

¼ teaspoon salt

6 tablespoons cold butter

⅔ cup buttermilk

½ teaspoon vanilla extract

Preheat the oven to 350 degrees. Butter a 3-quart oven-to-table baking pan. To make the filling: In a large bowl, place all the berries, lemon juice, and liqueur. In a small bowl, mix the sugar and cornstarch together. Add to the berries and combine gently. Transfer to the prepared baking dish and set it aside while preparing the dough.

To make the dough: In a large bowl, place the dry ingredients—flour, ⅓ cup sugar, baking powder, baking soda, and salt. Whisk to combine. With a pastry blender or 2 knives, cut the butter into the flour mixture until crumbly.

In a cup, mix the buttermilk and vanilla, and add it all at once to the dry mixture. Mix gently until all the flour is absorbed. Do not overmix.

Spoon 6 mounds of dough evenly over the berries and sprinkle with the remaining tablespoon of sugar. Bake for about 35 minutes, or until the top is golden and the fruit is bubbling. Let cool before serving. It can be served topped with vanilla frozen yogurt or ice cream.

MARSALA CREAM–FILLED STRAWBERRIES

A sumptuous, easy, and attractive dessert. The largest, most perfect, eye-catching strawberries you can find are cut into a flower and filled with Marsala cream.

SERVES 4

12 very large strawberries, rinsed, dried thoroughly, and caps removed

½ cup heavy cream

1 tablespoon confectioners' sugar plus additional for garnish

1½ tablespoons dry Marsala wine

Place the strawberries, hull side down, on a work surface and from the pointed end, split each berry into eighths. Do not cut through to the stem end. Set aside.

In a chilled bowl, using a hand beater, whip the cream until partially whipped. Add the confectioners' sugar and whip until almost stiff. Add the Marsala and complete the whipping process. Gently spread the berries open, being careful not to separate the sections. Fill each one generously with the cream, using either a heaping teaspoon or piping from a pastry bag fitted with a half-inch star tip. Serve within 30 minutes so that the whipped cream remains stable. Dust with confectioners' sugar just before serving.

Marsala Cream-Filled Strawberries

UNTRADITIONAL HAZELNUT AND RASPBERRY PIE

A cross between a cake and a pie, with raspberries sandwiched between the 2 hazelnut layers. Other berries such as blueberries, blackberries, and strawberries can also be used, but you will miss the special tantalizing scent of raspberries baking and perfuming your entire house.

SERVES 6

6 ounces hazelnuts, toasted and skinned

8 tablespoons (1 stick) butter, slightly softened

½ cup light brown sugar

½ cup flour

⅛ teaspoon salt

2 egg whites, lightly beaten

2 cups raspberries, dried thoroughly on paper towels

1 teaspoon Chambord, kirsch, or Cointreau

1 tablespoon sugar

Crème fraîche, whipped cream, or nonfat frozen vanilla yogurt

Preheat the oven to 350 degrees. Butter the inside of a 9-inch tempered glass or ceramic pie pan. In the bowl of a food processor, chop the nuts until fine. Transfer to a bowl and set aside.

In the same unwashed food processor bowl, place the butter and sugar, and process until creamy. Add the flour and salt, and combine. Add the nuts and process a few strokes, just to blend. Remove ½ cup of this mixture and set aside. Add the egg whites to the processor and blend thoroughly. Scrape the mixture into the prepared pie pan and spread evenly with a spatula on the bottom and up the sides of the pan. Heap the raspberries in the center. Sprinkle with the spirits and then the sugar. Top the raspberries with the reserved ¼ cup of the flour-nut mixture in small dollops.

Bake for 35 to 40 minutes, or until the bottom is golden. Cool on a rack and serve with your choice of cream on the side of the plate.

BLACKBERRY AND ALMOND CREAM TART WITH SHORTBREAD AND HONEY CRUST

For those who have a fear of making pastry, this tart has an easy crust made with shortbread cookies.

SERVES 6

CRUST:
6-ounce package Scottish shortbread
　cookies

3 tablespoons light mild honey
Butter for pan

ALMOND CREAM:
4 ounces almond paste, cut into small
　pieces
2 tablespoons softened butter, cut into
　small pieces
¼ cup sugar

¼ teaspoon salt
2 tablespoons cornstarch
1½ cups milk
1 egg, lightly beaten
1 teaspoon vanilla extract
¼ teaspoon almond extract

BERRIES:
⅓ cup seedless blackberry jam or
　currant jelly

1½ cups blackberries

Preheat the oven to 350 degrees. To make the crust: In a food processor, process the shortbread cookies until crumbs form. There should be about 1⅓ cups. Add the honey and process until combined. Butter a 9-inch tart pan with a removable base. Press the honey crumb mixture into the bottom of the pan and ¾ inch up the sides. Place the pan on a baking sheet and bake for about 10 minutes, or until lightly brown. Set aside to cool completely on a wire rack. While the crust is cooling, prepare the almond cream and berries.

　To make the almond cream: Process the almond paste and butter in a food processor until combined. Mix the sugar, salt, and cornstarch together in a cup, add it to the food processor, and combine. Transfer to a 3-quart nonstick saucepan, and over medium heat, gradually whisk in the milk. Bring it to a boil, stirring constantly, until thick and bubbling, about 5 minutes. Remove a ladleful of this hot mixture and whisk it into the egg. Scrape it back into the saucepan and stir constantly until thick, about 2 or 3 minutes. Remove from the stove, add the flavorings, and let cool completely. Scrape it into the tart crust.

To prepare the berries: Melt the jelly in a small saucepan over low heat. Combine with the berries and let cool for 5 minutes. Spoon the berry mixture in the center of the almond cream, leaving a border of filling showing. Remove the sides of the pan but keep the tart on the rigid base to serve.

CRANBERRY GRATIN WITH
ORANGE ZABAGLIONE

Tart, sweet cranberries are bathed in a rich and frothy sauce spiked with orange zest and Grand Marnier.

SERVES 4 TO 6

¾ cup sugar

¼ cup water

12-ounce bag cranberries (about
   3¼ cups fresh or thawed frozen)

2 large eggs at room temperature

1 egg yolk at room temperature

¼ cup sugar

1 tablespoon grated orange zest
   (1 large)

½ cup cold heavy cream

1 tablespoon Grand Marnier

Preheat the broiler. In a 2-quart saucepan, place the sugar and water, and stir over medium heat until dissolved. Stir in the cranberries, bring to a boil, and lower the heat; cook only until the berries begin to pop, about 5 minutes. Put the berries in a single layer in a 10-inch oval baking dish.

Heat ½ inch of water in a medium saucepan in which a stainless-steel mixing bowl fits snugly but doesn't touch the water. With an electric hand beater, whisk the eggs, yolk, sugar, and orange zest in the mixing bowl until frothy. Place the bowl over simmering water and continue to beat until the mixture is pale, has tripled in volume, and forms thick ribbons when the beater is lifted, about 8 minutes.

Remove the bowl from the heat and beat the mixture until slightly cool, about 1 or 2 minutes. Whip the cream until stiff, fold it into the zabaglione, and pour evenly over the berries. In the preheated broiler, 5 or 6 inches from the source of heat, broil about 1 minute, or until lightly golden in color. Serve warm.

Tropical Fruits and the Not So Tropical Fruits

Baby Bananas with Kahlúa and Espresso Sauce

Fresh Figs Filled with Mascarpone in Ginger Sauce

Papaya and Lime Relish with Grilled Shrimp

Mango and Chile Butter with Bluefish

Kiwis and Pineapple in Ginger Plum Wine Sauce

Stars and Striper

Rhubarb Soufflé with Orange Cointreau Sauce

Persimmon Spice Pudding with Bourbon and Pecans

Quince Spoon Sweets

Fresh figs, dates, melons, pomegranates, and persimmons, formerly exotic to us in the Northern Hemisphere, have always been a large and important part of the food supply of the tropical world. More recently, with jet transportation from the Southern Hemisphere, we've been blessed with a fall and winter bounty, not only as imports but also from growers in Florida, California, and Hawaii.

Some are unfamiliar strangers, looking as if they were grown on Mars, while others—like the ubiquitous banana—have been in our markets for a lifetime.

BANANAS

There are about three hundred varieties of bananas worldwide, with rich, subtle flavors and a range of exotic sizes and textures. One of the most prolific and versatile plants on earth, the banana has remained one of the best fruit buys. They have a year-round availability and a low price, allowing Americans to consume an average of twenty-five pounds per person per year. Multiplying that by about 300 million people makes for a lot of bananas!

SHOP SMART

- ◆ Peeling a banana is like doing a striptease, but rather than slowly revealing hidden secrets, it is the peel that actually tells us the ripeness of the fruit that lies under it:
- ◆ *Slightly green tipped* bananas are partially ripe and ideal for cooking, though they can be ripened further until the green disappears completely.

- ◆ *All yellow* bananas are ripe and ready to eat, yet firm enough to cook. When a banana is flecked with brown (as Chiquita Banana used to say) and has a golden hue, it is fully ripe and very sweet. This is a "top banana"—ready to mash, bake, drink, or slice. Just remember: Store it in the refrigerator *crisper* to retard over-ripening and then serve at room temperature. (It is not true that you never put a banana in the refrigerator!)

FRESH DATES

Dried dates are available year-round, but fresh dates, sometimes called "tree candy" because of their high sugar content, appear in early fall and throughout the winter. Truly a lush dessert, they are light, and have a honeyed taste and a single removable pit. They cry out to be filled with fois gras, wrapped with bacon and grilled, served with tart yogurt, or baked into pastries, bread, and cake.

The best, the most popular, and the largest date is the Medjoul, which has luxurious flesh and good flavor. They're often sold in specialty shops. Khadrawy is a soft, smaller date that ripens early. Deglet Noor, often labeled the *California date*, has a distinctive date flavor and makes up 95 percent of the California crop.

FRESH FIGS

Figs are believed to have originated in the Near East and the Mediterranean area, where the summers are not too hot or humid and the soil is somewhat barren. Most of the figs grown in the United States are cultivated by people with strong Mediterranean backgrounds—from Greece, Italy, and the Middle East.

A sensual fruit, fresh figs resemble soft, leathery pouches and have colors that vary from the pale jade green of the fragrant, honey-scented Kadota fig to the small Mission, with just a hint of bloom on a dusty black-purple skin. The Calymyrna figs, a later California variety, show off green/amber skin with flesh that ranges from pale to ivory to pink. Amber-colored Celeste and Brown Turkey are two of the most popular home-grown varieties.

SHOP SMART

- The skins of figs are thin and the fruit highly perishable, so they must be carefully packed and handled. If possible, choose soft, dry fruit that has just begun to shrivel, and the fig will be ripe and sweet.
- Avoid those with a sour smell, indicating overripeness. If the figs are not quite ripe when you buy them, keep them at room temperature until they become soft and ready to use. Then use them as soon as possible.
- Figs should never be refrigerated.

Notes for the Cook

ON FRESH FIGS . . .

- Try them with prosciutto or baked with roasted pork, with cheese for dessert or cut them in half to fill a baked tart shell.

PAPAYAS

One of the most healthful of all fruits, papayas grow prodigiously in tropical and semitropical regions. When green and not yet ripe, the papaya contains an enzyme called papain that acts as a digestive aid and has the ability to break down protein. It is frequently listed as an ingredient in meat tenderizers.

Papaya pack a punch of eye appeal with an enchanting flavor, and the flesh ranges from golden to an intense, gorgeous salmon. They ripen at room temperature, with the skin changing from green to yellow-orange. Gentle pressure will tell you when it is ripe. We find that the Strawberry papaya, when available, is an especially good variety.

Notes for the Cook

ON PAPAYAS . . .

- When cut open, the cavity reveals gelatinous black seeds, closely resembling fine caviar. When the papaya is eaten raw, the seeds are discarded, but they can be toasted in a low oven for 20 minutes until they resemble peppercorns, and they do have a peppery bite when added to sauces and salads.
- The best way to serve papaya is raw, with a wedge of lime, or filled with shrimp salad combined with other fruits or made into a relish for grilled seafood.

MANGOES

Long a household staple in the tropics, the mango has now gone mainstream in America with year-round availability and over two thousand varieties worldwide—from the tiny Thai yellow mango to the 1½-pound Caribbean. Some are oval and rather flat with a flattish central pit and a somewhat stringy pulp. We much prefer the fatter mangoes with their finer, peachy pineapple flavor. The most popular and flavorful is the Tommy Atkins from Belize. It is easy to eat and much less fibrous than the others.

An unripe mango can be disappointing, so keep them at room temperature until the fruit "gives" easily. The thin, tough skin may be speckled with brown, but that only means ripeness, not spoilage.

Notes for the Cook

ON MANGOES . . .

A ripe mango will generously drip its juices when cut. It can be daunting unless you know a few tricks:

- The large, flat central pit runs almost the length of the fruit, so holding a mango horizontally makes it easier to handle.
- Cut the mango in half with a serrated grapefruit knife, slicing the fruit away from the seed with the curved end. Slip the knife under the flat pit to release the other half.
- Either serve it with a spoon to scoop it right from its skin or score the flesh of each half into 1-inch cubes, making sure not to cut the skin. Fold each half back to fan out the cubes and serve with a knife and fork to release the bite-size pieces.

Mangoes make sensational sorbets and sauces for ice cream. You can try a mango slice wrapped in prosciutto or add it as a keynote sweet to counter peppery salsas.

MELONS

Most people are mad about melons. Many previously imported varieties are now being cultivated in California, and the choices have begun to be almost delightfully overwhelming. All are best eaten raw, mixed with other melon varieties or with berries, in desserts and in salads.

The Melon Family

HONEYDEW: These are large, some weighing over 5 pounds. The larger ones are more delicious. They have pale ivory skin, not netted, and their flesh is lime green, sweet, and soft when ripe.

ORANGE-FLESH HONEYDEW: A hybrid melon with the rich, sweet taste of papaya-like undertones, it is pale peach and has a slightly netted skin with papaya-colored flesh.

CANARY: A very sweet, large, oval melon with a flavor that is reminiscent of honey. Smooth orange skin and pale green flesh distinguish this vivid melon.

SANTA CLAUS: A large oval with skin that is striped and mottled dark green and gold. The dense, soft, pale green flesh has a slight refreshing tang.

CASABA: Originally from Turkey, it has a large, wrinkled, orange skin that harbors a delicate flesh and flavor. It has very little fragrance even when ripe.

CRENSHAW: A large, slightly oval, golden melon with striated skin and delicate, sweet, pale greenish yellow flesh. When ripe, the skin turns golden yellow.

MUSKMELON: The United States incorrectly calls these cantaloupe, but they are sold under both names. They have closely netted green skin with slight wedge-shaped indentations, covering a peach-colored flesh with a sweet smell and taste.

CHARANTAIS: A small, fragrant, expensive, and elegant miniature with pale gold-green skin that is defined by a darker wedge and a luscious orange flesh with an alluring musky scent. It is native to the south of France and is grown in the Cavaillon region near Avignon. They are sometimes identified as Cavaillon melons. These melons are now imported from Guadaloupe and are also grown in California. You can recognize the French imports by their high price tag and superior flavor.

WATERMELON: Everybody's hot weather treat, they are sold all over the world—three billion pounds in this country alone! Fifty varieties are grown in the United States, all pleasantly fruity and thirst quenching. Choose picnic melons, so-called because they are the largest, weighing between fifteen and fifty pounds. Round or elongated, they have crimson flesh; they are also available with yellow flesh, a variety that has recently gained popularity.

Smaller "icebox" melons weigh between five and fifteen pounds and were developed to fit into refrigerators. The sugar baby variety is the most popular.

SHOP SMART

Since ripeness is such a critical key, here is some advice on how to choose a winner:

- ◆ Press the nearest stem end while holding it close to your nose. It should give slightly and relinquish a sweet, flowery, honey scent. Grab it and rush home to eat it as soon as possible!
- ◆ If not quite ripe, it will eventually ripen at room temperature. Very few melons are vine-ripened, unfortunately, except for some local ones that are picked and sold at their peak.

POMEGRANATES

A mythic fruit favorite of the ancient gods, it was the symbol of fertility, eternal life, hope, and prosperity. It has been cultivated in the Middle East since 4000 B.C. Once opened, the pomegranate is one of the most beautiful and exotic of fruits. Its round, leathery skin is packed with tiny, juicy, jewel-like, tart garnet seeds, each encased in a white cushiony protective pulp.

Notes for the Cook

ON POMEGRANATES . . .

- ◆ Getting at the seeds: The best way to keep them intact is to first slice off the little blossom and crown on top, then score the skin vertically with a sharp knife without penetrating to the seed layer. Gently break the fruit apart at the score lines, grasp the corners, and carefully turn each section inside out, pulling the seed clusters away from their white pithy cushion and putting them into a bowl. Loosen any remaining seeds with the tip of a knife. By submerging the seeds in cold water and gently breaking them apart under the water, you can avoid staining your fingers. Also, working on a sheet of aluminum foil will prevent the staining of your counter or work surface.
- ◆ Take a tip from the inventive cooks of Mexico and the Middle East. Use the tart seeds to scatter over grain and fruit salads, and with fish and poultry.

PINEAPPLES

Though grown in many areas of the world, it was first introduced in the United States in the late eighteenth century. Hawaii is the leading producer of the fruit.

Two major varieties are now available in the United States: The long, cylindrical, golden yellow variety with long swordlike leaves sprouting from a single base, and the squat-shaped variety with reddish gold skin and leaves that grow in clusters.

Both have tufted, diamond-patterned skin and weigh between two and five pounds. The Mexican sugar loaf variety is larger and sweeter, but it doesn't ship well, so it is not usually found here. It has a golden fibrous flesh, is very juicy, and has a tangy, sweet-tart flavor.

SHOP SMART

Pineapples must be picked when ripe, since once off the plant, the starch doesn't convert to sugar. They must be soft to the touch and have crisp green leaves when purchased. Some markets do offer peeled and cored fruit at a more expensive price.

- Before buying, tug at one of the central leaves. The fruit is at its best if the leaf comes out easily.
- Its strong fragrance demands that it be tightly enclosed in plastic wrap when refrigerated. Keeping a slightly underripe pineapple at room temperature will reduce its acidity but will not increase sweetness.

Notes for the Cook

HOW TO CUT A PINEAPPLE:

- Grasp the pineapple, and using a chef's knife, cut off the leaves about 1 inch from the top. Turn the pineapple over and slice 1 inch off the bottom.
- Stand the pineapple up and slice off the skin, cutting down from top to bottom.
- Remove the "pips" or eyes by cutting out tiny wedges, following the natural diagonal line.
- Firmly hold the trimmed pineapple horizontally and cut off ¾-inch-thick slices.
- Cut out the center core hole from the middle of each slice.

And please note: Be forewarned. Pineapple and kiwi contain a natural enzyme that prevents gelatin mixtures from setting, so don't use them for molded desserts or salads.

KIWIS

Native to China, they were originally known as Chinese gooseberries. They got their current name after their introduction to New Zealand where they were dubbed "kiwi" after the flightless native bird of that country. Oval-shaped, the brown hairy skin is deceptive, for when it is peeled, it reveals a soft, vivid emerald green flesh with a center of tiny edible seeds. The flavor is rather delicate and sweet, a combination of strawberries, watermelon, and grapes.

SHOP SMART

Kiwis are available throughout the year in varying sizes and quantities. For best flavor select the soft ones. If they're quite firm, keep them at room temperature until they soften and then refrigerate them.

Notes for the Cook

ON KIWIS . . .

- ◆ They are best eaten raw and do not profit from cooking.
- ◆ Peel and slice them crosswise or in quarters or halves. Add them to fruit medleys and fruit drinks or serve them with custard. They are also a bright addition to cakes and tarts and as a garnish for many dishes.

CARAMBOLA (STAR FRUIT)

This is an oval, five-ridged fruit with a waxy yellow color. When cut horizontally, they yield a perfect five-pointed star, hence their aliases: Star Fruit or Chinese Star Fruit or Five-Angled Fruit. They were grown for centuries in India and southern China as well as in other tropical countries, but virtually all of the United States supply comes from Florida.

SHOP SMART

The carambola can be either sweet or tart depending on the variety. Sweet carambola are large and have the floral, fruity taste of an orange-pineapple combination. Tart varieties are smaller and have the clean, fresh flavor of citrus. Both are very juicy, have crisp, translucent flesh and an edible skin, and are ripe when the ridges turn brown.

Notes for the Cook

ON CARAMBOLA . . .

◆ To reveal their star shape, slice them crosswise.
◆ Float them in a punch bowl or garnish a tart.
◆ Use the small carabambola variety baked over fish or grilled atop sea scallops.

RHUBARB

Although botanically a vegetable, rhubarb is treated like a fruit. When hothouse grown, they have rather long, celery-shaped stalks in pink to pale red, but they are closer to cherry red with thicker stalks when field grown. The green crenelated leaves, with their high oxalic acid content, are poisonous, and grazing animals (as well as humans) leave them alone.

At one time the appearance of rhubarb was a harbinger of spring, but now they appear in the marketplace as early as January and are available for several months. Field-grown rhubarb generally appears in March, and the crop continues through the summer, giving those of us who love it a long, continuous supply.

SHOP SMART

When buying rhubarb, avoid limp stalks. The deeper the color, the sweeter the rhubarb.

Notes for the Cook

ON RHUBARB . . .

Rhubarb has a refreshing, tantalizing tang, and it must be cooked with sugar to make it palatable. We find that when it is combined with strawberries, a fruit with which it has a natural affinity, we can reduce the amount of sugar needed to produce an absolutely ambrosial dessert. It can also be flavored with ginger and orange zest.

Its tartness goes well with rich poultry such as duck as well as pork and fois gras.

ON COOKING RHUBARB . . .

- Trim and slice the stalks into ¾-inch or 1-inch pieces.
- Rhubarb is very juicy, so use very little water when cooking and don't overcook. It should be tender, not mushy.
- Cook over medium-low heat and test after 10 minutes.
- The juices can be thickened with cornstarch or arrowroot. Or cook the rhubarb with 1 tablespoon of minute tapioca, whirled in a blender, to thicken it.

GRAPES

It was not until the time of the Renaissance that grapes were raised for the table rather than for the wine market. In Spain, some years back, we were taught to eat twelve grapes right before midnight on New Year's Eve, one for each chime of the clock. Good luck would come to us if we finished before the final stroke.

Table grapes are usually thin-skinned and have less acidic juice, but are not as sweet as the wine grapes. The flavors vary, depending on where the grapes are grown and based on the tannin content of the skins. Because of the number of varieties, there is a steady supply of table grapes all year round, with June through December as the peak months.

After you buy them, keep them unwashed in a plastic bag in the refrigerator, then wash and dry them right before using to eliminate any insecticide spray that may have been used. They will keep well for up to a week.

A PARTIAL GLOSSARY OF GRAPE VARIETIES

BLACK CORINTH (also known as the tiny "Champagne" grape): They are very delicate and the size of currants. In fact, they are also used for dried currants. They are sweet and spicy, and they are lovely in tarts or served with mascarpone cheese.

CONCORD: The source of most grape juice and jelly. Robust, winy, tangy, and sweet. They are round, dark blue-black, and rather small, with a dusty blush and tough skin.

GREEN SEEDLESS (such as Thompson Seedless): Light green, rather long ovals available year-round. They vary in flavor from tart to super sweet. Best poached or eaten as is.

HIMROD: Round, small, seedless green grapes. They are tart and juicy and are sometimes called "summer grapes."

MUSCAT: Fat, oval, and amber-green with a musky aroma and a sweet flavor. Used for sweet raisin wines such as Valformosa and muscatel, and when dried, a large winy Muscat raisin results.

RIBIER: Large and a smoky black; mild and sweetly perfumed. Their skins are thick, and they have seeds.

RED SEEDLESS: Available year-round and very popular. They are dark red in color and have a fat round shape with hazy skin. They are good with blue cheese.

PERSIMMONS

Eaten with pleasure for hundreds of years throughout the Orient, the flame-orange, silken-skinned persimmon has not yet realized its full potential here in the United States. One reason may well be that the astringency of the unripe Hachiya persimmon, the most commonly available, has given it a bad press. The unripe fruit has harsh tannins that pucker the mouth dryly and render the fruit inedible. But when the fruit matures, the tannins soften, and both the sugars and the luscious flavors develop fully. A really ripe Japanese Hachiya rewards us with its butter-soft, sensually textured, sweet-flavored flesh.

In the last few years another variety of persimmon has appeared: the squat, four-lobed Fuyu, which looks like a flat tomato. It can be eaten when fully colored, but it will still be firm and slightly crisp. Our preference is to wait for the Hachiya to fully ripen, since the texture is so much a part of the eating pleasure.

Notes for the Cook

ON PERSIMMONS . . .

- Ripeness is crucial. Unblemished, firm Hachiya will ripen in three to six days in a tightly closed brown paper bag. Place an apple or banana in the bag along with the persimmon to hasten the process.
- Eating a persimmon with or without peeling it first is a matter of personal choice.
- Since persimmons are usually available from October through January, you can freeze them whole, tightly wrapped in plastic, and defrost before using.
- When Hachiya persimmons are cooked or baked, the pulp should be combined with baking soda before adding other ingredients to avoid any trace of lingering astringency.
- You can slice or dice persimmon into compotes and fruit salads, or make them into preserves.

QUINCE

The quince is among those fruits that have been around for centuries, appearing mostly in Middle Eastern cookery as a foil for rich meats such as game, lamb, and pork. A large, round, or sometimes pear-shaped fruit with a nippled stem end, it is golden in color and has a rather wooly-surfaced skin that covers a hard pulp that is dry and inedible when raw. When cooked, however, the pulp softens and becomes an attractive shade of pink. Like apples, they must be skinned, cored, and dropped into water that has been acidulated with lemon juice to prevent discoloration. It is a highly aromatic fruit when ripe, and a bowlful can perfume a room.

SHOP SMART

They are usually available from October through winter, and the large ones are the best. Avoid small, knotty quince with spots or bruises.

Notes for the Cook

ON QUINCE . . .

- Their high pectin content makes them perfect for cooking down with sugar into preserves or as a paste. The French make a version of quince paste called *cotignac*, a sort of confection, while the Spanish version of quince paste is served with salty cheese. The Greeks use them to make their famous spoon sweets (see recipe, page 404).

◆ Quince are wonderful served with sweet spices or kept in a rough puree and added to whipped cream for a beautifully scented fruit fool. Or add them to an apple or pear pie for a haunting flavor.

BABY BANANAS WITH KAHLÚA AND ESPRESSO SAUCE

We constantly seek out the very sweet, small bananas called niños, *and they're very popular with kids, whose small hands can hold them easily.*

SERVES 4

1¼ pounds baby bananas (about 12), 4 inches long, or 4 medium-size, firm, ripe bananas

1 cup water

1 tablespoon instant espresso granules

½ cup light brown sugar

3 tablespoons butter

¼ cup Kahlúa

Vanilla frozen yogurt

Mint sprigs for garnish

If using *niños*, peel and leave them whole. If using regular medium-size bananas, peel and cut into 3-inch pieces. Set aside. In a 10-inch nonstick skillet, bring the water to a boil over medium heat. Add the espresso and sugar, and stir until the sugar dissolves. Add the butter and stir until it melts. Cook for 10 minutes, until slightly reduced and syrupy. Add the bananas, lower the heat, and simmer for 2 or 3 minutes. Turn the bananas once and simmer 2 or 3 minutes more.

Add the Kahlúa and transfer the bananas to 4 serving plates. Place a scoop of yogurt in the center of the dish and then trickle some sauce over the bananas. Top with a sprig of mint.

FRESH FIGS FILLED WITH MASCARPONE IN GINGER SAUCE

This simple dessert looks festive and stunning when served on a fig leaf or on a crystal dish.

SERVES 4

12 large, fresh figs such as Black
    Mission or Kadota
6 ounces mascarpone cheese
2 tablespoons finely minced preserved
    stem ginger

1 tablespoon sugar
2 tablespoons water
2 tablespoons syrup from preserved
    ginger

Cut each fig crosswise ¼ of the way down from the stem end. Using a small demitasse spoon, carefully scoop out the soft pulp containing the seeds, making a cuplike well to hold the filling. Set aside the pulp.

Place the reserved pulp, cheese, and minced ginger in a small bowl and beat well to combine. Spoon some of this mixture into the fig cups and replace the tops on the filling. Place 3 stuffed figs on each of 4 plates and set aside.

Place the sugar and water in a small saucepan and cook over medium heat until the sugar dissolves. Add the ginger syrup, raise the heat, and bring to a boil. Boil hard for 2 or 3 minutes, until the sauce has thickened slightly. Remove from the heat, let the bubbles subside, and baste the figs with the sauce to glaze them. Serve with a very sharp knife and a fork.

PAPAYA AND LIME RELISH WITH GRILLED SHRIMP

A tropical uncooked relish that is prepared several hours before to blend its flavors. Perfect with grilled shrimp or sea scallops on a hot day, since the seafood takes only a few minutes to cook. Serve on hot rice, if desired.

SERVES 4

2 ripe papaya (about 1 pound each)

4 to 5 large limes

1 large red sweet pepper (about 8 ounces), seeded and cut in ½-inch dice (about 1 cup)

1 medium (4-ounce) onion, finely diced (about ¾ cup)

3 tablespoons roughly cut cilantro leaves

2 tablespoons lemon juice

4 or 5 drops Tabasco

⅛ teaspoon cayenne pepper, or more to taste

Coarse salt to taste

1¼ pounds shrimp (or sea scallops), peeled

1 tablespoon olive oil

1 large clove garlic, coarsely chopped (1½ teaspoons)

Cut the papayas in half. Scrape out the seeds with a spoon and discard. Peel and dice the papaya into ½-inch pieces, place in a bowl, and set aside.

Peel 2 limes, removing the white pith at the same time as the peel. Cut the limes into small pieces and add to the papaya. Squeeze the juice from 1 large lime (about 2 tablespoons) into another small bowl and set aside. Add the onion and cilantro to the papaya mixture. Add the lemon juice, Tabasco, cayenne, and salt to the lime juice and whisk to combine. Add to the papaya mixture. Marinate at room temperature for at least 6 hours.

Combine the shrimp, oil, garlic, and salt 30 minutes before grilling and let marinate. Pan-grill the shrimp in a hot, heavy skillet until opaque—about 2 minutes on each side—turning once. Serve the shrimp with the relish spooned over.

MANGO AND CHILE BUTTER WITH BLUEFISH

A lovely peach-colored sauce with a sweet, hot edge that takes bluefish to another dimension.

SERVES 4

1 teaspoon olive oil

1 tablespoon coarsely diced jalapeño chile (1 large)

⅔ cup seeded and coarsely diced red sweet pepper (1 medium)

1 tablespoon coarsely chopped shallot (1 medium)

3 tablespoons red wine vinegar

½ teaspoon mild honey

⅛ teaspoon cayenne pepper

Salt to taste

1 large mango, peeled, pitted, and cut into chunks (about 1 cup)

4 tablespoons butter, cut up

2 tablespoons corn oil

Flour for dredging

Pepper to taste

4 bluefish or red snapper fillets (about 8 ounces each)

Cilantro for garnish

Heat the olive oil in an 8-inch skillet over medium-low heat. Add the jalapeño chile, red pepper, and shallot, and sauté for 2 minutes, stirring, until soft. Stir in the vinegar, honey, cayenne, and salt. Turn the heat to low and simmer until the liquid evaporates, about 2 or 3 minutes. Cool the mixture completely.

When cool, add it to a food processor and process until fairly smooth. Add the mango and puree until smooth. Add the butter, incorporate it in the mixture, and transfer to a small saucepan.

In a 12-inch skillet, heat the corn oil until very hot but not smoking. Dredge the fish in flour mixed with salt and pepper, and sauté quickly, turning once, about 3 or 4 minutes on each side.

When the fish has been turned over, heat the sauce over low heat, stirring, for about 2 minutes, just to warm it through. Transfer the fish to a serving plate, spoon some sauce over the fish, and garnish with a sprig of cilantro.

KIWIS AND PINEAPPLE IN
GINGER PLUM WINE SAUCE

The smoky, sweet taste of Japanese plum wine and the bite of fresh ginger counterbalance the tart, sweet kiwi and pineapple for a refreshing, easy dessert.

SERVES 6

1 cup Japanese plum wine
1 teaspoon sugar
2 teaspoons peeled and finely minced
    ginger root
3-inch cinnamon stick

1 small pineapple, peeled, cored, and
    cut into chunks
5 medium-size kiwis, peeled and cut
    vertically into quarters

In a 1-quart saucepan over medium heat, combine the wine, sugar, ginger, and cinnamon stick. Cook, uncovered, until reduced by 1/3, about 5 minutes. Discard the cinnamon stick. Combine the pineapple and kiwis in a serving bowl. Spoon the sauce over all, cover with plastic wrap, and refrigerate for at least 1 hour, stirring once.

STARS AND STRIPER

Deliciously different. Black stripes made of olive puree are drizzled on a white-fleshed fish and then accentuated with star-shaped, citrusy carambola (star fruit) slices.

SERVES 4

1 tablespoon melted butter

1½ pounds striped bass, blackfish, or snapper fillets, cut into four 6-ounce portions

1 tablespoon lemon juice (1 small lemon)

2 tablespoons olivada (black olive paste)

3 tablespoons olive oil

1 teaspoon fresh thyme leaves, plus a few sprigs for garnish

Black pepper to taste

1 carambola (about 4 ounces), ends trimmed and cut into ¼-inch slices and seeds removed

Preheat the oven to 400 degrees. Place the butter in an oven-to-table baking pan large enough to accommodate the fish in 1 layer. Turn the fish over in the melted butter to coat both sides and place in the pan.

In a small bowl, whisk the lemon juice and olive paste together. Stir in the oil, thyme, and black pepper. Spoon the sauce in a striped pattern on the fish and place the carambola slices between the stripes. Without basting, bake for 10 to 12 minutes, or until the fish tests done with the point of a knife. Tuck in a sprig of fresh thyme for garnish.

RHUBARB SOUFFLÉ WITH ORANGE COINTREAU SAUCE

A custardy layer of orange sauce is hidden as a surprise under slices of ruby rhubarb, which is topped with a light soufflé.

SERVES 4 TO 6

1 large navel orange (about 1 pound) or 2 smaller ones	1 tablespoon water
1½ pounds rhubarb, trimmed, washed, and cut into 1-inch pieces	2 tablespoons butter
	2 large eggs, separated
1¼ cups sugar	⅓ cup flour
1 teaspoon cornstarch	⅔ cup milk
Pinch of salt	1 tablespoon Cointreau

Preheat the oven to 350 degrees. Wash and dry the orange and grate the zest (about 1 tablespoon). Squeeze the juice into a cup (about ¾ cup). Set aside.

In a 3-quart oval oven-to-table casserole, place the rhubarb and ½ cup of sugar mixed with the cornstarch and salt. Stir to combine and sprinkle with the water. Cover with aluminum foil and bake for 20 minutes.

About 10 minutes into the baking time, cream the butter and the remaining ¾ cup of sugar in a food processor and process until light and fluffy. Add the egg yolks to the food processor, 1 at a time, and combine. Add the flour, orange zest, milk, orange juice, and Cointreau, and process until combined. Transfer the mixture to a bowl. In another bowl, beat the egg whites along with a pinch of salt with a rotary hand beater, until stiff but not dry. Fold into the orange mixture. Spoon over the partially cooked rhubarb and return to the oven.

Bake, uncovered, for 25 to 30 minutes, or until the top is golden and the edges bubble.

PERSIMMON SPICE PUDDING WITH BOURBON AND PECANS

With a scattering of bright orange flecks, this soft, moist, spicy pudding, spiked with bourbon and textured with toasted pecans, is one of the sensual joys of autumn.

SERVES 6 TO 8

3 large, very soft, ripe Hachiya
    persimmons (about 8 ounces each)
½ teaspoon baking soda
¾ cup brown sugar
4 tablespoons melted butter
2 tablespoons bourbon
1 egg
1 cup buttermilk

1 cup flour
⅛ teaspoon salt
1 teaspoon baking powder
1 teaspoon ground cinnamon
½ teaspoon each nutmeg and ginger
¼ teaspoon ground cloves
1 cup roughly chopped toasted pecans
Whipped cream (optional)

Remove the green stems from the persimmons and discard. Quarter the persimmons (no need to peel) and puree with the baking soda in a food processor. There should be about 3 cups of puree.

Butter a 2-quart soufflé dish. Boil a kettle of water and preheat the oven to 400 degrees. Add to the puree the sugar, melted butter, bourbon, egg, and buttermilk, and combine well in the food processor. In a large bowl, place the flour, salt, baking powder, and all the spices, and whisk to incorporate. Add the contents of the food processor and whisk until combined. Stir in the pecans and scrape the mixture into the soufflé dish.

Set the pudding in a larger pan and pour boiling water halfway up the sides of the soufflé dish. Bake for 55 minutes, until the pudding shrinks from the sides of the dish and the top is golden. Serve warm with whipped cream if you wish.

QUINCE SPOON SWEETS

The offering of spoon sweets is a symbol of Greek hospitality. Set out on a tray that is usually covered with a beautiful hand-embroidered napkin are small crystal bowls of various fruit sweets—quince, cherry, grape, fig, and so forth—with a spoon and a glass of water. Take a spoonful of the sweets, drink the water, place the spoon in the empty glass, and wish your host happiness and good fortune.

MAKES 1½ QUARTS

3 cups water

1 large lemon

3 pounds quince (about 5 large)

3 cups sugar

1 tablespoon brandy (see Note)

In a heavy-bottomed 5-quart Dutch oven, place the water and the juice of ½ lemon. In a large bowl, squeeze the juice of the remaining ½ lemon and fill the bowl ¾ of the way with water. Wash and peel the quinces, dropping the peels only into the pot and the whole quinces into the bowl.

Cover the pot and bring the peels to a boil over high heat, then lower the heat and cook for 5 minutes. Strain and reserve the liquid, discarding the peels. Quarter and core the quinces, then cut them into eighths, returning the sections to the bowl of acidulated water. When all the quinces are cut, remove the fruit with a slotted spoon and transfer to the pot, layering sugar and fruit alternately. Slowly pour the reserved peel water over all. Cover the pot and bring to the boiling point over medium-high heat. Lower the heat and simmer, uncovered, stirring once or twice while cooking. Do not overstir, or the fruit will break into small pieces.

Cook until the fruit is very tender, amber colored, and shiny, with the liquid the consistency of light honey, about 1¼ to 1½ hours. Do not overcook. The mixture will thicken as it cools.

Remove from the heat, stir in the brandy, and let stand at room temperature overnight. Transfer the spoon sweets to a covered container and refrigerate. It will keep for 2 to 3 weeks.

You can also try it spooned over yogurt with a few pistachio nuts scattered over all.

Note: At the whim of the cook, sometimes the brandy is replaced by
1 or 2 rose geranium leaves, which can be added while the mixture
is cooking.

Nuts and Dried Fruit: Highlights of Flavor

Whole Wheat Date and Walnut Bread

Chestnut and Rum Cloud (Monte Bianco)

Hazelnut and Chocolate Tart

Dried Fruits Baked in Apple Juice with Bay Leaf and Vanilla Bean

Italian Pine Nut Cookies with Orange Zest

Pistachio Nut and Almond Pudding

The world's oldest confection, almond marzipan, is probably four thousand years old, although nuts probably became a part of the culinary diet as far back as forty thousand years ago. Cooks such as Marcus Gauius Apicius, who lived in Rome in the first century, made liberal use of nuts—almonds, beechnuts, hazelnuts, chestnuts, walnuts, and pine nuts—in such gourmet dishes as sauces for ostrich, crane, and flamingo as well as stuffed marrows and Lucanian sausages. But for many of the home cooks who followed, the major use for nuts has been in pastries and cakes.

But limiting the use of nuts, as Tennyson wrote, to "after dinner talk across the walnuts and the wine," leaves a world of culinary pleasure undiscovered and untasted. We love nuts, and we use them freely throughout this book. Their versatility is almost infinite. They can be eaten whole, halved, sliced, chopped, minced, shaved, broken, pounded to a paste, raw or dry-roasted, oil-roasted, smoked, candied, flavored, salted, and salt-free!

GOING NUTS

A Guide to Choosing, Buying, Measuring, and Using Nuts

Although most nuts are available year-round, fall and winter are the peak harvest seasons. Keep in mind that nut measurements are always approximate since the size, shape, and density of whole shelled nut meats can vary widely.

VARIETY AND DESCRIPTION	HOW MARKETED	USE
ALMONDS: BOTANICALLY, A STONE FRUIT (PEACH, APRICOT). WE EAT THE PIT, A HARD, OVAL NUT WITH A STRAW-COLORED SHELL, RUSSET SKIN, AND OFF-WHITE KERNEL.	In shells, shelled, whole with skin, and blanched without skin, sliced horizontally, slivered vertically, chopped. Nonpareil are short and plump. Jordan are long, plump, and sometimes sugar-dipped for weddings. Almond paste is usually in 7-ounce rolls or larger cans. Almond extract is made with bitter almonds. 4 ounces shelled and blanched = ¾ cup	With dried fruit, all baked goods, grains, candy, vegetables, fish, poultry, meats, and salads. Included in many ethnic cuisines.
BRAZIL NUTS: LARGE, HARD, DARK BROWN, TOE-SHAPED. CRINKLED OUTER SHELL; THIN, CLINGY BROWN SKIN. RICH CREAM-COLORED NUT MEAT WITH HIGH OIL CONTENT AND CRISP TEXTURE.	Whole in shells and whole with some inner skin clinging. Also in pieces. 8 ounces shelled = 1½ cups whole nutmeats	Soups, grains, baked goods, and snacks.

VARIETY AND DESCRIPTION	HOW MARKETED	USE
CASHEWS: KIDNEY-SHAPED; CREAMY BEIGE. CRUNCHY, SWEET WITH HIGH FAT CONTENT.	Whole, skinned; raw, roasted, salted, unsalted, in pieces, or as cashew butter. 8 ounces = 1½ cups whole nut meats	Liberally used in many ethnic cuisines, such as Chinese, Indian, Middle Eastern. With poultry, grains, vegetables, and in stuffings.
CHESTNUTS: SHINY, ROUND, RED-BROWN NUT WITH ONE FLAT SIDE. SLIGHTLY SWEET TASTE WITH MEALY, FLOURY TEXTURE AND LOW-FAT CONTENT.	In shell, shelled in syrup, shelled in cans or in jars with no syrup. Dried, made into flour. Glacéd and pureed. 1 pound in shell = 2½ cups nut meats	Ice cream, pastries, confections, and stuffings; as flour in crepes. Roasted, steamed, in soups, and with grain and game dishes.
COCONUTS: AN ANGULAR, THICK HUSK IS USUALLY REMOVED BEFORE SHIPPING. HARD, ROUND FURRY-HAIRED BROWN SHELL HAS THREE INDENTATIONS ("EYES"). HEAVY FOR ITS SIZE, AND WHEN SHAKEN, YOU CAN HEAR LIQUID SLOSHING WHEN RIPE.	In shell or commercially shelled, shredded, flaked; moist in cans and air-tight packages. Sweetened, unsweetened, frozen. Coconut milk and coconut cream in cans. Frozen and powdered coconut milk. High in saturated fat. 1 medium size = 3 to 4 cups grated	Sweetened flaked or sweetened coconut milk can be used in breads, coconut macaroons, and with other tropical fruits. Coconut cream only for desserts and drinks. Unsweetened coconut milk in tropical and Asian dishes, soups, sauces for poultry, seafood, cakes, and puddings.

HAZELNUTS (FILBERTS):

SMALL, ROUND, LIGHT TO DARK BROWN WITH REDDISH CAST. BOTTOM SLIGHTLY POINTED; TOP HAS TEXTURED ROUND CAP. BROWN PAPER SKIN COVERS CREAMY, DENSE, FRAGRANT KERNEL.

Sold in bulk: in shells and shelled with papery skins. Also sold in plastic containers, jars, and cans. Hazelnut oil and hazelnut paste, called "nutella."
6 ounces whole shelled nut meats = 1 cup

Less oily than pecans and walnuts. Light and fluffy when ground. Major ingredient in famous nut tortes of Central Europe. Also in pastries and candies with chocolate. With fish, vegetables, vinaigrettes, and the classic hazelnut butter, *beurre de noisette*.

MACADAMIANS (QUEENSLAND):

FAT, ROUND, CREAM COLOR WITH CRISP, AIRY TEXTURE AND CREAMY RICH FLAVOR.

Sold out of shell, whole, and in pieces; in jars, cans, raw, roasted, and roasted salted. Also chocolate covered.
4 ounces = 1 cup whole nut meats

Chopped as a crust for fish and chicken; with vegetables, seafood salads, ice cream, desserts, and baked goods.

PEANUTS (GOOBER OR GROUND NUT):

TECHNICALLY LEGUMES AND GROW IN THE GROUND. TAN, PAPERY, CORRUGATED SHELL CONTAINS TWO OVAL, SPLIT-CENTER "BEANS" WITH A PAPERY RED SKIN. A VARIETY, SPANISH PEANUTS, ARE SMALLER, ROUND, WITH RED SKINS.

In and out of shell; in bulk, jars, cans, plastic bags. Roasted and coated with sugar and vanilla; raw or roasted and salted. Boiled in shells in salted water. Peanut butter, peanut oil, and peanut brittle.
12 ounces in shell = 8 ounces shelled

High in unsaturated fat. Used in most Asian cuisines as well as in African dishes. Soups, stews, salad dressings, and snacks.

VARIETY AND DESCRIPTION	HOW MARKETED	USE
PECANS: SMOOTH REDDISH BROWN SHELL SHAPED LIKE A LONG OLIVE. TWO-PART TAN NUT MEAT WITH CONVOLUTED SHAPE, THE HALVES SEPARATED BY A THIN LAYER OF FIBROUS MATERIAL. VERY SWEET, RICH, AND OILY. SCHLEY VARIETY HAS PAPER SHELL. STUARTS ARE LARGER WITH A THICKER SHELL.	Sold in bulk in shell or out of shell. Also in halves, pieces, and chopped. In cans and raw; roasted and both salted and unsalted. 2 pounds in shell = 1 pound shelled 1 pound shelled = 4 cups nut meat "Jumbo" pecans = 300 to 350 halves per pound "Mammoth" = under 200 halves per pound	Pecan tarts, coating for fish and poultry, with vegetables, stuffings, breads, cookies, and praline candy.
PINE NUTS (PIGNOLI, PIÑON, CHINESE PINE NUTS): SMALL, 1/4 to 1/2 INCH, ELONGATED SHAPE. CREAMY COLORED. HARVESTED FROM PINECONES AND LOOK LIKE PUFFED RICE CEREAL. SWEET, OILY, AND FLAVORFUL.	Shelled whole nuts in plastic containers and in bulk. 4 ounces = 3/4 cup	High oil content and best when toasted lightly. Use with fish, grain dishes, and sauces; in Middle Eastern and Mediterranean cuisines; with basil for pesto sauce and with vegetables; in desserts, candies, and cookies.

PISTACHIOS:
SMALL OVAL NUT WITH
BRITTLE, SMOOTH, TAN
SHELL. THE KERNEL HAS A
REDDISH PAPERY INNER
SKIN. THE COLOR OF THE
NUT RANGES FROM
YELLOW-GREEN TO BRIGHT
ACID GREEN. FRESH,
SWEET FLAVOR AND SOFT
TEXTURE.

Best to buy natural colored shell in bulk. Sometimes dyed red or encrusted with white salt. Shell is usually slightly open. Out of shell in jars and cans. The best flavored are the light green from Turkey and the dark green from Sicily.

1½ pounds in shell = 8 ounces shelled

An addictive snack food. Used in pilafs, ice cream, pâtés, Middle Eastern pastries, and candies.

WALNUTS (ENGLISH OR PERSIAN):
HARD, ROUND, TAN SHELL
WITH A CENTER RIDGE
MARK FOR DISSECTION.
IRREGULAR LIGHT TAN NUT
WITH TWO HALVES JOINED
BY A FIBROUS INEDIBLE
BARRIER. NUT MEAT IS
SWEET WITH A SLIGHTLY
BITTER EDGE.

In shells in bulk, and shelled in bulk and in cans and packages. In halves and broken into pieces. In syrup and as walnut oil.

4 ounces shelled = 1 cup

Used in salads, Chinese food, meat loaf, breads, cakes, pastries, with grains, cheese (such as Stilton), vegetables, fruit, desserts. Green, immature walnuts are pickled.

SHOP SMART

The wonderful flavor of nuts is derived from their fat content, unsaturated and cholesterol-free, except for coconuts, which are high in saturated fat. But that very fat content causes nuts to turn rancid fairly quickly. Therefore . . .

- Nuts in their shells, sold in bulk or by the pound, usually keep longer than shelled nuts.
- We prefer to buy shelled nuts in containers, cans, or jars rather than select them loose from storage bins. If you do buy them loose, make sure the shop has a frequent turnover and taste one to check for rancidity and flavor.
- Make sure shelled nuts are plump and not shriveled, firm, and not oily looking. If they don't meet those standards, they have either been stored badly or have been kept too long.
- At home, protect all nuts from light, heat, moisture, and air, in whatever form they've been purchased. They'll keep in the refrigerator for about four months in tightly closed containers. You can store them in the freezer for about eight months, taking a few out when you need them and refreezing the rest.

The real secret is keeping them cold to prevent loss of quality. And we strongly suggest toasting them before you use them to bring out their true flavor.

Notes for the Cook

ON NUTS . . .

TOASTING: There are two basic ways to bring out the flavor of nuts:

1. In the oven: Preheat to 300 degrees. Spread the nuts in a single layer in a shallow pan and roast for 5 to 10 minutes, shaking and stirring the nuts until they are just lightly golden. To prevent further browning, spread the nuts out on paper towels to cool.
2. In a skillet: Use a heavy skillet. Over low heat, warm a small amount of butter and sauté the nuts, stirring constantly, until they are light brown. Remove the nuts immediately from the pan and transfer to paper towels.

SKINNING: Nuts such as almonds can be purchased already skinned (blanched), but hazelnuts and pistachios must be skinned at home before chopping, grinding, or leaving them whole.

- *Hazelnuts,* if finely chopped or ground, do not need to be skinned first. But when left whole or coarsely chopped, the papery skins may cause choking, so it is best to remove them. Toast the nuts in a preheated 350-degree oven for 10 minutes, or until the thin skins begin to flake. While still hot, wrap the nuts in a kitchen or cotton towel and let them steam 5 minutes more, or until cool. Take the towel to the kitchen sink to avoid a mess and rub off as much of the papery skin as you can.
- *Pistachios* can be shelled Greek style, which will save your fingernails. Use half of the shell of one nut to pry apart the slightly opened shells of the others. Pistachios are then treated the same way as hazelnuts: Put them in a preheated oven, and when the skins look dry, place them in a towel.

CHOPPING: A food processor is still the fastest and easiest way to chop nuts coarsely or finely. Use the on/off switch (or pulse) to pulverize the nuts, but don't overprocess or they get pasty.

When adding nuts and/or dried fruits to any bread, cake, or pancake batter, combine them first with the dry ingredients, which coats them and prevents them from sinking to the bottom.

TO SHELL AND SKIN CHESTNUTS

Two easy methods are as follows:

1. Using a sharp knife, cut an X on the convex (round) side. Place the nuts in a steamer and steam for 15 minutes. Remove a few at a time with a slotted spoon. When they are cool enough to handle, peel off the outer shell and the inner skin with a knife or your fingers. If the skin is stubborn, rinse the chestnuts under cold water, return them to the covered steamer for a few minutes, and then try again.
2. After cutting an X in each nut, place them in a preheated 350-degree oven in a single layer on a large cookie sheet or in a pan. Roast for 25 minutes, shaking the pan several times. If you wish to eat them out of hand, roast them for an additional 25 minutes for best flavor and tenderness.

Once the chestnuts are shelled and skinned, most recipes then give specific instructions. They can be cooked in broth, sautéed in butter, cooked in milk or water, kept whole, chopped, or pureed.

Notes for the Cook

COCONUT: IT'S A HARD NUT TO CRACK

- Insert a sanitary ice pick or screwdriver into two of the three "eyes" of the coconut and drain the milky water (not to be confused with coconut milk or coconut cream). The water can be drunk or used as flavoring.
- Bake the coconut at 350 degrees for 20 to 40 minutes, or until the shell cracks.
- Place the coconut on a towel in the sink to steady it and hit it with a hammer to crack it open.
- Use a swivel blade vegetable peeler to remove the clinging inner brown skin.
- Grate or shred the white meat in a food processor, using the shredder blade, or use a hand grater. One medium coconut yields between 3 and 4 cups grated.
- To make coconut milk: Combine equal parts of grated coconut and water—or substitute unsweetened packaged coconut—and simmer until foamy. Strain through cheesecloth, squeezing as much liquid from the coconut meat as possible.
- For coconut *cream*, combine one part of water to four parts of grated coconut. (Milk can be substituted for a richer result.) Proceed as with coconut milk above.

RAISIN D'ÊTRE . . . AND OTHER DRIED FRUITS

We have always loved the story (probably apocryphal) about the California grape grower about a hundred years ago who shipped a bountiful harvest to the East, only to find that the long hot journey on airless boxcars had dried out his entire crop. Advertising the shriveled remains as a new "delicacy" straight from the vineyards of Peru—the "raisin"—he sold the entire batch in two days! Great story except that dried fruits have been around since biblical times.

The Middle East is the birthplace of a wonderful concoction: dried apricots rolled into paper-thin sheets. As kids we used to buy these as "shoe leather." In the early days of the American frontier, the pioneers made peach leather and apple leather, flattened and dried in the sun for two or three days to preserve their harvest.

The procedure has not changed much today. Before drying, the fresh fruits are allowed to ripen for a long period of time, thus increasing the sugar and fiber content. Then through either sun-drying or dehydration under controlled temperatures, about three-fourths of the moisture is removed. Flavor increases in intensity, and there are more concentrated amounts of vitamins, carbohydrates, and minerals. It takes about six pounds of fresh apricots, three pounds of prunes or figs, and four pounds of grapes to make the final one pound of dried fruit. But it also means that the calorie count can easily go from about 200 to over 1,000!

The most common dried fruits are apple, apricot, blueberry, cherry, cranberry, currant, date, fig, grape, mango, papaya, pineapple, peach, pear, plum, strawberry—just about everything that we normally buy fresh.

SHOP SMART

- ◆ Buy prepackaged dried fruits in tightly sealed containers or vacuum-packed cans.
- ◆ Store them in a cool, dark place, sealed tightly. They deteriorate quickly when exposed to air.

Notes for the Cook

ON DRIED FRUITS . . .

- ◆ They can be difficult to chop since they are often sticky. Use a pair of sharp scissors with lightly oiled blades to snip large, whole dried fruits. Some (pears, peaches, dates) can now be found precut. Or use a food processor, either lightly brushing the blades and inside of the bowl with a bland vegetable oil or tossing the fruit in a small amount of the oil before processing.
- ◆ Unless the fruit is unusually tough or leathery, presoaking (other than called for in the recipe) should not be required. To presoak very dry fruit, either use hot water for 15 minutes or plump them in a steaming basket over boiling water, tightly covered, for about 3 or 4 minutes.
- ◆ When stewing fruits, cover with water, add any whole spices (such as cinnamon stick, vanilla bean, and whole cloves) and citrus zests, and cook over medium-high heat, tightly covered, until tender. Add a small amount (under 4 tablespoons) of sugar or honey only during the last 5 minutes of cooking, or the fruits may toughen. The use of sweet spices allows you to use less sugar, so taste before adding any sweetener.

WHOLE WHEAT DATE AND WALNUT BREAD

*We have been baking and refining this date nut bread for many years, and
we think we have finally perfected it. Try it warm, thinly sliced, and spread
with a bit of creamy ricotta cheese for complete Nirvana.*

MAKES 1 LOAF

1½ cups pitted and chopped dates
  (8-ounce package)
¾ cup water
1 teaspoon baking soda
2 cups whole wheat flour
½ cup all purpose flour
½ teaspoon salt
1 tablespoon baking powder

5 tablespoons butter, cut into pieces
1 tablespoon finely minced
  orange zest
¾ cup sugar
4 ounces toasted and coarsely broken
  walnuts (about ¾ cup)
1 egg, lightly beaten

Preheat the oven to 300 degrees. Butter and flour a 9 x 5 x 3-inch loaf pan and set it aside. In a 1-quart saucepan over medium-low heat, combine the dates and water, and slowly bring just to the boiling point. Remove from the heat and stir in the baking soda, which will bubble up. Let it cool.

In a medium-size bowl, sift both flours, salt, and baking powder together. With a pastry blender, cut the butter into the dry ingredients until crumbly. Stir in the orange zest, sugar, and nuts. Add the beaten egg to the cooled date mixture and then add that to the flour mixture. Mix thoroughly with a wooden spoon to form a stiff, fairly dry batter. Scrape the batter into the prepared pan, smooth the surface, and bake in the lower part of the preheated oven for about 1 hour 20 minutes, or until the loaf is firm and shrinks slightly from the sides of the pan.

Cool completely in the pan on a wire rack, then invert to remove the loaf. Wrap in aluminum foil and keep for 1 day before using to mellow the flavors and in order to slice it more easily. This bread will keep, well wrapped in the refrigerator, for 2 weeks, and it freezes well. If it comes directly from the refrigerator or freezer, it tastes best when a few slices are wrapped in aluminum foil and warmed.

CHESTNUT AND RUM CLOUD (MONTE BIANCO)

The Italians call it Monte Bianco, and we first tasted it in Rome. It is airy, light, and very rich, and we call it divine!

SERVES 4

1 pound chestnuts (about 35), shelled
   as directed on page 413
Milk (about 2½ cups)
Vanilla bean
⅓ cup sugar
¼ cup water

2 tablespoons dark rum
1 tablespoon soft butter
1 cup heavy cream
2 tablespoons confectioners' sugar
1 ounce sweet chocolate

Put the shelled chestnuts in a nonstick 2-quart saucepan with enough milk to cover. Cut off a 1-inch piece of the vanilla bean, split it, and scrape the tiny seeds into the pot. Add the scraped vanilla bean pod. Simmer for 30 minutes, or until the chestnuts are very soft. Drain the chestnuts, reserving the vanilla milk but discarding the pod. Put the chestnuts in a potato ricer to make a mound of puree in a bowl and moisten it with the reserved vanilla milk. Set aside.

In a 1-quart nonstick saucepan, combine the sugar, water, and another 1-inch piece of vanilla bean, split and scraped. Cook the syrup over medium-high heat without stirring, until the mixture forms a soft ball when a little is dropped into cold water or it registers 234 degrees on a candy thermometer.

Discard the vanilla bean and combine the hot syrup with the chestnut puree. Beat vigorously until it forms a soft paste. Beat in the rum and let cool to lukewarm. Add the butter and then put the paste through a potato ricer again, forcing it into a neat mound on a serving platter. Chill in the refrigerator for at least 1 hour before serving.

When ready to serve, whip the cream with the confectioners' sugar. Pile the cream on the chestnut mound with a spatula, grate about 2 teaspoons of chocolate over the cream, and serve.

HAZELNUT AND CHOCOLATE TART

Hazelnuts have a deep affinity for chocolate and are paired in many French and Italian desserts. This tart can easily be made in two stages, so it is not a daunting recipe. It's worth the effort when the accolades are offered.

MAKES ONE 10-INCH TART

BASIC RECIPE FOR TART PASTRY:

1 ¼ cups flour

⅛ teaspoon salt

1 tablespoon sugar

7 tablespoons cold butter, cut into
    small pieces

1 egg yolk

3 tablespoons cold water

1 teaspoon vanilla extract

FILLING:

4 ounces good-quality bittersweet
    chocolate

4 tablespoons butter

5 tablespoons sugar

½ cup heavy cream

1 tablespoon mild light honey

2 cups hazelnuts, toasted, skinned, and
    very coarsely chopped with a large
    knife (see procedure on
    page 413)

To make the pastry: In a food processor, combine the flour, salt, and sugar. Add the butter and pulse about 7 or 8 times. In a small bowl, whisk the egg yolk, water, and vanilla together. Add to the food processor and pulse only until the dough is moist and holds together but hasn't formed a ball. Flour your hands, gather up the pastry, and knead with the heel of your hand for 1 or 2 strokes. Slam the pastry down on a piece of aluminum foil to get out the air bubbles and flatten it into a disk. Wrap in the foil and chill for 1 hour. Allow the pastry to warm a bit before continuing.

Roll out the pastry to fit a 10-inch tart pan that is 1 inch deep and has a removable base. Freeze the pastry in the pan for 20 minutes. Preheat the oven to 425 degrees. Line the pastry with aluminum foil and fill it with pie weights or beans. Bake for 15 minutes, then lower the heat to 325 degrees. Remove the foil and weights, prick the bottom of the shell all over with a fork, and return it to the oven to bake until golden. Let cool completely. The pastry can be prepared several hours or even a day in advance.

When you are ready to prepare the filling, preheat the oven to 325 degrees. In a small nonstick pot, melt 3 ounces of the chocolate with 1 tablespoon of butter, stirring slowly over low heat. With a pastry brush, paint a thin layer of warm chocolate on the bottom of the baked crust. In a 1½-quart saucepan, melt the remaining 3 tablespoons of butter. Add the sugar, cream, and honey, and bring slowly to the boiling point over very low heat, stirring to dissolve the sugar. Boil for 2 minutes and then stir in the hazelnuts. Spoon into the prepared tart shell and bake for about 10 minutes, or until golden.

After 5 minutes, place a piece of aluminum foil on the bottom of the oven to catch any spills while the tart is baking. Remove the tart from the oven and cool completely on a rack. Melt the remaining 1 ounce of chocolate and drip a free-form design on top of the tart, à la Jackson Pollock.

DRIED FRUITS BAKED IN APPLE JUICE WITH BAY LEAF AND VANILLA BEAN

After the fruits of summer have gone on vacation, a baked dried fruit compote claims an easy elegance as an appropriate conclusion for an autumn or winter dinner.

SERVES 6

1 teaspoon soft butter
4 ounces bite-size pitted prunes
8 ounces dried peaches
6 ounces dried apricots
6 ounces dried apples
2 ounces dried tart cherries
1 bay leaf
3 long strips lemon zest made with
  vegetable peeler (1 medium lemon)

2 tablespoons lemon juice
½ vanilla bean, split (about
  2½ inches)
2 cups apple juice
1 cup water
1 cup dry red wine
¾ cup firmly packed dark brown sugar

TOPPING:
¾ cup sour cream
1 teaspoon fine sugar

¼ teaspoon ground cinnamon
6 teaspoons sliced almonds (optional)

Butter a 3-quart oven-to-table baking pan. Add the prunes, peaches, apricots, apples, cherries, bay leaf, and lemon zest and juice. Scrape the seeds from the vanilla bean and add them, along with the pod, to the dried fruit. Combine well and set aside.

In a 3-quart saucepan over medium heat, combine the apple juice, water, wine, and brown sugar. Bring to a boil and cook for 30 seconds. Pour over the fruit mixture, cover with aluminum foil, and let stand for at least 8 hours to marinate.

When ready to bake, preheat the oven to 375 degrees and bake, covered, for 30 minutes, stirring after 15 minutes. Remove with tongs and discard the bay leaf, lemon strips, and vanilla bean pod.

Serve in large wine goblets, warm or cool. For the topping, combine the sour cream, sugar, and cinnamon, and spoon a bit over the fruit. Scatter sliced almonds over all if you wish.

ITALIAN PINE NUT COOKIES WITH ORANGE ZEST

Flavored with almond paste and citrus peel and studded with tiny cream-colored pine nuts, these cookies are fun to make but expensive to buy. Although they can be stored in an airtight container for a week, at our house they seem to disappear in about a day.

MAKES 24

7-ounce roll of soft almond paste, cut into small pieces
½ cup sugar
1 tablespoon finely grated orange or tangerine zest (1 large tangerine or medium orange)

⅛ teaspoon salt
½ teaspoon vanilla extract
2 egg whites plus 1 extra for dipping
5 or 6 ounces pine nuts
Confectioners' sugar for dusting

Lightly butter two 14 x 17-inch baking sheets and line with parchment paper. (The butter holds the parchment in place.) Set aside.

In the bowl of a food processor, place the almond paste, sugar, zest, salt, and vanilla, and process until combined. Add the 2 egg whites and process until smooth. Transfer the mixture to a bowl and stir in ⅓ cup of the pine nuts, reserving the rest for the tops of the cookies.

Chill the mixture in the refrigerator for about 15 minutes to firm up. Preheat the oven to 300 degrees. In a small bowl, lightly beat 1 egg white until foamy. Place the remaining pine nuts in a pie pan. Using a heaping tablespoon, roll the paste into balls between your palms. Dip each ball in the beaten egg white and then roll in the pine nuts. Transfer to the prepared sheets, 12 to a sheet, spaced about 1½ to 2 inches apart. Flatten slightly with your fingers, pressing the surface nuts so that they adhere. Bake for 15 to 18 minutes, or until lightly golden. Switch the baking sheets on the oven shelves midway through the baking.

Slide the parchment sheets onto a rack and cool completely. Carefully remove each cookie using a wide spatula dipped in water. Dust the cookies lightly with confectioners' sugar. If you wish to store them, place in an airtight container between layers of waxed paper so they don't adhere to each other. They can be stored for about 1 week.

PISTACHIO NUT AND ALMOND PUDDING

For special occasions in India, a version of this pudding is served with a top layer of gold or silver leaf called vark. *It's a lovely, unusual dessert that is thickened with fine vermicelli and flavored with saffron and orange flower water.*

MAKES SIX 4-OUNCE SERVINGS

¾ cup plus 2 tablespoons shelled
    pistachio nuts
⅓ cup skinned whole almonds
4 tablespoons butter
2 tablespoons very fine vermicelli
    pasta, broken into 1-inch pieces
2½ cups milk

⅓ cup heavy cream
⅛ teaspoon crumbled saffron threads
4 tablespoons sugar
Pinch of salt
¼ teaspoon orange flower water
6 teaspoons flaked coconut for garnish

Toast the pistachio nuts in a 350-degree oven for 5 to 10 minutes. When cool, put in a towel and rub their papery skins off. Remove 2 tablespoons of the pistachio nuts, chop them coarsely, and set aside for garnish. Add the remaining ¾ cup of pistachios and the almonds to a food processor and process until fine but not a paste. There should be some texture and about 1¼ cups. Set aside.

In a 3-quart nonstick saucepan over low heat, melt the butter and add the vermicelli. Cook, stirring constantly, until it is golden in color. Add the milk, cream, and saffron, and bring to the boiling point over medium-low heat. Stir in the sugar, salt, and ground nut mixture. Lower the heat and simmer for 15 minutes, stirring frequently, until thick and blended. Remove from the heat, stir in the orange flower water, and let cool slightly.

Spoon into glass dessert dishes or goblets and sprinkle with flaked coconut and the reserved pistachios. Refrigerate for at least 1 hour and serve cool or at room temperature.

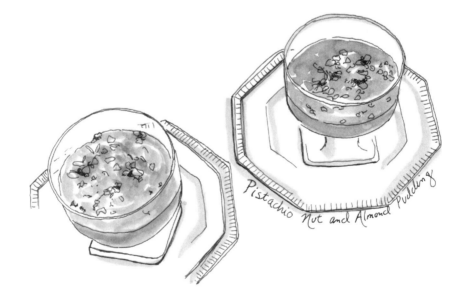

Pistachio Nut and Almond Pudding

The Big Cheese

*Tortillas with Jalapeño Jack Cheese, Green Olives,
and a Cilantro Tomato Sauce*

Gruyère and Onion Puree with Cloves and Nutmeg

*Spanish Potato Gratin with Tetilla Cheese, Red and Yellow Peppers,
Black Olives, and Saffron*

Col Legno Tiramisu

Saganaki

Fresh Goat Cheese Tarts with Serrano Ham and Grilled Pears

Asiago Cheese Ramekins with Anchovies

Four Quick European Cheese Desserts:

Greek: Manouri Cheese with Thyme Honey and Toasted Walnuts
Italian: Taleggio Cheese with Acacia Honey and Toasted Pine Nuts
Spanish: Manchego Cheese with Manukka Raisins and Honey
French: Fromage du Brebis with Walnut Bread and Black Cherry Preserves

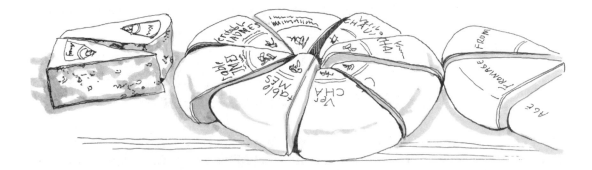

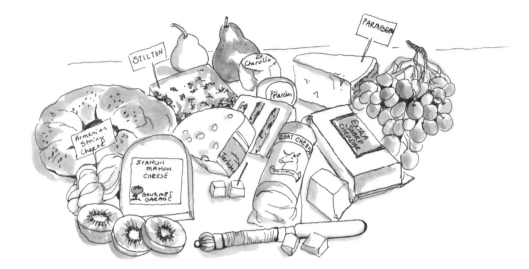

Cheese may be made from the milk of a cow, a sheep, a goat, or water buffalo—or even the milk of a yak, a camel, or a zebra! Or the cheese maker may decide that blending the milk of a cow along with that of his sheep and goats would be the way to go—just as they do with the Queso Iberico of Spain.

Whatever the choice, the basic beginning of cheese making is very much the same— the curdling of the milk by adding a rennet, either an enzyme taken from the stomach lining of ruminants or a vegetarian substitute. The curds are then compressed to form a solid. The resulting cheese will depend not only on the animal from which the milk was taken—and whether she was milked in the morning or evening—but what the animal was fed, the complexity of the local soil, whether the milk is pasteurized, how the curds are cut and shaped, whether it is finally washed in water or alcohol or even buried in ashes, the temperature and humidity during ripening, and how long it has been aged. And these are but a few of the elements, making the study of cheese a lifetime undertaking.

There is now a positive explosion of imported and domestic cheeses available to the consumer. Italy is said to produce over four hundred varieties of cheese, mostly sold in the villages in which they are produced. France can probably boast even more varieties—Charles de Gaulle once claimed that it was impossible to govern a country that offered so many cheeses. At Gourmet Garage alone there are four huge counters brimming with the products of fifteen countries.

CHEESE 101—A PARTIAL PRIMER

At a cocktail party, a selection of cheeses can appear (and rapidly disappear) as we stand, drink in hand, like so many hungry mice nibbling the samples right to their very rinds. After dinner that very same cheese assortment becomes the catalyst for lingering around the table, chatting in a relaxed fashion as we sip an aged tawny port or a mellow sherry. Or we cut into a juicy pear or a succulent fig and crack a few nuts. We punctuate our conversation while eating little bites of cheese and tear off hunks of a crispy baguette.

Cheese can also be the lone star as a dessert course, and we have included several easy European combinations, all of which can be put together in minutes.

And there are the everyday uses of cheese that we take for granted: freshly grated Parmigiano-Reggiano over pasta, goats' milk cheese or blue cheese with our salads, or a creamy fresh mascarpone whipped into a silky rich tiramisu for that special occasion.

What follows is a respectful account, sort of a primer, to acquaint you with some of our personal favorites. We've listed them in categories for composing a selection for a cheese tray and how to use them for cooking.

FRESH CHEESE

These cheeses are just a step away from being milk. They are unripened and generally mild in flavor. Although there are many different styles with varying fat content, their texture is always soft, ranging from spoonable to sliceable.

CREAM CHEESE AND COTTAGE CHEESE: These cheeses are so common that they need no explanation.

FETA: A white Greek cheese that is slightly salty, earthy, and a bit sour. It is made entirely from sheep's milk in order to be authentically Greek. The Bulgarians produce a firmer feta with a blend of 70 percent ewes' milk and 30 percent, more or less, goats' milk. Feta can either be soft and creamy or firm and crumbly. In Greek the word *feta* means "a slice," and indeed a slice of it or a bit crumbled appears with every taverna Greek salad.

MASCARPONE: A soft, pale, ivory-colored Italian cows' milk double-cream cheese with a slightly acidic flavor and a silky smooth texture very much like heavy whipped cream. A rich breakfast or dessert treat with berries, or a last-minute addition to pasta sauces instead of cream. It is a major ingredient in tiramisu, that bit of Italian heaven on a dessert plate.

MOZZARELLA: Originally made in Italy from the milk of the water buffalo, it is now made and marketed mixed with cows' milk as *mozzarella di bufala*. Curds, called *fior di latte*, are stretched in hot water, and the mass is then shaped into ovals, small balls, or braids. Stretching gives the cheese its characteristic springy texture and layered structure. Keeping it in its liquid whey results in a mild and slightly tart taste that has become synonymous with pizza but is equally good sliced and alternated with tomatoes, basil, and olive oil. Good mozzarella is glossy and the color of fine porcelain, and it is best eaten as soon as possible. It can be stored for a day or two by putting it into a container, along with milk to cover, and keeping it in the refrigerator. It should be brought to room temperature again before serving.

PETIT-SUISSE: A French double-cream cheese with a moist texture and delicate flavor, somewhat like mascarpone.

QUARK: A curd German cheese made from either skimmed or whole cows' milk or buttermilk. A white, smooth-textured, delicately sour cheese, it is used widely for baking pastries in Germany and for spreading on dense, moist, dark pumpernickel bread.

RICOTTA: An unripened whey cheese with a fine granular consistency and a mild, lightly sweet, unsalted flavor. Now made from cows' milk, it was originally made in Italy from ewes' milk. A versatile cheese used in baked pasta dishes, for Italian cheesecake, or eaten merely sprinkled with powdered coffee, sugar, and shaved chocolate.

SOFT RIPENING OR SOFT RIND CHEESE

These cheeses are characterized by the formation of a soft rind (which is edible) during the maturation period. There are two types: white (or blooming) crust and washed rind. The white crusted type is treated with mold spores that cause the covering to develop; an example is Brie. The washed (or orange rind) cheese is rinsed in salt water to keep it supple and allow the salt to penetrate the cheese. These cheeses ripen from the outside in, and it is important to buy them in their prime—not too hard or too soft in the center. At room temperature the centers ooze, which is part of their charm.

BRIE: The most internationally recognized and popular of the French cheeses, Brie has been around since the thirteenth century. A cows' milk cheese with a high butterfat content, it is aged for three or four weeks and ripens quickly. When it is at its best, the flavor is full and mildly tangy. The longer the aging process, the stronger the flavor. Brie is produced throughout France. Look for two special varieties made with unpasteurized milk for a special treat: Brie de Meaux has a slightly golden rind and a straw-colored interior, and is aged for four to six weeks, and Brie de Melun is sold at various stages of ripening, from six to ten weeks old. The latter is the strongest smelling and has the tangiest flavor of the Bries, a great table cheese eaten as is—at room temperature, of course.

KASSERI: A Greek, semi-soft, pale yellow sheeps' milk cheese, similar to Italian Fontina but with a pronounced sheep's milk flavor. The cheese should be smooth textured and resilient. Good for melting or as a table cheese, it is used to make the famous Greek appetizer of fried cheese called Saganaki.

PONT L'EVÊQUE: Probably the oldest of Normandy's cows' milk cheeses, it is unpasteurized and named after the town in Calvados that became its major distribution point. It is square shaped with a full, savory scent, a tender golden yellow center, and a ridged light tan rind.

CAMEMBERT: Another great cheese that originally was from Normandy but is now made all over France and accounts for almost 25 percent of the country's cheese production. More assertively flavored than a regular Brie, but like Brie, the center of the cheese should bulge but not run when lightly pressed.

REBLOCHON: A semi-soft cows' milk cheese with a pale brown rind and a creamy interior that has a mild floral flavor and a supple texture. It is usually ripened in five weeks.

TALEGGIO: A *stracchino*-type cheese much like the Robiola from Lombardy. The word *stracchino* is a generic one in the Lombard dialect describing the milk from "tired cows"—those that are returned to the plains after grazing all summer in their Alpine pastures. This new change in their diet imparts a distinctive flavor to the cheese, which is named after a town in the hills of Bergamo. It is a salted cows' milk cheese, six to seven weeks old, soft, smooth, supple, creamy, and the color of pale straw. It can be recognized by its square, squat shape and a thin, soft, washed rind with a grayish golden crust. The flavor is fruity, tangy, and mild, and it gets stronger with age. It is easily spread as a table cheese and melts quickly when cooked.

There are several other wonderful double- and triple-cream cheeses that have become our personal favorites:

EXPLORATEUR: An exceptional triple-cream cheese created in the '50s. Ripened for three weeks, it is rich, mild, and creamy.

MORBIER: From the French Jura Mountains, this raw milk cheese has a tangy, milky flavor. It is produced in much the same manner as Saint-Nectaire but is distinguished by a thin, edible ash layer that separates the morning and evening milkings.

SAINT-ANDRÉ: A drum-shaped rich cheese from the south of France that has a downy white rind.

SAINT-NECTAIRE: A smooth, slightly nutty cheese from the Auvergne, it is firm, mellow, and golden. The flattish disks are pressed and then ripened for two to four months. Traditionally it is made from two separate batches of milk, one from the morning and one from the evening.

SEMI-HARD AND HARD CHEESE

These giant wheels of cheese are deliberately made extra large to account for all the moisture that will be lost during the aging process. The process of aging cheeses originated in the mountainous regions of Europe. The cheeses were produced on the farms in late spring and part of the summer when the animals' milk was at its richest from their grazing on the freshest green grass.

These cheeses go through many stages before they reach their final form. The milk is first curdled, then drained to separate the curds from the whey (the watery liquid that is drained from the curds). The curds are then cut up into small pieces and pressed into a form or a mold. At this point the curds may be crushed, pressed again, or heated. The longer the cheese remains under pressure in its mold, the more moisture is drained out. This aging process is what determines the character, flavor, and sliceability of the cheese, making some of them great for grating.

CHEDDAR: A natural golden yellow or cream color, it gets its name from a process called "cheddaring" whereby blocks of curd are stacked and turned to facilitate draining, giving the cheese its firm, close texture. It results in a cheese that is sliceable when young and has a range of flavors from mild to sweet. And when dense and mature enough for grating and cooking, it changes to become mellow and nutty and then sharp. It is widely made in Canada and the United States (Vermont, upstate New York, Oregon, and Wisconsin) as well as in England, which has only a few farms left that produce this cheese with quality and by traditional methods. Unfortunately, we rarely get to taste English cheddars outside of their home country.

EMMENTALER: A semi-hard, nutty, fruity cheese with holes, one that we in America call "Swiss cheese." Other countries have tried to make reasonable facsimiles, but genuine Swiss Emmentaler, made only from unpasteurized cows' milk, is stamped "Switzerland" all over its rind.

GRUYÈRE: Switzerland's second most famous cheese is cooked using a similar process but with a slightly different technique from Emmentaler. The result is a rather sweet-flavored cheese, mild to sharp, with a nutty aroma and a texture that is a bit drier and firmer than Emmantaler. An excellent cooking cheese, it is used in gratins and provides a crusty cover for French onion soup, the bistro classic. Comté is one of the French Gruyère family of cheeses, but it is richer and fruitier and has a darker, tougher rind. Raclette is also produced in Switzerland, and it's a firm, smooth, buttery, easy melting cheese with a full fruity flavor. It's the main ingredient in the traditional Swiss dish that is also called raclette. In this dish cheese is placed near an open fire, and as it toasts and melts, it is scraped off and eaten immediately with boiled potatoes or fire-toasted bread.

MANCHEGO: Probably one of Spain's most famous sheep's milk cheese. Its rich, tangy flavor, ivory color, grainy texture, and saltiness can vary greatly depending on the age of the cheese. It is sold in various stages of maturity and according to law can only be made from the milk of the Manchego sheep that graze on the plains of La Mancha.

A Triumverate of Great Italian Grating Cheeses

ASIAGO: Produced outside Vicenza since the Middle Ages, it is creamy white to golden yellow in color with small compact holes. This part-skim cows' milk cheese has a smooth texture. Two types are available: Asiago d'Allevo, aged with a sharp, complex flavor and typically used for grating or eating as is, and Asiago Pressato, a hard, slightly sweet, younger cheese with a creamier texture, preferred in Italy as a table cheese. We have cooked with both and feel that they are interchangeable.

PARMIGIANO-REGGIANO: With its name branded all over its golden brown rind, pressed with a consortium seal guaranteeing its quality and minimum ripening time of twenty-four months, this straw-colored cows' milk cheese from the Emilia-Romagna region is exported virtually all over the world. It is a noble, aristocratic cheese that has been made for over seven hundred years by hand and with love. In Italy nothing is wasted; respectful, frugal cooks even add a chunk of the leftover rind to their rich bean pasta soups for fabulous depths of flavor. Once you have tasted it, you will never again buy a "reasonable facsimile" of Parmesan.

PECORINO: In Italy the word *pecorino* denotes any cheese made from sheep's milk. The most famous and popular is Pecorino Romano, although there are also Pecorino Sardo, Pecorino Siciliano, and Pecorino Toscano, all slightly different in flavor; they have a grayish white interior, are slightly salty, and have a rind stamped by the consortium that checks the authenticity. The flavor is sharp, and the texture is rather dry.

GOATS' MILK CHEESE

These are sold as fresh or aged cheese in a variety of shapes: buttons, cylinders, truncated pyramids, and logs. They can be marinated in oil or herbs or rolled in charcoal ash to absorb surface moisture and preserve them. Depending on the time allowed for maturing, goats' milk cheese may be soft, medium dry, dry, hard, or even blue, and they range from mild to aggressively flavored.

France, with more than a million head of dairy goats, has by far the greatest variety of production styles. And recently in the United States many unique goat cheeses made by craftsmen on small farms have been produced and marketed to fill the requirements of restaurant chefs who often feature warm goat cheese in salads.

COACH FARM: A fresh American artisanal farmstead cheese shaped as a log *(bûche)*. Moist, soft, mild, and creamy, it should be sliced into rounds for serving.

CROTTINS DE CHAVIGNOL: One of the oldest and most popular of chèvres from Berry in central France, it comes in small 2-inch disks with a slightly wrinkled rind that darkens as it matures. The interior is dry, firm, full-flavored, and very sharp, with a strong, goaty smell. At its freshest, it is very mild and nutty and only slightly fragrant.

SAINTE-MAURE: A cylindrically shaped chèvre from the Touraine region of France. Soft and creamy, it is distinguished by a straw through the center, a pinkish rind, and a full-bodied smell and taste.

TAUPINIÈRE: A dome-shaped, full-flavored goat cheese with a dense, rich flavor and an exterior crust that is slightly wrinkled, soft, and bluish as a result of its ash coating.

VALENÇAY: Pyramid-shaped, with the top shaved off and covered with blue-gray wood ash. It is smooth, creamy white, and has a slight farmlike smell. When serving, cut it into neat quarters.

BLUE CHEESE

These cheeses are injected with mold spores to produce their characteristic blue-green veining. Most of them were originally the result of an accident because the mold spores were naturally present in the cool, damp caves and cellars where the cheeses were made and aged.

ROQUEFORT: It is revered as the "King of Cheese and the Cheese of Kings." It is the oldest blue-veined of them all and has an international reputation. This crumbly, slightly salty, and strongly flavored unpasteurized sheep's milk French cheese is still produced in exactly the same manner as it has been for centuries. Look on the foil-wrapped cheese for a label with a red sheep printed on it for authenticity.

Other blue cheeses from around the world combine some of the properties of the soft-ripening cheeses and are made mostly of cows' milk. They appeal to those who prefer a milder flavored cheese than Roquefort. Most blues are round in shape and range in size from a hefty sixteen-pound standard wheel of wonderful English Stilton to smaller flat-disk French blues such as Bleu de Bresse and Bleu de Gex (a raw milk cheese). A tall, cylindrical blue cheese has been made in the Auvergne since the Middle Ages; it is called Fourme d'Ambert. Pipo Crem' is similar in shape and flavor.

Some of the blues are rindless, while others are crusted. And the blue-green veining also varies—from sparse to intricate. The textures can be crumbly to creamy, with color ranging from ivory to gold or even reddish orange, such as the English Blue Cheshire. They slice well and melt to a satiny finish when cooked. Here are some other examples:

CABRALES: Spain's lovely member of the blue cheese family, from the Asturias in the north. It is made primarily with cows' milk with sometimes a bit of goat and sheep milk for added richness and aroma.

CASTELLO BLUE: Another Danish, even milder, lush, triple-cream, spreadable, blue-veined cheese.

GORGONZOLA: Originated in the Italian village of the same name just east of Milan and is still produced in Lombardy. There are two types: Gorgonzola Naturale, which is moderately strong, drier, more crumbly, and pungent, and Gorgonzola Dolcelatte, which is a smooth, creamy, spreadable cheese that has been aged less than three months.

MAYTAG BLUE: Made since the 1940s at the dairy farms in Newton, Iowa, which are owned by the family that started the Maytag washing machine business. The cheese is smooth and has a pleasant sharpness and creamy texture.

SAGA BLUE: A Danish soft-ripening, Brie-type, creamy, ivory interior with intermittent blue veins. It is a rich double-cream cheese, mild and full-flavored.

And if you really have "the blues," try the Irish Cashel Blue or the Greek Kopanisti.

 SHOP SMART

- As with wine and seafood, look for a reputable market or specialty shop with a good turnover. Although cheese is produced under the most exacting standards, nature's whims take a hand in the end result, and cheese will deteriorate if left too long on the shelf.
- A serious cheese merchant will be willing to offer advice and will usually carry labels that have brief descriptions of the origins, textures, and flavors.
- If you are offered a taste sample, always accept it. It is the only way to discover new cheeses or to see if the familiar ones are the best they can be.
- Many cheeses are available only in huge wheels, and storage can become a problem for the proprietor unless the shop sells nothing but cheese. There-

fore, many cheeses are precut and wrapped. Check the date on the label that indicates the final day of sale before you buy the wrapped cheese. When you open the package, if the cheese smells of ammonia or is very acidic, it's overripe or has been badly stored or frozen. Return it.

◆ As soon as you get it home, place the cheese in the crisper of your refrigerator. Refrigeration slows down the natural aging process. Fresh, soft cheese such as ricotta and fresh goat cheeses should be used as soon as possible after purchase. Double and triple creams will keep well for one or two weeks, hard cheeses for as much as a month or more.

◆ After using, always wrap the remaining cheese in fresh aluminum foil or plastic wrap.

◆ If mold forms on semi-hard and hard cheeses, recognize it as part of the aging process. Just cut it off, discard it, and use the good cheese underneath. Soft fresh cheeses and processed supermarket sliced and wrapped cheeses that grow moldy should be discarded.

◆ On Serving Cheese ◆

◆ Always serve cheese at room temperature. Cold cheese has less flavor and texture.

◆ Suggest to your guests how cheese should be cut: When serving a platter with various cheeses, start a few cuts, wedges, or slices in each piece by following the natural lines of the cheese. Our pet peeve is the attack on cheese without regard to its form, leaving hollowed rinds or wedges with their tips cut off.

◆ Don't forget to provide a separate knife for each cheese.

Notes for the Cook

ON COOKING WITH CHEESE . . .

Sometimes when we're cooking, cheese separates or curdles, leaving a puddle of oil and a rubbery, globby mess. The culprit is too much heat for too long a time. A few tips should help avoid a minor kitchen catastrophe.

To avoid curdling and stringiness:

◆ Grate or cut the cheese into small pieces so that less time and less heat will be needed.

◆ Sometimes just the residual heat of a cooked dish such as cream sauce, soup, or hot cooked pasta will melt the added cheese smoothly. So add the cheese and then remove the pot from the heat before stirring.

◆ Stirring grated cheese into the boiling liquids of a casserole or gratin, which require long heating times, can result in curdling. So before you add the cheese, stir in a slurry of water and a bit of either flour or cornstarch; then add the cheese to help keep it smooth. Cheese added to a béchamel sauce of flour, butter, and milk already has the flour in it, and that will stabilize the cheese.

◆ A squeeze of lemon juice added to grated mozzarella or Emmentaler before it is added to a sauce avoids stringiness. Remember to add and stir over *low* heat.

◆ When preparing a gratin where the dish is to be slipped briefly under the broiler, always add the cheese toward the end of the cooking process. To help melt and spread the cheese evenly and to dapple the crust with a desirable flavor, adding a few bits of butter along with the cheese will do the trick.

◆ Fresh cheeses such as soft goat cheese have a higher moisture and a lower fat content, and they will keep their shape when heated. They are best just warmed through. If you cook with them, add a bit of cream or a high-fat creamy cheese such as mascarpone. Fresh cheese will not brown or develop a crisp surface when grilled, such as the harder types like Gruyère and Parmesan.

◆ Some cheeses are naturally saltier, so take this into account when cooking. Taste and adjust the salt in the dish. You may need only a bit after the cheese is added.

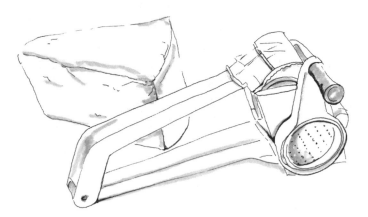

TORTILLAS WITH JALAPEÑO JACK CHEESE, GREEN OLIVES, AND A CILANTRO TOMATO SAUCE

You can prepare the sauce in advance. The assembly is quite fast. It then takes only ten minutes in the oven. Your vegetarian guests will love its slightly hot tingle.

SERVES 4

3 large scallions, trimmed and cut into 1-inch pieces

1 cup loosely packed cilantro leaves plus 2 sprigs cilantro for garnish

Two 1-pound cans Italian plum tomatoes

¾ teaspoon ground cumin

Salt and black pepper to taste

10 yellow corn tortillas

½ cup pitted and sliced green olives such as Atalanta or Agrinion

7 ounces Jalapeño Jack cheese, very thinly sliced

Sour cream for garnish

Place the scallions and cilantro leaves in the bowl of a food processor and chop until fairly fine. Add the tomatoes and process until smooth. Stir in the cumin, salt, and pepper. Transfer the mixture to a bowl and set aside.

Preheat the oven to 450 degrees. Use a 9 x 14-inch rectangular oven-to-table baking dish. Spread ½ cup of the sauce on the bottom of the dish and top with 2 tortillas placed side by side to start 2 separate stacks. Sprinkle each tortilla with a few olives and a few slices of the cheese. Add ¼ cup of the sauce over each stack. Repeat this process of layering 3 times, ending with sauce and cheese on top. Bake for 10 minutes.

Remove from the oven and top with a dollop of sour cream and a sprig of cilantro. Cut each stack in half with a very sharp knife and serve while hot.

GRUYÈRE AND ONION PUREE WITH CLOVES AND NUTMEG

A side dish that is perfect with roasted veal and tastes surprisingly like a good, old-fashioned French onion soup. Prepare it early and slip it in the oven just before serving.

SERVES 4 TO 6

4 tablespoons butter plus extra for the gratin dish

1½ pounds large, sweet Bermuda or Vidalia onions (about 2 large), peeled and thinly sliced

Coarse salt to taste

⅛ teaspoon fresh black pepper to taste

⅛ teaspoon cayenne pepper

¼ teaspoon freshly grated nutmeg

⅛ teaspoon ground cloves

⅓ cup heavy cream

2 tablespoons dry white wine

3 to 4 thin slices sourdough bread, toasted

½ cup grated Gruyère cheese

In a 12-inch nonstick skillet, melt 2 tablespoons of the butter over low heat. Add the onions and sauté slowly, stirring occasionally, until the onions are soft and golden, about 20 to 25 minutes. After 10 minutes, stir in the salt, pepper, cayenne, nutmeg, and cloves, and continue to cook.

Preheat the oven to 400 degrees and butter a 2-quart shallow oven-to-table gratin dish. When the onions are cooked, puree them in a food processor along with 1 tablespoon of the butter, the cream, and wine. Place slices of toasted bread on the bottom of the casserole, sprinkle with 3 tablespoons of the cheese, and spread the onion puree over the top. Sprinkle the remaining cheese on the surface and dot with the remaining butter. Bake for 10 to 15 minutes, then raise the heat to broil. Slip the casserole under the broiler until the cheese is flecked with brown. Serve at once.

SPANISH POTATO GRATIN WITH TETILLA CHEESE, RED AND YELLOW PEPPERS, BLACK OLIVES, AND SAFFRON

The sexy-looking Spanish cheese from Galicia, Tetilla, in the shape of a slightly flattened breast, is a mild, fast-melting, creamy cheese. It tops a lovely and colorful potato gratin with all the typical flavors of Spain. It is a perfect accompaniment to simply grilled fish or poultry.

SERVES 6

4 large russet baking potatoes (about 2 pounds)

5 tablespoons olive oil

2 large, sweet onions, Bermuda or Vidalia, peeled, halved, and thinly sliced

Salt and pepper to taste

1 teaspoon dried thyme

1 large, sweet red pepper, cored, seeded, and cut into ¼-inch strips

1 large yellow pepper, cored, seeded, and cut into ¼-inch strips

½ cup pitted black Kalamata olives

1¼ cups hot vegetable broth

¼ teaspoon saffron threads

4 ounces Tetilla, Ulloa, or San Simón cheese, cut into cubes

3 tablespoons minced parsley

Peel the potatoes and slice them ⅛ to ¼ inch thick. Drop the slices into a bowl of cold water and set aside. In a 12-inch sauté pan, heat 3 tablespoons of the olive oil over high heat. Add the onions, salt, and pepper, and cook, stirring constantly, for about 5 minutes. Turn the heat to low, and when the onions start to brown, add the thyme. Cook, partially covered, for 25 to 30 minutes, until the onions are soft and golden. Drain the potatoes and gently stir them into the onions.

Place the peppers in a bowl and toss with the remaining olive oil.

Preheat the oven to 400 degrees. Butter a 10 x 14-inch oval gratin dish. Spoon the onion-potato mixture into the baking dish, pressing lightly to form an even layer. Layer the peppers over the potato-onion mixture and scatter the olives around evenly.

Combine the broth and saffron and let stand for 5 minutes, then add to the gratin dish. Cover with aluminum foil and bake in the center of the oven for 1 hour, or until the broth has been absorbed by the potatoes and the peppers are tender.

Remove the foil, scatter the cheese cubes over the top, and raise the heat. Slip the gratin dish under the broiler to melt the cheese and dapple it golden brown. Scatter the parsley over all and serve hot.

COL LEGNO TIRAMISU

Many restaurants have tiramasu on their menus. However, the best we've ever tasted is this one from Col Legno, a small local restaurant we frequent that is located in the East Village in New York City.

MAKES 9 PORTIONS

8-ounce cup espresso coffee
  (see Note)
3½ tablespoons dark rum
26 Savoiardi (Italian ladyfingers)
12 ounces mascarpone cheese

¾ cup confectioners' sugar
1 pint heavy cream
½ teaspoon vanilla extract
2 tablespoons dark cocoa for garnish

Prepare the coffee. Add 1½ tablespoons of the rum and set aside to cool in a tempered glass pie pan. Quickly dip 13 Savoiardi on both sides and place them on the bottom of a 2-quart 8 x 8 x 2-inch tempered glass dish. Set aside the rest of the coffee and Savoiardi. (You may need to trim 3 of them slightly for each layer in order to get a tight fit.)

In a large bowl, place the mascarpone, confectioners' sugar, cream, the remaining rum, and the vanilla. Beat with a handheld electric beater until the surface ripples and the mixture is fairly stiff. Spoon half of this mixture over the coffee-dipped ladyfingers and smooth the surface with a rubber spatula. Dip the remaining Savoiardi in the rest of the coffee mixture and repeat, making another layer. Top this with the remaining cream mixture, then cover with plastic wrap and chill for a minimum of 4 hours and up to 8 if necessary.

When ready to serve, cut it into equal squares. Place them on serving plates and sift the cocoa over the surface, allowing some to dust the plate. Serve cold.

Note: We used an estate blend espresso called Illy, and we prepared the coffee by using a paper filter with the drip method. However, any good, freshly made, strong espresso can be used.

SAGANAKI

A simple Greek taverna mezze, an appetizer that owes its name to the small two-handled pottery gratin dish in which it is served. It is tricky to make unless the cheese is very, very cold and the clarified butter is very hot. The frying time is very brief. The results? A hot, crispy, golden crust encasing a warm, oozing creamy center.

SERVES 4

1 pound cheese, either Kasseri or Kefalograviera or Graviera
Cornstarch for dredging
4 tablespoons clarified butter (see page 439)

4 tablespoons lemon juice
1 tablespoon minced fresh mint (optional)

Cut the cheese into four 4-ounce slices about ½ inch thick and freeze for at least 30 minutes (or longer if convenient) before frying. When the cheese is very cold, rinse the slices under cold water and shake off the excess water. Sift some cornstarch onto a piece of waxed paper, lay the cheese down, and sift more cornstarch over the tops. Wipe off the excess, making sure all sides are covered with cornstarch. Keep chilled while heating the butter.

In a 10- to 12-inch well-seasoned black iron skillet, over medium heat, heat the butter until very hot, almost to the smoking point. Add the cheese slices and raise the heat to high. Fry on one side until the bottom is lightly golden and the center just begins to ooze. Carefully turn the cheese over and fry on the other side until golden. It takes about 2 to 3 minutes for each side.

Transfer to a warm plate or "Saganaki" gratin dish. Spoon 1 tablespoon of lemon juice over each slice and top with a few shreds of mint if you wish. Serve immediately while hot.

◆ Clarified Butter ◆

The reason for using clarified butter is that it can be heated to very high temperatures over a long period of time without burning. It is one of the secrets of Saganaki and is easy to make ahead of time.

Melt 8 tablespoons (1 stick) of sweet butter slowly in a heavy saucepan over low heat. Turn off the heat when the butter is melted and let it stand for 5 to 10 minutes. Using a spoon, carefully skim off the foamy white butterfat that is on the surface. The clear, golden liquid beneath is the clarified butter. Spoon the liquid into a plastic container, leaving the remaining milky residue in the bottom of the pot. Clarified butter can be refrigerated for a month and used as needed. One-quarter pound of butter makes ⅓ cup of clarified.

FRESH GOAT CHEESE TARTS WITH SERRANO HAM AND GRILLED PEARS

We created and served these elegant little tarts for a Sunday brunch. We prepared them ahead of time and warmed them just before serving. Our guests took one bite and immediately asked for the recipe—a compliment if we ever heard one.

SERVES 4

CRUST:
½ cup skinned almonds
2 English muffins, torn into small pieces
¼ teaspoon dried oregano

¼ teaspoon almond extract
2 tablespoons melted butter

FILLING:
4 ounces fresh goats' milk cheese
1 tablespoon milk
⅛ teaspoon black pepper
4 ounces Serrano ham or smoked ham,
    cut into very thin strips

1 tablespoon olive oil
2 pears such as Bartlett or Bosc
Small lemon wedge
⅓ teaspoon fresh thyme leaves plus
    4 sprigs for garnish

Preheat the oven to 375 degrees. To make the crust: Process the almonds in a food processor until fairly fine. Add the English muffins and process again until fine. Add the oregano, almond extract, and butter, and process once more until well combined. Butter four 4-inch tartlet pans with removable bottoms. Spoon about 3 tablespoons of the crust mixture into each pan and press against the sides first and then evenly on the bottom. Place the pans on a baking sheet and bake for 8 minutes, or until the crust is light brown around the edges. Remove and cool on a wire rack. This can be done well in advance.

To make the filling: In a small bowl, beat the goat cheese, milk, and pepper with a wooden spoon until smooth. Using a spatula, gently spread about 1 tablespoon of cheese on the bottom of each cooled crust. Scatter about 1 tablespoon of ham strips over the cheese and set the tartlet pans aside.

Preheat the oven to broil. Spoon the olive oil onto a flat plate. Core the pears, keeping the skin on, and thinly slice them. Dip them in the olive oil on both sides and then place them on a baking sheet. Squeeze the lemon wedge over the pears and slip the sheet under the source of heat. Grill until the edges of the pears start to turn brown, then turn off the oven. Remove the sheet and arrange about 6 pear slices in a spiral over the ham. Sprinkle the pears with fresh thyme and return the tartlets to the warm oven for about 5 minutes, just long enough to warm through. Garnish with a sprig of thyme. Gently remove the sides, slide each tartlet off its base onto a plate, and serve.

ASIAGO CHEESE RAMEKINS WITH ANCHOVIES

A soothing, delicate cheese custard bakes over a layer of crisp croutons with just a hint of anchovy, a singularly delicious first course.

SERVES 4

8 flat anchovies
¼ cup milk
2 tablespoons butter
2 slices peasant bread, crusts trimmed
    and cut into ½-inch cubes (about
    2 cups)
¼ teaspoon dried thyme

2 eggs
1 cup milk
Salt and pepper to taste
⅛ teaspoon nutmeg
8 ounces Asiago cheese, grated
    (Gruyère can be substituted)
Paprika for garnish

Soak the anchovies in the milk for 5 minutes, then drain and dry on paper towels. Set aside. Melt the butter in a 10-inch skillet over medium heat. Add the bread cubes and thyme, and sauté, stirring frequently, until crisp and golden.

Butter four 1-cup ramekins (individual soufflé cups). Distribute the croutons among the 4 cups and top with some anchovies.

Preheat the oven to 375 degrees and boil a kettle of water. In a bowl, whisk the eggs, milk, salt, pepper, and nutmeg together, then stir in the cheese. Ladle ½ cup of the egg mixture over the croutons in each ramekin. Place the ramekins in a 9 x 13 x 2-inch roasting pan and pour boiling water into the bottom of the pan until it is halfway up the sides of the ramekins. Bake for 15 to 18 minutes, until the custard is firm. Remove the ramekins from the water bath, sprinkle the tops with paprika, and serve hot with spoons.

FOUR QUICK EUROPEAN CHEESE DESSERTS

GREEK

MANOURI CHEESE:

From the Isle of Crete, a velvety white, creamy sheep's milk whey cheese is featured here. For 4 people, allow about 8 ounces of cheese. Cut into 4 slices. Trickle each slice with thyme honey and scatter 2 tablespoons of coarsely broken toasted walnuts over each portion. Try it after a dinner of Greek-style wood-grilled fish with lemon.

ITALIAN

TALEGGIO CHEESE:

A cream yellow cows' milk cheese that is slightly salty and tangy. For each person allow 3 ounces of cheese. Trickle with 1 tablespoon of clear acacia honey and scatter 2 teaspoons of lightly toasted pine nuts over all. This simple and elegant dessert is a study in pale colors.

SPANISH

MANCHEGO CHEESE:
From the plains of La Mancha, this ivory, slightly salty sheep's milk cheese is traditionally served with large Manukka raisins and honey. The light, milky fresh, soft junket-like cheese from Catalonia, sold in tubs called *Mató*, is sometimes available in the United States, and when eaten with raisins and honey, it is called *Miele y Mató*.

FRENCH

FROMAGE DU BREBIS:
A Basque sheep's milk cheese from Languedoc is served with walnut bread and black cherry preserves. Combine them as desired and eat with mad abandon!

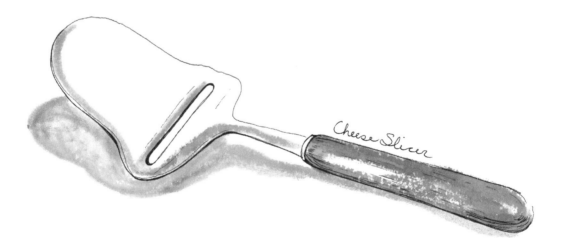

Olives: The Pit Stop

Pissaladière

Cheddar Cheese Olive Puffs

Black and Green Olives with Roasted Red Peppers

Cherry Tomatoes Stuffed with Egg and Black Olive Tapenade

Grown in rocky soil under arid conditions, the silvery green, gnarled olive trees are part of almost every Mediterranean landscape. Some say that olive trees are ageless and immortal, for they predate the written history of Greece. The olives and their oil have been renowned in Italy since the time of the Romans. In the Middle East, North Africa, and Spain the landscape has been dotted with them since 4000 B.C., and today in Spain there are over 200 million olive trees still growing and still producing.

As the olive matures on the tree, the colors turn from green to reddish purple, a deeper wine-color red, blackish red, and finally to a pure glossy black. Since color is a result of the ripening process, they can be harvested at any stage. But before they are cured, olives contain an intensely bitter, almost obnoxious compound called "oleuropein." And although it is quite harmless, if you have ever been tempted to bite into an uncured olive, as we did on a recent trip to Greece, the instant reaction is to spit it out immediately.

Curing olives affects their flavor, texture, and appearance, and many different methods are used. A rapid method of curing puts the olives in a strong lye solution for several hours, after which the bitterness disappears but most of the flavor is leached out as well. A more gentle method soaks the olives in a gentle bath of water and wood ash (a weaker form of lye), which does less damage and is the preferred method of the two.

A still slower method is brine curing, where the olives are steeped in salt water for several months. Some producers combine both procedures, with an end result that maintains the shape of the original olive as well as its moisture and flavor balance.

Dry-cured olives are either sun-dried or oven-baked first, then packed in coarse salt to leach out their bitterness. They are then washed and steeped in oil. These are the olives that have a leathery, somewhat shriveled appearance and a more intense flavor than those that have been brine cured.

After curing, producers may then add other finishing touches: oil or wine, vinegar, garlic, chiles, herbs, spices, or citrus peels. And because of the vast range of methods, growth patterns, origins, and personal preferences of growers, there is a great deal of confusion in the way that olives are named and marketed. Sometimes they are named for the curing method, other times for the region in which they grew. Olives with exactly the same name may appear as black or green.

It was not long ago in the United States that only canned or jarred, pitted black and green olives were available. That, luckily, is no longer true. There is now an astonishing international variety of olives from which to choose—in sizes from tiny to mammoth, instilled with flavors that are oily or smoky, in shapes that are shriveled, plump, oval, or round, and with textures that run the gamut from soft to firm and crisp. Gourmet Garage and many specialty shops around the country keep containers filled with olive samples—alongside a container in which to stash the pits. We love the ever-changing supply of olive varieties, and the tasting buckets of olives help us make our own decisions.

Notes for the Cook

ON OLIVES . . .

- ◆ Keep olives moist and in their brine, tightly covered and refrigerated if you plan to store them for more than 2 weeks.
- ◆ A cool room temperature will keep them for 1 or 2 weeks.
- ◆ Always serve olives at room temperature for the fullest flavor.

AN OLIVE SAMPLER

These are just a few of the popular varieties. However, the particular olive you want may not be available because of season or the whim of the importer or retail merchant. Therefore, in our recipes, we have suggested substitutes.

VARIETY	DESCRIPTION
	Spanish
ARBIQUENA	Small, reddish green, brine-cured with a fresh, herbal, smoky taste. They have tough skins, are not too fleshy, and are sometimes sold with stems and leaves still attached. An eating olive, it is also used for making olive oil.
MANZANILLA	Small to medium size, light green taupe, called the "little apple" in Spain for its toothsome, crisp texture and resinous flavor. Also grown and sold in California, pitted and stuffed with pimientos or almonds.
SEVILLANO	Large, green, brine-cured variety, grown in both Spain and California, where they are marketed as "queen size" or "super colossal." Have a tart flavor and are difficult to pit.
	Greek
AGRINION	Huge, light green olives from northwest Greece, cracked and brine-cured. They have firm, tangy flesh, are easily pitted, and are sometimes confused with "Greek Green," a dull green, fat, and juicy olive with softer flesh.
AMPHISSA	Large, round, dark purplish brown, with a meaty, winy flavor. They are marinated in wine or vinegar or grape must.

ATALANTA   Medium size and greenish brown with a complex, earthy, sharp taste. Tender, meaty flesh. Sometimes sold pitted. Good for cooking, tapenades, and olive paste (*olivada*).

ELITSES   From the island of Crete, they are small, brine-cured, nibbling olives with pointed ends. They are a bit larger but similar to the French niçoise, which is rounder in shape. The color ranges from olive to drab to jet black, and they have a rich lemony flavor.

IONIAN GREEN   Large, plump, olive green, meaty, crisp, lemony, and fresh tasting. Not overly salty and an olive lover's joy.

KALAMATA   Lustrous, almond-shaped, medium-size black-purple olives from the Peloponnese. Firm, with a robust flavor and a fruity aftertaste. They are sun-ripened, cured in brine, and then enhanced with red wine vinegar or olive oil. Easily pitted, they are sometimes sold pitted. They are wonderful, easily attainable, all-purpose olives.

NAPHLION   Medium size, khaki green or black, glossy, tender/firm, with a salty, tart taste. Usually cracked before brine-curing and then packed in oil. Easy to pit.

GREEK BLACK   Large, purplish brown cured olives with soft, pulpy flesh and winy flavor. Good for pureeing.

ROYAL OR VASILIKES   Huge round olives, light brown to dark red in color. They are slit, brine-cured, and then marinated in vinegar and olive oil. Soft, pungent, and salty taste. Easily pitted.

Italian

BARESI DOLCI   Hail from Bari, the region at the heel of Italy. Medium size, elongated, dull green. They are ash-cured, crisp, and have a sweet taste. Low in salt and difficult to pit.

VARIETY	DESCRIPTION
BELLA DI CERIGNOLA	Huge green and black. Bright leaf green, they are meaty and crisp with delicate, mild flavor. These ash-cured olives from Apulia are difficult to pit. The inky black variety is a ripe version and a bit softer in texture, more intensely flavored, and easier to pit.
GAETA	Small, salt-cured, unpredictable olives. Sometimes smooth and purple, sometimes slightly wrinkled and black. Difficult to pit. They have a sour, salty, winy flavor. They are also available marinated with lemon, bay leaf, rosemary, and thyme.
SICILIAN GREEN	Many olives are called by this name, while others are named after their region, Castelvetrano. "True" Sicilian green olives are brownish green, very large, and brine-cured. They have very fleshy soft fruit and are easy to pit. Their flavor is sharply assertive and slightly bitter. At times they are spiced with hot pepper flakes, sliced garlic, or fennel and oregano.
	French
NIÇOISE	Tiny, shiny, brine-cured olives that range in color from purplish brown to black. These Provence olives have a pungent, herbaceous taste with more pit than flesh.
NYONS	Round, slightly shriveled, medium-size brownish olives from the south of France. Shiny, meaty, sometimes dry-roasted for a smoky, pleasantly bitter taste, and at other times brine-cured. Easy to pit.
PICHOLINE	Medium or small submarine shapes with tapered ends. Pale green, brine-cured olives, sometimes packed in lemon juice. They have a crisp, salty flavor and flesh that is hard to pit.

MOROCCAN   Medium or small, jet black, shriveled, and shiny, sun- or heat-dried, then salt-cured and preserved in oil. Sometimes enhanced with rosemary and sliced garlic. They are meaty and moist and easy to pit. Similar to the oven-dried, oil-preserved Italian roasted (*al forno*) olives, with a fruity, sweet, spicy flavor. (Note: To remove some of the bitterness, these olives can be simmered in water for 10 minutes or dressed with strong spices.)

Chilean

ALPHONSO   Huge, unique, purple-black to pale brown, soft and very meaty. Extremely flavorful, these brine-cured olives are steeped in wine or wine vinegar for marinade after curing. They are not overly salty and easy to pit.

Other Varieties

They are cultivated all over the world and occasionally pop up in the marketplace. They come from Jordan, Lebanon, Turkey, and Tunisia—some green and some black. Mixtures from Tunisia are marinated in a colorful assortment of harissa or hot chiles and are powerful, soft, and very spicy.

PISSALADIÈRE

A flavorful, sophisticated option for the ubiquitous Italian pizza, made here with flaky frozen puff pastry. The first bite will whisk you back to the south of France.

SERVES 8

1½ tablespoons olive oil

1½ pounds onions (about 3 or 4 large), thinly sliced

1½ teaspoons dried thyme

3 large leaves fresh sage, finely minced

1 teaspoon sugar

1 teaspoon balsamic vinegar

Salt and pepper to taste

14-ounce package frozen puff pastry, thawed (10 x 13-inch sheet)

Flour for dusting

1 egg plus 1 teaspoon water for egg wash

6 tablespoons grated Parmesan cheese

6½-ounce jar roasted red pimiento peppers, drained, blotted dry, and cut into thin strips

16 to 18 pitted black olives such as Nyons or Kalamata, cut in half

In a large nonstick skillet, heat the oil over medium-low heat and sauté the onions for 5 minutes. Add the thyme, sage, and sugar, and cook 20 minutes more, stirring occasionally, until golden. Add the vinegar, salt, and pepper, and set aside. Can be prepared in advance up to this point.

Rub a stick of butter over a 14 x 17-inch baking sheet and press a sheet of baking parchment paper on the buttered surface. Unfold the pastry and dust lightly with flour. Turn over and place flour side down on the prepared sheet. Dust again with flour. Roll the pastry into a rectangle approximately 11 x 14 inches. Brush a 1-inch border around the edges with egg wash and prick the inside surface all over with a fork. Fold the sides over ½ inch and brush this border with the egg wash as well. Cover completely with plastic wrap and chill a minimum of 20 minutes until ready to assemble and bake.

Remove the plastic wrap and sprinkle 3 tablespoons of the cheese within the borders of the pastry. Spread the onions evenly over the cheese and sprinkle 3 more tablespoons of the cheese over them. Arrange the red pepper strips diagonally, forming a lattice surface, and then place half an olive in the center of each diamond shape. If you are preparing the pissaladière well ahead of time, cover again with plastic wrap and keep chilled.

Preheat the oven to 375 degrees. Remove the plastic wrap and bake in the upper third of the oven for 25 to 30 minutes, or until the border of the pastry is puffed and golden. Cut into 8 portions with a very sharp or serrated knife and serve hot.

CHEDDAR CHEESE OLIVE PUFFS

A fun, easy-to-make hors d'oeuvre with a surprise olive in the center. They seem to disappear as quickly as a snowflake on a warm sidewalk.

MAKES 4 DOZEN

8 ounces sharp cheddar cheese
1 cup flour
½ teaspoon sweet paprika
¼ teaspoon cayenne pepper

6 tablespoons soft butter, cut into small pieces
48 small Spanish Manzanilla olives stuffed with pimiento

Grate the cheese using a shredder blade in a food processor. There should be 2 cups of grated cheese. Change the food processor blade to the steel chopping blade. Add the flour, paprika, cayenne, and butter, and pulse about 6 or 8 times, just until the mixture holds together. Remove the cheese mixture, cover with plastic wrap, and chill for 15 minutes.

While the cheese mixture chills, preheat the oven to 400 degrees. Rub some butter lightly over two 14 x 17-inch baking sheets and line the sheets with a piece of parchment paper. (The butter will help the paper adhere to the sheet.) Flour your hands and shape a heaping ½ teaspoon of cheese mixture into a ball. Push your small finger into the center of the ball to make a deep depression. Insert an olive and reshape the cheese mixture around the olive to fully cover it. Repeat until the 48 olives are prepared in the same way. Place on the baking sheets, allowing space between them. Bake for 12 to 15 minutes, until baked but not brown. Serve hot.

BLACK AND GREEN OLIVES WITH ROASTED RED PEPPERS

A colorful, versatile condiment that is great on sourdough toasts. Or try a few spoonsful over a grilled chicken breast or fish fillet. Tuck some into a baked potato over a cube of melted cheddar cheese or spoon a trail over steamed asparagus.

MAKES 2 CUPS

1 cup pitted black olives such as
    Kalamata, Nyons, or Gaeta
1 cup pitted green olives such as
    Manzanilla or Agrinion
½ cup finely diced roasted red
    peppers, drained if used from a jar
    or can

⅓ cup finely minced red onion
    (1 small onion)
¼ teaspoon crushed dried oregano,
    preferably Greek
Black pepper to taste
2 tablespoons olive oil

Add the olives to the bowl of a food processor. Pulse 4 or 5 times to coarsely chop the olives. Scrape them into a bowl and stir in the red peppers, onion, oregano, pepper, and oil. Cover with plastic wrap and chill for at least 1 hour, or prepare it the day before you plan to use it. Bring it to room temperature before serving.

CHERRY TOMATOES STUFFED WITH EGG AND BLACK OLIVE TAPENADE

Bound with a hard-boiled egg, this tapenade is devoid of any harshness or the excess salt found in many others.

MAKES 3 DOZEN

1 large hard-boiled egg
1 cup olives such as Kalamata or black Nyons, pitted
4 medium anchovy fillets, rinsed in cold water and dried on paper towels
1 small clove garlic, roughly chopped (about 1 teaspoon)
1 heaping teaspoon Dijon mustard

2 tablespoons nonpareil capers, rinsed and dried
1 tablespoon lemon juice (½ small lemon)
⅛ teaspoon black pepper
36 large cherry tomatoes, about 1 inch in diameter (a mixture of red and yellow if possible)
Parsley leaves for garnish

In the bowl of a food processor, chop the egg finely, pulsing about 4 or 5 times. Transfer to a small bowl and set aside. Place in the food processor the olives, anchovies, garlic, mustard, capers, lemon juice, and pepper, and process until pureed, scraping down the sides of the bowl frequently with a rubber spatula. Return the egg to the food processor and combine using 1 or 2 pulses. Transfer to a bowl, cover with plastic wrap, and refrigerate until ready to use. (Can be made 1 or 2 days in advance. Makes 1 cup.)

Cut a ¼-inch slice from the bottom of each tomato, using a very sharp knife. Leave the stem end intact. Carefully scoop out the pulp and seeds with the tip of a knife, using a circular motion, and discard. Place the tomato shells on paper towels to drain.

Fill each tomato with a heaping ½ teaspoon of tapenade and arrange on a serving dish. Insert the stem of a parsley leaf in each one for garnish or, alternatively, use 12 filled tomatoes to surround the remaining tapenade in a small dish, accompanied by melba toasts.

Caviar and Smoked Fish:
What Foods These Morsels Be

Miniature Potato and Scallion Pancakes with Red Caviar

Star-Spangled Red and Black Caviar

Smoked Trout with Fennel, Oranges, and Mint

Smoked Whitefish Pâté with Shallots

Cullen Skink: A Scottish Chowder of Smoked and Fresh Seafood

Smoked Salmon Parcels with Chives and Cream Cheese

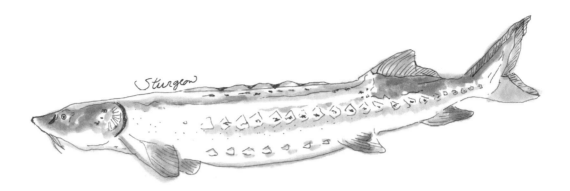

CAVIAR

You either love it or hate it. If you hate it, chances are your first experience with caviar was with "lumpfish caviar"—an oxymoron if there ever was one. Lumpfish, a pasteurized overly salty roe, is usually from Irish or Scandinavian waters, where it is immersed in a dye that makes it look like caviar. Incidentally, this process also blackened the reputations of cost-cutting caterers because the black dye leaks onto the white paper doilies lining silver trays.

For most of us, caviar is synonymous with elegance and extravagance. Every important event, every special red-letter day is made more so when good caviar is served along with the welcome addition of Brut champagne.

All caviar is made from fish roe, but not all fish roe can be called caviar. Caviar refers only to salted sturgeon eggs that come from only three of the more than twenty species of this prehistoric fish. About 90 percent of the world's best, true caviar comes from sturgeon that swim between Iran and the former Soviet Union in the Caspian Sea. The top season is late fall to early spring when the finest roe comes from fish caught in the most frigid waters.

The roe is first sieved to remove the surrounding connective membranes, and we can begin to understand the cost when we realize that the finest varieties are processed by hand. The roe are then graded for quality and cured with noniodized salt. The results are tiny, moist, sparkling beads of various colors, sizes, and textures.

A Personal Primer

When your purchase is going to be extravagant, it pays to be practical and know the differences among the three best varieties.

BELUGA: The roe comes from the largest of the Caspian Sea sturgeons and is the most scarce of the major types. The Beluga sturgeon can weigh up to two thousand pounds and grow to a length of twenty feet. It takes twenty years out of a fifty-year life span for the female to mature enough to produce the largest, most delicately flavored (and thus the most expensive) caviar. The size of the eggs does not necessarily dictate the quality of the caviar. The texture must be buttery, yet firm. The color range is fairly uniform, from pearl gray to charcoal gray. The flavor is clear and delicate.

OSETRA: The second largest Caspian sturgeon weighs one hundred to three hundred pounds and is about six or seven feet long. It matures in twelve to fourteen years and produces medium-grain, firm eggs that are grayish brown to greenish gold and black. Osetra has a distinctive nutty, earthy, or herbal taste. For value and flavor, this is our choice.

SEVRUGA: The most plentiful and smallest species of the three, this sturgeon weighs between thirty and fifty pounds, is about five feet long, and matures in seven years. The eggs are naturally small-grained, medium gray to off-black. The texture is firm and the flavor distinguished by a slightly more assertive brinyness. Russians and many European connoisseurs select sevruga as their primary choice.

SHOP SMART

Top-quality caviar is generally sold in bulk or packed in tins. It should have a subtle saline flavor but not a fishy taste and a texture that is silken, not flaccid. Plump, round, separated eggs should have a delicate sheath, allowing you to crush them on the roof of your mouth in a sensual orgy.

- You'll also find sturgeon caviar available pasteurized in jars, and there are jars of pressed, pasteurized damaged eggs with a somewhat jamlike consistency.
- Fresh caviar, when labeled with the Russian word *malossol*, which means "little salt," is about one-third salt by weight. However, vacuum-packed and pasteurized caviar contains twice the amount of salt to prevent spoilage and to flavor less-than-perfect eggs.
- Once you have purchased fresh caviar, treat it with respect. Keep it under refrigeration in the coldest spot or on ice, and eat it within two or three days. If there are leftovers, press a piece of plastic wrap gently over the surface to squeeze out any air and then refrigerate it.

Notes for the Cook

ON CAVIAR . . .

We are purists who prefer to splurge for special occasions and to eat our caviar straight up, with only a squeeze of lemon juice. We serve it totally unadorned and present it in a glass pedestal bowl of crushed ice, along with a tiny horn or mother-of-pearl spoon. Silver is a no-no since it alters the taste of the caviar and gives it a metallic overlay. Spoon it on freshly made toasts, not too crisp, so that the crunch of the roe and the flavor of the caviar shine through like a beacon.

A ROE BY ANY OTHER NAME

Overfishing and pollution have almost eradicated the American sturgeon, but with tighter international laws the industry has begun to stage a comeback, which has produced some interesting roe from Japan. All are much less expensive than the three top imported caviars. Roe from salmon, whitefish, carp, pike, mullet, and shad are all available, each with its own flavor characteristics and popularity.

Currently, a pressed, salted, and sun-dried mullet roe from Sardinia, southern Italy, and Greece, called *Bottarga*, is having its day on the menus of some of the more expensive restaurants, where it is shaved over pasta and incorporated into salads. Salmon roe (called Ikura in Japan), comes from coho and chum salmon eggs. They are bright bubbles the size of small peas, with an exquisite golden orange color. They pop pleasantly in the mouth and leave a refreshingly mild, briny taste. They have become a popular addition to sushi trays, along with some others:

Crab roe (*Masago*) is crunchy and has a bittersweet flavor. Flying fish roe (*tobiko shiozuke*) and cod roe (*ajitsuke tarako*) are all tinted with food coloring in various shades of pink, gold, and red. Cod roe tastes a bit like anchovy paste, while flying fish roe is very crunchy and has a slight fishy flavor.

The most popular roe from Greece is the pale pink cod roe, sometimes with a bit of food coloring. *Tarama* is sold in jars in the refrigeration section of the market, and it is used to make *taramasalata*. The roe is whipped up with bread or potato, some garlic, olive oil, and lemon juice, and is served with pita.

Golden whitefish roe from the Great Lakes consists of small, crunchy, sunny-colored eggs with a mild, unremarkable flavor. However, it's pretty when used as a garnish.

SMOKED FISH . . . GOING UP IN SMOKE

The process of smoking seafood—whether by the cold method of professionals that uses brine, salt, and low temperatures or the mostly amateur method of brine and hot smoking in our backyards—helps to bring out tempting and original flavors in the product. Of course, some successful fishermen just love to smoke their catch with chips of hickory, alder, peach, cherry, or even corncobs. We have tried it, but it is a long and messy process that we prefer to leave to the pros.

The commercial selection is fairly constant, with salmon, whitefish, trout, mackerel, sturgeon, eel, oysters, clams, and mussels being the most common.

SHOP SMART

- At the fish counter, check to see that the fish looks moist and firm. If it looks dry, it is probably past its prime.
- If the seafood is vacuum-packed, check the date on the label while still at the store. It can be kept in the refrigerator for weeks, but once you open it, either eat it or repack with tightly wrapped plastic and return it to the refrigerator; eat it within the next two or three days.
- Some smoked fish, such as whitefish, comes in small (chub) size as well as much larger sizes. There is a lot more moisture and generous meat on the larger ones.

Notes for the Cook

ON SMOKED FISH . . .

- Smoking does not preserve for long periods of time. As with fresh fish, keep your selection in the refrigerator. To get the most flavor, take it out about 30 minutes before serving. If it comes in very thin slices (such as smoked salmon), separate the pieces while still cold, then allow to mellow to room temperature before serving. Hot- or cold-smoked fish can also be kept in the freezer for three to four weeks.
- If your fisherman neighbor smokes a big catch and gives you some, eat it within a day or two. For commercially smoked fish, such as salmon or whitefish, serve within six or seven days.

MINIATURE POTATO AND SCALLION PANCAKES WITH RED CAVIAR

Do you know anyone who doesn't love potato pancakes? Topped with a touch of crème fraîche and the orange jewels of salmon caviar, they are a mouthful of paradise.

MAKES 18 TO 20

1 pound Idaho potatoes (about
   2 medium), peeled.
¼ cup finely minced scallion (about
   1 thin scallion)
1 large egg, lightly beaten
Salt and freshly ground pepper
   to taste

Corn oil for frying
⅓ cup crème fraîche or sour cream
2 ounces red salmon caviar
Small sprigs of dill

In a food processor, process the potatoes until they are medium-fine in texture. Transfer to a plastic strainer set over a bowl. Let stand for a few minutes and then press out all the liquid into the bowl. The creamy white potato starch will settle to the bottom of the bowl. Pour off the surface liquid but keep the starch and add it to the potatoes. Add the scallion, egg, salt, and pepper.

In a heavy 10-inch iron skillet, heat the oil until it is hot but not smoking. Drop the potato batter into the oil, 1 tablespoon at a time, and flatten the pancakes at once with a spatula until they are thin. Fry until golden and crisp, then turn over and fry until golden on the other side. Drain on paper towels and keep warm in a low oven.

Spoon about 1 teaspoon of crème fraîche in the center of each pancake and flatten it slightly. Top the crème fraîche with ½ teaspoon of caviar, place a small sprig of dill on top, and serve.

STAR-SPANGLED RED AND BLACK CAVIAR

A veritable galaxy of caviar stars! They are fun to make and look gorgeous on a silver hors d'oeuvres tray.

MAKES 16 PIECES

1 loaf firm white bread or challah (1 pound), sliced	1 ounce black caviar, sevruga or osetra
Melted butter	1 ounce red salmon roe
⅓ cup crème fraîche or sour cream	Few chives, snipped in 1-inch pieces
	Small lemon wedge

Using a 3-inch star-shaped cookie cutter, cut out a star from the center of each slice of bread. There should be 16 stars. Place on a cookie sheet to dry for a few hours (see Note). Brush the surfaces with melted butter and slip the tray under the broiler for about 30 seconds. Watch carefully to see that they don't burn. Turn the stars over, brush with butter, and toast the other side.

Put a small dollop, about ½ teaspoon, of the crème fraîche in the center of each star. Top with ½ teaspoon of caviar—some red and some black. Squeeze 1 to 2 drops of lemon juice over the caviar and top only the red caviar with 2 crossed pieces of chives.

Note: For thrifty cooks, the bread scraps can be used for any recipe in the "Born Again Bread" chapter (page 467).

SMOKED TROUT WITH FENNEL, ORANGES, AND MINT

One of the simplest and most refreshing first-course salads, this has licoricy fennel, sweet tart citrus, smoked trout, and cooling mint.

SERVES 4

1 ½ pounds fennel (2 small bulbs),
    trimmed and very thinly sliced
    (about 4 cups)
2 large navel oranges
8 ounces smoked trout fillet, broken
    into bite-size pieces

Freshly ground black pepper
3 tablespoons olive oil
20 arugula leaves
2 tablespoons finely minced
    fresh mint

Place the fennel in a large bowl and peel the oranges over the same bowl to catch any juices. Remove the skin and white pith, slip a sharp knife between the membrane sections of the oranges, and dislodge the orange segments. Cut the segments in half crosswise and add them to the bowl. Squeeze whatever juice remains in the membrane shells over the fennel.

Add the trout, pepper, and olive oil, and toss lightly. Arrange 5 arugula leaves on each of 4 plates like the spokes of a wheel. Distribute the salad among the plates and sprinkle with some of the mint.

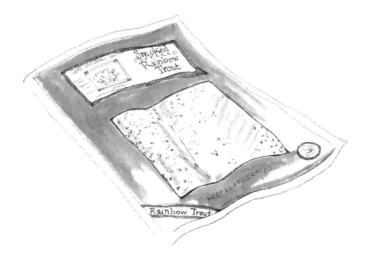

SMOKED WHITEFISH PÂTÉ WITH SHALLOTS

A standby quickie that we frequently prepare for guests who drop by for a chilled glass of wine on a warm summer evening.

MAKES 1½ CUPS

6 ounces boneless and skinless smoked
    whitefish, cut into small pieces
1 teaspoon lemon juice
¼ cup mayonnaise
1 tablespoon sour cream

3 or 4 drops Tabasco
¼ cup finely minced shallots (about
    3 large)
Rye melba toasts

Place all the ingredients in a medium bowl and combine with a wooden spoon, keeping a coarse texture. Do not overmix. Mound on a serving plate and serve with small pieces of the toast.

CULLEN SKINK: A SCOTTISH CHOWDER OF SMOKED AND FRESH SEAFOOD

In a tiny restaurant (whose name now escapes us) in Glasgow, we ate and loved this simple Scottish chowder that is seasoned with tomatoes, fresh thyme, and smoked fish, and laden with chunks of fresh fish and scallops. We thought that the smoky flavor was unusual since we in the United States rely on bacon for the same flavor in our New England chowders. This seemed a fine alternative for our vegetarian friends.

SERVES 4

1 tablespoon butter
⅔ cup finely chopped onion
2 cups peeled, boiled, and diced
   potatoes such as Yukon Gold (about
   1 pound)
3 sprigs fresh thyme
1½ cups dry white wine
3 cups milk
1 cup skinned and diced tomatoes
   (about 2 large)

4 ounces smoked whitefish, skinned
   and torn into bite-size pieces
12 ounces firm white-fleshed fish such
   as Chilean sea bass, tilefish, or
   monkfish, cut into ¾-inch chunks
6 ounces large sea scallops, cut into
   quarters
Salt to taste
Lots of freshly ground black pepper
4 teaspoons finely minced parsley

Heat the butter in a 5-quart pot over medium-low heat. When the butter has melted, add the onion and cook, partly covered, until the onion is wilted and tender but not brown, about 2 or 3 minutes. Stir in the potatoes, thyme, and wine. Bring to a boil, covered, then lower the heat and simmer for 15 to 18 minutes, or until the potatoes are soft and the wine is almost all absorbed.

With a potato masher, crush the potatoes coarsely in the pot. Add the milk, stirring slowly, and bring to a simmer, about 5 minutes. Simmer gently 5 minutes more, keeping the heat low or the milk will curdle. Add the tomatoes, smoked fish, and firm-fleshed fish, and simmer for 6 minutes. Add the scallops and cook 4 or 5 minutes more. Remove the sprigs of thyme and discard them. Season with salt and pepper. Serve hot, sprinkled with 1 teaspoon of parsley over each bowl.

SMOKED SALMON PARCELS WITH CHIVES AND CREAM CHEESE

Thinly sliced smoked salmon wrapped like a present conceals a tiny square of chive-laced cream cheese, tied with a "string" of chive—each bundle a gift to your mouth.

MAKES 12

4 ounces cream cheese
1 tablespoon finely snipped chives plus
    12 long chives

8 ounces smoked salmon, thinly sliced
Small lemon wedges

Cut the cheese with a wet knife (so that it doesn't stick) into twelve 1¼ x 3 x ¼-inch squares. Sprinkle with minced chives, pressing so that the chives adhere to the surface. Chill the cheese until firm.

Evenly trim each slice of salmon if the edges are ragged. Enclose each cheese square in a slice of salmon. Blanch the long chives under hot water to wilt them and use to knot the parcels. Trim the chive "string" neatly at an angle and serve the parcels with a tiny wedge of lemon.

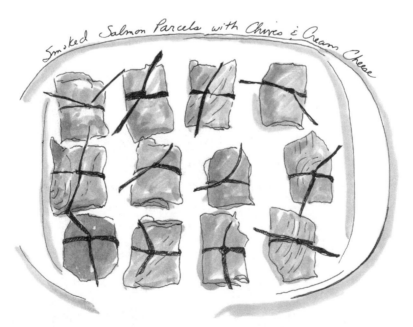

Smoked Salmon Parcels with Chives & Cream Cheese

Born Again Bread

Rustic Autumn Fruit and Bread Pudding with Rosemary and Lemon

Fattoush Bread Salad

Panzanella (Tuscan Bread and Tomato Salad with Basil)

Portuguese Sopa Alentejana (Bread and Garlic Soup with Egg)

Bread carries with it a mystique, a history, a universality as a basic staple in countries on every continent. We know of it as "the staff of life," and the lack of it has been the catalyst for famine and for revolution. It plays a role in religion, in ceremony, and in our social lives. We bless our daily bread. We break bread together. We offer bread (along with salt) for the new homeowner.

In the past few years there has been a veritable "yeast feast" everywhere, as new, original, very talented bakers have begun to offer a vast range of crusty breads in bakeries and specialty shops like Gourmet Garage. And so we find it easier to shop for our bread while baking our own less frequently than before.

We have also been inspired by thrifty cooks all over the world who have created many ways to utilize leftover bread. Stale bread cubes swell up to absorb juices. Bread can be added to thicken simple peasant soups. It can live again in baked puddings or in French toast. The versatility of bread crumbs is unmatched: feeding the birds, topping casseroles, and filling seafood.

Every culture also has its own brand of finger foods that start with bread, no doubt originating during hard economic times. Made from recycled crusty bread a day or two old, many have crossed the ocean from Europe to America, and all are easy to make. The Tuscans designed *Fettunta*, a fancy name for garlic bread, celebrating the first pressing of the olives. *Bruschetta* is a more complex fettunta and is slathered with various toppings—sautéed onions, diced tomatoes, chopped olives or mushrooms.

Called *croutons* in France, the *crostini* of Italy are little toasts sprinkled with Parmesan cheese and floated on a vegetable-rich ribolitta or minestrone soup by the Italians. There are sliced baguettes that the French bathe in melted Gruyère cheese for an onion *panade* (a bread and onion soup). They are also used as a little boat to hold the *rouille*, the spicy, garlicky, red pepper puree that is part of the Provence seafood ragout.

In Spain the *pa amb tomàquet* is born-again bread that reigns supreme: a Catalan snack that is merely thick country bread toasted over a wood fire and then rubbed with a ripe tomato, drizzled with olive oil, and sprinkled with salt.

So stale breads can indeed have a rebirth. Here are some of our born-again bread recipes.

RUSTIC AUTUMN FRUIT AND BREAD PUDDING WITH ROSEMARY AND LEMON

Apples, pears, and grapes reflect the abundance of a fall harvest. Here they are married with Tuscan country bread and the surprise of fresh rosemary and lemon.

SERVES 6

¼ cup golden raisins

1 tablespoon dark rum

1 tablespoon water

3 eggs

⅓ cup sugar plus 2 tablespoons for the top

2 cups whole milk

Pinch of salt

1 teaspoon vanilla extract

1 teaspoon grated lemon zest

2 tablespoons flour

3 cups trimmed and roughly torn stale Tuscan peasant bread or challah

1 small sweet apple such as Fuji or Empire, peeled, halved, cored, and thickly sliced (about 8 ounces)

1 small pear such as Bartlett, peeled, halved, cored, and thickly sliced

About 6 red and black grapes, seeded and halved

2 tablespoons lemon juice

1 tablespoon butter, cut into small pieces

2 teaspoons coarsely chopped fresh rosemary

Preheat the oven to 350 degrees. Butter a round 10-inch-diameter baking pan that is 2 inches deep. If possible, use earthenware since it looks lovely with this dessert.

In a small cup, soak the raisins in the rum and water and set aside.

In a large bowl, whisk the eggs until light, then add the ⅓ cup of sugar, milk, salt, vanilla, lemon zest, and flour. Whisk for a smooth batter. Stir in the raisins along with their soaking liquid and then the torn bread. Pour the mixture into the prepared pan.

Alternate apple and pear slices in the center to cover the surface, leaving space around the outside for the grapes. Arrange a ring of grapes around the outer rim, alternating red and black. Sprinkle with lemon juice and the remaining 2 tablespoons of sugar. Dot with butter and sprinkle evenly with the rosemary.

Bake for 1 hour, until the pudding is puffed and shrinks away a little bit from the sides of the pan. Cool slightly before serving.

FATTOUSH BREAD SALAD

This light yet filling Middle Eastern bread salad is made with a mixture of sturdy lettuce, cucumbers, tomatoes, and scallions, and showered with lots of mint and parsley. The tangy lemon dressing is absorbed by crisp pita triangles, and every chunky forkful has some sort of taste surprise.

SERVES 6

3 medium-size pita breads

2 to 3 hearts of romaine or iceberg
   lettuce (about 12 ounces), cut into
   1½-inch pieces

2 medium English cucumbers, unpeeled
   and cut into ¾-inch chunks

4 plum tomatoes or 2 large tomatoes,
   cut into ¾-inch pieces

3 to 4 scallions, thickly sliced

1 cup loosely packed mint leaves

¾ cup loosely packed parsley leaves

6 tablespoons lemon juice (about
   2 large lemons)

½ cup olive oil

Salt and pepper to taste

1 tablespoon baharat (see Note)

Preheat the oven to 300 degrees. Cut the pita bread into wedges and split them open. Place on a baking sheet in a single layer and toast until dry and crisp but not brown, about 5 minutes. Set aside.

In a large salad bowl, place the lettuce, cucumbers, tomatoes, and scallions, and combine. Add the mint and parsley leaves to the bowl of a food processor, pulse until coarsely chopped, and add to the salad bowl. In a small bowl, whisk the lemon juice and olive oil to combine. Add salt, pepper, and baharat, whisk to combine, and spoon over the salad. Toss gently. Add the pita triangles and toss again before serving.

Note: *Baharat* is a spice blend from the Middle East that smells like a bazaar in a jar. Although the ingredients vary slightly in Lebanon, Syria, and Iraq, it basically contains the following spices in varying proportions: nutmeg, black and cayenne pepper, coriander, cumin, cloves, cinnamon, allspice, and cardamom. It can be purchased in Middle Eastern specialty shops.

PANZANELLA

(Tuscan Bread and Tomato Salad with Basil)

A simple Italian bread salad that relies on the ripest tomatoes and the freshest basil of summer, along with a good peasant bread.

SERVES 6

4 cups ¾-inch dry bread cubes made from 8 ounces trimmed, coarse-textured country bread 1 or 2 days old (see Note)

2 pounds fully ripe beefsteak tomatoes (about 3 or 4 large)

1 medium red onion (about 6 ounces)

22 large basil leaves, roughly torn

1 scant teaspoon coarse salt

1 large clove garlic, peeled

6 tablespoons olive oil

2 tablespoons red wine vinegar

Freshly ground pepper to taste

Place the bread cubes in a large bowl. Cut 1 tomato in half and squeeze the juice from this tomato over the bread, just enough to moisten it slightly. Cut the remaining tomatoes into bite-size pieces and add to the bowl. Cut the onion in half and slice it very thinly. Add the slices to the bowl along with the basil leaves and stir to combine.

Place the salt on a cutting board and place the garlic on top. Smash the garlic with a meat pounder or the side of a heavy knife blade. Using the back of a wooden spoon, crush the garlic with the salt to form a smooth paste. Add to a small bowl along with the olive oil and vinegar, and whisk to combine. Add to the tomato-bread mixture and mix thoroughly. Set the salad aside for 30 minutes to 1 hour at room temperature to develop flavors and to allow the bread to absorb both the dressing and the tomato juices.

Serve at room temperature with a few grindings of fresh pepper over the surface.

Note: If the bread is too fresh, you can cheat and dry out the cubes by placing them in a 250-degree oven for 10 minutes.

PORTUGUESE SOPA ALENTEJANA

(Bread and Garlic Soup with Egg)

In its original and simplest form, this soup is composed of bread, garlic, olive oil, and water. But there are also more enhanced, luxurious ways of preparing it, varying from region to region. It even spills over the Portuguese border into Spain, where it is called Sopa de Ajo al Heuvo.

SERVES 4

6 cups chicken or vegetable broth

10 to 12 large peeled garlic cloves, roughly chopped

Two 2-inch strips lemon zest, cut into rough pieces

1 teaspoon coarse salt

⅛ teaspoon cayenne pepper

⅔ cup tightly packed cilantro leaves

4 tablespoons olive oil plus 4 teaspoons for garnish

4 thick slices rustic country bread or Portuguese Broa

Few drops of vinegar

4 eggs

In a 5-quart pot, heat the broth to the boiling point over medium-high heat. Meanwhile, add the garlic, lemon zest, salt, and cayenne to the bowl of a food processor and process until fairly fine. Add ½ cup of the cilantro leaves and 2 tablespoons of olive oil to the food processor and continue to process until fine. Add this mixture to the boiling broth, lower the heat, cover the pot, and simmer very gently.

While the soup is simmering, brush both sides of the bread with 2 tablespoons of olive oil and fry or grill the slices until toasted on both sides. Keep them warm.

Fill a 12-inch skillet with salted water and vinegar, and bring to a simmer. Place the eggs, 1 at a time, in the bowl of a soup ladle and then slide into the water. Poach gently until the white of the egg is cooked but the yolk is still soft. Remove the eggs with a slotted spoon and place each one on a slice of toast.

Ladle the soup into bowls, preferably earthenware, and sprinkle the remaining cilantro leaves over the soup. Float the toast and egg on top. Trickle 1 teaspoon of olive oil on each egg and dust with a little cayenne if you wish.

Index